Nehrewr,

As I looked [illegible] for the perfect gift [illegible] up with this. The last book he was reading. Bookmark with water marks on it from reading in the tub. ☺

My father loved you, and he "knew" we belonged together till the day he died. Prayerful, hopeful. He never wanted you to experience the pain he experienced when he lost "our" mother.

When my mother passed so did half his spirit, Something we all knew...

Keep him in your thoughts and remember him in your prayers. As he did the same for you.

Hassan bint Dawud Salahadd

1/19/05

Our Land Before We Die

Our Land Before We Die

THE PROUD STORY

OF THE SEMINOLE NEGRO

Jeff Guinn

JEREMY P. TARCHER/PUTNAM

A member of Penguin Putnam Inc.

New York

While the author has made every effort to provide accurate telephone numbers and Internet addresses at the time of publication, neither the publisher nor the author assumes any responsibility for errors, or for changes that occur after publication.

Most Tarcher/Putnam books are available at special quantity discounts for bulk purchases for sales promotions, premiums, fundraising, and educational needs. Special books or book excerpts also can be created to fit specific needs. For details, write Putnam Special Markets, 375 Hudson Street, New York, NY 10014.

Jeremy P. Tarcher/Putnam
a member of
Penguin Putnam Inc.
375 Hudson Street
New York, NY 10014
www.penguinputnam.com

Published simultaneously in Canada

Library of Congress Cataloging-in-Publication Data

Guinn, Jeff.
Our land before we die : the proud story of the Seminole Negro/Jeff Guinn.
p. cm.
Includes bibliographical references and index.
ISBN 1-58542-186-3
1. Black Seminoles—Florida—History. 2. Indian scouts—Florida—History. 3. Black Seminoles—Texas—History. 4. Indian scouts—Texas—History. 5. African Americans—Relations with Indians. 6. Black Seminoles—Government relations. 7. Seminole Indians—Government relations. 8. United States—Relations—Mexico. 9. Mexico—Relations—United States. I. Title.

E185.93.F5G85 2002 2002020362
975.9004'973—dc21

Printed in the United States of America
1 3 5 7 9 10 8 6 4 2

This book is printed on acid-free paper. ♾

Book design by Michelle McMillian

For Bill and Alison Skokan,
in thanks for Nora and for being themselves;

and for Miss Charles Emily Wilson and
Willie Warrior, who have devoted their lives
to keeping the Seminole Negro history alive.

PROLOGUE

miss charles speaks

MISS CHARLES EMILY WILSON, last survivor of the Seminole Negro camp on Fort Clark across from Brackettville in South Texas, doesn't organize the Seminole Heritage Days celebration anymore. She has what her Brackettville friends call "the Alzheimer's," and has been moved seventy miles away to a niece's home in Kerrville.

It was eighteen years ago that the ninety-one-year-old retired schoolteacher, known to everyone as "Miss Charles," declared there had to be an annual Brackettville event celebrating the rich history of the Seminole Negro. With the tribe's modern-day young people getting so distracted by television and video games, Miss Charles warned, the storytelling tradition of the Seminole Negro was fast disappearing. Tribal descendants had scattered around the Southwest after the terrible day in 1914 when the United States Army, having run out of uses for scouts on horseback, evicted them from the shady Las Moras Creek village on Fort Clark land where they'd lived for more than forty years. Miss Charles herself was the last one left who'd been there when the empty wagons arrived, who saw the soldiers with their guns and heard the old people crying when they were left on the Brackettville streets to survive or starve—the army didn't care anymore. The story of the Seminole Negro was so glorious, going back to the days when the Spanish owned Florida and escaped slaves eagerly ran south. There was so much everyone, not just the Seminole Negro children, should know about the great chiefs, the great battles—how the Seminole Negro fought the U.S. Army in Florida, then helped the Mexicans guard their borders, then returned to Texas to show the Americans how to finally beat down the Apache. Whole history books could have, should have, been filled with these things.

But historians overlooked the Seminole Negro. Only tribal bards told the stories, and there were fewer of them as years passed and people died or drifted away. Now, Miss Charles said she was getting on, her memory might weaken at any time, and after she was gone, knowledge of all those great and terrible times still had to be passed down from one generation to the next, or else everything that had happened to the Seminole Negro would be forgotten, and the blood and tears shed over centuries would come to nothing.

So they chose the third Saturday in September, when the blast-furnace South Texas heat abates a little. Miss Charles and other tribal elders conferred with Brackettville leaders. Traditionally, whites among the 1,700 or so town residents never cared much for their dark-skinned neighbors, whose numbers had steadily dwindled over the years, though many Brackettville Hispanics, comprising about half the population, had some Seminole Negro blood in them. But times had changed enough so everyone agreed it would be good for the community as a whole to have a Seminole Negro celebration. Miss Charles orchestrated everything—a parade, the wearing of traditional turbans and cloaks, gospel singing, dancing in the cool of the evening, and, above all, time for the children to hear the tales of Abraham and John Horse, of the slaves who ran away to Florida and the Seminole tribe that welcomed them; about fighting the American army to a bloody draw in the early 1800s, then relocating to Indian Territory; the treachery that awaited the Seminole Negro there, and the amazing exodus to Mexico that, 150 years later, still seems almost impossible to comprehend, it was so awful and yet so brave; then the fine service to the Mexican government, and the request from the Americans to come back to Texas. Help us defeat the Apache and we'll give you land of your own, that was the promise, and, though the promise was broken by the white men, the tribe's children needed to know, to be proud, that their ancestors, the Black Indian scouts, more than kept their part of the bargain.

For thirteen years, Seminole Days went almost according to plan. The thirty-five or so Seminole Negro families left in town were joined by a few hundred scout descendants who came back to visit from Oklahoma or Mexico or wherever they had drifted, some from as far away as California and Illinois. They didn't come for the scenery—Brackettville is a charmless hamlet between Uvalde and Del Rio that ceased to have a reason to exist when Fort Clark was shut down in 1946. The surrounding countryside is flinty and desolate. When John Wayne wanted to film *The Alamo* someplace so isolated that nobody would bother his cast and crew, where he could blow up buildings and not have to worry about scarring the countryside, he chose a ranch just outside town. Filming ran three weeks over schedule in part because hundreds of rattlesnakes had to be cleared off the set every morning. Brackettville is a place most people don't go on purpose, except for the oasislike grounds of adjacent Fort Clark, and rights to any of that land were unceremoniously taken from the Seminole Negro in 1914.

No, scout descendants came because they loved Miss Charles—she had taught most of them, or their parents, or their cousins, in elementary school—and because the Seminole Negro value family ties with a devotion almost unimaginable to outsiders who haven't shared their generations of incredible struggle. If the crowd never seemed to include as many young people as Miss Charles had hoped, well, perhaps they would be more interested next year. Saturday's events went on from morning until dark, and on Sunday there were outdoor services in the tiny tribal cemetery outside town, the only property the Seminole Negro have been able to retain. Four Medal of Honor winners are buried in that cemetery, but their descendants must ask permission before visiting the Fort Clark site where Adam Payne, John Ward, Isaac Payne, and Pompey Factor once lived.

So for years the annual get-together was a success. Occasionally people would talk about how Miss Charles was looking frail, probably it was time for somebody else to really jump in and take over, but it is human nature to take people like her for granted. Then Miss Charles turned ninety, and suddenly she couldn't remember anyone's name. Now she's brought down from Kerrville as guest of honor, but it isn't the same. Nobody can tell the old stories like Miss Charles, except maybe Willie Warrior, and he's in his seventies, has heart disease, and doesn't get along well with the younger officers of the Seminole Indian Scouts Cemetery Association, the group organized by Miss Charles to tend the cemetery and serve as de facto keepers of the tribal flame. So the speakers now are less interesting—they lack rhythm, and they take an hour to say what Miss Charles or Willie Warrior could have told better in ten minutes. The heat seems more oppressive, too, and the teenagers still don't come. A cynic might even point out more people ride in the parade than line up to watch it; Brackettville's nontribal citizenry apparently has better things to do with its third Saturday morning every September.

But the beer is free. Area Budweiser and Coors distributors make generous donations. The barbecued goat is tasty, and old friends enjoy seeing each other again. Though Willie Warrior isn't fond of him, current association president Clarence Ward is a great genial bear of a fellow. And there, all dressed up and looking pretty, is Miss Charles, now gaunt instead of plump but still, at age ninety-one, able to sit on a parade float and wave vaguely at old friends she can no longer recognize. Most of the "floats" are just pickups dotted with flowers fashioned from Kleenex, but Miss Charles's float is an elaborate, if tiny, reproduction of the wood huts in which the scout families used to live along Las Moras Creek. She sits in front of the hut on a high-backed chair, looking regal.

After the parade is over, everyone troops to the tiny park Brackettville has set aside for the Scout Association. Ninety minutes are given over to well-meaning speakers who are more confusing than informative when they try to pay tribute to the Seminole Negro's noble history. Awards are given for the best parade floats. Two staffers from San Antonio's Institute of Texan Cultures make remarks—at least they get the facts right, though their presentations are more scholarly than entertaining. With the Seminole Negro storytellers all but gone, the institute's exhibit delineating the tribe's past may soon be the best record that they ever existed.

Through it all, Miss Charles sits quietly on a metal folding chair in the front row. Each speaker makes a point of praising her. When she hears her name mentioned, she smiles and waves. At one point she's even called to the microphone—"This wouldn't be Seminole Days without a word from Miss Charles," somebody cries. In a reedy voice, tottering in the warm breeze, Miss Charles says everybody looks nice. Then she sits back down.

After the program, many of the men head for the free beer. The women hug each other and exclaim over dresses and jewelry. There is endless talk involving family—who married who, where they might be living now—trying to learn the whereabouts of as many third cousins as possible. The few children in attendence amuse themselves playing on some rickety swings and climbing bars. Even in mid-September, it is still blazingly hot, as it has been since May. A few weeks earlier, using the weather as an instructive example, the marquee of Brackettville's Frontier Baptist Church noted, "Hell Is A Lot Hotter!!!" Now, Miss Charles sits on her metal chair, perspiring but still smiling.

"So nice to see you, Miss Charles," she is told over and over. "You look so well."

"Thank you," Miss Charles responds politely. Her eyes are cloudy.

Then, gradually, the memories return. The reason she proposed Seminole Heritage Days is somehow back burning in her mind. Miss Charles twists a little in her chair, looks up at the people all around, most now turned away from her and chatting about jobs and families and who's had three of those free beers already when, Lord, it isn't much past noon.

"Our people . . ." Miss Charles begins. Her voice fades for a moment, but her eyes seem to focus better, and she sits up straight and tries again, talking to people's backs and elbows and not caring, because the words are so important to her, it is crucial to get the story told the right way, with all the good and bad things that happened.

"Our people were originally from Africa," Miss Charles declares. "We came to America as slaves hundreds of years ago. Soon many of us chose to run away. We fled south, to Florida, and there were taken in by the Seminole . . ." Her voice weakens. She slumps a little. But her eyes remain bright. She is remembering. If she can just get her breath, she'll try telling the story again.

"They ran," Miss Charles says, softly but clearly. "They ran, and finally they saw—"

chapter one

THE FIRST THINGS THEY SAW, as they followed a path through the prickly brush into a clearing, were the fields. Corn was being grown there; the stalks waved in the soft breeze. The air was rich with the odors of tilled earth, animal droppings, cooking food, and oranges and lemons.

At least, that's the way it probably was. Miss Charles always admitted she couldn't be certain what those first runaway slaves saw, or even who they were. No records were kept then, not by escaping slaves or the Seminole who took them in.

"But we know they ran there and were welcomed," Miss Charles recalled in 1994 on the first morning that I met her. We sat in the darkened living room of her clapboard house in Brackettville. Like most houses there, it was box-shaped with a tiny yard whose spiky grass had been blasted a dull yellow color by the relentless sun. The living-room curtains were drawn and only one dim light was on. As a retired schoolteacher who had to be careful with her pension dollars, Miss Charles kept a watchful eye on her electricity bill. Like everyone else in Brackettville, she was already expending endless wattage that summer on air-conditioning. At 10 A.M., the temperature outside was already in the mid-90s. Miss Charles's house was cooled by a couple of cranky window units. The one in the living room, straining to combat the heat, groaned rather than hummed. The noise almost drowned out Miss Charles's hushed voice.

I'd come to Brackettville on assignment from my newspaper. Like many Texans, for years I'd heard fragmentary tales about a black Indian tribe down by the Texas-Mexico border. They were supposed to have helped the army defeat the Comanche and Apache. There were Medals of Honor involved, and a cemetery. But for most of us, these Seminole Negro, whoever they really were, remained more rumor than legend.

When I finally took time to consider it, the black Indian story seemed interesting enough to follow up. There was surprisingly little reference material about the Seminole Negro in the downtown Fort Worth library. From the limited sources of a few articles from scholarly magazines and a mention in *The Handbook of Texas,* published by the Texas Historical Association, it seemed the tribe's history broke down into well-defined sections. Its origin involved runaway slaves reaching Florida and being adopted by the Seminole Indians. After the Second Seminole War, the Seminole Negro were shipped off to Indian Territory in Oklahoma. Persecuted and miserable there, they embarked on a lengthy escape across Texas and down into Mexico, where they fought Indians for the Mexican government. After the Civil War, the Seminole Negro came back to Texas, where their men served as scouts for the United States, tracking marauding Comanche and Apache. Several scouts won the Medal of Honor. In 1914, the army eliminated the scouts, some of whose descendants still lived in the tiny West Texas town of Brackettville. There was just enough sketchy information to be intriguing—at least, enough for the basis of a Sunday feature story and the chance to get out of the office for a couple of days.

I flew from Dallas/Fort Worth International Airport to San Antonio, rented a car, and drove southwest for almost two hours. The land became progressively harsher. Brackettville, when I arrived, was disappointing. The town itself was a small, depressing conglomeration of clapboard shacks, roadside convenience stores, and more than a few shuttered shops that had closed for lack of business. There was a huge sign by the highway touting Alamo Village, a vast ranch about six miles north where John Wayne made his epic, if historically inaccurate, movie, and other Westerns like *Lonesome Dove* needing desolate, harsh-looking locations had later been filmed. There was also a formal entrance to Fort Clark Springs. The old military installation adjacent to Brackettville had been turned into a combination residential community/golf resort. I took a room at the motel there—the charge came to less than $40 a night—and drove to Brackettville's tiny combination City Hall/police station, where I asked a heavyset Hispanic woman at the front desk who I should talk to about the Seminole Negro.

"That would be Miss Charles Emily Wilson," she said immediately. "You're from a newspaper? She's their leader. A retired teacher, you know. Lovely lady. I'm sure she'll be glad to see you." She turned her back and made a quick phone call. I could hear a few words—"reporter" was emphasized. Then the woman turned around and said Miss Charles would be glad to see me. I was given directions to her house. They weren't complicated. Brackettville doesn't have many streets.

Though I'd later learn she had once been heavy, the eighty-four-year-old woman who greeted me now had a bony frame. She wore a print dress—its hemline reached halfway down her shins—a gold necklace, and just a touch too much of the sort of sweetish perfume favored by elderly ladies everywhere. Miss Charles—"Call me that or Miss Wilson, but Miss Charles will do"—also retained a teacher's air of authority. She invited me inside, pointed to the living-room chair where she wanted me to sit, and, after establishing which newspaper I represented and that I intended to write a *nice* story about her people, said she would tell me all about it.

"I'll tell you just what I always tell our children," Miss Charles said. I had to lean forward to hear her. The window air-conditioning unit was very loud. "Do you know about our Seminole Days celebration in September? Do you have children of your own? You could come back then, and bring them to hear the stories."

So Miss Charles began, saying her people had originally been slaves in the American colonies, and that they escaped from their white masters, ran south, and were taken in by Seminole in the Spanish colony of Florida.

"When did the first slaves escape and do this?" I interrupted, scribbling in my notebook. "In what year? What were their names?"

"Oh, no one knows," Miss Charles replied, sounding slightly impatient.

"Who was there to write down such things? I know what my mother and father told me, which was what their parents told them, and so on back through the generations. Just listen to the story. For the first part, the names don't matter much."

"Well, do you know how many escaped to the Seminole? Just one or two at first? Did they come in groups or separately?"

Miss Charles was clearly not pleased. Adopting the tone she must have used for decades with especially recalcitrant students, she said, "It's not certain. I believe they may have come in small groups. Perhaps six. Half a dozen. That's as good a number as any." Irritation made her voice slightly more audible above the laboring air conditioner. Miss Charles began her story again. On this occasion, as on the others that followed, her reedy tone gradually took on a near-hypnotic rhythm. She spoke with her eyes closed and her head swaying slightly, no doubt imagining, as she always hoped her listeners would imagine, the great saga as it unfolded.

"The six runaways came into a clearing," Miss Charles said again, "They looked about them, and then they saw . . ."

They weren't certain what to expect. They fled south because, like many blacks in American bondage, they heard there was freedom if you could elude pursuit and get to what white men called "the Floridas." But this substantial village surprised them; they stared at it, almost unable to believe it could be real.

The so-called Revolutionary War had just ended. American colonists had overthrown British rule, but it made no real difference in the lives of their slaves. These half-dozen Africans, all men, perhaps ran away from a South Carolina plantation months earlier. They came more than three hundred miles south, mostly moving at night, stealing food from farms they passed, staying alert for the sound of hooves or hounds that would indicate pursuit. Every unexpected noise or movement could have meant the slavers were on them, those men with their guns and chains, eager to drag them back to where they'd run from. Capture would have meant certain agony, for runaway slaves could be punished at the discretion of their masters. No law limited the severity of the discipline—nose-slitting or lashings

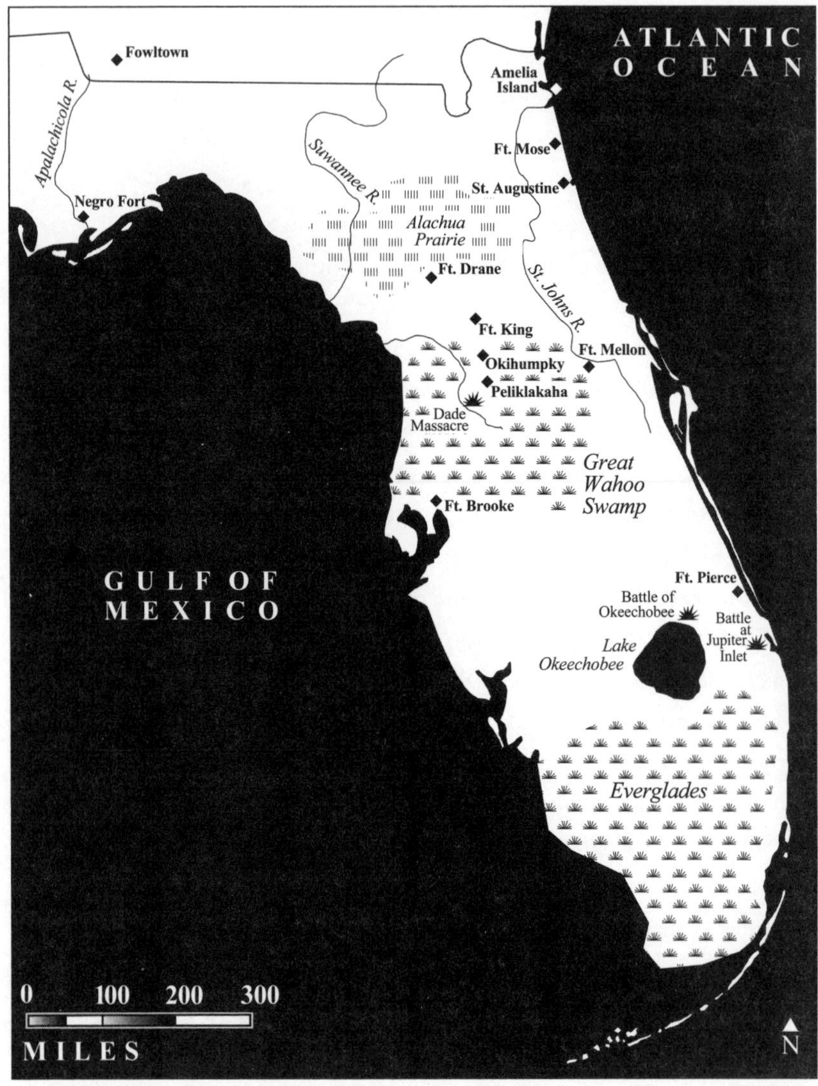

(MAP BY BROC SEARS)

that left backs permanently torn were the most common. They could each have had an ear cut off as punishment, or, if their South Carolina master was sufficiently furious, they might have been castrated. Hanging was less common, though not unprecedented, if a master wanted to make a lasting impression on his remaining slaves. But these six were not captured.

Instead, they ran south until, finally, they came to the fabled Spanish town of St. Augustine, revered by American slaves as the place where white men allowed black men to be free and gave them tools for farming and even guns to help protect Florida from invaders. These newcomer slaves were puzzled when, with signs and broken English, it was indicated by the white men in St. Augustine that they should keep going south and west. They did as they were told, and there was relief in knowing they were probably safe from any American pursuers.

And now this! It was more than a camp, more than a village—a town, a much grander one than the shacks and mucky streets that comprised many white American communities. Looking past the fields and the hog pens, the runaways saw many long cabins built from palmetto planks and thatched with fronds, and they somewhat resembled the huts with leafy roofs some of these Africans remembered from their native homelands.

This grand community was undoubtedly the Seminole town of Cuscowilla on the Alachua Plain, fifty miles southwest of St. Augustine. I deduced this later from old maps and history books, not Miss Charles, who, when her tale involved early tribal events in Florida, was much less specific than she would be regarding the Seminole Negro experience in Indian Territory, Mexico, and Texas. For purposes of pegging Cuscowilla's location, the modern-day city of Gainesville is in approximately the same area.

Although the newcomers didn't know it, the Seminole were relatively recent Florida arrivals, too. Chief Cowkeeper established Cuscowilla thirty years earlier, making his peace with the British when they acquired Florida from Spain in 1763. Had these slaves arrived at Cuscowilla while Cowkeeper was still chief, in the days before the Americans won their freedom and chased the English back into Canada or across the great ocean, they would have had a different reception. Cowkeeper was loyal to the British and would have returned runaway slaves to their colonists. But in 1783, with the British reeling from the loss of their American colonies, Spain took control of the Floridas again. Cowkeeper was dead. His successor, King Payne, made friends with the Spanish, and welcomed, as they did, escaped blacks.

"Didn't the Seminole make the blacks their slaves?" I asked Miss Charles.

"You'll see," she replied, her eyes still closed, her mind still picturing it all. "It took a while for everyone to figure out what was what."

The six black men were directed into town, toward the larger huts in the center of the village. There they were formally greeted by a particularly well-dressed man who might have been King Payne. If he didn't happen to be present, there would have had subchiefs on hand for such duty. The blacks felt relieved. The extent of the welcome made them hope they would be allowed to stay. Conversation proved impossible. Besides their own native Muskogee dialect, the Seminole may have had a few words of Spanish. The runaway slaves probably knew some English—white slave-owners did their best to keep slaves ignorant of anything that might help them to escape—and, of course, their own native tongues, but they were not all from the same region of Africa and had a hard enough time communicating among themselves.

Then there was a commotion off at the north end of the village, and happy shouting. Someone else had arrived, several others from the sound of all the voices, and then the runaways nearly reeled with shock, because walking up to them were other black men, dressed in the same bright colors as the Seminole. These Indian-Blacks greeted the runaways in an odd language that included some English. It was astonishing.

The six newcomers were urged to their feet. Friendly hands on their shoulders filled in gaps left by unfamiliar words. The Indian-Blacks led them out of Cuscowilla, back into the brush, and the runaways wondered if they were being sent away to fend for themselves. But their new guides made it clear they were to all stay together, and there was a path they followed through the brush and past the lemon and orange trees until, in a clearing perhaps a mile from Cuscowilla, there was a second village, a smaller one, but the fields and pens and herds looked the same and the huts were bigger, built better. There was another, more amazing sight: The men and women and children rushing to greet them were all black, every one! Some held hoes and other farming implements. A few men had bows and arrows. One or two cradled muskets. Since being removed from their native lands, the runaways had not seen black men with weapons. The sight made them proud.

There were main huts in the center of this village, too, and the newcomers were ushered to them. A stooped black man in bright finery stepped out of one and walked to the runaways with his arms wide in greeting.

The six new arrivals looked around. After so many years in bondage, it was hard to comprehend the possibility of free black people in their own homes.

"Where are?" one runaway asked, summoning his best pidgin English.

The man considered. "*A casa,*" he finally said. "Home."

And so six runaway slaves needed to run no farther. In the days ahead, they would be assimilated into village life. They would be given tools to cut palmetto trees and build huts, parcels of ground for fields, seed to sow, weapons for hunting. If they found willing women, they could take wives. There were rules, of course, in this first camp of the Seminole Negro, these runaway slaves who aligned themselves with the Indian tribe. The newcomers had much to learn about their complicated relationship with their Seminole hosts, and about the Seminole relationship to the Spanish.

While they forgot about their old masters for a while, there was little chance the Americans would let their valuable property get away quite so easily. The relative tranquility of Cuscowilla and the adjacent Seminole Negro camp was not going to last much longer. The Americans wanted their slaves back, and they also wanted Florida. They would be coming soon.

In the decades and centuries ahead, critical events in history would often impact the Seminole Negro, almost always to their detriment. This moment, this speck of time in the 1780s, might have been when they were closer to happiness than any time before or since. Protected by the Seminole, they were relatively safe. Their numbers grew slowly but gradually as more escaped American slaves made their way into Florida. They proved themselves excellent hunters, good farmers, fine builders—their fields yielded more crops than the Seminole's, their huts were built better, because in their time of bondage to the white man they became skilled in such useful arts. Seminole treated their slaves better than the white man did. It is easy to understand why the Seminole Negro valued their relative freedom so much and why, soon, they fought desperately to keep it.

After an hour or so, Miss Charles began to wear down. Her voice lost its rhythm; her breathing became thready. When I suggested a break, she didn't argue.

"Are you here for some time?" Miss Charles asked. "Will you come back in the afternoon?"

I stayed in Brackettville for five days and came back again afterward. The more I learned about the Seminole Negro, the more I wanted to know. Besides doing my own research, I spent several mornings and afternoons with Miss Charles in her dark living room and many more hours with Willie Warrior, her old pupil who succeeded her as tribal historian. They were really the only two Seminole Negro descendants left who knew enough to be mesmerizing storytellers. But even their knowledge had gaps, mostly concerning the tribe's early years in Florida. Once the great U.S.–Seminole Wars concluded and the Seminole Negro were transferred to Indian Territory, there were government records, many letters, and a few books and other documentation. But of the Seminole Negro in Florida very little was recorded, and, apparently, the early tribal storytellers didn't provide much detail. Recourse to history books and non–Seminole Negro historians, though, provided me with background to more fully appreciate Miss Charles's first tales of the anonymous half-dozen slaves, and to flesh out what she and Willie told me later. The existence of the Seminole Negro resulted, as most cultures had to, from merging forces of history. That there were blacks seeking freedom; that they fled to Florida more than to other regions of the North American continent; that the Seminole tribe was there to greet and shelter them—these were separate elements that, through chance or some higher design, came together in that place and time.

Later, when I shared what I'd learned with Miss Charles, she listened raptly, leaning forward but usually with her eyes closed. I could easily imagine her sorting through what she was hearing, deciding which facts could be incorporated into her own tale-telling. It had been necessary, I said, to go back some 350 years from the time the first slaves ran to the Seminole in Florida. To understand all that was going to happen, I'd needed to begin with the development and eventual collision of three historic facts—slavery in the New World, the colonial ambitions of Spain, and the decision by members of the Creek tribe to break away and form their own nation.

"Oh, yes," Miss Charles said. "Let me get some paper." She rummaged in a desk drawer and brought out a pad and pencil. Then she gestured for me to begin.

Slavery came first. In 1415, Portugal became the first European nation to actively participate in the slave trade. Spain and the Netherlands became heavily involved. For a long time, France and England participated to a lesser extent. In Europe, there was limited use for uneducated African slaves. There was not an endless amount of land to be tilled and harvested. But, across a great ocean, there were new economies that could only flourish with an immense influx of slave labor.

Early on in their New World colonies, the British didn't dabble in the African slave trade. As in England, indentured servants provided the first labor for American colonial masters. When British colonists did experiment with slave labor, they used captured Native Americans. That plan failed miserably. The Indians were still in their homeland; it was easy for them to escape. Members of their tribes often skulked about and stole them back. So when Indians didn't prove suitable, and the number of available indentured servants dropped off—this New World was, by wide repute, a dangerous place, and poor young Englishmen were reluctant to gamble on a period of indenture in return for eventual freedom if they survived—African slaves suddenly seemed necessary.

In a very real sense, blacks were brought to America from Africa to die. Three or four Africans in ten died on the slave ships crossing the Atlantic Ocean. The average slave who survived the voyage lived five years after arriving in the British colonies. Measles and influenza killed them. Living in shanties and rough lean-tos, many died of exposure. Some were worked to death, with no more value assigned to their lives than those of mules that dropped in the traces of a plow. A percentage died from beatings, and it was not unknown for slaves to commit suicide.

So slaves faced hard choices. Once sold to an owner and put to work on his property, each captive African could, of course, accept his or her sad fate and work resignedly until freed by death. Fighting back was almost certainly fatal. A single armed slave was easy for whites to subdue and execute; rebelling in a group only meant more Africans would die. Trying to run away, individually or as part of a group, was also risky. Recapture would certainly mean terrible punishment, and even if white pursuers could be eluded there were hostile Indians everywhere who might either kill Africans or enslave blacks themselves.

But among the three choices—work until death, fight until death, run until captured or free—the last one had, in modern jargon, the best upside. The healthiest, strongest slaves looked for chances to run away. The potential penalties for a failed escape—beating, mutilation, even execution—weren't that much worse than everyday pain endured in the fields. So, many slaves tried to run.

"How many?" Miss Charles asked.

"I don't know," I admitted. "Most people then didn't keep accurate records."

"I told you," she said, grinning. "But they all wanted to come south, didn't they? To Florida."

Africans fleeing masters in northern colonies could try for Canada. But there were fewer blacks in the north, and towns were closer together. There was less room to hide, and dark skin was more conspicuous. To the west were the Allegheny Mountains, and Indians who were as dangerous to runaway slaves as the masters they were fleeing. To the east was the Atlantic Ocean—no hope there.

But to the south was Florida, territory of the Spanish, and many black slaves in the British colonies dreamed of escaping to Florida, where Africans were allowed to be free.

From the moment in October 1492 when Christopher Columbus and his crew spied land—not mainland America, of course, but an island, which Columbus named San Salvador—the Spanish were eager to conquer and occupy as much New World territory as possible. While the British wanted land and the French pursued trade, Spain wanted everything, especially the fabulous treasures its explorers believed were waiting to be taken from the native people who had accumulated them.

In the so-called New World, Spain concentrated on Mexico—"New Spain"—and the north and west South American coasts (there was an agreement with Portugal that left the interior of South America for Portuguese occupation). But the Spanish had one other colonial holding.

In 1513, Juan Ponce de León landed near the spot where, one day, Jacksonville would be built. Having come to the New World as a member of Columbus's first colony on Hispaniola, Ponce de León had a grant from the king to find and settle additional new lands, with any natives being forced into slavery and given as property to Spanish colonists. Not an especially observant explorer, Ponce de León thought he had landed on an island. He sailed his ships south and west, charting a unique, finger-shaped coastline, and named the "island" Florida.

Spain's main colonial focus was elsewhere. New Spain and its South American holdings held the promise of gold, or at least access to further vast expanses of land to conquer. Florida was oddly shaped, cratered with swamps, and full of angry natives who declined to be conquered. But Spain needed Florida. England was in the process of establishing colonies all down America's Atlantic coast and extending west with the colony named Georgia. Spain required its own foothold in this portion of the American continent. In 1565 King Philip II's colonists built St. Augustine on the east Florida coast between the Atlantic Ocean and the St. Johns River. The settlers there were able to stave off initial Indian attacks and gradually began making friends with the natives. Catholic priests were sent to St. Augustine with specific instructions to bring red-skinned heathens to Christ, but soon lacked potential converts. Florida Indians seemed especially vulnerable to European diseases. Within a few years, these native tribes—the Tocobaga, Chilucan, Yustaga, Oconee, Pensacola, and several others—virtually disappeared. Perhaps one thousand Native Americans were left in all of Florida.

Spain allowed its Florida colonists to own black slaves. The few remaining Native Americans were tolerated, not annihilated. The central Florida plains offered some opportunity for farming, and game was plentiful. Besides deer, there were bear and wild pigs and even panthers. Lush citrus fruit was readily available. It became apparent Florida had great potential as a place to live, raise crops, and hunt. The quirky Florida coastline offered all sorts of possibilities for ports. Fishing in its coastal waters was prime.

None of this escaped the notice of English colonists who spread down the Eastern seaboard. Settlers in South Carolina and Georgia felt no obligation to stop moving south. As more slaves were imported into these British colonies, their owners had greater interest in expanding their land holdings. In the 1680s, British colonists in Georgia and the Carolinas approached the Creek nation, one of the largest among all Native American confederations, with the suggestion that the Creek raid Spanish settlements in Florida. The Creek were well-organized and essentially autocratic. Chiefs—called *miccos*—required taxes from their subjects, using the crops collected in this way to benefit poorer tribal members. The Creek also kept slaves, including some Africans sold or given to them by white colonists. The British/Creek alliance was a substantial danger to Spanish Florida.

Since the British and Creek made a habit of raiding Florida, the Spanish wanted armed manpower more than slave labor. They not only welcomed escaping slaves, they encouraged them to send word back to the Carolinas and Georgia that there were opportunities in Florida for runaways to be completely free. They would have to take instruction in Catholicism. And they would, of course, have to be willing to bear arms on behalf of their new Spanish friends.

In 1704, Governor Jose de Zuniga y Cerda of Florida's Apalachee Province declared that "any negro of Carolina, Christian or not, free or slave, who wishes to come fugitive, will be (granted) complete liberty, so that those who do not want to stay here (in this area of Florida) may pass to other places as they see fit, with their freedom papers which I hereby grant them by word of the king."

Miss Charles asked me to spell the governor's name for her. When I did, checking it carefully against my notes, she wrote it down on her own notepad. I asked why she wanted to know.

"I know about Ponce de León, of course," she said. "But not this Governor Cerda. Now, if one of our children asks me about him, I can answer."

"I don't think any of them will ask you that," I said.

"Children are a wonder," Miss Charles replied. "Someday, one of them might."

In February of 1739, Florida Governor Manuel de Montiano built a coastal fortress a few miles north of St. Augustine. He invited free blacks to populate it; Gracia Real de Santa Teresa de Mose, more commonly known as Fort Mose, was the first free black community in North America. Spain did its best to make Fort Mose attractive to Africans. Seed and tools for farming were provided, and food was sent in until the first crops could be raised. There was a priest assigned to the fort for religious instruction. Cannon were placed on the ramparts. Muskets were issued to men who wanted them, and most did. The only obligation placed on the Africans living there was to help defend Florida against invaders.

Word about Fort Mose spread quickly to slaves in the Southern British colonies. The colonists and the English army personnel stationed in the southern regions of their American colonies decided they had only one option—to invade Florida, destroy St. Augustine and Fort Mose, and, hopefully, drive out the Spanish colonists forever. All they needed was an excuse.

In October they got one. Britain declared war on Spain over Spanish harassment of English shipping. It was known as the War of Jenkins's Ear, because British sea captain Robert Jenkins supposedly had his ear hacked off by Spaniards near the coast of Cuba. British colonists in America marched south into Florida and attacked St. Augustine. They were amazed to find the city's defenders included several hundred black soldiers. The Africans received the same pay and benefits as Spanish enlistees and fought under the command of black officers.

Though St. Augustine withstood the attack, Fort Mose didn't. Enough of its buildings were destroyed so that the Africans living there had to be relocated to St. Augustine. It was 1752 before it was rebuilt and became an African stronghold again.

Britain's colonies in the New World eventually had trouble on two fronts. In 1754, the extended French and Indian War broke out between the English and France. England was trying to extend its colonies west of the Allegheny Mountains, and the French felt they already had claimed the land there.

Even with the British also fighting France, and even with its contingents of black soldiers, Spain was still handicapped in efforts to retain Florida. Colonists in Georgia encouraged the Creek to stage hit-and-run attacks on Spanish colonies; the Creeks especially welcomed the raids because they enabled them to capture Africans who would serve as tribal slaves.

Eventually, the Treaty of Paris in 1763 temporarily ended both the English-Spanish and English-French conflicts. But by the time the War of Jenkins's Ear was over, there was a new player in Florida, perhaps the critical mass in the violent explosion of war that would come fifty years later.

"This is where the Seminole come in, isn't it?" I asked Miss Charles on my first day with her.

"I know something about that, but Willie Warrior knows more," she said. It was late in the afternoon. After leaving Miss Charles earlier, I'd looked around Brackettville to find someplace to eat. I knew there was a restaurant on the old fort grounds near my motel, but I didn't want to drive back across the highway. Instead, I cruised the limited blocks of Brackettville and found exactly one cafe. It was called the Krazy Chicken. The menu consisted of a few things fried in grease. I ate a hamburger there and was immediately sorry. Afterward I poked around town, killing time until I thought Miss Charles had had sufficient time to rest. I passed one grocery and two video stores. There was a small public library, but no bookstore or movie theater.

When I got back to her house, the temperature outside was well over 100 degrees. The air conditioner in the living room window couldn't compete with such heat. The air inside was warm and sticky. Miss Charles blotted herself with a Kleenex.

"Willie and some girl from a college were talking about where the Seminole got their name," she said. "She was telling him things, and he was laughing at her. I think he said nobody knows about the name, they just think they know. Have you talked to Willie yet?"

I said I was going to see him the next day in Del Rio, a town some thirty miles west of Brackettville. I'd called from a pay phone outside the Krazy Chicken—the helpful woman at City Hall had given me his phone number, too. A man with a deep voice on the other end of the line identified himself as Dub Warrior, and when I asked for Willie Warrior he said that was his name, too.

"He's a good one," Miss Charles said proudly. "He and his wife, Ethel, are both in the Scout Association. He goes to schools all the time to give talks. He can tell you all about the Seminole."

Historians have argued for years where the name *Seminole* comes from. Some believe it is a bastardized term from the old Creek language. Others insist it is a corrupted pronunciation of the Spanish word *Cimarron*. Most agree Seminole is supposed to mean *runaway*. What is important is why there was a newly formed Indian conglomerate known collectively as the Seminole, because it would directly effect the eventual relationship between the Seminole and the black runaways the newly hatched tribe took in.

Early in the 1700s, the Spanish realized they needed more inhabitants in the Florida lands between Georgia and the Carolinas and St. Augustine. This would make it more difficult for the English colonists to conduct raids. Runaway slaves weren't numerous enough to occupy sufficient territory. Prospective Spanish colonists were mostly sent to New Spain and South America. So the same European power that gleefully slaughtered natives by the hundreds of thousands in New Spain rolled out the proverbial welcome mat in Florida to Indians who wanted to come and live there. As it happened, there were some Indians who were pleased to be invited.

Small bands began breaking away from the Lower Creek nation; these pushed south and east into Florida. Various struggles between colonists and Indians to the north drove additional Native Americans south. So long as they would comply with Spanish rule, they were welcome in Florida.

Cowkeeper and his Oconis established primacy among the newcomers, who were also joined by surviving members of Florida's indigenous tribes. A less stringent form of Creek government was enacted. Each village chief, or *micco,* could assess taxes from crops and generally oversee daily life. Designated from among the village chiefs would be a few principal chiefs, who collectively would make decisions on behalf of the entire tribal nation. "Nation" might give the impression of greater numbers than were initially in Florida. Perhaps two thousand Seminole lived there by the end of the 1700s. The tribe's numbers continued to swell as more Indians left the Creek and migrated east.

These newcomers were allowed to build on land unoccupied by the Spanish. Unlike many tribes in the Western plains and Southwest, the Seminole built permanent villages. They meant to stay. They were primarily farmers and hunters.

And, from the beginning of their Florida existence, the Seminole had slaves. Their system of vassalage was more benign than that of the Creek. Slaves, captured in battles with other tribes, had their own lands, huts, and weapons. They were required to give a portion of their crop to their owners. Slaves and owners intermarried, most often Seminole men and slave women. Monogamy was not required of Seminole males.

Different tribes joining to form the Seminole nation spoke different languages. It would be the 1820s before the Muskogee tongue of the Lower Creeks became the most common means of verbal communication. They learned some Spanish, too, but in 1763 they abruptly needed to learn English, when European powers met, negotiated, and ended up trading large tracts of land in the New World. Spain received the French holdings west of the Alleghenies. Spain also received Cuba from England. England got Florida from Spain.

Immediately, the Spanish shipped most of their black Floridian allies off to Cuba and other island holdings. English colonists from the Carolinas and Georgia rushed into Florida searching for runaway slaves, and some were recaptured. But many black refugees stayed in the Florida swamps; other freedmen booked passage to Spanish islands in the Caribbean.

As English settlers swarmed in, they brought slaves with them. The British made friends with the Seminole, who had no reason to particularly miss the Spanish. The Indians noted how ownership of Africans conferred social status on English owners. The richer Seminole began to buy occasional black slaves for themselves. The British also made a habit of awarding slaves to various Seminole chiefs. These were known as "King's gifts."

From the beginning the Seminole had to decide what to do with their slaves. They certainly had no intention of imposing the same harsh rules as the white men and Creek did. The Seminole-owned Africans were given tools and instructed to build huts of their own, in villages adjacent to but separate from those of the Indians. The blacks had seed to plant their own crops. Some even received a few cattle or pigs to start their own herds. They were expected to share part of their harvests with their owners, but in all, blacks quickly discovered that being a slave among the Seminole was far preferable to white man's bondage. On a daily basis, they were as free as the Seminole themselves, and most often called *Seminole Negro*—Black Seminole.

Word of this spread among slaves still held in the Carolinas and Georgia, and to slaves of white masters in Florida. These Africans kept running away, running south and east—but now they were running to the Seminole, not to the Spanish. Some of the chiefs who were especially loyal to Britain, Cowkeeper in particular, returned runaway slaves. But other chiefs didn't.

The outbreak of the Revolutionary War in 1776 uprooted many landholders in the Carolinas and Georgia who had remained loyal to the British. These people—and their slaves—took refuge in Florida. But in the Caribbean and other places, the French and Spanish fought the British as well. It was only in 1783, with yet another Treaty of Paris, that all hostilities in the New World ended, at least for a little while. Once again, the

European superpowers traded colonial holdings, and this time the new American nation also was a participant. And, while America gained certain fishing rights off the Newfoundland coast, and other rights regarding passage and exploration along the Mississippi River, there was one aspect of the treaty that infuriated Americans, particularly those with land and slaves in Southern states. Spain had taken Florida back from Britain.

This meant that runaway slaves were welcome in Florida again. Spain had no particular stake in the prosperity of the so-called United States. While America had won its freedom from Britain, the fledgling nation was far from a global superpower. Spain intended to hang on to Florida this time.

"This is where you always start your story, Miss Charles," I said one afternoon as we sat in her living room. I can't remember what time of year it was, but the window air conditioner was emitting its usual roar because it was so hot outside. It almost always is hot in Brackettville.

"Yes," she replied sleepily. It was obvious she was tired. I offered to leave, but she said she wanted to "visit" a little more. "It happened just like I told you, didn't it?" she asked.

"Just like you said," I agreed.

The Spanish began encouraging runaway slaves to go to Seminole villages. The Indians' lenient tribal system of vassalage suited Spanish aims perfectly. The blacks would be part of the Seminole, and the Seminole could help fight Americans if and when it became necessary. By aligning the Indians and Africans, Spain increased its defenses without having the responsibility of providing for the runaways.

Outraged American slave owners in the South did what they could to retrieve their human property from Florida. They entered into new treaties with the Creek, and those chiefs promised to return the Florida runaways. The problem, of course, was that the Seminole now considered themselves separate from the Creek and in no way bound by that tribe's agreements. Such Seminole recalcitrance worsened relations between the tribes.

Blacks living with Indians or in their own camps were commonly called "Maroons" by the whites. In some history books, the Seminole Negro are identified only as Maroons. They were also called Black Seminoles or

Black Indians. But Seminole Negro—the latter word pronounced NAY-gro, not NEE-gro—seemed to suit them best.

Early letters and trading documents telling of visits to Seminole Negro villages describe inhabitants as hard workers. Certainly, the life they had in Florida with the Seminole was infinitely better than existence as slaves of white men on their Southern farms and plantations. But they weren't entirely happy. They were better off than before, but they still belonged to someone else. They were still *property.* And the Seminole, though benevolent masters, had no intention of ever giving up the slaves they owned.

The most telling measure of the very real division between the Seminole and Seminole Negro was the separation of their villages. There was always space—a mile, two miles—between them. Put simply, the Seminole Negro were considered allies, but not blood kin. The Seminole clearly felt themselves to be superior.

Such class distinctions developed over the years. The Seminole Negro spent these relatively quiet times assimilating some of the Seminole culture and developing their own. In particular, they gradually created their own language, *Gullah,* a mixture of English, Spanish, and various African dialects. Slaves on America's southeastern seaboard also formed variations of Gullah, and future linguists would spend entire careers rooting out the origins of individual words.

Seminole Negro religion incorporated aspects of African faiths, Indian beliefs, and American Christianity. Through the addition of runaways and some intermarriage with the Seminole, the tribe grew more numerous. Eventually there were several "Maroon" towns in northern Florida and along the Alachua Plains. Perhaps, if left alone, the Seminole Negro would have indefinitely stayed allied with, but subservient to, the Seminole. They might eventually have declared their freedom in much the same way the Seminole separated from the Creek. Certainly there were Maroon communities in the Caribbean where they would have been taken in, or they might have established their own lands further south along the Florida peninsula, somewhere the Seminole hadn't yet reached and the Spanish settlers didn't want. But there wasn't enough time for such possibilities to play out, because a decade into the 1800s America decided to take Florida away from Spain, precipitating tragic events that followed one upon another like bloody footprints across history.

"All that happened so long ago," Miss Charles commented late in our first day together. "That's why our kids at Seminole Days don't want to listen. They think if something's old, it's not important."

Later, when I'd learned more about her own remarkable history, I thought Miss Charles could have spent that first day telling me all about herself—how she became the first scout descendant to go off to college, how she earned not only an undergraduate but a graduate degree as well (this in a time when young black women rarely completed high school), how she'd spurned opportunities for life in big, exciting cities to come home to seedy Brackettville and work with her people there. Miss Charles not only ruled the Scout Association, she'd founded it. She not only survived segregation in Brackettville, she was eventually named the town's citizen of the year. Charles Emily Wilson was one of the first black teachers in Texas to teach integrated classes. All this, and the only personal reference she made that first day was how, as a four-year-old child, she'd cried in 1914 when the army marched the Seminole Negro off Fort Clark grounds at gunpoint.

"Willie Warrior will tell you interesting things in Del Rio tomorrow," Miss Charles promised as she escorted me to her front door. "What we've talked about today is only the beginning of my people's history. Come back after you've seen Willie."

chapter two

WILLIE WARRIOR said he'd meet me in a Dunkin' Donuts shop in Del Rio, a border town about thirty miles west of Brackettville. Willie was already there when my photographer and I arrived. It was easy to pick him out at the counter. He was a big, thick-chested man with a black mustache and narrow beard. He shook hands, squeezing a little too hard for comfort, and immediately began questioning me: Which newspaper did I write for? How long would my story be? When would it be printed?

"I'm not getting any younger," he said. "Got to get the word out while I can." I thought he might be in his midforties. In fact, he was sixty-seven.

We spent all morning and most of the afternoon with him. Willie initially talked in rapid-fire bursts, referring to people—General Jesup, Abraham—and places—Fort Moultrie, Nacimiento—I wasn't familiar with. When I'd ask him to explain, he looked surprised, as though everyone should know his tribe's history as well as he did. My initial impression was that, as a Seminole Negro storyteller, he was the exact opposite of Miss Charles. She coaxed listeners in; Willie put both hands between your shoulder blades and shoved. That difference came, probably, from their professions. As a former teacher, Miss Charles was used to plenty of classroom time to build up student interest bit by bit. Willie was a retired trucker, paid during his working life for getting from point A to point B as quickly as possible. Too, Willie often encountered his listeners along the region's Kiwanis/Lions Club/Rotary Club lunch circuit. He usually had no more than fifteen or twenty minutes to first get his audiences interested, then hit all the Seminole Negro history high points before his very limited time was up. He was much more of an entertainer than Miss Charles. Describing the Seminole Negro defending themselves against white soldiers, his eyes would flash and he'd brandish an imaginary rifle. Willie was, in particular, a master of tossing in small, fascinating details. Discussing his teen years working on ranches around Brackettville, he told wonderful anecdotes about "wild-eyed, hammer-headed crazy horses" he was given to ride; how, when nature called, it was safer to "piss over the whithers instead of climbing down. Those damn crazy horses would bite the hell out of you, then run off."

Mostly, that first day, we talked about two subjects. Willie was deeply concerned about the modern-day plight of his people, with some living in poverty in Mexico and many of the rest not doing much better in and around Brackettville. But he also talked about the early days in Florida, when runaways who'd become Seminole slaves suddenly found themselves fighting Americans determined to drag them back into much crueler bondage. This wasn't his usual area of discussion.

"Florida's important, I know," he said. "If I lived there I'd tell more Florida stories. But when I talk to people in Texas, see, they want stories about Texas. But wherever we were, we ended up having to fight, because everybody all along the way would lie and do us wrong."

"Like in Florida," I said, hoping to bring him around to the point in Seminole history I wanted him to discuss first. I'd learn, over the next seven years, that Willie Warrior was at heart an incredibly gentle man, tender with his wife, children, and grandchildren, endlessly thoughtful regarding anyone he considered even a marginal friend. But the part of his life devoted to the history of his people brought out different traits. He'd suffered as a child in Jim Crow Brackettville, then spent so many frustrating adult years standing up in front of any audiences willing to listen and trying, not always successfully, to make them care about things that happened to a struggling tribe of black Indians whose tribulations could scarcely be comprehended by more well-heeled people. His anger about the past seethed into the present; there were no gray areas, no points of discussion or dispute about Seminole Negro history where Willie would consider compromise. Whenever, during our many subsequent meetings, I'd mention some book or historical document that indicated Willie's version of something might be skewed or even inaccurate, he'd contemptuously snort, "That's not *right,*" and go on with whatever he'd been talking about without further acknowledgment that he could have been even marginally wrong. This insistence on being right carried over into his relationships with younger would-be leaders among the tribe's Scout Association; future clashes threatening the solidarity of the Seminole Negro descendants eventually—inevitably—occurred.

And on this first of many days I spent with him, Willie had more generalities to offer on early Seminole Negro days in Florida than actual facts and dates. These would have to come later, from outside historians, books, and government records. But Willie was adamant on a first, important point: The early Seminole Negro tribesman living among the Seminole in Florida never considered surrendering meekly to their former white masters.

"They were ready to die rather than go back," he noted. "God knows they had reason to feel that way."

But as he picked up the story where Miss Charles had left off the day before, it was obvious to me that there was more involved, in 1811, than a simple desire on the part of the newly formed U.S. government to chase down some escaped slaves. The members of the fledgling Seminole Negro tribe had the bad luck to be in the wrong place at the wrong time, when American settlers wanted to expand south to Florida and found Spain and the Seminole in their way.

In January 1811, the U.S. Congress took its first step toward snatching Florida away from Spain. President James Madison was given the authority to use whatever force he believed necessary to take over part or all of

Florida if any other foreign power tried to occupy it, or if "local authorities" requested American assistance.

Congressional permission for Madison to send troops to Florida was the equivalent of a mandate. Almost immediately, American squatters in East Florida made it clear they were requesting military support. By summer, Madison had delegated General George Mathews to go to the area and help Americans there organize their own separate government—in effect revolting against the legitimate Spanish authorities.

Mathews knew the region well. He had been governor of Georgia, and his prejudices against the Spanish, Seminole, and runaway slaves were a perfect match with those of the squatters he was ordered to assist. Once the upstart East Florida government was in place, it was a logical next step to request the presence of American troops, just in case the Spanish might have the bad manners to object.

Mathews imported those troops from his home state of Georgia. Most were volunteers whose burning desire to protect the interests of a provincial East Florida government was surpassed only by personal greed. The occupying troops certainly could stake out some Florida land for their own. Just to be certain their motives were perceived as pure, they named themselves "the Patriots," and, in March 1812, they used federal gunboats to capture Amelia Island, which is northeast of today's Jacksonville. The occupation was underway.

It's possible, had the Patriots stopped there, that Spain might have let the whole thing pass. Losing a tiny chunk of a marginal colony meant very little. It was obvious England and America would soon be at war again, and with the Americans distracted the Spanish might have been able to easily roust them out of Florida. But Amelia Island didn't satisfy the invaders. Mathews brought his rabble south and surrounded St. Augustine with troops. If he could take St. Augustine, the rest of Florida, or at least the portion the Americans wanted, would lay open before him.

For too long, Spain had let the city's defenses languish. Mathews led well-armed besiegers. St. Augustine had fewer than five hundred defenders, and most of them were civilians who weren't certain which end of a gun to point at the enemy. St. Augustine might hold out for a few weeks or months, but its fall to the Americans was almost inevitable.

Almost. Mathews wasn't worried about Spain's Seminole allies—he reportedly told King Payne he would drive him from his land—and he certainly discounted any threat from the runaway American slaves who now considered the St. Augustine region their home.

"We were always great fighters, you know," Willie Warrior said proudly. "We never got whipped up on. We always did the whipping, though sometimes it took us a while. In Florida, in Mexico, here in Texas. Anybody who underestimated us got his butt kicked."

"That's what happened early on in Florida, didn't it?" I asked.

"That's right," he said, laughing. "They made those fools *pay*."

Mathews was indeed a fool to take the Indians and their slave allies so lightly. Though they were estranged from the Creek, the Seminole were still in constant contact with them. They had seen the Americans befriend the Creek in Georgia, then gradually push them out of the best land there. The last thing the Seminole wanted was for Americans to begin encroaching on their territory, too.

The Seminole Negro were even more opposed to the American invasion, and for the obvious reason. Once in place and in power, the Americans could turn their attention to rounding up every black man, woman, and child. Even free blacks would probably be included. Blacks who could, under American law, be proven the property of specific white owners would be returned to them and receive the inevitable punishments, or even death. Blacks who couldn't be claimed would be handed off to slavers and sold in the markets of New Orleans or Charleston.

The Seminole Negro had been able to escape from white slavery to Florida because they were strong, because they were skilled in matters of survival. Now they knew it was necessary to support the Spanish and save St. Augustine. They sharpened their knives, primed the powder in their muskets, and prepared for war.

Inadvertently, the Americans helped. In April 1812, Madison came under intense pressure from Northern congressmen to call off the blatantly illegal siege. Congressmen from Maine, New Hampshire, New York, and other points north of America's lower states had little interest in annexing East Florida and retrieving a few hundred slaves. In another two months, America would declare war on England. That inevitable conflict, protesting congressmen believed, deserved more attention than St. Augustine. As a sop, in May, Congress annexed *West* Florida into the so-called "Mississippi Territory."

Madison agreed it was foolish to antagonize Spain while preparing to fight England. He relieved Mathews and replaced him with David B. Mitchell, who happened to be the current governor of Georgia. Had Madison then ordered Mitchell to withdraw American troops from Florida, subsequent terrible events might have been avoided. But Madison didn't.

Instead, Mitchell chose to keep the American troops in place until the Patriots were granted complete amnesty for their actions by the Spanish. Further, Mitchell could call up the Georgia militia and bring them into Florida if he deemed it necessary. He did.

But while Mitchell assumed authority from Mathews, the Spanish bolstered St. Augustine's defenses with five hundred free blacks. At the same time, the Seminole and Seminole Negro began to mobilize. Mitchell, preoccupied with St. Augustine, apparently didn't notice. Even if he did, he probably dismissed any threat from Indians and blacks. What possible damage could they cause a well-equipped army of white men?

Instead, Mitchell began complaining that Spain was obviously willing to arm every negro in Florida. He also considered it unsporting that Spain was bringing in black soldiers from Cuba. Not that these dusky troops could ever defeat his army, but the concept of uppity blacks parading around with rifles would undoubtedly inspire even more runaways from American farms and plantations. Mitchell actually wrote the Spanish governor of Florida that this should have "induced you to abstain from introducing them into the province."

By summer, King Payne decided the Americans weren't going to go away. He knew very well where they would head next after St. Augustine fell. A war party of some two hundred Seminole and fifty Seminole Negro left their villages and attacked American East Florida plantations along the St. Johns River. Some of St. Augustine's besiegers were from those plantations. They immediately deserted, weakening Mitchell's forces. Joint Seminole/Seminole Negro bands also assaulted American supply trains. Cut off from provisions and gunpowder, the Americans ended their siege.

"Should've quit while they were ahead," Willie Warrior chuckled. "They just couldn't believe a bunch of Indians and blacks could lick them."

But the Americans didn't end their invasion. It was obvious now where their real enemies were to be found. It was no secret that the Seminole and Seminole Negro had their most substantial villages on the Alachua Plain. Major Daniel Newman was instructed to destroy those towns. There weren't that many U.S. troops available. Many militia enlistments were up, and American soldiers had now witnessed firsthand just how well the Seminole and Seminole Negro could fight. Newman could only muster about 125 men.

Still, they went and soon ran into King Payne, his brother Bowlegs, and some one hundred Seminole and Seminole Negro warriors. Days later, the remnants of Newman's force staggered back to the American camp in East Florida. The survivors reported they'd had to subsist on gophers and alligators while retreating. More than half of their original number were dead or severely wounded. And, by the way, the Indians were good fighters, but their negroes were better. The savagery with which the Seminole Negro fought astounded the Americans.

Newman's defeat stalled American plans. There was no immediate retaliation. But it was still a costly victory for the winners. King Payne was killed in the fight, and the invaders were now grimly determined to subdue the Seminole and eradicate the Seminole Negro. With St. Augustine no longer under seige, Spain was happy to let the Americans and Seminole/Seminole Negro alliance slug it out.

Word of America's defeat spread to the Southern plantations. It conjured the worst fear among slave owners—armed blacks willing and able to kill whites. Rumor surely exaggerated the Seminole Negro numbers. But panic spread: What if those murderous negroes, thousands of them, maybe tens of thousands, decided to march into Georgia or South Carolina and free the rest of their black people? Every white person in the vicinity would undoubtedly be slaughtered!

John McIntosh, the latest leader of the Patriot forces, put it bluntly in a letter to Secretary of State James Monroe: Unless something was done immediately about the Seminole and their black allies, word of their prowess would spread throughout America's slave community and "bring about a revolt of the black population of the United States."

As it happened, some crack troops were available to order into Florida. Andrew Jackson had spent the summer of 1812 putting together Tennessee troops to fight the British at their stronghold of Mobile. This army included two hundred well-armed cavalrymen. After Newman's defeat, that cavalry unit was sent into Florida, where it combined with forces under U.S. colonel Thomas Smith, and prepared to march on the Alachua Plain.

It was one thing for the Seminole and Seminole Negro living there to conduct guerrilla attacks on supply lines and plantations. Combined, they still could gather only a few hundred warriors. A concerted American attack on their villages could not be beaten back, and they realized it. Led now by Bowlegs, the Seminole contacted the Creek Indian agent and asked for peace talks. They were turned away.

In February 1813, the Americans began their campaign. About eight hundred soldiers and cavalrymen made up the invading force. The commander of the Georgia militia underscored the real purpose of the mission by declaring that every negro found bearing arms would immediately be executed.

Their red and black enemies were wise enough to retreat into the swamps where they knew they probably would not be pursued. By the time the Americans arrived at Bowlegs's principal town, it was deserted. They burned it to the ground. Then they moved on to the adjacent Seminole Negro village, where an incredulous U.S. officer reported destroying 386 huts and 1,500 to 2,000 bushels of corn.

The Seminole and Seminole Negro were permanently driven from the Alachua savanna. Their food reserves were destroyed. Some of them would starve in the swamps. American settlers swarmed into the fertile area the Indians and blacks had abandoned. As far as the United States was concerned, it had won.

But other events gradually swelled the Seminole numbers and encouraged both Indians and blacks to continue the Florida fight. First, federal troops withdrew soon after victory on the Alachua. The Patriots were back on their own. About six months after the Alachua battle, America began a bloody war with the Creek. The U.S. Army was led by Andrew Jackson. Davy Crockett was a scout for Jackson's troops. The United States won; its numbers and firepower were overwhelming. Many of the Creek put down their arms and agreed to a one-sided peace treaty that eventually included relocation to so-called "Indian Territory" in Oklahoma and Arkansas. Rather than surrender, some Creek warriors fled to Florida and linked up with the Seminole in the swamps. This vastly increased the fighting ranks of the Seminole fugitives.

Then the British came to Florida. They, too, had noted the effectiveness of black fighters there and wanted their U.S. foes to have to focus at least some of their military force on an enemy other than England. In 1814, Major Edward Nicolls (some historians identify him as Colonel Nicholls) came ashore proclaiming that all Florida blacks who joined England in its war against America would be given free land in the West Indies afterward. They would never have to worry about being returned to their former masters. Nicolls even ran up the British flag next to Spain's. Spain responded by naming Nicolls its own area military commander. The remaining Creek, Seminole, and Seminole Negro were ready to join him. Some three thousand Indians and four hundred blacks rallied to Nicolls. He armed them, trained them, and built them a fort.

It was a beautiful fort, seemingly indestructable and holding a key position. The Indians and blacks had conceded northern Florida from the east banks of the Suwannee River to the west banks of the St. Johns River. But they and the Spanish still held land west of the Suwannee and east of St. Johns (the location of St. Augustine). Nicolls built his new fort about 150 miles east of Pensacola, near the mouth of the Apalachicola River where it emptied into the Gulf of Mexico. The spot chosen on the eastern bank was known as Prospect Bluff.

The Treaty of Ghent was signed on Christmas Eve 1814. America and Britain were suddenly at peace. That treaty, of course, had no effect on America's relations with the Seminole and Seminole Negro. Nicolls was recalled to London. The British government rebuffed his suggestion that the Indians and blacks be considered permanent allies. Any promises to give blacks land in the West Indies were forgotten.

But about three hundred blacks still held British Post, along with a handful of Creek and Seminole. They had plenty of ammunition, thanks to Nicolls, and they also had cannon that the British left behind. They plowed fields outside the fort and began raising crops. It was obvious to white observers that they had no intention of leaving. Within a few months, "British Post" became known as "Negro Fort." A black named Garson commanded there.

All this was unacceptable to Americans. After eighteen months, they demanded that the Spanish do something about it, but the Florida governor, probably with ill-disguised glee, said he simply didn't have the time or manpower to act. The Americans would have to deal with Negro Fort themselves.

Andrew Jackson, now military commander of America's southern territories—expanded hugely by the Louisiana Purchase in 1803—was nothing if not decisive. Since Spain wouldn't shut down that damned fort and its negro defenders, he would. He ordered General Edmund Gaines to destroy Negro Fort and return any surviving blacks from it to their original owners.

At this point, Willie Warrior stopped enjoying the story so much. Though the Seminole Negro were great fighters, Andrew Jackson and his crack troops were obviously going to be too much for them, at least to begin with. Though Willie never hesitated to tell about tribal defeats—"If we tell the story, we got to tell the whole thing, the bad along with the good"—I still had the sense that, among all the foes the Seminole Negro ever faced, he most hated Andrew Jackson, along with Indian agent Marcellus Duval, who came later, and the modern-day Seminole nation that, he insisted, "is screwing us today as bad as anything anybody did to us before." Within a few years, news of just how the Seminole were still doing that would make the front page of the *New York Times*.

Certainly, how Jackson carried out his assault on Negro Fort, then on the Seminole and Seminole Negro, fully qualified him to Willie as a particularly implacable enemy. Jackson ordered Gaines to make his way down the Apalachicola and build his own fort a few dozen miles north of the black stronghold. In mid-July 1816, Gaines sent soldiers under the command of Duncan Clinch down the river to move back and forth in front of Negro Fort until its occupants fired on the Americans, which would offer the United States sufficient justification to attack. Eventually some shots were fired. On July 27, American gunboats assaulted the fort. At first, their cannonballs couldn't crack the thick walls. But then a lucky shot hit the fort magazine, and the subsequent explosion killed almost everyone inside. Black survivors were sent back into slavery. The exception was Garson, who was shot after being captured.

While Jackson and the United States had been preoccupied with Negro Fort, many of the Seminole and Seminole Negro reestablished villages along Florida's west coast, mostly in the area that is now Tampa Bay. To a certain extent, this was fine with the whites. American settlers now held the Alachua Plain. Spain retained control of the eastern Florida seaboard. Neither the United States, Spain, or the Seminole/Seminole Negro coalition had much interest in Florida's swampy south.

But the blacks and Indians weren't through fighting. With hindsight, it's easy to say they should have kept quiet and stayed in their new villages, though I could never get Willie to even consider that alternative. He argued that surviving Seminole and Seminole Negro realized Americans would always keep coming. Sooner or later, white men would want all the land, not just parts of it. Better to fight them now while at full strength and perhaps convince them to steal land from other, less warlike people. The final straw was the continued presence of invading slavers, who picked off any blacks they could.

"Maybe we paid for it later, but at least we hit back," Willie said, sounding proud. "They knew they'd been in a scrap. Our people always did enjoy a fight."

The reprisal raids began mostly in Georgia. The Seminole Negro were at the forefront. Bowlegs was the principal Seminole chief recognized by the blacks, who chose his head slave, Nero, as their own war leader. Nero was assisted by two British military men, Alexander Arbuthnot and Robert Armbrister, who claimed they had come to fight in Florida out of sympathy for the negroes being enslaved there. Soon whites were jarred by the news that a massive troop of up to six hundred blacks was being trained in sophisticated modern military maneuvers. When slaves weren't being stolen from plantations during Seminole/Seminole Negro raids, they were running to Florida of their own volition.

In August 1817, Kenhadjo, one Seminole chief whose band was not actively fighting the Americans, received a message from General Gaines telling him to give up any blacks he had. Kenhadjo replied that he had no blacks and would fight any Americans on his land. He was luckier than Neamathla, a Seminole who led the small Indian village of Fowl Town in Georgia. When Neamathla sent a similar reply to the Americans, they came and burned Fowl Town to the ground. Though Neamathla and most of his people escaped, both sides understood this action to be the opening attack in a full-scale assault. The First Seminole War is considered to have begun here. For the rest of 1817 and through the early months of 1818, whites, Indians, and blacks skirmished, mostly along the Georgia-Florida border.

In January 1818, Andrew Jackson named himself the new American field commander and built a stronghold on Prospect Bluff where the Negro Fort once stood. Jackson called the new facility Fort Gadsden, and he made it his headquarters. Jackson soon believed many prominent Seminole and Red Stick chiefs, plus Ambrister and Arbuthnot, were meeting with Spanish officials in the town of St. Marks, which was some hundred miles east of Fort Gadsden on the Florida Gulf Coast. Except for the Red Sticks, the Creek still hated the Seminole, so Jackson recruited almost two thousand of their warriors, who he combined with fifteen hundred of his own white soldiers. He led these troops to St. Marks and occupied the town. No one fought back. There were no Seminole, Seminole Negro, or Red Sticks present. So Jackson kept going.

His new targets were the Seminole and Seminole Negro villages on the west bank of the Suwannee. Outnumbered three to one, the Seminole wisely led their families across the river and into the adjacent swamps before Jackson's force arrived. Bowlegs's town and the Black Seminole village were about one mile apart. On April 16, the blacks sent their women and children into the swamps, too, and then assumed responsibility for covering both villages' flight. The two hundred or so Seminole Negro men had no chance to defeat Jackson. Their goal was to hold his troops off until all their noncombatants had escaped, plus the vast majority of the Seminole warriors. Only a few Seminole stayed to fight beside their black allies. Perhaps Bowlegs ordered his tribe's "slaves" to sacrifice themselves as a rear guard. Maybe the Seminole Negro men realized they, as superior fighters, could buy more time for their loved ones to run than Seminole braves could have managed. Whatever their reasoning, they stayed to fight and die.

"A great battle," Willie Warrior said dreamily. "You think our men couldn't fight? Think they weren't brave? And they fought Jackson's army to just about a damn draw."

The battle was awful. The muskets owned by the Seminole Negro were no match for the better U.S. guns. The Americans charged from the west, and the setting sun behind them blinded the Seminole Negro warriors as they tried to aim. Still, they held off Jackson until their people were safely into the swamps; then they, too, turned and ran. The Americans stopped to burn the villages. The Creek charged into the swamps after the Seminole Negro. For several miles the blacks fought and retreated, until finally they broke into small groups and the Creek abandoned pursuit.

Meanwhile, Jackson captured both Ambrister and Arbuthnot. He hanged Arbuthnot and shot Ambrister, and later wrote they were "legally convicted as exciters of this savage and negro war; legally condemned, and most justly punished."

Essentially, that ended the First Seminole War. The Indians and Seminole Negro were scattered in the swamps. American settlers were everywhere in East Florida and the Alachua. West Florida had already been annexed into the United States. Spain's hold was increasingly tenuous. It was time for them to get out, after having bargained what they could from the Americans in exchange.

In February 1819, Spain and the United States negotiated what became known as the Transcontinental Treaty. Spain ceded America all its lands east of the Mississippi in return for American promises to leave Texas to Spain forever. This promise lasted less than twenty years. As for Florida, the separately designated Adams-Onis Treaty found Spain selling Florida to the United States for $5 million, with a clause requiring the Americans to treat its Native American inhabitants kindly. This promise, too, would soon be broken.

chapter three

WHEN WILLIE WARRIOR and Miss Charles told their tales of Seminole Negro history, they sometimes sacrificed specifics for dramatic effect. Describing a pitched battle, Willie might say an American general had "a mess of troops, and we had only a handful." Miss Charles's description of land given to the Seminole and Seminole Negro for a Florida reservation was confined to "an awful place in the swamps" without any further information about how many acres or where exactly the awful place was located. And it was certainly true that otherwise their listeners, whether Seminole Negro children or visiting journalists, might have soon felt bored by extraneous details.

I wanted to write the story of the Seminole Negro through the voices of Miss Charles and Willie. But spoken stories, even wonderfully engaging ones like theirs, often don't translate well into print. I knew that for a good newspaper story, I'd have to find some additional sources of facts. I'd already learned that my city library couldn't provide these. Neither Willie nor Miss Charles had collections of printed documentation. There was a tiny museum on the Fort Clark grounds, but it was dominated by exhibits about the white cavalry there. The Seminole Negro items, mostly a half-dozen grainy photos, had been donated by Willie, with the exception of a few from "the collection of Ben E. Pingenot." On my third or fourth day in Brackettville, someone—a clerk at the Fort Clark motel, I think—said Ben Pingenot lived right on Fort Clark. After the army closed the fort down in 1946, it was sold to a series of civilian companies and eventually converted into a residential/golf community. Some of the barracks were rebuilt into boxy motel rooms and others into economy-priced housing. The old officers' quarters, an impressive array of smallish stone buildings ringing the parade grounds, were sold as higher-ticket residences. Pingenot, a former president of the Texas State Historical Association, lived in one.

Since it was impossible to call him from my motel room—none of the rooms in the Fort Clark motel have phone lines—I walked a half-mile across the parade ground and knocked on his door. Ben was a friendly, slender, sixtyish man in poor health. He had an endless fascination with the Seminole Negro and a voluminous library of magazine articles about them clipped from magazines few people other than lifelong historians would have read. He'd written several articles on the Seminole Negro himself, mostly for similarly obscure scholarly journals. But his interest was in the entire spectrum of Texas history, from the saddle tack used by cowboys to the china settings at the first governor's dinner table. All his old books and Xeroxed documents and yellowing photos were carefully sorted. Whole tall file cabinets and dozens of bookshelves were crammed with items. Every inch of wall space was decorated with old photos and maps. Ben approached Texas history with real reverence, and his home was nothing less than a shrine to it. Hearing I'd spent time with the two foremost Seminole Negro tribal historians, he nodded approvingly.

"Miss Charles is a treasure," he declared. "Willie Warrior, too. They just embody that fine Native American tradition of storytellers preserving tribal history.

"Dub, I know, has told you the army deceived his people. He believes there was always an agreement in place that, after serving as scouts, the men would be given land here. Instead, they supposedly were rounded up and thrown off the fort after there was no further need for them. Betrayed by the army. Do you think that's true, or not? I don't, personally, but that misunderstanding is the crux of the whole story at Fort Clark. Of course, there are other areas of historical disagreement—what the Seminole Negro were promised in Florida if they'd stop fighting the Americans, for instance."

"I'm really wondering right now about Florida," I told him. "Miss Charles and Willie—Dub—have stories about it, but they don't always know all the facts or dates."

Ben said he understood. Regarding the Seminole Negro in Florida, he said, there was a wonderful old book written by an American army officer, Woodburne Potter, who'd been right in the middle of things.

"Most of history is written down somewhere; it's a matter of knowing where to look," Ben said. "None of us who call ourselves historians know all those places. So we talk to each other and share information, or at least we should. Beware anyone who says he knows everything about anything. No single source of history is definitive."

Over the next few years, as I drove thousands of miles and talked about the Seminole Negro to several historians recommended by Ben and others I discovered on my own, there was time to ponder the advantages and disadvantages of oral and printed history. Short term, storytellers like Miss Charles and Willie had all the best of it. They could stick to the highlights, embellish a little here and there, and base much of what they said on what they intuited individual audiences wanted to hear. Willie, in a church, might discuss the Seminole Negro devotion to spirituality. Addressing a gathering of war historians, he'd regale them with stories of bloody clashes.

But anyone taking more than a superficial interest would eventually want more than this—not just *what* happened, but also the *how* and *why.* Any moment in history is the culmination of other events. Ben told me the Seminole Negro's chances for freedom and land arguably ended in 1588, when the Spanish Armada was destroyed by the English. This was the beginning of Spain's military downfall all over the globe, he said, leading to its inability to keep Florida out of British, then American, hands, with the resulting disasters for the Seminole Negro there.

"So you can't really write about the Seminole Negro without writing

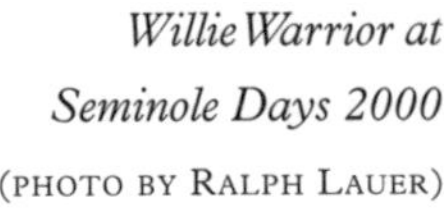

Willie Warrior at Seminole Days 2000
(PHOTO BY RALPH LAUER)

about the Armada," Ben said. "And to do a proper job of it, you have to explain why the Armada was put together, and how the English defeated it, and how things were between England and Spain that brought them to that point."

Yet such extended detail would cause the eyes of even dedicated readers to glaze over long before they got to the chapters where the Seminole Negro fought the American army in Florida. Overreliance on dates and names—"list history," historian David Halberstam once described it to me—sucks the descriptive juice out of any printed record.

"Ben knows all the names and dates," Miss Charles told me. "I don't know that he understands all the *feelings*. He tells it his way, we tell it ours."

After I wrote my newspaper story about the Seminole Negro, I knew I had to eventually do something more than provide a quick sketch of the historical highlights, with commentary from Willie and Miss Charles. There was a book to be written, one that combined the best of oral history

Miss Charles Emily Wilson at Seminole Days 2000
(PHOTO BY RALPH LAUER)

with supplementary, *complementary* detail from books, documents, maps, treaties—Miss Charles and Willie leading the way, providing a framework strengthened with outside sources. Where oral and printed history disagreed, I'd simply note the disagreement and let readers decide for themselves. Telling the story would get easier once the tribe left Florida for Indian Territory; Miss Charles and Willie had heard these and subsequent stories from the lips of men and women who'd actually been there. As for Florida, well, there were some old records and the very detailed account provided by Woodburne Potter, plus some additional insights from Willie Warrior about the beginnings of the Second Seminole War.

"Jackson figured he'd whipped us for good," Willie noted. "And things *did* look pretty bad. But we came back up after being knocked down, just like always."

Cautiously, around 1820 and 1821, the Seminole and Seminole Negro emerged from hiding. Their old villages had been burned. Some of the tribes from the western edges of Spain's old Florida territory drifted east and built new towns not far from Bowlegs's former property on the Alachua. Bowlegs's people, driven south by Jackson, rebuilt about a hundred miles away. Scattered Seminole tribal offshoots remained around Tampa Bay. Some were east of St. Johns River.

The blacks who remained with the Seminole once again built their towns near, but not adjacent to, those of the Indians. Many free blacks, fearing the American slavers, got passage on cargo boats headed for the Bahamas. Others built their own canoes and sailed south. Everyone involved—white, black, and red—had a good idea of what would happen next.

The Americans had never hidden their intention toward Indians in Florida or anywhere else. Red savages had to be removed from land the white men wanted. They could go voluntarily, or they could be forced to leave. This was, Americans believed, eminently fair. There were more whites than there were Indians. Majority ruled.

Immediately after making the Louisiana Purchase, Thomas Jefferson suggested the Mississippi River would make a good natural divide between red savages and civilized whites. Gradually, Jefferson believed treaty or war would require Indians to give up their homelands and move west beyond the Mississippi. Besides discovering a passage to the Pacific, the goal of the Lewis and Clark expedition was to encounter Indian tribes and convince them to bend to the will of the white man. Jefferson noted in a message to one reluctant chief that *all* white Americans were "gun-men," and his tribe had better cooperate at peril of being destroyed.

In Florida, Americans believed the Seminole had been broken. Having taught the savages a military lesson, it was now time to negotiate a treaty that required the defeated Indians to move somewhere whites weren't interested in settling. But American representatives approached the Creek, believing the Seminole were still part of that tribe.

In January 1821, the Creek and the United States signed the Treaty of Indian Springs. The tribe gave up about five million acres of land; they were allowed to keep sixteen hundred acres. In return, the Creek got $40,000 right away, then a few thousand more each year for thirteen years. In all, the Creek were paid about seven cents an acre for their land, cheap even by 1821 standards.

A decade later, the Creek allowed themselves to be relocated to the newly designated "Indian Territory," a huge mass of land mostly in what later became the state of Oklahoma. For the time being, not many white settlers were interested in moving there.

The Seminole ignored the treaty. They denied that any promises made by the Creek obligated them. It took nearly two years, but finally the Americans decided to begin dealing directly with the Seminole.

The major issue to be determined involved the Seminole Negro. American slave owners still wanted their property back. There was limited support for this among the Seminole themselves. Some Indians blamed the Seminole Negro for the war. If the whites hadn't wanted their slaves back, they reasoned, they never would have invaded the Alachua. It was only logical, to these Seminole, that after returning every black to the white man—perhaps in a way that might bring a profit to the Indians—there would be a better chance the Americans would subsequently leave the Seminole alone.

"This was an important moment," Willie Warrior told me, tapping his thick finger on my arm for additional emphasis. "The Seminole could have said right there that, 'hey, these people are *our* people.' But they just saw us as slaves, the same way the white people saw us as slaves. And that set up all the crap that came later on. 'Sell the slaves, let's save ourselves'; that was the idea, I guess."

"It was a hard time for the Seminole," I suggested.

Willie glared at me.

"Damn sight harder for the Seminole slaves," he snapped.

Bowlegs died shortly after Jackson's assault on the Suwannee towns. His place as principal chief of the Alachuas was taken by his son Micanopy, who owned Seminole Negro slaves. One of these was named Abraham, a tall man, perhaps in his early thirties, who might have been considered handsome except for one crossed eye. Historians believe Abraham, a full-blooded black, served under Major Nicolls and perhaps survived the Negro Fort explosion of 1816. He certainly was an excellent public speaker, one who liberally sprinkled his messages with references to God. This earned him a nickname: "The Prophet." Since Nero was gone, probably killed in Jackson's attack on the Alachua, the Seminole Negro were without a leader. Abraham quickly stepped forward.

An intelligent man, he understood exactly what would happen if the Seminole agreed to every treaty term the Americans were bound to suggest. So Abraham ingratiated himself to Micanopy, while continually exhorting the Seminole Negro to resist any settlement with the whites that involved tribal blacks being returned to the white man.

"Abraham was our first great one," Willie Warrior enthused. "He was right in the middle of the action, making things happen."

Micanopy's new village was named Okihumpky; the Seminole Negro town built nearby was called Peliklakaha. Micanopy visited it often. Abraham was one of three chiefs there. The other two were named July and August. Together, the three made certain the Seminole chief was always made especially welcome. Eventually, Micanopy spent most of his time in Peliklakaha rather than Okihumpky. He probably kept wives there.

Two other major Seminole Negro villages were Mulatto Girl's Town and Bucker Woman's Town. Another, Payne's Town, had the largest black population—perhaps three hundred. An estimated 120 lived in Peliklakaha. But since one of those 120 residents was Abraham, it was the most influential of the four Seminole Negro communities.

Abraham intended to participate when the Americans and Seminole met to determine the fate of the blacks. Cannily, he learned sufficient English to serve as Micanopy's interpreter—and the Alachua chief soon needed one, since the United States decided to open negotiations by taking a census of Florida's Indian population.

U.S. Indian Agent John Bell spent a year wandering Florida, counting Seminole and quietly trying to estimate the Seminole Negro population. This was the first time Americans knew for certain that Indians and blacks lived in separate villages. Bell eventually reported thirty-five Seminole towns and the four black villages. About 5,000 Indians were counted. He believed there were some 500 blacks "in a state of half slavery to the Indians." Of those 500, 150 were warriors, a far cry from the 600 or so armed Seminole Negro who were supposed to have been on the rampage during the recent war. In fact, neither the Americans, the Seminole, nor the Seminole Negro probably knew for certain how many blacks were in Florida.

The numbers reported by Bell didn't frighten the Americans. James Monroe was now president; his administration felt great pressure to move the Seminole somewhere away from white settlers and to take back every Seminole Negro "slave." Agents were instructed to identify the principal Seminole chief and negotiate a treaty with him.

But no single Seminole chief spoke for the entire tribe. Gradually, the Americans were able to convince leaders of most major Seminole towns to come together, and in September 1823, several of the important chiefs—Micanopy, Neamathla, Mulatto King, Jumper, King Philip, and a few others—signed what became known as the Treaty of Moultrie Creek. Under its terms, the Indians had to move south, to a five million–acre reservation that the Americans knew was mostly swamp and the Indians probably didn't, since it was not their custom to scout land far from areas they currently occupied. The reservation's boundaries did not include any portion of the Florida coast, to discourage the Seminole from consorting with pirates. The Indians would be given $5,000 a year for twenty years. There would be a little more money to build schools, and money to pay a blacksmith and gunsmith.

The Indians had to pledge they would no longer take in escaped slaves; instead, they would return them to their white masters and receive bounty payments. An oblique reference to the Seminole Negro required the Indians to return any blacks *they did not own* to the whites. The Seminole believed they owned every black living in or near their tribal towns. Neamathla, somehow considered by the Americans to be the most important Seminole chief, was asked to submit a list of current Seminole towns, plus the number of Indians and blacks living in them. After consultation with the other chiefs, Neamathla returned with a list of thirty-seven towns inhabited by a total of 4,883 Indian men, women, and children. Significantly, he did not list the major Seminole Negro villages, or any of the Seminole Negro.

The American negotiators, led by Florida governor William Duval, wrote U.S. Secretary of War John C. Calhoun that the treaty made the best of a bad situation: "It was a misfortune to Florida, as a frontier territory, and with her maritime exposure, to have any tribes of Indians within her boundaries."

The Seminole Negro issue troubled U.S. observers. One report to the secretary of war noted, "The negroes who dwell among (the Seminole) as their slaves are intelligent, speak the English language . . . and have great influence over the Indians. They fear being again made slaves under the American government and will omit nothing to increase or keep alive mistrust among the Indians, whom they in fact govern. If it should be necessary to use force with them, it is to be feared the Indians would take their part."

Abraham couldn't have described his strategy better. But the next part of this message, written by someone named Jedidiah Morse, is proof the Americans always intended to snatch the Seminole Negro back, though they didn't mention it anywhere in their peace treaty with the Seminole. "It will, however, be necessary to remove from the Floridas this group of lawless freebooters," Morse wrote. "Among (them) runaway negroes will always find refuge."

The first Seminole and Seminole Negro Indians to arrive at the new reservation were appalled. The marsh was unsuitable for growing crops. There was nothing to hunt. The Seminole custom was to build permanent villages, but there wasn't enough solid ground for even that. The Americans were also supposed to provide food for the Indians while they planted their first crops and waited for harvest, but most of the food was never delivered. So the Indians complained—to each other, to the white men, and to Neamathla, who was lucky enough to be living away from the useless land.

Soon after the Moultrie Creek treaty had been signed, the U.S. government established the Bureau of Indian Affairs. The new department's task was to negotiate treaties with Indian tribes and then see that terms of the treaties were enforced. The Seminole knew nothing of this new bureau, which at least in theory was supposed to represent the tribe's best interests. Neamathla appealed to Duval instead. The Florida governor's response was to suggest to Secretary of War Calhoun that the Seminole chief be sent to Washington, since he had "no precise knowledge of the strength and power of our country." Calhoun declined the opportunity to have Neamathla as his guest. Duval was instructed to make the Seminole behave.

Meanwhile, there was a new problem. As the various Seminole bands reluctantly moved south, the Americans seized the opportunity to relieve them of any blacks whose status was remotely questionable. Hungry, desperate, the Indians began grudgingly to give up some of what they still considered their property. Most of the blacks gave up hope the Seminole would protect them.

Neamathla became disgusted with the Americans. He began suggesting to other chiefs that combined resistance might be preferable to starving. Governor Duval was not a fool. He had informants in most Seminole camps. Someone told him of Neamathla's ingratitude, and Duval took an armed war party to the chief's village in 1826. His own report had Duval taking Neamathla by the throat and shaking him, which the Indian and his outnumbered warriors would probably never have allowed. ("He'd have been a pincushion," was Willie Warrior's comment.) But Duval did inform Neamathla he was no longer a chief. John Hicks, a more pliable resident of Neamathla's village (and probably Duval's informer) would take over.

The people living on the reservation began to starve. Duval ignored their protests until white settlers to the north began complaining the godless red heathens were stealing their cattle. Duval investigated. The Seminole didn't deny it. They had to feed their children something. The secretary of war asked Duval what was happening.

Duval's response was to blame the area Indian agent ("I fear he has lost all influence over them"), request federal money not to feed the Indians but to pacify their accusers ("I hope you will recommend to Congress to make some provision to indemnify the citizens for their losses"), and ask for a little help in slapping the pesky Seminole down ("If I had the command of two hundred regulars . . . I could, without danger of bloodshed, make all the Indians return to their boundary. These people have great confidence in me, yet they fear me as they should").

The Indians and blacks did the best they could. They planted where the ground was least soggy. When they had a successful hunt, they shared the meat. But there was grumbling around every campfire. Relations between the Seminole and Seminole Negro were tense. Slavers made regular raids, and the white soldiers looked away rather than offering protection. Even when the Indians stayed on the reservation, they were blamed for the loss of every white settler's cow that fell into a bog or was dragged away by a panther.

Not all white men were as unsympathetic as Duval. Lieutenant Colonel George M. Brooke sent an official report to his superiors that perfectly described the Seminole plight: "The major part of the nation are, and have been, suffering for some time in extreme want. Some have died from starvation, and many have lived on the roots of the sweetbriar as a substitute for bread . . . I can assure you they are in the most miserable situation; and unless the Government assists them, many of them must starve, and others will depradate on the property of the whites in the Alachua and St. John's settlements."

Brooke's report was sent slowly up through proper military channels. Meanwhile, the Indians and blacks on the reservation continued to suffer. Abraham did his best to boost the spirits of the Seminole Negro. But it was a dreadful time. For the moment, there was no coherent plan among the Indians or the blacks to try and fight the Americans.

Complaints from American settlers—occasional raids on their livestock certainly were the work of reservation blacks and Indians—caused the U.S. government to move troops south. Brooke, who at least cared about the suffering Seminole and Seminole Negro, was part of this contingent. The soldiers under his command established an outpost they called Camp Brooke.

It was then, in the fall of 1826, that the Seminole Negro's greatest leader first made himself known. Abraham the Prophet clearly led the blacks for the present. He would be an integral part of their history for some time to come. But another man eventually surpassed him.

Willie Warrior and Ben Pingenot may have disagreed about some things, but they were in complete agreement about John Horse. They both called him a genius.

"Keep in mind you're talking about the little boy of an Indian's black slave," Ben said. "No books in his hut, certainly. No one to teach him arithmetic. Yet this incredible man still emerges. I would say without qualification that he was the intellectual equal of just about anyone in our nation's history. He was that special."

John Horse was born in 1812 to a Seminole Negro woman and Seminole man. Probably the father was Charles Cavallo, whose last name was a bastardization of the Spanish *caballo,* or *horse*. Because Seminole lineage is traced through the mother, baby John was, from birth, a slave. He and his mother, whose name is lost, first lived in a black village on the Alachua. A sister, Juana, was born sometime after John.

Jackson's attack in 1818 drove John's family south. They settled in a village some dozen miles from Camp Brooke. The Indians and blacks who lived there wanted to be near the soldiers; they hoped this would afford them some protection from slavers, and, besides, Brooke and his men were generous with extra rations if anyone was hungry.

Even as a child, John Horse was a prodigy. He became an excellent linguist, who spoke Muskogee, English, and Spanish. Yet he was almost certainly self-taught. In the tumultuous years after his birth, what literate adult had the time or opportunity to tutor a ragged black Indian boy? And young John's abilities went beyond the written and spoken word—he was excellent with sums. His only obvious defect was an occasional tendency to stammer.

Over the next half-century, he would be known by several different names. John Cavallo, John Caballo, and John Horse were the most common. But his first name among the whites, and one he used among them

Drawing of Chief John Horse

(COURTESY OF THE INSTITUTE OF TEXAN CULTURES AT SAN ANTONIO)

for the next two decades, was *Gopher John,* given to him by Lieutenant Colonel Brooke.

Brooke had a black cook named Andrew. On a bright fall morning, Andrew informed Brooke that a Seminole Negro boy was in camp with fresh land turtles to sell. For some reason, Americans referred to these turtles as "gophers." Brooke sent for the boy. The youngster was clearly the product of Indian and Seminole Negro parents. He had curly hair and skin that was equal parts black and copper. The boy introduced himself as John, and Brooke was impressed by his clear, grammatical English. They bargained, and Brooke bought the turtles for twenty-five cents. (Miss Charles thought it might have been a dollar, but that would have been an outrageous price in those days.) John said he could regularly supply more. Brooke said that would be agreeable. The next day the boy said he had two additional turtles. The American officer gave him another twenty-five cents. This went on for several more days, until Brooke began wondering why a pen he'd built to hold the "gophers" never had more than two turtles in it at a time. Confronted, John confessed he'd been reselling the same two land turtles each day. Another white man might have had the boy beaten. Brooke simply told him not to do it again and nicknamed him Gopher John.

The next few years found the Seminole and Seminole Negro floundering, but John Horse managed to do well for himself. Somewhere he acquired a few head of cattle. With careful handling, they grew into a herd of almost ninety. He was also a crack shot. While still in his teens, he even managed to marry into Micanopy's family. It was rare for Seminole Negro males to be allowed to formally wed Seminole women. Obviously, John Horse had attained a great deal of respect among the Indians. He was one of the few blacks—or Indians—to thrive. Most were still near starvation on reservation lands.

Duval eventually visited the reservation himself. Even he found conditions there appalling. In one letter to the Bureau of Indian Affairs he admitted, "I think that a man who is a judge of land would not give more than one dollar per acre for the best of it." Duval complained about mosquitoes and a lack of decent drinking water. In all, he wrote, "the best of the Indian lands are worth but little; nineteen-twentieths of their whole country within the present boundary is by far the poorest and most miserable region I ever beheld."

Not that this knowledge caused Duval to go easy on the Indians and blacks. Calling the leaders of the Seminole together (the Seminole Negro leaders, including Abraham, were excluded), Duval threatened them.

"How is it, my red children, that many of you act wrong and very bad, that you kill the hogs and cattle of the white people, and that you take their potatoes and corn?" he asked, undoubtedly through an interpreter. "Do you not expect such actions will occasion war? Beware, in time, of your danger; for if you sit still and let your bad people continue such conduct, mighty evils will soon fall on the whole of your nation."

Then Duval raised the touchy subject of the Seminole Negro.

"Chiefs and warriors, you hold negroes in your nation that belong to the white people," he said. "By the treaty, you are bound to deliver all the negroes that do not belong to the Indians to the agent. You are not to mind what the negroes say; they will lie and lead you astray, in the hope of escape from their rightful owners."

"That was typical of the thinking then," Ben Pingenot noted. "The whites would bargain with the Indians, the Seminole, sort of on the basis of one man to another. But the Seminole Negro were always referred to as property, like cattle or chickens. By reducing them to that level in negotiations, it made it more likely that the Indians would hand them over."

But, Willie Warrior pointed out, "Things started to happen, and the Seminole started to have a bigger problem."

Instead of American soldiers invading the swampy Seminole reservation to round up every Seminole Negro, the U.S. government decided instead to separate the Indians and blacks by getting the Seminole out of Florida.

In 1830, President Andrew Jackson signed the Indian Removal Act, which essentially made into law Thomas Jefferson's old plan of moving every Native American west of the Mississippi River. The Creek were transplanted; so were the Choctaw. In the Carolinas, white settlers cheered when the Cherokee were forced away on what became known as the Trail of Tears. In the case of each tribe, little choice in the matter was given. Yes, they had been granted land in past treaties. But now the white civilization's expansion required them to move. Money was offered to cover expenses, and seed and rations were promised once the tribes arrived in their new homelands. But the Indians weren't being asked if they wanted to go.

The Seminole obviously had no love for the wet, stinking reservation they'd been given in Florida. But in 1832, when Colonel James Gadsden arrived to negotiate a new treaty, the Indians remembered too well how, the last time they'd bargained with the white man, they'd ended up with the worst land possible. Gadsden was informed by Micanopy, Jumper, John Hicks, and others that the Seminole weren't interested. Their interpreter was Abraham.

"Because," Willie Warrior noted almost gleefully, "Abraham was the *smart* one. Those Seminole wanted him negotiating for them."

I told Willie he seemed awfully concerned that I didn't have sufficient respect for Abraham.

"None of you people do," he replied. It reminded me, in an uncomfortable way, how Willie and the modern-day Seminole Negro still felt that life was basically a case of themselves against the rest of the world.

The Indians weren't in a position to hold out long; 1831 was a year of drought. They couldn't grow many crops on their reservation in the best weather, and now they basically had nothing to harvest. Gadsden and Wiley Thompson, the Seminole agent appointed by President Jackson, were aware of the tribe's plight. Gradually, they wore the Indians down.

The Seminole chiefs insisted they couldn't move to Indian Territory because the Americans wanted them to merge their tribe there with the hated Creek. Blandly, Gadsden and Thompson replied that the Creek very much wanted to welcome the Seminole back. The Indians argued that the land they'd be given next might be just as bad as the reservation in Florida. Well, came the answer, why didn't some of the chiefs go look at the proposed Indian Territory reservation and judge for themselves?

This seemed like a sensible suggestion. The Seminole designated seven leaders, including Jumper and Sam Jones, to go out to Indian Territory and report back. In a preamble to the Treaty of Payne's Landing, signed on May 9, 1832, the Americans wrote that the chiefs "and their faithful interpreter, Abraham . . . (shall) be sent at the expense of the United States as early as convenient to examine the country assigned to the Creeks west of the Mississippi River; and should they be satisfied with the character of the country, and of the favorable disposition of the Creeks to reunite with the Seminoles as one people," then the Seminole would agree to the treaty and gradually move to Indian Territory over a period of three years. In return, they'd be paid $15,400 for their reservation lands (Duval had speculated at least some of the five million swamp-ridden acres were worth $1 each!), $3,000 annually for fifteen years, and another $7,000 to make up for any slaves that might have to be returned to white masters.

The Seminole Negro were relieved that Abraham and Cudjo were part of the delegation. The Creek system of slavery was far more severe than that of the Seminole. If the tribes merged, certainly the Creek would insist that the Seminole adopt their draconian treatment of blacks, which usually consisted of either working them to death or selling them off to whites. Surely Abraham, at least, would persuade the seven Seminole chiefs to refuse to move!

Instead, word came back to Florida that, on March 28, 1833, the chiefs had signed an agreement stating the property was fine, the Creek were friendly, and the Seminole would move to Indian Territory. The whites rejoiced, the Indians wondered, and the Seminole Negro were horrified. What had happened in Indian Territory?

When the chiefs and their interpreters returned to Florida, it was obvious things weren't quite as they had seemed. Some of the chiefs claimed they'd been pressured into signing; while there doesn't seem to be a record of what means were used, physical intimidation is almost as strong a possibility as copious amounts of whiskey. The Seminole chiefs who made the Indian Territory trip were all, apparently, prone to drinking. Some of the Seminole Negro suspected they'd been sold out by their own; Abraham and Cudjo were paid $200 each by the whites for their services as translators. ("Didn't mean nothing," Willie Warrior said.)

Abraham probably didn't betray his people. Certainly, his role in the coming war indicates he was as opposed to the Indian Territory move as anyone. But he also took the white man's money, and the Americans weren't paying him to encourage Seminole and Seminole Negro resistance to relocation.

Abraham was an intelligent man; he couldn't have mistaken the $200 for anything other than an unsubtle bribe. Perhaps, once he was positive the seven chiefs would sign the agreement—whether under duress or not—Abraham saw no reason not to take the money and pretend to go along. It would have been the practical thing to do, and this possibility was Ben Pingenot's best guess. Or he may have wanted the money for another reason. If the Seminole moved to Indian Territory, Abraham had no illusions about his own fate, let alone that of all the other Seminole Negro. They'd either be given back to the whites before the move, or sold back to them by the Creek after they'd arrived in Indian Territory. Either way, the relatively free lives enjoyed by blacks under the Seminole would be over. Abraham probably wanted the $200 so he could at least buy his own freedom if the relocation ever did take place.

If the treaty was enforceable, the Indians should have been moved out over a three-year period beginning in 1833. But Duval and Thompson weren't able to bring all the Seminole chiefs together in one place. Instead, they held a series of meetings with several tribal leaders at a time. It became obvious Seminole Negro politicking against the relocation was the cause of the delay. In frustration, Duval wrote to the Bureau of Indian Affairs that "the slaves belonging to the Indians have a controlling influence over their masters and are utterly opposed to any change of residence."

Bribed or not, once he'd returned to Florida Abraham actively opposed the proposed relocation. A U.S. officer noted that "Abraham dictated to those of his own color." He wasn't the only one. John Caesar, another Seminole Negro owned by King Philip, went to St. Augustine to recruit runaways and free blacks there. The fact his master let him do this meant the Seminole chiefs knew war was coming, too.

Meetings between white and Indian leaders didn't help. A Seminole subchief named Osceola was especially vehement; not only did he refuse to leave Florida, he promised to fight if necessary. One tale, perhaps apocryphal, has Osceola waving a knife at Thompson and screaming, "The only treaty I will ever execute will be with this!"

The Seminole had an additional argument. The original Treaty of Moultrie Creek still had seven years to go. They'd consider accepting the Payne's Landing agreement only after the earlier treaty ran its course. It was clearly a delaying tactic; reports from Duval's spies indicated the Indians had begun buying large amounts of ammunition.

The government considered another approach. It was obvious the

Seminole Negro were complicating what should have been a clear-cut issue. Why not take a simple step to remove them entirely? General Richard Call captured President Jackson's attention with the suggestion that the U.S. government just buy all the Seminole Negro from their Indian masters and give the blacks back to white slave owners. But Wiley Thompson fought the recommendation, risking his own career in the process. While the Seminole Negro were encouraging the Seminole not to relocate, Thompson wrote the secretary of war: "I have given (the Seminole) a pledge I will do everything in my power, consistent with the rights of others, to save Blacks from worse bondage . . . with the most respectful deference to the Department, I should consider any other (action) an abandonment of the principles of the Treaty, and Humanity. Should this happen and be tolerated, God only knows what the consequences will be."

Thompson's response didn't impress the secretary, who wrote back that he'd heard rumors Thompson planned to seize the blacks for himself. Call's plan was to be followed—but, as it turned out, there wasn't enough time for that.

Osceola continued his warlike orations. In June, Thompson arrested him. Six days later, the Seminole made it known he'd changed his mind. He'd move his followers to Indian Territory and encourage other chiefs to follow his example. Thompson was delighted; he released Osceola and even gave him a new rifle.

A handful of chiefs suddenly agreed to relocate. Charley Emathla, Hadjo, Holata Emathla, and Econchatomico weren't as influential as Micanopy, Jumper, Sam Jones, or Alligator, but their cooperation was enough to encourage Thompson. He declared that all the Seminole should be ready to leave Florida on January 8, 1836. Micanopy, Alligator, Jumper, and other recalcitrants were told they were no longer Seminole chiefs. The Indians and their black slaves were to report to Tampa Bay by that date, and then the government would send them off on ships.

Osceola sent his own message to tribal leaders: Any chiefs who cooperated with Thompson and agreed to go to Indian Territory would be killed before they ever left Florida. Near the end of November, a large party of

Seminole and Seminole Negro arrived at Charley Emathla's village. Ominously, its leaders were Osceola and Abraham. They had determined that Charley Emathla was the key chief favoring emigration, and they demanded that he reconsider.

Here, for the first time, there is an extensive written record. Second Lieutenant Woodburne Potter was stationed in Florida and kept a detailed diary about what he saw and heard during 1834 and '35. In 1836 he published *The War in Florida,* identifying himself only as "a late Staff Officer." Much of what Potter recorded was hearsay, both from white soldiers and Indian prisoners. He certainly despised Osceola, who he called "Assiola." Potter believed the Seminole was a cunning liar who fooled Thompson and agitated the rest of the Seminole into going to war—and that is indisputably true. That Osceola was responding in kind to white treachery is something Potter never took into consideration.

But Potter, despite his dislike for Osceola, was often in sympathy with the Seminole and the Seminole Negro, pointing out how the United States failed to honor its treaty promises and emphasizing repeatedly how lawless American settlers stole land and slaves from the Indians. In all, his seems the most complete, objective account of events in late 1835.

On November 26, Potter wrote, Osceola and Abraham led four hundred Indian and black warriors to Charley Emathla's village. There they informed Charley he could either refuse to emigrate or die. Osceola was especially angry that Charley had sold his cattle to the Americans, taking this as a sign he had more interest in U.S. gold than the welfare of his people.

"But that Indian nobly replied that he had already pledged his word," Potter wrote. "He said that he had lived to see his nation a ruined and degraded people, and he believed their salvation was in removing to the west; he had made arrangements for his people to go, and had delivered to the agent all their cattle, so they had no excuse now for not complying with their engagements."

His visitors weren't moved. Charley was told he had two hours to change his mind. Bravely, he replied that two hours weren't necessary.

He'd given his word to the white man, and he meant to keep it. Osceola raised the rifle he'd been given by Wiley Thompson. Abraham interceded, suggesting to Osceola that they needed to talk more before killing one of their own. Osceola momentarily agreed; Potter writes that he left, but almost immediately came back and shot Charley to death. Since Potter got his information from some of Charley's people, who, after seeing their chief killed, ran to nearby Fort King seeking protection from the soldiers there, some subjectivity is involved. But it's certain that, after Charley died, the Americans took no immediate action against Osceola for the shooting. Thompson noted that "the consiquences [*sic*] resulting from this murder leave no doubt that actual force must be resorted to for the purpose of effecting removal, as it has produced a general defection."

U.S. soldiers had nicknamed the upper reservation area "The Long Swamp," an apt description for an extended swath of mud, dingy water, alligators, and poisonous snakes. Knowing the white soldiers would hesitate to come near it, Micanopy, Jumper, King Philip, Sam Jones, Osceola, and other tribal leaders chose that location to meet. Desperate as they were, they did not automatically decide to fight.

Americans had demonstrated their military might twenty years earlier. The Seminole and Seminole Negro had been soundly defeated by Jackson. Defying Thompson's orders to move would be tantamount to inviting another white invasion. The Americans had promised the Seminole could keep their black slaves, and that, in Indian Territory, the Creek would not impose their laws on the newcomers.

But, after Moultrie Creek, the chiefs had also learned how little they could trust the white man's promises. Their Florida reservation was uninhabitable. White slavers seemed to raid their villages at will; afterward, the soldiers wouldn't do anything about it. When the whites didn't like the wording of the Payne's Landing treaty, they changed it to suit their purposes. Agent Thompson even told the Indians who their chiefs were and weren't. Once they were in Indian Territory, everyone realized, their ability to fight would be even more limited. The Creek would align themselves with the whites as they had before. The Seminole and Seminole Negro would be on unfamiliar ground. Better to fight in Florida, where they knew the land and could use the swamps to their advantage.

There was another good reason to fight as soon as possible. The army had pulled most of its soldiers out of Florida; Potter's book notes that, at the end of 1835, there were just 489 white soldiers in the state. A few intense, well-coordinated attacks might at least force the Americans to wonder whether a second Seminole war was worth the trouble.

The perspective of Abraham and the Seminole Negro was more clear-cut. If the Indians moved, the blacks would be taken away from them, either by the Americans before ships sailed west from Tampa Bay or by the Creek once the Seminole arrived in Indian Territory. Either way, the Seminole Negro would face new lives of great degradation and killing workloads. It was preferable to die fighting.

It may have been at this meeting that a younger subchief first stepped forward. He was tall, aggressive, and very charismatic. A full-blooded Seminole, his tribal name was *Coacoochee,* which Americans translated as *Wild Cat.*

"Wild Cat's another one who doesn't get respected enough," Willie Warrior said, sipping from his ever-present cup of coffee. We were sitting in the living room of one of the Fort Clark enlisted men's barrack areas, which had been converted into housing. Willie and his wife, Ethel, also a former president of the Scout Association, had bought a home on the same fort grounds where their ancestors had been evicted eighty-five years earlier.

"So you think there are some good guys in this story besides your people?" I asked, laughing.

"Not too many, but some," Willie said. "With Wild Cat, I don't deny he did some bad things to us. But without him, God knows what would have happened in Oklahoma. He was a sharp one, in his way. Too ambitious. Drank too much. But he was mostly our friend."

The circumstances of Wild Cat's birth are unknown, but his lineage isn't. King Philip married one of Micanopy's sisters. Somewhere around 1810, she gave birth to a son. King Philip was an influential chief. Micanopy was probably the nominal Seminole leader, and Osceola forced his way to the front of most war parties, but Philip, a direct descendent of Cowkeeper, certainly ranked high in the second tier of Seminole chiefs. This essentially made Wild Cat a sort of tribal prince. He was welcomed into the most influential circles, and his philosophies mirrored Osceola's. Given a choice between surrender to the white man's wishes and war, Wild Cat never hesitated.

It's impossible to be sure, but in these crucial last days of 1835, Wild Cat and John Horse may have met for the first time. Superficially, they would have had little in common. Wild Cat was a lordly Seminole chief, and John Horse was, despite his possessions, a black Seminole slave. But Abraham had proven a canny Seminole Negro could wield considerable influence, and, in terms of intellect, John Horse was clearly Abraham's superior. More than any other moment in the history of the tribe, whenever it was that Wild Cat and John Horse recognized each other's skills and became friends would impact the future of the Seminole Negro. Theirs would become a uniquely powerful, long-lasting partnership.

The Seminole chiefs' decision to fight was immediately put into practice. During Christmas week of 1835, King Philip, Wild Cat, and John Caesar raided plantations along the St. Johns River. There had been sporadic armed skirmishes between whites and the Seminole/Seminole Negro coalition since Charley Emathla's murder. King Philip's raid was the first overt sign that Indians and blacks had an overall war strategy. Wiley Thompson's assignment was still to calm his red and black charges and get them out of Florida. Extra troops were on the way from other Southern states and territories. In his office just outside the walls of Fort King, about in the center of the North Florida panhandle, Thompson spent December 28 doing paperwork and worrying. Most of the fort garrison had been sent out in response to King Philip's raids. Thompson had been warned not to go outside the fort; after all, the blacks and Indians were on the warpath, and they hated him. Abraham had predicted more than once that Thompson would die by native hands. But Thompson apparently believed the Indians and blacks still thought he was their friend.

Drawing of Wild Cat

(COURTESY OF THE INSTITUTE OF TEXAN CULTURES AT SAN ANTONIO)

Sometime that afternoon, when Thompson and a few other army personnel had finished dinner and were strolling around the area, shots rang out. Osceola and his warriors are credited by historians for the attack. They were bloodily efficient; besides Thompson, a lieutenant, the camp sutler, and two sutler's clerks were killed. Soldiers who'd remained behind at the fort rushed out, but the attackers were gone. Thompson's body looked like a sieve; besides fourteen bullet holes, there was a ragged knife wound deep in his chest. His hair had been ripped from his head.

The agent's death alone would have been sufficient outrage for declaration of all-out U.S. war on the Seminole, but forty miles south an even worse slaughter was taking place.

"Here's one we won," Willie Warrior said proudly. "The army ended up calling it the Dade Massacre. Those Seminole didn't do the real work that day. We did."

Initial American campaign tactics against the Seminole and Seminole Negro were the same used by Jackson in the First Seminole War. Well-armed soldiers were sent to find Indian and black towns, then ordered to burn everything they found there. In no way did the United States really consider these enemies to be particularly dangerous on the battlefield. They'd broken and run quickly enough when Andrew Jackson tore into them.

Major Francis L. Dade volunteered to take about one hundred troops from Fort Brooke near Tampa Bay north to Fort King, which could serve as a new base for the soldiers while they raided nearby villages. The expedition was well-armed. All the soldiers had fine rifles, and a six-pound cannon was towed along on a wagon. Dade was guided by Luis Pacheco, a slave who spoke both English and the Seminole dialect. Later, some would claim Pacheco was a spy for the Indians, and that he betrayed Dade to them. But Pacheco always denied it.

Whether Pacheco warned them or not, the blacks and Indians knew Dade was coming. This time, they didn't respond to an American invader by retreating into the swamps. Instead, they went to meet him. Osceola wasn't part of the attack—he was too busy slaughtering Wiley Thompson. Micanopy and Jumper led the combined force of Indians and blacks that moved south into the Great Wahoo Swamp. They knew very well what trail the whites would be taking to Fort King. Jumper sent out scouts, who reported back that the white soldiers were coming. In all, about 180 Indian and black braves were ready for battle.

About eight A.M., perhaps eight or ten hours before Wiley Thompson died, Dade and his soldiers approached a field "of high grass," according to Potter, who heard everything second- or third-hand. The first shot fired killed Dade. The gunfire directed at the Americans came in massive, deliberate volleys. About half of Dade's force died during the battle's first half hour. The Indians and blacks, mostly concealed by trees and swamp vegetation, screamed war cries.

But their enemy was brave. The remaining officers rallied the white soldiers. A grove of palmetto trees was nearby, and the Americans used it for cover. Someone remembered the cannon; it was loaded and fired. The first cannon shot unnerved the blacks and Indians, but they soon saw that the cannonballs weren't landing anywhere near them. During the brief interval before the Seminole and Seminole Negro decided the cannon was ineffective, the Americans built a small breastwork of logs, mud, and grass. For the next few hours, the blacks and Indians inched closer to the barricade. One by one, most of the remaining Americans fell. By 2 P.M. the survivors were out of ammunition, and the Seminole Negro charged over the breastwork.

Not every white soldier died. Three played dead, and, despite severe wounds, eventually crawled back to U.S. forts and safety. Their accounts are the basis for descriptions of what the black warriors did when the shooting had stopped. Even allowing for exaggeration—and "official" army reports had Dade's band wiped out by one thousand Seminole and Seminole Negro, five times more than participated in the ambush—what came next was horrible.

Based on testimony from survivor Ransom Clarke, Potter reported that the Seminole backed away, and the Seminole Negro came forward to finish the slaughter: "The negroes came inside of the breastwork and began to mutilate the bodies of those who showed the least signs of life, when (Lieutenant) Bassinger sprang upon his feet and implored them to spare him; they heeded not his supplications, but struck him down with their hatchets, cut open his breast and tore out his heart and lungs; such is the report of Clarke."

The Seminole Negro not only finished off the white soldiers, they enjoyed doing it. Surely some of their actions expressed the frustration of generations—here, finally, black men could treat white men as horribly as they remembered white masters treating slaves. But another element had to be in play, too.

No historian seems to have wondered why, amid all the slaughter, the

Seminole Negro somehow allowed not one, but three soldiers to escape. If Micanopy took part in the battle, Abraham could not have been far away. With hostilities finally commenced, certainly the last thing the Seminole Negro leader wanted was for the Indians to fight a few battles and then, honor partially restored, sue for peace. But blacks committing such gratuitous atrocities—mutilating the heroic white dead, of all things!—and then letting a few soldiers live to tell about it, would only inflame the Americans to a point where they might never accept a cease-fire. The longer the war lasted, the better for the Seminole Negro. That must be why the blacks specifically took on the role of butchers. ("Could be," was Willie Warrior's only comment. Miss Charles never specifically discussed the Dade Massacre with me.) Based on what they were told by the survivors, Americans were both infuriated and intimidated. It took nearly two months for a relief expedition to go to the massacre site and recover the decaying bodies. Potter was part of it.

The carnage Private Clarke reported was more descriptive than accurate. Potter, an objective reporter, took pains to point out Bassinger's corpse wasn't nearly as mutilated as Clarke described it: "I must confess that the appearance of (Bassinger's) body on the 20th of February did not seem to indicate that such violence had been committed on him." Still, there were plenty of other horrible things done by the Seminole Negro to the dead: "One of the slain, a private, was found in a truly revolting condition—a part of his body had been cut off and crammed in his mouth!" Delicacy prevented Potter from saying which part, but we can guess.

Up to this point in the Florida portion of Seminole Negro history, Ben Pingenot frequently suggested research materials, other historians to talk to, and, of course, wasn't shy about offering his own opinions. I enjoyed his company; he was a charming man. But during my next few visits to Brackettville, he was away, speaking at or simply attending historical conferences. On my early Brackettville trips I always saw Miss Charles. Usually I saw Willie Warrior. Ben and I exchanged notes—I sent him a copy of my newspaper article, which he said he liked—and maybe three telephone calls. I assimilated his comments and Seminole Negro research into my own expanding pile of notes and followed through in contacting a half-dozen other Texas historians he'd recommended as knowing something of value about the Seminole Negro. They were all very friendly, and their insights helped provide a fuller picture of the tribe.

Then, gradually, I began neglecting Ben. Using a Fort Clark motel room as a base, I made long, time-consuming side trips to Eagle Pass and across the border into Mexico, tracing Seminole Negro migration, and into parts of West Texas where, as scouts, men of the tribe had fought the Comanche and Apache. I'd get back to my tiny motel room late at night, too tired to walk across the parade grounds to Ben's home.

Finally, in late 2000, I remembered—guiltily—how long it had been since we'd spoken. I was going down to Brackettville again, and I called Ben to say I was coming and would like to get together. His wife answered the phone and told me he'd died a few months earlier. She was in the process of selling his book collection, along with all of his files and photos. They were already boxed and on the way to the auctioneer, and so no longer available to me. She was sorry to give me such bad news—she remembered Ben talking about me.

Ben Pingenot had given me so much information about the Seminole Negro. He'd generously shared his library, his thoughts, the names and phone numbers of his historian friends. But there were questions I'd still wanted and meant to ask him, and now the chance was gone.

That's how bits of history get lost.

chapter four

MISS CHARLES loved children with a gentle intensity bordering on obsession. She *knew,* she told me every time we met, that if only the Seminole Negro kids would become interested in their tribal history again, everything would turn out all right. Miss Charles's definition of "all right" was vague. Sometimes she talked about a hundredth annual Seminole Days celebration and all the festivities she was certain would be associated with that. Other times there were references to Seminole Negro kids growing up to be mayor of Brackettville or superintendent of the town schools—important people, *bosses,* in position to tell other people what to do instead of taking orders.

"It's the television and those video games," Miss Charles would add mournfully. When she was a child, she'd note, amusement for youngsters "of an evening" was sitting at the knee of older Seminole Negro spinning tales of great adventures in Mexico and west Texas. But modern children preferred more sophisticated amusements. "Someday, though, I'll find one kid," she promised. "There'll be one who'll listen to me, who'll get excited by the stories. John Horse and fighting and medals of honor, all these things. And that kid will carry it on when I'm gone."

In 1994, there was little chance Seminole Negro youngsters would learn anything about their unique heritage in a classroom. One of Willie Warrior's particular peeves was that the Brackettville public schools didn't teach students about Seminole Negro history.

"It's right there for the kids to learn about," he grumbled. "In Brackettville they teach 'em about the Alamo because there's a fake one around the corner, and all about things that happened thousands of miles away. But nothing about us. I do programs in schools in Del Rio and San Antonio and anywhere else they want me to, but they never asked me in the Brackettville schools, not once."

On a late summer day in 1994, I drove to the one long building that housed Brackettville's combined elementary, junior high, and high schools. Summer vacation was about to end. A secretary told me Steve Mills, the Brackettville superintendent, was meeting with his teachers in the school library. I said I'd come back later when he was free, but she said she'd just peek in and see if he could talk to me right away. A minute later she was back, bringing him with her.

"I think maybe we do some Seminole units in the elementary building," Mills said, squinting in the bright sunlight. We talked outside on the sidewalk; a narrow roof overhead didn't do much to deflect the glare. "I guess I could check for you."

"You don't know if you do or not?"

Mills sighed. "Look," he said, sounding more resigned than impatient, "It's not a topic completely forgotten. Besides, if our Seminole students aren't learning about their past, shouldn't their parents take responsibility for providing that education?"

Mills said he'd never met Willie Warrior. He thought he might have "run into" Miss Charles somewhere. I said I thought Brackettville was small enough for everyone to know everybody else, and he said he had to get back to his meeting. Later, Willie told me he'd met Mills several times: "He didn't mean to be, but that man was just about *Klan*! I think he lived on the fort, but I don't think he ever got into the history of it."

After talking to Mills, I went to the cramped Brackettville public library. Cindy Lockwood, who'd worked there for three years, said she always helped schoolkids working on research papers and other class assignments, "but I haven't heard about any they've done about the Seminoles."

"Do you think you'd know if there had been any Seminole-related assignments?"

"Oh, yes," she said. "The kids would have told me. But there haven't been."

I gave up for the afternoon and holed up in my phoneless motel room to read articles Ben Pingenot had Xeroxed about the Second Seminole War. I had Woodburne Potter's book with me, too. It was hard to believe the Brackettville school district couldn't find time to teach students even a little Seminole Negro history. The Second Seminole War alone had all the elements—violence, courage, treachery—that would have mesmerized any class assigned to study about it. Over the next few days, I felt mesmerized myself as I learned, through reading and talking with Willie and Ben Pingenot, what happened after the first few days of the conflict.

Coupled with the assassination of Wiley Thompson, the Dade Massacre forced the American army to respect the Seminole and Seminole Negro as ferocious, dangerous enemies. After their impressive victory on December 28, the Indian and black warriors gleefully embarked on a bloody series of hit-and-run attacks on Florida plantations and smaller settlements.

According to Potter, they "spread themselves in small parties for the purpose of devastating the country. They appeared simultaneously in the south part of the peninsula, and from the extreme east below St. Augustine to the west, carrying off everything that was useful to them and destroying the remainder."

Usually the richest planters were at least able to save their families, sending them to the various Florida forts or north to friends in Georgia or South Carolina. Families on smaller farms had to trust to luck. The Seminole and Seminole Negro were not merciful. They killed whatever whites they could.

But it was the owners of major plantations, wealthy men with political connections, who railed to officials in Washington that the Indians and blacks had to be stopped, whatever the cost to taxpayers. Their lucrative businesses were losing money.

There was also the matter of slaves. Throughout the American South, blacks were eager to run to Florida and join the Seminole Negro—a chance not only to escape, but to fight the white man! And, as the Seminole Negro attacked Florida plantations and farms, they found willing recruits among slaves there. According to Potter, in the St. Johns River area alone "it is supposed more than three hundred negroes have been carried away."

The government responded. General Duncan Clinch was permitted to call on the governors of Georgia, South Carolina, and Alabama for state militia. Volunteers flocked to Florida, too: "With a spirit which does honour to the American character, hundreds of the bravest sons of these states flew with eagerness to the standard and superseded the necessity of drafts being made," Potter noted.

This influx of white fighters didn't escape notice by the Seminole and Seminole Negro. Indian forces combined probably didn't total more than one thousand warriors. The Seminole Negro had perhaps 350 fighting men. Whenever American forces had full engagements with the enemy, Indians and blacks were blasted into retreat. The United States supplied its soldiers with better weapons. Their rifles fired straighter and further. The Seminole and Seminole Negro mostly relied on hit-and-run tactics, which could effectively burn a plantation but couldn't repulse a well-armed white regiment.

Realizing they could never decisively defeat the Americans, and hopeful their short-term success against the whites might result in more favorable terms, even the fiercest Seminole leaders soon were willing to consider a peace treaty. There were sporadic peace talks, but nothing came of them. So General Winfield Scott, later to become the hero of the U.S.–Mexican War, was sent to Florida to put down the uprising for good. Scott had nearly five thousand soldiers under his command, about four times the number of Indian and black warriors combined. Scott's plan was to divide his forces into three groups and send them south. When they found the enemy, they would surround and annihilate every one. Part of the process would be to destroy the main Seminole and Seminole Negro villages. The locations of Okihumpky and Peliklakaha were no secret. Once enough havoc had been wreaked upon them, Scott was certain, the Seminole would beg for a cease-fire and gladly hand over all their black slaves, if that was what the conquering Americans demanded.

But the Seminole and Seminole Negro didn't fight according to Scott's plan. They set up ambushes for the American troops, they hid in the swamps if faced with too great an opposing force, and, when their villages were burned, they shrugged. These tactics wore down the U.S. troops. By early fall, Osceola and his warriors even temporarily occupied an American fort.

Florida governor Richard Call decided it was time for reinforcements. He hired 750 Creek warriors as mercenaries, shipping them in to Tampa Bay and promising they would receive "such plunder as they may take from the Seminoles." By plunder, he meant Seminole Negro. The Creek very much wanted slaves, less for their personal use than for sale to the ubiquitous slavers in and around Indian Territory. In instances when the Creek captured Seminole Negro who were proven to be property of white owners, they would be paid a bounty of twenty dollars for each black they turned over.

The Seminole were outraged by the Creek arrival. The two tribes had long hated each other, and Seminole opposition to the Payne's Landing Treaty had mostly been due to having to rejoin the Creek nation. But the Seminole Negro, knowing what their fates would be if they fell into Creek hands, were even more determined to fight to the death.

They got the chance soon enough. Unlike the rigid, failed battle plan of starchy General Scott, Call let his combined white and Creek forces adopt the opposition's tactics. When, confronted by superior numbers, the Seminole and Seminole Negro retreated into the swamps, the Creek went in after them. There was a final, pitched November battle in the Great Wahoo Swamp. Call's force of about two thousand met four hundred Seminole and two hundred Seminole Negro. It resulted in a blood-drenched stalemate. Call's men eventually retreated, hopeful that sufficient damage had been inflicted on the outnumbered enemy to convince them to give up. But the Seminole and Seminole Negro decided to fight on.

At that point in my reading, I began wondering again why modern Seminole Negro kids weren't demanding to know more instead of ignoring their heritage. Of course, so far I only had the word of Miss Charles and Willie Warrior about that. Maybe those two storytelling veterans were wrong about such youthful apathy. So I went into town to find some Seminole Negro kids and see what, if anything, they knew about the history of their people—specifics like the battle in the Great Wahoo Swamp, or even basic information about runaway slaves in Florida. I didn't think they'd be hard to find.

But downtown Brackettville in the evening is hardly a social magnet for youngsters. There's no mall to wander, no multiscreen movie theater to offer glimpses of a more exciting outside world. No kids were hanging around the Krazy Chicken. But there was a video store, and when my photographer and I went in we found a nineteen-year-old girl working the cash register. It was very hot in the store. No Brackettville air-conditioning, it seemed, was equal to the summer heat.

The girl told us her name was Monika Cruz. She'd grown up in Brackettville and gone through the school system there—"First through twelfth grade," she volunteered. Her dream in life was to go to junior college in nearby Uvalde, where they had a movie theater and a tiny mall. And no, Monika couldn't remember any of her Brackettville teachers talking about the Seminole Negro.

"I think it would have been interesting if they'd told us about those scouts or something, but they never did," she said. It was broiling in the corner of the store where Monika perched on a stool behind the cash register. There weren't any shades on the wide windows facing the street. All the plastic cassette covers on display were faded from direct exposure to sunlight. Monika's forehead was beaded with sweat, and she was wearing a very skimpy halter top and cutoff shorts.

Miss Charles had said most Brackettville Hispanics had at least some Seminole Negro in them, and Monika had the same high cheekbones and strong nose that Miss Charles and Willie Warrior did. But, when I asked, she insisted she wasn't "even one bit Seminole. I have two uncles that are buried in their cemetery, but I'm not Seminole at all."

"Your uncles are in the scout cemetery? Were they Seminole?" I asked.

"Mmm-hmm," Monika replied. The conversation was beginning to bore her.

"Were they blood relations, or just related through marriage?"

"Blood relations."

"But you're not Seminole?"

"No. Not a bit."

And, Monika added, she'd never been to a Seminole Days program. I could imagine Willie Warrior standing behind her, saying to me angrily, "See? What did you expect?" We thanked her for her time and spent another half hour poking around looking for other kids. There were none to be found. Monika had said all her friends were probably at home watching TV, or more likely off in Uvalde "where you can have fun." For the first time I began to have a real sense of what Miss Charles and Willie Warrior were up against. You can't teach kids who don't want to learn, and you can't even try to teach kids who aren't around. I couldn't think of anything else to do but go back to the motel and read more about the Second Seminole War. Woodburne Potter was handy, even if Seminole Negro youngsters weren't.

What Potter wrote supported what Ben Pingenot and, later, several other Texas historians, told me. After one year, the war was no closer to resolution. The Seminole and Seminole Negro were tenacious. Their fighting skills were sufficient to hold off the American army, though they weren't numerous enough to actually defeat the United States. Some new strategy had to be brought into play, and the next commander of American forces in Florida came up with it.

Major General Thomas Sidney Jesup was a pragmatic man. Willie Warrior whistled when he talked about him, showing appreciation of, if not admiration for, a worthy foe. Where Winfield Scott had expected textbook battles from like-minded opponents, when Jesup arrived in Florida in December 1836, he took the time to study the enemy. Obviously, the Seminole and Seminole Negro strategy of fighting, then running, worked. According to the most optimistic U.S. records, only 136 enemy Indians and blacks had been killed in the first year of the war. Even with their limited numbers, that still left most of their warriors alive to fight.

Jesup knew he had the edge in manpower. He also believed he knew why the Seminole were really fighting: "This, you may be assured, is a negro and not an Indian war," he wrote soon after arriving. "And if it be not speedily put down, the south will feel the effects of it on their slave population before the end of next (planting) season." The blacks had the Seminole's collective ear, and their counsel was to fight on rather than surrender. So long as the Seminole Negro remained at large and kept winning impressive battles against white foes, slaves throughout the Southern states would be inspired to run away, too. In Florida, and even into portions of Georgia, Seminole and Seminole Negro raiding parties kept crops from being planted and harvested on schedule. Somehow, Jesup had to find a way to apply more effective pressure to Seminole chiefs than their black slave-allies could bring to bear.

His solution was action-specific: Capture as many Seminole women and children as possible. It would be nice to catch warriors, too, but if enough Seminole braves wanted their families released from captivity, they might not listen as much to black warriors urging them to keep fighting.

Using scouts and informants, Jesup spent a few weeks locating the larger Indian/black bands. In the first weeks of the new year, he took troops and attacked, focusing less on killing warriors than on capturing women and children. In this, he succeeded; about one hundred Indian noncombatants were taken, along with a few blacks. At the same time, a contingent of Creek mercenaries raided a Seminole camp and captured relatives of Micanopy.

Jesup fretted that "not a single first-rate warrior has been captured, and only two Indian men have surrendered. The warriors have fought as long as they had life, and such seems to me to be the determination of those who influence their councils—I mean the leading negroes."

Then Jesup got lucky. Abraham agreed to meet with him. He arrived at

Jesup's Fort Dade headquarters on January 31. The two men probably sat down in a rude, whitewashed office. An oil lamp would have provided flickering light. Jesup would have on his dress uniform—lots of braid, and maybe some dangling medals. Abraham, in contrast, would undoubtedly have worn ragged deerskin, the sartorial legacy of fighting and hiding in the swamps.

They talked for hours. When they were done, whatever had been said, Abraham became Jesup's ally. He promised to go back to the Seminole and convince their principal chiefs to at least come in and parlay.

And what did Jesup promise Abraham? His freedom, certainly. Abraham would have wanted his wife's freedom guaranteed, and that of his children. Money may have changed hands. Abraham had taken U.S. dollars before. But he would not have agreed to help Jesup unless he believed the general would keep whatever promises he made to the Seminole and Seminole Negro, Willie Warrior insisted. By representing Jesup to his Indian masters, Abraham was risking his life. Osceola had shot Charley Emathla for cooperating with the whites. Abraham would not have forgotten that.

Abraham left Fort Dade; just a few days later, he returned with Jumper and Alligator. The two chiefs found Jesup's arguments persuasive enough to agree to further talks. Jesup wanted Micanopy, Osceola, King Philip, and the rest of the principal Seminole chiefs to attend. He was wise enough to realize that every important Seminole leader had to agree to a treaty this time. Also, while Jesup worked toward a settlement at Fort Dade, other Seminole and Seminole Negro leaders were conducting a new series of raids against the plantations along the St. Johns River. The young chief named Wild Cat was particularly active.

Jumper and Alligator agreed on February 18 as the date of the peace talks. Because of the St. Johns raids, Jesup worried that a significant number of the Seminole still wanted to fight.

Abraham had the same concern. He spent his days seeking out every Seminole chief he could find, trying to persuade them to come to Fort Dade on the eighteenth. Apparently, he had further conversations with Jesup, too, stressing that the Seminole Negro had to be satisfied with terms of a new agreement. If they weren't, he warned, the Seminole would never cooperate with the Americans.

On the appointed day, Jesup was ready early. Long tables piled with food and liquor were set up inside the fort. Soldiers were alerted not to shoot any Indians and blacks who arrived bearing white flags. But no hostiles came that morning. It was February 24 before the Seminole leaders arrived and, when they did, Micanopy wasn't with them. Neither was Jumper. Abraham told Jesup that Jumper was sick. Micanopy sent his son Holatoochee. Perhaps the absence of two such important chiefs was a Seminole ploy. Certainly, opening negotiations didn't go smoothly. Jesup said the Indians had to leave Florida. Holatoochee said Micanopy wouldn't go. Jesup insisted the move to Indian Territory was nonnegotiable, but added it would be possible to include treaty stipulations that protected the Seminole interests against the Creek. Hearing that, Holatoochee said it was necessary now for him to report back to Micanopy. They could talk again with the American general in early March. Jesup was agreeable, but wanted the Seminole to leave behind a dozen hostages as proof they intended to negotiate further, and in good faith.

The Seminole delegation left. When they returned on March 4, John Horse joined Abraham as an interpreter. This clearly indicates that somehow, somewhere, during the war, he had assisted the Seminole and impressed them sufficiently to trust him during these critical negotiations.

Jumper came this time. Micanopy still was absent; Holatoochee was his spokesman again. Ominously, Osceola wasn't there, either. But Abraham assured Jesup that enough Seminole leaders were present to effectively make a quorum. If an agreement could be reached, all the Seminole and Seminole Negro would abide by it.

After two days of intense bargaining, they reached one. For public relations purposes, Jesup called it the "Capitulation of the Seminole nation of Indians and their allies." The Seminole agreed to stop fighting at once and to accept removal to Indian Territory on or about April 10. That gave the Americans what they wanted—a Florida free of Indians.

But the Seminole and Seminole Negro apparently got what they wanted, too. To them, the key clause of the treaty was Article 5: "Major

General Jesup, in behalf of the United States, agrees that the Seminole and their allies, who come in and emigrate West, shall be secure in their lives and property; that their negroes, their bona fide property, shall also accompany them West . . ."

There were other considerations. The Americans promised to pay fair value for the horses and cattle the blacks and Indians had to leave behind. All relocation expenses would be paid by the government. Once in Indian Territory, the United States would provide rations for one year, plus seed to plant crops.

But the vagueness of some treaty terminology somehow escaped immediate notice. Did *allies* just mean free blacks, or also recent runaway slaves who'd enlisted in the Seminole cause? *Bona fide property* was open to even wider interpretation. The Seminole believed that any blacks they owned at the time of the treaty agreement fit that category, whether it was a Seminole Negro who had been part of a Seminole family for decades or a slave taken from a Florida plantation in recent weeks. Abraham and other Seminole Negro leaders apparently believed the same thing. Otherwise, they would never have agreed to the treaty.

Jesup knew that. After the treaty signing, he wrote that "the negroes rule the Indians and it is important that they should feel secure; if they should become alarmed and hold out, the war will be renewed."

Initially, things went well. On March 18, Micanopy finally arrived. He pronounced himself satisfied with the agreement and signed it. King Philip sent word he and his people were on the way in. As the Indians and blacks arrived, they were set up in a camp outside the fort grounds, since the fort itself didn't have enough room to house all the new arrivals. Everyone got along well enough. The army issued some rations, and the Seminole and Seminole Negro hunters shared what they brought back to camp with the soldiers.

There was one obvious absentee. Jesup stressed to the other chiefs that it was their responsibility to make Osceola agree to the treaty and come in with his warriors.

But Osceola wasn't the only recalcitrant. Jesup had believed Florida citizens, including the major plantation owners, would be overjoyed by the treaty. The hated Seminole and their even more despised black cronies were being shipped out of the territory, never to return. Peace was at hand; plantings and harvests could resume. But for many of the Florida whites, as well as landowners in Georgia, South Carolina, and Alabama, it wasn't enough.

They wanted their slaves back. It didn't matter whether they sought grandchildren of blacks who escaped in the 1700s, or field hands who'd recently run away. They demanded their property and discounted any claims the Seminole might feel they had on them.

The firestorm of demands began with former Seminole agent Gad Humphreys. He had originally been replaced by Wiley Thompson when white Florida settlers believed Humphreys was too sympathetic to the Seminole. Now Humphreys claimed that the treaty deprived him of a number of Seminole Negro he'd acquired during his tenure. Angry planters rode in, demanding financial restitution and the return of missing slaves.

Jesup could have rebuffed them. He could have ordered them off fort property, perhaps promising to ask the government to reimburse them for any lost slaves or goods. He could have pointed out the main American goal was to get the Seminole and Seminole Negro out of Florida, then worry afterward about who owed what to whom. But he didn't. He caved in. A meticulous chronicler of events, on March 29 Jesup wrote that "I have some hopes of inducing the Indians and the Indian negroes to unite in bringing in the negroes taken from the citizens during the war." Suddenly, Jesup decided, recent runaway slaves who'd joined the Seminole and Seminole Negro were no longer classified as allies. By April 8, Jesup had secret agreements with a few Seminole chiefs, Alligator in particular, to go along with that convenient philosophy.

We can be certain he asked Humphreys, Cooley, and the others to be patient—he was working things out. But they didn't want to wait. By the first week in April, hired slavers were ringing the Seminole camp adjacent to Fort Dade, on the lookout for blacks who could be snatched up. Belatedly, Jesup issued an order forbidding nongovernment whites from coming near the fort. But too many were already there.

Rumor had it that the Florida militia was getting ready to march on the fort, with the intention of taking back blacks at gunpoint. Jesup wrote a pleading letter to the militia commander, claiming, "There is no disposition on the part of the great body of Indians to renew hostilities and they will, I am sure, faithfully fulfill their engagements if the people of Florida are prudent; but any attempt to seize their negroes or other property would be followed by an instant resort to arms."

Jesup was stalling for time; two dozen ships were on the way to Tampa Bay to transport the emigrants. About eight hundred Indians and blacks were in camp, ready to go. But the Seminole and Seminole Negro were becoming nervous. Many of their chiefs—Micanopy, Holatoochee, Wild Cat, Abraham, John Horse—were there, and they were unwilling to see the Seminole Negro so harrassed by the slavers. Wild Cat and John Horse, both roughly in their middle twenties, had become especially close friends. We know this because people who were with them in the camp told Miss Charles's parents that they did. When Wild Cat and John Horse discovered that some of the Seminole chiefs had made a secret agreement with Jesup to return at least some blacks to white Florida masters, they were furious. Many Seminole Negro chose not to wait and see what happened; they fled the Fort Dade camp, heading back into the swamps. Because they had been allowed to come and go fairly freely, some Seminole leaders, including Wild Cat, also chose to stay away from the camp.

Jesup didn't give up. After all, he still held many of the principal Seminole chiefs hostage, including Micanopy and Jumper. Abraham and John Horse, the leaders of the Seminole Negro, remained in friendly custody. Jesup ordered them all to meet with him on June 2, when they would decide how to induce the remaining Seminole chiefs to come in and somehow lure back the missing Seminole Negro, too.

But the Indians and blacks didn't come to the scheduled conference, and that night Osceola, leading at least two hundred warriors, sneaked into the Fort Dade camp and led away almost all the Indians and blacks there, including Micanopy, Jumper, and John Horse. It's possible Osceola forced some of them to leave. Micanopy later told an Indian agent he'd asked to be killed rather than go back on his word to stay and emigrate, but was placed on a horse and taken against his will. It is far more likely Micanopy was glad to go with Osceola. Once again, the white man's word had proven false.

Afterward, Jesup blamed John Horse: "Wherever John Cavallo was, foul play might be expected." Osceola and Wild Cat were also identified as principal perpetrators.

Abraham wasn't. He stayed in the camp. There was really no other option for him. So far as the Seminole, especially Osceola, were concerned, Abraham had guaranteed the white general would keep all his promises, including the ones allowing the Indians to keep their blacks. Jesup's lie, in their minds, became Abraham's lie. To them, he was now allied with Jesup, and, under the circumstances, Abraham really had no other choice than to cooperate with the American general. If he'd gone back to the Seminole, Osceola would almost certainly have killed him.

The Seminole hadn't lost much through the failed treaty. But the Seminole Negro were weakened, though not devastated. Nearly two hundred of their people were lost, either through abduction by slavers or appropriation by the army as lost property of white masters. Abraham, their former leader, was now allied with Jesup. That left John Horse as the new Seminole Negro headman.

While the escaped Seminole and Seminole Negro regrouped, Jesup felt obligated to inform his superiors that his boast of the war being over had proven premature. His anger was directed at the Seminole and Seminole Negro rather than himself.

"I believe the emigration of the Seminoles to be impractical under any circumstances," he wrote the commissioner of Indian Affairs. "The country can be rid of them only by exterminating them." The next week, Jesup asked for seven hundred Florida militiamen to assist his troops because "if the war is carried on it must necessarily be one of extermination. We have, at no former period in our history, had to contend with so formidable an enemy."

Jesup also mentioned Abraham to the Indian Affairs commissioner: "I have promised Abraham the freedom of his family if he be faithful to us, and I shall certainly hang him if he be not faithful."

In the next months, Jesup came up with various schemes. He suggested the Seminole Negro could be shipped to Indian Territory, but other Florida property—hopefully better than the previous swampland—could be given to the Seminole as a new reservation. He hinted to Creek volunteers that, if they'd defeat the Seminole, they might be allowed to keep Seminole women and children as slaves besides whatever blacks they captured. He sent to Washington lists of the Seminole and Seminole Negro he'd captured, with greatly exaggerated descriptions of how prominent each was within the tribe. Eventually, that exaggeration became fact. Led by a Seminole Negro informer, U.S. soldiers captured Wild Cat's father, King Philip, and forty-eight of his people. Wild Cat wasn't present. About a month later, in late October, Wild Cat was concerned enough about his father to bring Osceola, John Horse, and other leaders in for new peace talks. More than two hundred armed Florida militiamen emerged from hiding and took the Indians and blacks captive. Their prisoners didn't try to fight back. They knew they were outnumbered and outgunned. Jesup proudly informed his superiors that "nearly all the war spirits of the Nation" were in custody. Osceola, Wild Cat, John Horse, and their companions were marched off to St. Augustine. Along with twenty other detainees, the three men identified by Jesup as ringleaders were locked in an underground cell that measured eighteen by thirty-three feet. The only sunlight came through a narrow window high on one wall. They had to relieve themselves in buckets. They slept on a wooden platform. Each day, they were allowed to wander for a few hours in the courtyard.

Then unexpected visitors arrived. The U.S. government had asked Chief John Ross and other leaders of the Cherokee to come to Florida and plead with the Seminole to stop fighting and come to Indian Territory. The land there was decent for farming, the Cherokee promised. The Creek would not oppress the Seminole. Fighting the white man was futile. Osceola, worn down by imprisonment, agreed he was tired of fighting. Hopeful of imminent peace, the white soldiers then escorted the Cherokee away, sending them to Fort Mellon, where another Seminole delegation had been invited to come in under a white flag and hear what the visiting Indians had to say. When these Seminole arrived, Jesup had them arrested, too.

The general was especially anxious to have more Indian and black prisoners, because he had just lost several of the more famous ones. On November 20, John Horse, Wild Cat, Wild Cat's two brothers, and two women escaped from their cells in the St. Augustine dungeon. Their method of escape was classic. Someone smuggled in a file; the prisoners gradually cut through a bar in a high window, tied strips of sheeting together for a rope, and climbed on other prisoners' shoulders to wriggle their way through the tiny new opening and lower themselves down the outside wall. Osceola didn't escape with them. He was sick, probably with consumption.

So Jesup focused on getting other prominent prisoners. Micanopy was recaptured. Osceola's family turned themselves in. The Cherokee delegation filed an outraged protest with the commissioner of Indian Affairs, claiming they'd been used to betray the trust of the Seminole. But Jesup was getting desperate.

Few generals are devoid of ambition, and it was obvious to Jesup that his inability to end the Seminole war was making his superiors in Washington unhappy. As usual, he tried to place the blame on others, including the Cherokee. Responding to their claim they'd been unwittingly used to betray the Seminole, Jesup wrote the secretary of war that he "authorized no assurance(s) to be given to the Indians that they were to come to my camp and be permitted to return. I promised protection and kind treatment. If the Cherokee promised more it was on their own responsibility and without my authority."

To counter accusations that he was keeping his Indian prisoners in dank cells, Jesup transferred them to nicer confinement at Fort Moultrie in South Carolina. Osceola became gravely ill. Despite this, he was trotted out for interviews with newspapermen, where he said he was ready to ask his people to stop fighting, so long as they could keep living in Florida. Osceola even posed for a portrait by artist George Catlin, who made the dying chief look strong and determined on canvas.

When Osceola died in prison on January 30, 1838, he was buried near the gates of the fort. A few nights later, his grave was dug up, the coffin ripped open, and "persons unknown" cut off Osceola's head and took it away. Later it was supposedly displayed at the Stuyvesant Institute in New York City.

A few months after Osceola's death, the Indians at Fort Moultrie were forced onto a ship and transported to Indian Territory. King Philip died on the trip.

Back in Florida, Jesup found himself stymied. The Seminole and Seminole Negro no longer trusted him. Wild Cat and John Horse were loose, and Seminole chief Sam Jones, who had become more prominent with Micanopy, Osceola, and King Philip in white custody, sent word to Jesup that he had never made a treaty and never would; he and his people would fight it out forever.

Then Jesup did a clever, if unethical, thing. The basis of the relationship between the Seminole and Seminole Negro had always been one of convenience. The Seminole wanted slaves, and, sometimes, war allies. The Seminole Negro yearned for freedom; they never wanted to be permanent vassals of the Seminole. So Jesup sent several Seminole Negro prisoners out to find John Horse and other black Indian leaders. Tell them, Jesup instructed, that he promised complete freedom to them and their Seminole Negro people "on their separating from the Indians and surrendering." The blacks didn't respond, but, Willie Warrior believes, "that got their attention."

Jesup didn't send Abraham on this mission. The old Seminole Negro was wary, certain he was hated by the Seminole and perhaps by his own people. His spirit broken, access to Jesup denied now that he had no particular use, Abraham finally wrote a poignant note asking to please be sent west with his family, although in the note he made passing, perhaps sarcastic, reference to Jesup's habit of verbal but unwritten promises.

"We wish to get in writing from the General, the agreement made with us," Abraham wrote. "We do not live for ourselves only, but for our wives and children who are dear to us as those of any other men. When we reach our new home we hope we shall be permitted to remain while the woods remain green, and the water runs."

It was another eighteen months, though, before Abraham and his family were finally sent west in early 1839.

Meanwhile, another American officer was sent to Florida. While Jesup schemed, future U.S. president Zachary Taylor, then a colonel, was ordered to find and fight the Seminole and Seminole Negro. Taylor was surprised that many of the Indians and blacks he first encountered wanted to surrender. They were often affiliated with Micanopy, who had sent orders from prison that his people should give themselves up.

In late December 1837, Taylor and the thousand men under his command met Seminole and Seminole Negro who weren't inclined to put down their weapons and surrender. Wild Cat, Sam Jones, and John Horse, with about four hundred combined warriors, stood and fought on Christmas Day along the shore of Lake Okeechobee. The battle lasted almost three hours. Taylor sent his troops against the Indians and blacks in straight, traditional battle lines. His opponents fired, changed position, fired, moved again, and, as had happened so often in the past, they confounded their American foes and decimated them. Twenty-six American soldiers died; 112 were wounded. Seminole and Seminole Negro losses were less than a dozen. When they'd exhausted most of their ammunition, the Indians and blacks jumped into canoes and paddled away.

Two more clashes ended just as decisively in favor of the Seminole and Seminole Negro. On January 15, 1838, they fought off the U.S. Navy in a battle beside Jupiter Inlet on the coast of the Atlantic Ocean. About a week later, Jesup led troops against two hundred Seminole warriors; the Americans were badly battered. Jesup himself was wounded—a bullet shattered his glasses and cut his cheek. In February, Jesup's senior officers asked to meet with him. Enough was enough, they said. Declare a truce. Find a way to let the Seminole stay in Florida, if that's what it would take to end the war.

Once again, Jesup sent messengers asking the Indian and black leaders to come in and talk. Without asking his superiors in Washington for permission, Jesup suggested to the Seminole that they might be given new reservation lands south of Lake Okeechobee. This property would not be a swampy bog, but good, arable ground. However, Seminole already in American custody would be sent to Indian Territory.

The Seminole Negro heard different inducements. Jesup promised that all blacks who had been Seminole property, "but who separated themselves from the Indians and delivered themselves up to the Commanding officer of the Troops" would be free. He was using common sense, Jesup told critics among fellow officers and civilians. Losing their black allies would significantly weaken the ability of the Seminole to fight. And, though he was willing to let some of the Indians remain in their homeland, the blacks were all going to leave: "They should be sent to the west as a part of the Seminole nation and be settled in a separate village, under protection of the United States." The obvious contradiction there—that the Seminole Negro would be free, yet, in Indian Territory, still somehow be part of the Seminole nation—wasn't an issue anyone raised. Perhaps Jesup only mentioned the first part of his scheme to the Seminole Negro.

Incredibly, many of the Seminole and Seminole Negro trusted Jesup enough to come in to white forts, surrender their weapons, and be assigned to a general campground near Fort Jupiter. They waited patiently, and they waited in vain. On March 17, Jesup received word from the secretary of war that his plan to keep the remaining Seminole in Florida was unacceptable. All Indians, as well as all black Indians, were to be sent to Indian Territory.

Jesup could have gone to the Seminole and Seminole Negro leaders, telling them honestly his promises couldn't be kept, but that, for the good of their people, they ought to cooperate anyway. It might have worked. But now, humiliated, Jesup reverted to his old ways. He let his native guests continue to believe what he'd originally told them. Then, in the middle of the night on March 21, he surrounded their camp with soldiers and took them all prisoner—513 Seminole and 161 Seminole Negro. Many of the captives were warriors. Jesup could truthfully claim this time that the power of the Indians and blacks was significantly reduced.

There were still a few formidable bands at large. Wild Cat led one, Sam Jones had another, and Alligator and John Horse were virtual co-chiefs of the only combined Seminole/Seminole Negro forces left. Since Osceola was dead, Jesup felt he could send Abraham out to find John Horse and talk him into surrendering. Both Abraham and Holatoochee joined Zachary

Taylor in a search for the remaining Seminole Negro leader. Abraham hadn't lost his touch as a negotiator; on April 4, John Horse surrendered, and so did Alligator. They brought in with them eighty-eight Seminole and twenty-seven Seminole Negro.

At this point, Seminole Negro opposition to the Americans was essentially over. Wild Cat and Sam Jones didn't have any black warriors with them. Some wars have neat, conclusive endings, but this one didn't. Various bands of Seminole fought the whites in Florida for another four years. Since this is the story of the Seminole Negro, not the Seminole, just two final details are necessary here.

First, as the fighting in Florida dwindled down, it was clear the relationship between the Indians and blacks had changed. Though they had fought the Americans as allies, they did so for vastly different reasons. The Seminole wanted to keep their land and their slaves. The Seminole Negro fought to avoid returning to a worse form of slavery, so when Jesup promised them their freedom in return for surrendering, they believed there was no reason to resist anymore. Unconditional freedom in Indian Territory trumped benign slavery in Florida. Many Seminole Negro loved their Indian masters. But most of the blacks moving on to Indian Territory were no longer willing to be property.

The second detail involves the Seminole instead of the Seminole Negro, but it is instructive about how sincere the government really was in making treaty promises, and it also has direct bearing on events involving the Seminole Negro after they arrived in Indian Territory.

In May 1838, Jesup was replaced as Florida field commander by Zachary Taylor, who'd been promoted to general. Jesup went back to Washington, where he eventually became quartermaster general of the army. Taylor treated the Seminole Negro honorably. While they were in Florida camps waiting to be shipped off to Indian Territory, Taylor insisted each black be considered a full-fledged prisoner of war, which meant whites who claimed ownership of them were not allowed to try and take them back. Slavers were driven away from the camp.

Taylor was in charge for about a year, until another promotion took him away. The new Florida commander was Brigadier General Walker K. Armistead, who was replaced a year after that by Colonel William J. Worth. Armistead and Worth spent much of their tenures chasing the remaining Seminole around Florida.

In 1840, though, General Alexander Macomb, commander in chief of the U.S. Army, came to Florida himself to negotiate peace terms with as many warring Seminole chiefs as possible. Macomb sent word he wanted to parlay, and on May 18 about 150 Indians showed up to talk.

An army surgeon was present and took notes. Macomb told the Seminole that "the Great White Father in Washington" loved his red children as much as his white ones: "Let the Indians lay down the scalping-knife, rifle and the tomahawk. Let them go south of Little Peace Creek (in Florida), and their great father would see they were left tranquil and undisturbed." At a second meeting, the Indians were all "fed, clothed, and whiskied extensively." They agreed to move where Macomb had requested. Staying in Florida was the remaining Seminoles' sole objective.

On May 22, Macomb wrote the secretary of war, in effect telling him it was mission accomplished: "I (did not) think it politic at this time to say anything about their emigration."

It was all a trick. The Americans just wanted to herd the Seminole together so it would be easy to round them up and ship them off. The secretary of war wrote President Martin Van Buren that "I am of the opinion that the arrangement made by General Macomb will lead to the pacification of the country and enable me to remove the Indians from the Territory much sooner than can be done by force." Soon, the Indians learned they wouldn't be given a new Florida reservation after all, and so they kept on fighting.

It was William J. Worth, lately promoted to general, who finally concluded the war. He made it clear to most of the remaining Seminole combatants, especially Wild Cat, that the Americans would never let the Seminole stay. Wild Cat and his followers emigrated in late 1841. On April 9, 1842, Worth fought the last battle of the Second Seminole War, defeating a small Indian force near Abraham's old village of Pelaklakaha. Some

Seminole chiefs and their followers remained burrowed in the Florida brush, and the Americans were willing to leave them there for the time being. (A third Seminole War would break out in 1855.)

The Second Seminole War cost the United States dearly. Lasting seven years, it was the longest war in the country's history. To date, only the Vietnam conflict has dragged on longer. American taxpayers spent $20 million to defeat the Seminole and Seminole Negro—purchasing Florida cost just $5 million. More than fifteen hundred American soldiers died. Ten times that many were wounded. The price paid by white Americans for Florida was terrible.

They paid it and moved on. The Seminole Negro moved on, too, from Florida to Indian Territory. But they kept on paying. For them, things would only get worse.

chapter five

ON DECEMBER 23, 1846, about eight years after John Horse and the main body of Seminole Negro were moved from Florida to Indian Territory, the government-appointed subagent to the Seminole tribe traveled to Washington, D.C. Marcellus Duval had been on the job for a year. Originally from Alabama, he was an ambitious lower-echelon bureaucrat with a problem on his hands.

Back in Indian Territory, Duval was in the middle of an untenable situation. Despite General Jesup's promises to the contrary, the Creek had assumed they would once again be lords over the less numerous Seminole. Another Jesup promise hadn't materialized; far from being free, the Seminole Negro discovered their old Seminole masters still considered them to be property. There had been violent incidents and threats of many more. The army couldn't come up with a solution satisfactory to any, let alone every, side. So Duval had come to make his own case to President James Polk.

Duval wanted to talk to the president in person. In those days, such meetings between presidents and minor functionaries like Duval were possible. But Duval became ill after arriving in the capital, so he sent a letter instead.

"Sir," Duval wrote Polk, "I beg leave to lay before you the following statement of facts . . . which I believe now is necessary to settle, lest injurious results should follow. I allude, Sir, to the Seminole Negro question, and that you may know the grounds of the complaint of the Seminoles, I will here state what information I have on the subject."

Duval appealed to Polk on behalf of the Indians, not the blacks: Even if Jesup *did* promise the Seminole Negro they'd be freed in Indian Territory for abandoning their Indian masters in the Second Seminole War, Duval argued, Jesup also promised the Seminole that the blacks would still be their property afterward. The latter guarantee should take precedence, Duval explained to Polk, unless anyone "liked the Negroes better than the Indians. (The Seminole) assert (Jesup) promised them the safe delivery west of all their property, and that an order was subsequently made that all property removed with them, Negroes not exempted, should be safe from all claims of the whites or others. The Negroes were accordingly removed with them, and up to the summer of 1845 before I was appointed Sub Agt remained as their slaves."

Then Jesup visited Indian Territory and stirred up trouble, Duval complained: "General Jesup . . . hearing that the Seminole disposed of a few slaves, sent word to the Negroes that they were free."

Duval warned that the Creek, Cherokee, and other slave-owning tribes in Indian Territory were afraid freeing the Seminole Negro would tempt their blacks to run away. If the Seminole Negro were free, white citizens in the adjoining states of Arkansas and Missouri would never allow "300 free colored people" so close to their own borders. They'd have to be herded up and sent elsewhere. "Could this Gov't, of its own account, enter into the colonization of slaves?" Duval inquired. "I respectfully ask you to act as the only authority competent to settle the question at its present stage, as you consider proper."

Slyly, Duval ended his missive with a politely veiled threat. He hadn't included any information about the Seminole Negro problem in his annual report to Congress "although it was the most important subject connected to my sub agency," Duval noted, but if something wasn't done soon he'd have to reluctantly ask Congress for help. "I desire to avert the calamitous excitement which (this) would cause, shaking the Union to its center, a perfect firebrand to be thrown among the discordant & combustible materials on the floor of Congress."

So in eight years, the Seminole Negro had evolved from a persistent but regional problem in the swamps of Florida to a potential time bomb of racial violence in Indian Territory that could shake the Union to its core.

"It turned into a real damn mess up there," Willie Warrior said one morning during my first trip to Brackettville. "You're going to hear some *serious* stuff from me today." He'd driven in from Del Rio because he wanted to show me the old scout camp site along Las Moras Creek on Fort Clark. He promised I wouldn't believe what I saw. After we'd walked around, Willie said, we could talk about Indian Territory and Jesup's promises and Marcellus Duval, who Willie described as "a purely evil man." But he wanted me to see the old village site first, " 'cause it will help you really understand what got taken from us."

The Seminole Negro living in modern-day Brackettville have two special places. One is the old Scout Cemetery, a couple of sun-blasted acres about two miles south of town. They have complete access to it; it's theirs, apparently forever. The other is the site of the old scout village. Many of the scouts' descendants have never explored it, even though it's as close to their Brackettville homes as the cemetery. There's nothing of the huts and gardens and cooking pits left to see. The army burned or tore down most of the dwellings when they threw out the Seminole Negro in 1914. When Fort Clark was acquired from the government by civilians, the new owners turned the old fort into a vacation spa, figuring its natural springs and creek would entice visitors from Del Rio and Uvalde and maybe even San Antonio. When that didn't pan out, subsequent owners rebuilt the officers' quarters and enlisted men's barracks into quirky residences, and to supplement income from their sale turned much of the fort grounds' flat, snake-infested acreage into a golf course. A guard post was built at the highway entrance to the fort, and nobody gets onto the grounds without either a resident's permit or a visitor's pass, issued either to those who've paid to swim in the fort pool or whoever has reservations at the motel.

Seminole Negro descendants rarely qualify. But Willie, who'd donated photos to the fort museum and seemed to know everybody in charge there, was welcome.

My own first impression of the fort, having only seen the front portion, was that it reflected the nondescript town across the highway. The parade ground had been turned into a pitch-and-putt golf course. The old barracks and officers' quarters were briefly interesting—plaques pointed out where famous soldiers named Patton and Wainwright once lived—but a lot of the other fort property had been sold off to people who'd built blocky, cheap-looking homes. It seemed, from the FOR SALE signs sprouting in dozens of brownish front lawns, that many soon decided life in Brackettville wasn't worth the effort.

So when Willie said he'd take me to look at the old scout "homestead," I wasn't expecting much. We got into his truck and went slowly down the narrow Fort Clark streets, passing several elderly residents who preferred puttering around in golf carts to driving cars. As we moved south, away from the main fort grounds, I saw a couple of trailer parks. Soon, table-flat, yellow-grassed fairways extended along both sides of the road. People playing on them moved slowly in the heat.

"It gets better," Willie said, sensing how I felt. "Our people left this part of the fort to the white people. They were welcome to it. We got the best. Of course, it was because the whites wanted the scouts living as far away from them as possible."

I didn't see how. We drove a mile farther south. A clubhouse for the golf course loomed on the left. Then we went past the clubhouse, making a slight left turn that took us off the paved street and onto a stony road that soon swapped pebbles for dirt.

"Now," Willie said, and miraculously we were in a glade, the kind of tree-thick utopia found in California forests or the New England countryside, but never in West Texas. Suddenly everything seemed shady and cool; Willie nodded to our right, and I saw three—no, four!—deer watching us as they grazed nearby.

"Wow," I muttered. Willie chuckled.

"It still gets better," he said, and it did. Las Moras Creek, which had been gurgling along on our left, suddenly blossomed into a full-fledged pond. "They got a bird sanctuary on the other side of that water," Willie noted, and as he spoke some exotic-looking fowl swooped overhead. We drove another few hundred yards, and then Willie pulled to a stop.

"Your people really lived here?" I asked. "What a beautiful place. And it feels so peaceful."

"Well, the spirits keep it that way," he said. "And don't forget all we went through before we got here. Some of the old ones who made it from Florida to Indian Territory to Mexico to Texas said this place reminded them of Florida. But where they had to go when they first got moved out of Florida didn't please them a bit."

So we walked and talked about what happened when the Seminole and Seminole Negro reached Indian Territory.

On June 14, 1838, John Horse staggered off an American army boat in New Orleans. He and thirty Seminole Negro, along with 305 Seminole, had been transported by ship from Tampa Bay across the Gulf of Mexico into Louisiana. The voyage might have taken a few days or more than a week, depending on the weather. Even in sunshine and with relatively calm seas, most of the passengers would have been miserable. Acute seasickness afflicted all but the most veteran sailors on such voyages, and the blacks and Indians certainly were not accustomed to waves and rocking decks.

When they stepped off their transport ships in Louisiana, they entered hostile territory, the Seminole Negro far more than the Seminole. New Orleans was a hotbed of slave trading. Bedraggled Indians were a familiar sight in any city or town on the fringes of the American West. But a pack of negroes walking around unfettered was far less common.

The Seminole Negro were eager to get out of New Orleans as soon as possible. But they disembarked from one ship only to be ordered aboard another—a steamship, which would haul them up the Arkansas River to Indian Territory. In its own way, this was the riskiest portion of the journey, when weakened blacks and Indians often succumbed quickly to white man's diseases. Just months earlier, Micanopy's group of 1,069 Seminoles had lost hundreds of their people on the same trip, including Jumper and King Philip, Wild Cat's father. John Horse's mixed band of blacks and Indians proved far luckier—only one person died between New Orleans and Fort Gibson on the northeast boundary of Indian Territory.

As the steamship wobbled its way north up the river, the blacks and Indians stayed separate. There was little mingling between the races. "Those Seminole still acted like they owned us, but John Horse had Jesup's word they didn't," Willie explained. "So both sides figured when they got to Indian Territory, to wherever they were going to end up, the other side was going to find out it was wrong."

On August 15, when the ship finally docked and the Seminole and Seminole Negro were gently herded off to Fort Gibson, everyone was nervous. They soon learned the fort was still miles from the land they'd been promised. Fort Gibson, in fact, was in the part of Indian Territory reserved for the Cherokee. Some members of that tribe were on hand to offer greetings. The Cherokee still felt ashamed for unwittingly being part of Jesup's plot to bring in Seminole and Seminole Negro under a white treaty flag, then arrest them. So now they were effusive, offering food and promises of eternal friendship.

Almost immediately, John Horse and the Seminole Negro were alarmed. The white officers at Fort Gibson talked only about the Seminole land, a tract between the Canadian River and its North Fork. Micanopy and his Seminole were already there, the newcomers were told, building villages and planting summer crops and enjoying all the benefits of peace and friendship with the Americans. But nothing was said about separate land for the Seminole Negro.

"Even if Jesup had said to the Seminole Negro that they were no longer owned by anybody, he hadn't gotten that message to the officers at Fort Gibson," Ben Pingenot said later. "They wanted John Horse or somebody to show them that promise in writing. Of course, they didn't have that. So they were told to go on with the Seminole and follow their orders for a while longer, until things could get figured out."

The new arrivals set out west and south, passing through the Cherokee lands and noting the nice houses that tribe had built, the plowed fields, the smiles and waves. The Seminole Negro also noticed a disturbing number of black slaves, performing the same sorts of backbreaking labor they would have on white plantations.

Thankfully, they didn't see any swamps. Some of the dirt was redder than in Florida, there didn't seem to be groves of citrus trees, but there at least were lots of other trees, and hills, and rivers all around. During the two or three days the last leg of the trip took from Fort Gibson, the Seminole found much to smile about. The Seminole Negro, of course, worried about their status, but John Horse assured everyone he'd get things worked out. After all, they had General Jesup's word.

Then they arrived at the new homeland, and Micanopy and his people were, in fact, living there. So were the hated Creek.

The Creek land, in theory, was south of the wide Cherokee property and north of where the Seminole would live. But the confluence of the Canadian and North Fork pleased them and, after all, they had moved west fully expecting that their prodigal kinsmen, the Seminole, would soon come to Indian Territory and rejoin the Creek nation. Therefore, what belonged to the Seminole also belonged to the Creek. Chief Opothleyohola and his people built their village and, when Micanopy and his people arrived, showed no inclination to move north.

Micanopy could have protested. He had every right. But, trying to get along, Micanopy simply told his people they would build a Seminole village some distance away from where the Creek squatters were located. Fear of angering the Creek had much to do with the decision. Over the next several years, about four thousand Seminole would be moved from Florida to Indian Territory. The Creek there would outnumber them four or five to one.

The Creek were anxious to greet the Seminole arrivals, and they carefully inspected the Seminole Negro, too. Many Creeks believed they owned some of the black newcomers. They based their ownership on any of several claims—that the Seminole had stolen some of their slaves during the First and Second Seminole Wars; that many of their legally owned blacks had run away to join the Seminole Negro and therefore were, by terms of the Payne's Landing Treaty, to be immediately returned to their Creek masters; or, most often, that they'd captured Seminole Negro during the Second Seminole War and, under their agreements with the white officers, these captives, even if they'd found their way back to the Seminole, were still Creek property. That they'd been temporarily taken from the Creek and placed in a Florida emigrants' camp, then shipped on to Indian Territory as part of larger Seminole Negro contingents didn't change the fact they were rightfully owned by Creek masters.

A white American officer immediately made things worse. General Matthew Arbuckle, commander of the Second Detachment of the Western Military Divison, asked the Creek to help identify and turn over to the army any Seminole slaves claimed by U.S. citizens. White settlers in Arkansas and Missouri were worried, Arbuckle explained. Any "bad negroes" living with the Seminole might incite slaves to rise up against their American masters, or at least to run away. Arbuckle didn't want the Seminole Negro to create "a harbor for runaway negroes and horse-thieves."

In many ways for the Seminole Negro, it was like the worst days in Florida all over again. At least the Seminole pronounced themselves unwilling to hand over any blacks. Ben Pingenot suggested they stood up to the Creek less from devotion to the Seminole Negro than the fear that, if they gave in on this early issue, they would soon find themselves reabsorbed completely into the Creek nation. Willie Warrior, no fan of the Seminole, agreed. There was real danger of fighting between the tribes.

The numerical superiority of the Creek was the most obvious problem, but there was also the matter of the Seminole and Seminole Negro nearly starving again. Many of the farm tools and other supplies the Americans promised were late in arriving. The Indians and blacks often seemed too dispirited to use the few farm implements available to them. And, as other steamship loads of blacks and Indians docked in Indian Territory, the latest Seminole and Seminole Negro arrivals weren't as willing as Micanopy to settle side by side with the Creek.

During this time, John Horse was in Florida as much as in Indian Territory. He was so confident that the Seminole Negro would eventually be freed that he volunteered to go back to Florida and, as a translator, help the Americans talk the Seminole remaining there into moving west. He did this work well; eventually, John Horse was credited with bringing 535 Seminole back to Indian Territory. One of them was an old friend John Horse desperately needed for support. Worried about his status with the Micanopy-led Seminole back in Indian Territory, he wanted to persuade Wild Cat to move west so he, at least, if not all the Seminole Negro, would have a strong ally among Seminole leadership there.

Florida military reports from 1839 through 1842 make frequent mention of John Horse. Almost always, he is being praised—for being able to seek out Seminole leaders, for nimble negotiating tactics, and, perhaps too often, for his friendly attitude. He had elaborate public manners, ostentatiously rushing to each white officer he met to shake hands. The soldiers were impressed. The Indians and blacks being held in emigrant camps also noticed, and they were less pleased.

"For somebody who was supposed to be so smart, John Horse did some stupid things," I commented to Willie Warrior.

"Well, no law against smart people being stupid sometimes, too," he replied. "But I make sure when I tell the stories to kids in school or church groups that I put the bad in with the good. That's the honest way. And it makes it more interesting for them. A man with some faults is always more interesting than somebody perfect."

We stood looking at the pond for a while. Chirping crickets provided soothing background noise.

"This seems almost tropical," I said to Willie.

"Heaven is what it was for us, for a while," he replied. Then he talked some more about "old John Horse."

Even in matters of the heart, John Horse called too much attention to himself. Somewhere back in Indian Territory, John Horse had a wife, a relative of Micanopy. This didn't keep him from acquiring a new bride in Florida, a black woman named Susan. We know little about her, besides that her father was a Seminole Negro leader in Peliklakaha, and she and

John Horse stayed married for more than forty years. John's first wife simply disappears from history about this time. Perhaps she died in Indian Territory before he returned to Florida. More likely, he sent her back to her family. Micanopy would not have been pleased by this, but John Horse, at this point, was no longer concerned with what Micanopy thought of him.

In March of 1841, John Horse persuaded Wild Cat to surrender. The young Seminole leader came into the American camp, talked about being moved west, and promised to bring in the rest of his people. Either Wild Cat's followers weren't agreeable, or he wasn't entirely committed to emigration himself. Weeks went by, then months. Wild Cat made occasional visits to Fort Pierce, chatting with John Horse, telling U.S. officers he was gradually persuading other Seminole to come in. Eventually, Lieutenant William Tecumsah Sherman, later to become a national figure during the American Civil War, was sent out to bring Wild Cat back for good. Along with a dozen or so other recalcitrant Seminole, Wild Cat was clapped in irons and placed aboard a ship sailing west.

His voyage was interrupted; back in Florida, Colonel William Worth had been placed in charge of the army, and he wanted to talk to Wild Cat. When the Seminole chief's ship returned to Fort Brooke, Worth came aboard and brought John Horse with him to interpret. Worth's message wasn't a friendly one: Wild Cat should designate a few of his fellow prisoners to go back into the Florida wilds and convince the rest of Wild Cat's followers to surrender. If that didn't happen within fifty days, Worth would hang Wild Cat. We don't know if John Horse added any extraneous commentary; he certainly didn't want his main Seminole patron to be hanged. In any event, Wild Cat agreed. Within days, his people began to surrender, and he was allowed off the boat to meet them. Not long after that, Wild Cat began going with Worth and John Horse when they negotiated with other Seminole chiefs. In November 1841, he was sent to Indian Territory himself, along with about two hundred followers.

Wild Cat was appalled at what he found there. Creek living on Seminole land! Creek treating Seminole like poor relations! He flatly refused to set up camp between the Canadian and North Fork Rivers. Instead, he announced *his* Seminole—by inference, the *warrior* Seminole—would settle on Cherokee land near Fort Gibson. That this crowded the Cherokee didn't concern Wild Cat. After all, that tribe still owed a moral debt to the Seminole for their unwitting cooperation with General Jesup. Army officials threatened to withhold seed and other supplies from Wild Cat's people unless they moved to their designated land, but Wild Cat didn't budge. He and his followers were soon joined by other Seminole who didn't want cheek-to-jowl contact with the Creek. Eventually, some two thousand Seminole—almost half the tribe in Indian Territory—squatted on Cherokee land.

John Horse stayed behind in Florida, wholeheartedly cooperating with the American army. Colonel Worth appreciated John Horse, at least. By the end of April, he declared that, under any future circumstances, "Gofer John, his wife and increase" would be free.

Still, there was no question John Horse and his family were going back to Indian Territory. With the war winding down, John Horse was informed it was time for him to go back west. He was agreeable. First, though, he sold his Florida cattle, probably to a U.S. Army quartermaster. Then John Horse and 102 other Indians and blacks sailed west under the supervision of Lieutenant Edward Canby. The army had issued Canby just enough money to cover minimal trip expenses. But the Arkansas River was particularly low, so additional transportation costs were incurred. Canby ran out of money. It seemed his black and Indian charges were going to be stranded well short of Indian Territory. Magnanimously, John Horse offered to lend the young officer $1,500, which was later repaid by the government. The party arrived in Indian Territory in early September.

Once there, John Horse helped set up a Seminole Negro village along the North Canadian River. Though his friend Wild Cat skulked among the Cherokee, John Horse saw no reason he and other blacks shouldn't pick a fine place on Seminole-designated land and enjoy the first fruits of their freedom—after all, Jesup had set them free back in Florida, and John Horse personally had Colonel Worth's additional endorsement.

The Micanopy-led Seminole were quite happy to see John Horse and other newly arrived Seminole Negro. They believed their old slaves had rejoined them ready to assume their subordinate roles. In the three years John Horse had been in Florida, many of the Seminole Negro in Indian Territory had gradually been reassimilated into the Seminole tribe. Army officials in the West had yet to determine whether Jesup's Florida promises of Seminole Negro freedom were valid. The Creek, along with various white slavers, made frequent raids on Seminole Negro villages. There had been occasional clashes between Creek and Seminole concerning who really owned which Seminole Negro.

Pragmatically, the Seminole Negro more or less acquiesced to the Seminole, hoping all the while that the government would eventually uphold their claims to freedom. In Florida, they could have escaped into the swamps. In Indian Territory, they had nowhere to hide.

Soon after John Horse returned, William Armstrong, acting superintendent of America's Western Territory, wrote to his superiors that "(the Seminole) have many negroes that participated in the Florida war. In many cases the Creek claim negroes which are the property of the Seminoles. These negroes the Creek allege ran away from them before and during the Florida war, and were either captured with the Seminoles or came in under a proclamation from some of the commanders in Florida."

Jesup, stationed in Washington, D.C., as quartermaster general of the army, tried his best to help the Seminole Negro. He wrote Secretary of War William Wilkins: "I earnestly hope that the Executive will not permit the national faith thus solemnly pledged, and which as commander of the army I had the right to pledge, to be violated; but that all the Negroes who surrendered to me and have been sent away to the West, to be protected from capture by, or sale to either citizens, foreigners, or Indians, and that measures be taken to recover all who have been separated from their families and sold."

Wild Cat and John Horse were in regular contact. Wild Cat had problems of his own. He was angry that Creek villages were on Seminole land. His protests to American officials in Indian Territory were ignored. It was the Seminole's own fault, Wild Cat was told. If they'd come to Indian Territory immediately after signing the Payne's Landing Treaty, the Creek would not have had the opportunity to arrive ahead of them and squat on Seminole property. Besides, they pointed out, Wild Cat had no right to complain. He and many of his Seminole people were illegally occupying Cherokee land, and some of the Cherokee leaders were beginning to complain about it.

There was some good news for John Horse. In July 1843, Micanopy and the Seminole tribal leadership pronounced him to be free. But that didn't mean he really was. White slavers continued to raid Seminole Negro camps. If any of them captured John Horse, they'd treat him like a runaway slave, hauling him off to Memphis or New Orleans to be sold in the slave markets there. Despite Jesup, Worth, and Micanopy all declaring him his own man, John Horse still didn't have official papers designating him as a free black. So he moved himself and his family north to Fort Gibson in Cherokee land, where there were fewer slavers.

Once there, he realigned himself with Wild Cat. Both considered the Creek to be sworn enemies, and John Horse certainly did everything he could to keep Wild Cat feeling that way. If anything, the Creek helped him. In the spring of 1844, they began openly raiding Seminole settlements, taking blacks indiscriminately and claiming afterward that they were simply retrieving their rightful property. Roley McIntosh, the principal Creek chief, was a mixed-blood white-Indian whose philosophy of slavery would have been a match for the most extreme Southern plantation owner. Blacks owned by the Creek labored in fields, lived in hovels, and ate scraps. They were viciously punished for alleged transgressions and were sold or traded at the whims of their owners, often for nothing more than a bottle of whiskey or a nearly lame horse.

A Creek brave named Siah Hardridge was a particularly active raider. On one of his armed forays into a Seminole village, he captured a Seminole Negro man named Dembo, who had a good reputation among the blacks as a leader and fighter. Ostensibly, Dembo belonged to a Creek woman named Sally Factor, but she was living with the Seminole. The

Seminole Negro were outraged because one of their "free" tribal members had been kidnapped. The Seminole thought the Creek had stolen one of their slaves. Wild Cat asked the U.S. Army to take Dembo back. Reluctantly, the Creek returned Dembo, more to avoid conflict for the moment than anything else. But the incident greatly concerned both John Horse and Wild Cat. The Creek were becoming bolder. Something had to be done.

Talking about the Dembo incident made Willie Warrior sputter with indignation. This often happened when he had plenty of time to tell his stories, instead of some classroom or Kiwanis limit of twenty or thirty minutes. At first he'd stick to history, acting out parts and moving his story along, but gradually the injustices he'd describe would wear on him, and he'd begin interjecting comments about the unfairness of it all.

"You see the way we always were treated?" Willie blurted. "Nobody was really on our side, nobody! Seminole wanted slaves. Government didn't keep its promises. Don't tell me John Horse wasn't a hero."

Willie's eyes looked hard and bright. For all the jocularity he often displayed, laughing as he told his tales or smiling when asked a particularly good question about his people, there was always anger smoldering somewhere in him. Too much had been done *to* the Seminole Negro instead of *for* them. The pain of it, the insult of it, never entirely left Willie, even standing in the peaceful glade where his people once lived so happily.

John Horse risked his freedom going south to meet with Micanopy. He asked the Seminole chief to come with him to Fort Gibson, where Wild Cat and Alligator were preparing for a meeting with military leaders. They demanded Indian Territory land entirely separate from the Creek. Afterward, Wild Cat and Alligator put together a delegation of Fort Gibson–area Seminole and booked passage to Washington. There, they swore, they'd see Jesup in person and insist that the government honor everything he had promised to the Seminole and Seminole Negro in Florida. John Horse was enlisted both as leader of the Seminole Negro and as interpreter.

They left in April. In Washington, they met with various government officials and with Jesup. For all his underhanded dealings with the Indians and blacks in Florida, Jesup now treated them as friends. He invited them to his home—several books report his children sang to entertain them—and testified before investigative committees that he had promised the Seminole Negro they would be free.

Ultimately, it didn't matter. The Seminole and Seminole Negro got their meetings with government officials, who all promised they'd certainly look into things right away, and then it was over. The Indians and blacks headed back to Indian Territory having accomplished little besides airing grievances and hearing the Jesup children sing.

When they got back to Indian Territory, they discovered a flood had wiped out many of the fields planted by the Seminole squatting near Fort Gibson. Wild Cat's people were starving. He appealed to Lieutenant Colonel Richard Mason, the commander of Fort Gibson, for rations. Mason suggested that Wild Cat ought to move his people south, instead, and join Micanopy and the southern Seminole there.

John Horse had another urgent concern. He had only been back a few days when he was riding on horseback near Fort Gibson. A rifle shot rang out; the bullet grazed John Horse and killed his mount. Later, John Horse claimed his assailant was a Seminole brave, seeking revenge because he'd served the Americans in Florida. Others insisted someone shot at John Horse because, when among Indians and blacks, he always acted superior and obnoxious.

In any case, John Horse decided he was no longer safe in Indian Territory. His new goal became convincing the Americans to let the Seminole Negro return to Florida and settle there, far away from the Creek and the Seminole and the white slavers who plagued Indian Territory.

Mason allowed John Horse and his family to move into Fort Gibson. He contacted the secretary of war, asking what he should do next. Orders came back to hold the Seminole tribe responsible for the shooting; John wanted $30 for the dead horse, and the Indians should pay it.

Once again, Micanopy convened some Seminole leaders: Wild Cat and his militants were excluded from the gathering. After a vote was taken, Micanopy informed Mason that the Indians had nothing to do with the actions of "one man" who'd fired the shot. They had no idea who it might have been. They were willing to pay $30 for the dead horse, but, unfortunately, they didn't have the money. John Horse would have to seek payment elsewhere. He never did get the $30.

For the next five years, John Horse was a virtual prisoner. He spent most of his time inside the walls of Fort Gibson, only venturing out to serve as an interpreter and for another trip to Washington. At some point, there was a second assassination attempt, also unsuccessful.

Nearby, Wild Cat struggled to feed his people. The flood had been followed by a drought. The Cherokee sense of moral debt had been exhausted; now, their leaders insisted that the Seminole go away, preferably to the land originally assigned to them, but at least anywhere out of the vicinity.

Army leaders were pleased by Wild Cat's problems. If he and his followers were close to starvation, they might move south and take their chances with the Creek. In December of 1844, Wild Cat and Alligator agreed to negotiate. Creek leaders came north to participate; so did Micanopy. John Horse was ordered to interpret.

Wild Cat was ready to compromise. On January 4, 1845, an agreement was reached. All the Seminole on Cherokee land would move south, where they would join Micanopy's followers. The Americans promised they would provide all the seed and farm equipment Wild Cat's people needed; further, they would supply them with food for the next six months. No one would starve.

But all the Seminole, from Micanopy's band to Wild Cat's loyalists, would have to live between the Canadian and North Fork rivers, even though the Creek interlopers would also be allowed to stay there. In fact, the Creek were no longer interlopers at all. The Seminole, Wild Cat included, agreed to merge with the Creek nation. The Seminole could live separately, but they would be under Creek law. The Seminole would be allowed places on the Creek council, but their numbers there would be in the minority.

Nowhere in the treaty was there anything definite about the Seminole Negro. As always, their fate was left to be determined later. Some vague paragraphs noted that ownership of individual blacks could still be contested, but the Creek continued to believe most of the blacks belonged to them. The Seminole still considered all but a few of the Seminole Negro to be their property. The Seminole Negro insisted they were free.

But they moved south with the Seminole. They would have starved if they stayed at Fort Gibson, since the government wouldn't give them food. John Horse's pleas to Washington for Seminole Negro land in Florida were ignored. Once again, the Seminole Negro were going to be slaves.

As the Seminole and Seminole Negro moved south to join the Creek, John Horse made his second trip to Washington. He went seeking money he claimed was owed to him for service in Florida and got about $1,100. But he also brought a list of supposed crimes committed in Indian Territory against the Seminole Negro, mostly a list of blacks who had been kidnapped and sold off to slavers. Nothing was done about these complaints. And, while John Horse was off in Washington, the Seminole Negro's arch nemesis arrived in Indian Territory.

"Now, here comes old Duval," Willie Warrior said when he reached this part of the story. The controlled venom in his voice when he mentioned Andrew Jackson or General Jesup was missing as he named the most unlovable character in the entire Seminole Negro legend. It seemed that, like any good storyteller, Willie couldn't help but have affection for the ultimate bad guy in his tale. When I said I'd come across some of Duval's letters that had been preserved by the Oklahoma Historical Society, Willie was fascinated to hear about them.

"He was something, wasn't he?" Willie asked, seeming to derive pleasure from Duval's wicked ways. "Oh, he was a one!"

In fact, Marcellus Duval is something of a historical cipher. Based on what Willie and Miss Charles had to say about him, he was nothing less than a one-dimensional villain whose sole purpose in life was to thwart Seminole Negro hopes of freedom and take as many tribal members for his own slaves as possible. Neither Willie nor Miss Charles nor any of the dozens of historians I consulted had any idea what he looked like. Willie offered that Duval probably looked like a snake "because he always acted like one."

What we know of him comes from government records and his own letters, many of which are stored in the Oklahoma Historical Society's offices. These don't do Duval much credit. They constantly attack anyone who in any way supported the Seminole Negro. Their contents are intended to vilify anyone Duval didn't like, especially Jesup. He was a master at making enemies sound worse by pretending to objectively present their sides of any argument.

But it is also true that Marcellus Duval was representative of most white Southerners. In Alabama, he was surely raised to consider black people to be property rather than human. That he wanted to acquire Seminole Negro was typical; an ambitious white man in those days and in that region often measured his wealth, and his social standing, by the number of slaves he owned. That he would throw in with the Seminole against the Seminole Negro was inevitable. They thought of blacks as chattel, too. The irony of being an enslaved people themselves—after all, they were also ruled by white men—escaped them. If, as his letters and certain government records indicate, Duval connived with the Seminole to keep the Seminole Negro in bondage, it was because the white man and his red cronies mutually benefited from keeping them there.

Duval first appears in Seminole Negro history with expense reports he filed in mid-1846. Most items were typical—$2 a day, for instance, for twenty-eight days spent visiting various Seminole camps in Indian Territory. Duval also claimed $6 for "entertaining Wild Cat & others." John Horse and the rest of the Seminole Negro believed Wild Cat was their greatest ally among the Seminole. But this expense report and letters Duval wrote later indicate that, at least some of the time, Wild Cat was cooperating with a man whose goal was selling the Seminole Negro off to slavers at his earliest opportunity.

This relationship tells us as much about Wild Cat as it does about Marcellus Duval. Like John Horse, Wild Cat made foolish mistakes. But temporary alliance with Duval was not one of them, as later events would prove.

Some Seminole Negro had been hired to do chores at Fort Gibson. During a visit, Jesup assured them his promise of their freedom would eventually be enforced. After Jesup left, Duval began a campaign to undermine the general and his guarantee to the Seminole Negro. In correspondence to his superiors in Washington, Duval presented an example of a Seminole claim on slaves who considered themselves freed by Jesup.

First, Duval enclosed an August 11, 1842, bill of sale from one "A. Lefevre," who wrote, "I have this day sold and delivered to Halleck Tustenegger [*sic*] for six hundred dollars received, a negro woman named Elsa aged about 29, and her son Benjamin, aged about two years, both slaves for life, the title to them I warrant."

"Sir," Duval wrote to William Medill, commissioner of Indian Affairs, "Above you have a copy of a bill of sale of a Negro woman & child, sold to Halleck Tustenugger, Seminole Chief, by a white man named Lefevre. These Negroes . . . have been proclaimed free by Gen. Jesup, under what act of Congress by what authority, I have yet to be informed.

"This case is a particularly hard one on the Indian—he having bought the woman & child in good faith, and in part as an act of charity to her—being solicited by her to purchase & take her among those with whom she had been wed in Florida. She having been sold by some of those who first emigrated. Halleck Tustenugger was the leader of those who last removed, and was on his way up the river when he made the purchase."

In December 1845, Duval took pen in hand again. This time he wrote to Medill on behalf of Wild Cat: "Coah-coo-see or 'Wild Cat,' Seminole chief, has just been in to see me," Duval wrote. "[It was] relative to a negro boy named John [Philip] belonging to him, who was left in Florida with Genl. Worth as an interpreter.

"He desires that the boy may be sent West, as he requires him, and that Government should pay him [Coacoochee] for his services, while interpreting for the Army in Florida."

Wild Cat eventually got the boy, but only over the strong protests of Army captain J. T. Sprague, who indignantly opposed Wild Cat's claim in another letter to Medill. Sprague, commanding U.S. troops in Florida, argued that John Philip was legally freed by General Jesup. He misspelled both their names, but his intent is clear.

"John Phillip in the year 1838 surrendered to General Hernandez under the announcement made by General Jessup, commanding in Florida, that all Indian Negroes who gave themselves up would be considered free and protected by the United States," Sprague wrote, explaining that Wild Cat took John Philip captive when the boy came to him as a messenger sent by the Americans. "[Wild Cat], when sent from Florida, had his demands and claims adjusted before embarking. His only claim to this boy is his having taken him prisoner . . . and having retained him as such as long as in his power."

Relations between the Seminole and Seminole Negro became even more strained; the blacks staying at Fort Gibson completely cut off contact with the Indians. During most of 1846, John Horse pleaded for his people "to emigrate to any place where they can be free and unmolested." Duval wanted every Seminole Negro returned to Seminole slavery, even if they had to be rounded up at gunpoint. Soon, any black venturing outside the Fort Gibson stockade walls risked being kidnapped by the Seminole or the Creek or even white slavers, who blatantly came onto army property to snatch any blacks they could. There were still some Seminole Negro settlements along the Canadian River. In mid-1846, black warriors there had to fight off a Seminole war party that swooped down on their town. The situation grew more explosive every day, but no solution seemed forthcoming. Neither the army or Commissioner of Indian Affairs Medill seemed willing to act. So Duval made his trip to Washington and sent his letter to President Polk—who didn't act, either.

The Seminole Negro around Fort Gibson were hungry. They had no land on which to grow crops, hunting was limited, and their only income was from doing odd jobs around the fort. Occasionally, Lieutenant Colonel Gustavus Loomis, the current Fort Gibson commander, distributed army rations, which irritated Duval.

In October 1847, Duval sent Commissioner Medill a remarkable letter.

"Sir, I feel it to be my duty to call your attention to the course which Lt. Col. G. Loomis, USA Commanding at Fort Gibson, sees proper to adopt in regard to Negroes who happen to be at that post," he wrote. "I should not take it upon myself to call the attention of the Department to any act of Lt. Col. L's, unless it affected the Indians under my charge, and who have repeatedly complained to me relative to such acts. Nor should I even take notice of such complaints which I believed idly made, and therefore I made enquiries of those living at or about Fort Gibson, to learn if Lt. Col. L had been misrepresented; instead of which however, all with whom I have conversed on the subject have more than corroborated the statements as made to me. . . .

"The facts are these: There are a great number of Seminole Negroes. Those who according to Gen Jesup have a right to the benefit of his Proclamation in Florida, declaring them free, and a considerable number who are not believed to have any just claim to its benefits . . . reside in the Military Reserve of Fort Gibson under the protection of the Commanding Officer.

"These Negroes are not only protected by Lt. Col. Loomis from interruption by whites or Indians, but are granted immunities and privileges no where granted by law to slaves and 'colored persons' in a slave state or Territory. He himself, I am informed by credible persons, assists in teaching them how to read & possibly write; in fact, keeps school, a Sunday school, I believe to be sure, but the effects are the same, and felt by every man having slaves in this section of the country.

"There are various charges laid to Col. L. on this subject, but being hearsay, I do not feel warranted in asserting or giving publicity to them. The effect of all this schooling and petting of Negroes (as even grant they are free) are such, that every sensible man can see the evil of it. . . .

"I have no desire to injure Col Loomis; my intercourse with him has generally been on both sides courteous. Nor do I wish to deal in the slightest manner unfairly by him, and therefore shall send him a copy of this communication with the request to forward to the Adjt Genl USA, that he may have the opportunity of speaking in his own defense, and if possible, exculpating himself from any erroneous view of the case, if such there be, in my information."

There was little Loomis could say in his own defense. No record of any response by him to Duval's charges is available, but he did openly protect the Seminole Negro. It was certainly true that, even if Jesup's Florida "Proclamation" was upheld by the government, there were still many Seminole Negro in Indian Territory who didn't qualify for freedom under it. They hadn't left their Seminole masters in Florida to give themselves up to the Americans. They had, in fact, been shipped to Indian Territory with Seminole owners. Though the Creek inflated their war claims to some of the blacks, in Indian Territory they did buy many slaves from the Seminole. It was awful, but legal.

In late 1847, the Seminole pushed hard for resolution. They asked Duval to go to Washington and speak on their behalf. He said he couldn't; official duties kept him too busy. But he had a suggestion—his brother, attorney W. J. Duval, had already spent quite a bit of time in Indian Territory. W. J. Duval went to Washington for meetings with Medill and other government officials. Make a decision, he urged them. The Seminole and Creek won't peacefully endure such insolence from slaves much longer. He convinced Secretary of War Marcy to open an inquiry. Jesup was required to explain what exactly he had done in Florida, and why. His testimony was the same as it had always been: The Second Seminole War had to be ended. The Seminole Negro influence over their Indian masters was the reason it had lasted so long. As commander in Florida, it was his right to accept the surrender of enemy combatants and negotiate terms with them. The Seminole Negro who had stopped fighting and turned over their arms did so in exchange for a promise they would be free in Indian Territory.

Probably at Marcellus Duval's suggestion, the Creek countered Jesup's testimony by sending their own delegation to Washington. Endorse Jesup's Florida promise or don't, they told Medill. If the Seminole Negro are free, get them off Creek and Seminole property. If they aren't, return them to their tribal masters. In fact, the Creek delegation testified, the Seminole Negro "violate the laws of the United States and the laws of the Creek Nation with perfect impunity. They are idle and worthless, constantly engaged in bringing whiskey into the Nation, stealing and rioting, and offering inducements to the slaves belonging to the various surrounding tribes of Indians to run away; and when they are detected in crime, they at once take protection on the Government reservation where they are sustained by the commanding officer of the post."

Finally, in late spring, U.S. Attorney General John Mason was instructed to investigate, and then deliver a binding verdict. Were any of the Seminole Negro free because of Jesup's promise in Florida, or were all the blacks still slaves—and, if so, who owned them?

When he heard what was happening, John Horse made a final appeal to Jesup. The letter dated June 10, 1848, is proof of what Willie Warrior, Miss Charles, and several white historians insisted: John Horse, who never had any sort of formal education, was still a man of rare eloquence.

He wrote: "We have great many enemies, great many who think only of doing us injuries, many who fabricate false doing & who for a few guns or a little whiskey make false tales to our great annoyance; but the other day three of our people were stolen and more than a month has passed & have not yet been recovered. One of the principals in this theft has been placed before the law, and from some cause or other he has been let go. Some say there is no law against stealing Negroes; perhaps they say true. One thing however is certain, we are much annoyed, our people carried away, & our horses an object for many bad persons, so much so that we are now reduced to great poverty. Any fate is better than the great anxiety that overwhelms us. Thus you see, General, those who are ready to take advantage of us are many. You are the only man whose word has never failed us, and the only one where we can tell our tale of sorrow and have justice done us.

"Some say it is very probable we will be given back to our Old Masters, that (neither) the President nor the Congress will carry out the truce you made in Florida; be that as it may be, we know the law of the land is the Great Master of America, and if it denies us the benefits you promised us, we know it is no fault of yours."

Convinced Mason would rule in favor of the Creek and Seminole, John Horse couldn't resist a personal appeal. Though he was nominally free, he was afraid he might be swept up with the rest of the Seminole Negro and forced back into slavery. After all, the Indians hated him above all the other blacks.

"To prepare myself against all adverse chance," he noted to Jesup, "I thought it well to establish my claim on another title. The Seminole Nation in Council, with old Micanopy present, about five years ago, gave an order in council that from that day I shall be free, and had this put down on paper, all well signed and witnessed . . . this paper was taken to the Seminole Agency, once there recorded, a copy was given to me; but this copy is said to be no manner of use . . . the original cannot now be found in the office. Will you please do me the favor to . . . procure me if possible the original paper, that I may have it duly recorded in the County Courts office, and retain the original with me in case of necessity. Your Obt Svt, Gopher John."

Everyone had to wait until Mason reached a decision.

By the summer of 1848, many Seminole Negro had been in Indian Territory for ten years. For that entire decade, their legal status had been undetermined. They'd been the target of constant raids from white and Indian slavers. They still did not have land to call their own. Now all that stood between them and re-enslavement was one white man, this Attorney General Mason who represented the white government. The Seminole and Creek had Marcellus and W. J. Duval speaking for them. No one spoke for the Seminole Negro. Jesup supported the right of some of them to be free, but it was Jesup's decision in Florida that was being questioned. There is no evidence Mason ever talked directly to John Horse or any other member of the black Indian tribe. Loomis, who respected the Seminole Negro, apparently was not called upon to give his input, and by the time Mason began his deliberations Loomis had been replaced at Fort Gibson by Major B. L. Bonneville. Mason did hear the Creek tell about Seminole Negro drinking and thievery, and the Duvals describe unhappy Seminole robbed of their rightful slaves by one blundering army officer's unlawful act in Florida. Mason himself was a native of Virginia, a proud slave state. On June 28, 1848, Mason delivered the judgment that would be expected from a Southerner basing his decision on limited information and testimony.

Jesup, Mason ruled, had considered himself able to free the Seminole Negro by classifying the blacks as captured property in war. But if they *were* property rather than human beings, then the victorious American government could dispose of them as it wished. Taking into consideration all sorts of mitigating circumstances—the concern of white Americans that free Seminole Negroes would encourage other slaves to run away; the unhappiness of the Creek and Seminole after being deprived of their property; the official American treaty with the Seminole guaranteeing their removal to Indian Territory with all their property, slaves included—Mason ruled that all Seminole Negro not classified as free under U.S. or Indian law (as opposed to Jesup's "Proclamation" in Florida) must be returned immediately to their old masters: "My opinion is, that the Military authorities should be instructed to return the Negroes to the condition in which they were with the Seminoles, prior to the date of Major General Jesup's [action]."

President Polk promptly endorsed Mason's decision, and that was that.

In his letters to Medill, Marcy, and Polk, Marcellus Duval had frequently mentioned "300" Seminole Negro who had considered themselves free. That count was reasonably accurate. Of the three hundred, perhaps seventy-five were adult men who could fight. The rest were women, children, and old people. Another few hundred Seminole Negro already lived near or among the Indians, usually as slaves under the old system employed in Florida. In all, there weren't enough Seminole Negro to take on the Americans, Creek, and Seminole.

John Horse did something courageous. Despite Mason's verdict, even the Seminole agreed John Horse was free. Micanopy and other tribal leaders had released him from bondage. He could go—back to Florida, to Arkansas, to New York, or Washington, or anywhere else. He'd already proven to be an astute businessman. He could certainly have made a comfortable living far from the vengeful Seminole and Creek. But his family—wife, children, sister—were all reclassified as slaves. John Horse chose to stay with them in Indian Territory, knowing that his enemies among the tribes would be waiting to assassinate him.

Encouraged by the Duval brothers, the Seminole and Creek demanded that the Seminole Negro be returned immediately. The army was ordered by Medill to sort out which few Seminole Negro were really free, and deliver the rest to their rightful Indian owners, at gunpoint if necessary. To encourage the blacks to cooperate, the Seminole Negro could no longer be issued rations at Fort Gibson.

Bonneville, the fort commander, was ordered to return the Seminole Negro to the Seminole in August. But it took Bonneville until December to put together a list of 286 "free" Seminole Negro who had to be returned. Those names had to be turned over to the Seminole chiefs, who then had to decide who among their people owned whom. There were some disagreements concerning title. Micanopy said he owned seventy-eight. Nelly Factor claimed forty-seven, including John Horse's wife Susan. A half-dozen other Seminole put in multiple claims. Meanwhile, many of the Creek were impatient, arguing that some of the blacks being returned had already been sold to them by Seminole owners.

On January 2, 1849, a Seminole delegation arrived at Fort Gibson to meet with American officers. General William Belknap spoke for the U.S. government. John Horse led the Seminole Negro into the gathering and did the interpreting. Some Creek shouldered their way in; so did a few whites who wanted to establish their own claims on some of the blacks. And, of course, the Duval brothers were there. Sometime during the meeting, it became known that the Seminole had promised W. J. Duval one-third of the returned slaves as his fee for representing them in Washington.

Belknap stopped short of simply turning the blacks over to the Indians. Instead, he suggested the Seminole Negro be allowed to stay at Fort Gibson until spring, when the weather would be better for traveling. In front of the entire assembly, he told the Seminole they shouldn't sell their returned slaves to the Creek or whites—instead they should keep them and treat them well. But the Seminole Negro knew better.

So, as winter of 1848 turned into spring of 1849, Seminole Negro hopes seemed doomed. They might just as well have never run away from white masters, never fought the Americans in Florida, never trusted Jesup or boarded steamships or spent ten years fighting off slave raiders in Indian Territory. All the blood and sacrifice had come to nothing. They were almost back where they'd started. Seminole promises to Belknap that they'd keep their returned slaves and be kind to them meant nothing; the Seminole had already promised one-third of them to W. J. Duval as a legal fee! And what was Duval going to do with those eighty to one hundred Seminole Negro, if not haul them to the New Orleans or Memphis slave market in chains and sell them off to the same sort of white masters their parents and grandparents had run from in the first place?

The Seminole Negro spent the spring gathering their few belongings, and in April they moved away from Fort Gibson southwest to Seminole land. What happened next was entirely unexpected by the blacks, by the Seminole, and certainly by Marcellus Duval and the American government. John Horse was involved, but the main instigator was someone most of the Seminole Negro had long ago dismissed as unhelpful, if not an outright enemy.

Wild Cat had a plan, and the Seminole Negro were integral to it.

"You're gonna love what happens next," Willie Warrior promised. "The story gets better because this is where all the old folks used to really start telling it. Some of 'em, the old uncles and aunties who told these things to me, were alive when old Wild Cat and John Horse put their heads together and made their plan. They saw it happen. They *lived* it."

Willie and I spent a lot more time together. I knew I wasn't his only audience. Anyone with the slightest interest in the Seminole Negro eventually found their way to Willie's house. He undoubtedly spent as much time with other researchers as he did with me. Often, when I made contact with new Seminole Negro sources, they turned out to be old friends of Willie's.

"You'll write a book, maybe somebody else will write a book, finally there'll be a lot of books and maybe our story will get around," he told me. "Doesn't matter to me who writes them, just so they get written. Just so we've got it all on record."

Willie's bone-deep pleasure in walking around the shady glade on the south part of the vast fort grounds made him, on the several occasions we went there together, much more likely to smile and talk about little daily things in the lives of the scouts and their families who once lived there.

"They'd pull fish out of that water," he'd say, pointing to the pond. "Then they'd dig a little pit in the ground, cook the fish in the pit. Fish tastes so good fixed that way."

Over the next seven years I took many trips to Brackettville and, each time, no matter how hot it was in summer or freezing in winter, I made the long, slow drive out to the old village site. Almost always, I saw deer or wild turkey poking about the trees. It was, and still is, a sublimely peaceful place marred only by scattered picnic tables and trash left behind by picnickers and courting couples.

Maybe the shade creates the sense of tranquil wonder. There is no shade in the rest of Fort Clark or in Brackettville, no trees to block out the heat and glare. Brackettville is dust in the eyes and the danger of sunstroke. Anything moving seems to be scuttling along, hurrying to get inside a house or under a rock. Brackettville's colors are dirt-, not earth-, toned, all wind-blasted brown and sun-baked beige. But where the Seminole Negro scouts and their families once lived, the greenery is all the more startling for the contrast just hundreds of yards away. I loved being there, and thought, each time, about how happy the scouts and their families must have been living in such a special place, and how terrible it must have been to finally be ordered out at gunpoint by soldiers. Of course, before that happened, the Seminole Negro suffered other disasters, were badly treated by other people in other places.

Still, they had their glorious moments, too, and, as Willie Warrior pointed out, Wild Cat's Indian Territory plan was the catalyst for many of them.

chapter six

SOON AFTER I first met her, Miss Charles took me to the Scout Cemetery. It seemed to interest her much more than the old village site, which Willie Warrior obviously preferred. I decided, after a while, that their preferences demonstrated a difference between them. Willie loved the colorful history best. Miss Charles loved it, too, but she wanted something tangible to show the young people she so desperately wanted to succeed her as tribal historians. Headstones were something *their* Seminole Negro kids and visiting writers could see for themselves as proof of great people and great deeds, instead of having to imagine everything.

There was a sign to the cemetery beside the main highway—SEMINOLE SCOUT CEMETERY 3 MILES. That day, and every other time I took the road to the cemetery, I saw one or two bedraggled-looking Hispanics walking along it toward Brackettville. Later, I learned it was a popular route for illegal aliens who crossed the Rio Grande thirty miles south, around Eagle Pass. Brackettville had a Border Patrol office, and their trucks constantly whizzed around the area, but there were apparently more illegals than they could ever hope to round up. Certainly those I passed on the cemetery road didn't seem particularly concerned about being spotted.

"Here we are," Miss Charles said after a few minutes. The cemetery was on our left. There was a metal gate with the words SEMINOLE INDIAN

SCOUTS CEMETERY SINCE 1872 at the entrance. There was a state historical marker, too, something missing at the old village site. But then, that place belonged to the Fort Clark project, and the cemetery was property of the Seminole Negro.

Miss Charles wore a straw bonnet so massive she'd had to take it off to get into the car. Now she put it on again for protection from the sun. It was incredibly hot, 105 degrees officially but probably 10 degrees worse than that. There was no shade at all in the cemetery; the few scrubby, burned-looking trees were bunched at the back of a ratty chain-link fence that surrounded the few acres. A metal outhouse was placed near the trees. I couldn't imagine how hot it would have been in there, if someone was closed inside trying to use it. In between the front gate and the trees were several hundred graves, some marked with elaborate headstones and others with crude crosses made from lashed-together sticks or slabs of weather-warped wood with names and dates carved into them. Artificial flowers festooning some of the graves made colorful dots on an otherwise burned-out landscape.

"We must use the pretend flowers," Miss Charles said. "Real ones just wilt immediately in such heat."

She began pointing out names on headstones—July, Warrior, Wilson, names I'd begun to learn as part of the tribal history. There were four graves set apart—these honored the tribe's recipients of the Medal of Honor, the highest honor the U.S. military can bestow.

"No John Horse, you know," Miss Charles said. "He died in Mexico, no one knows quite where. Wild Cat died in Mexico and was buried there, too. I suppose you could say this is the resting-place of our more recent leaders instead."

"Are Wild Cat and John Horse buried together in Mexico?" I asked.

"Not at all," Miss Charles replied. "They went there together from Indian Territory, but they died separately and far apart."

For a while, though, the Seminole chief and the Seminole Negro leader formed an effective team. Though they'd known each other in Florida, the real moment they combined skills and ambition came in Indian Territory, when Wild Cat rode to visit John Horse and invited him to join in a risky plan that could save or destroy the followers of both men. Miss Charles was happy to tell about it.

Wild Cat had his faults, but lack of ambition was never one of them. In Florida, he assumed war leadership against the Americans after Osceola was taken prisoner, and no one among the Seminole challenged his right to do so. When Wild Cat finally arrived in Indian Territory, he refused to settle his followers anywhere near the land allocated to the Seminole by the white government because the Creek were living there, too, and Wild Cat refused to live under Creek rule.

So it isn't surprising that, from his first day in Indian Territory, Wild Cat began scheming. He felt he'd been defeated in Florida, but not conquered. He believed he was destined to lead his people back to freedom—it was only a matter of determining how and when.

Wild Cat came to Indian Territory in 1841 and squatted with his followers on Cherokee land. In 1844, he led the combined Seminole/Seminole Negro delegation to Washington to protest conditions and represented himself there as the Seminole lead tribal spokesman, which angered Micanopy. But Micanopy was a sickly old man. Under the arrangement most preferred by the Americans, "reservation" tribes had one principal chief with whom the whites would deal. For now, that was Micanopy. After he died there would have to be someone else. Wild Cat had no doubt who it *should* be.

It was a blow to Wild Cat's self-esteem when, returning from Washington, he found his followers starving and the Americans in position to force him to move south. All the Seminole had to submit to the Creek; Wild Cat was especially offended. That was probably one reason he insisted on having his former slave John Philip returned to him from Florida; both the Creek and Seminole considered slave ownership to be a status symbol. The more blacks a man owned, the greater he was. And Micanopy, now the principal chief in the eyes of his people as well as in the opinion of the Americans, owned the most.

So, for his own sake, Wild Cat wanted the Seminole Negro once again subjugated to the Seminole. He didn't consider his old friend John Horse a potential slave; Micanopy had freed him earlier. And, while John Horse bitterly resented most Seminole leaders and was hated in turn by them, he stayed on good terms with Wild Cat.

When Marcellus Duval arrived in 1845, Wild Cat, who certainly spoke some English by then, immediately ingratiated himself with him. Perhaps he just liked the white subagent, but more likely he considered him a useful pawn. Wild Cat was beginning to put a plan together, and he needed Duval's cooperation, since no Indians could leave the territory without an agent's permission.

Wild Cat envisioned a new confederation of Indian tribes, the Seminole joining not with the hated Creek or the mealy-mouthed Cherokee, but with the mighty Comanche, the wily Shawnee, the ubiquitous Kickapoo—tribes that still defied the whites to some extent, good fighters who, if gathered in sufficient numbers, could make the Americans think twice about offering misleading treaties and scrubland for reservations. All that was needed, Wild Cat believed, was for one charismatic leader to go to the chiefs of those tribes and put together an alliance. Surely they would grasp its potential and place at the head of their newly combined forces the man who'd conceived the plan in the first place.

Wild Cat had to fool Duval, but that proved easy enough. The subagent, he believed, was obsessed with getting control of the Seminole Negro. We know, from Duval's letters, that Wild Cat told the subagent General Jesup liked negroes better than Indians, a bit of helpful slander Duval immediately included in reports to Washington. Wild Cat certainly emphasized to Duval how unhappy the Seminole were at being deprived of their rightful property. And, at some point, Wild Cat had another suggestion: What about a trade delegation to go and meet with bands of nonreservation tribes like the Comanche? That could be a step toward bringing those Indians to heel; first they would trade with the whites, then they'd talk treaty with them, then they'd come in to some designated reservation.

On May 31, 1847, Duval wrote to Secretary of War Marcy: "Sir, I have the honor to inform you that many of the Seminoles propose visiting the Salt Plains to meet with the Comanches and other tribes. There will be present, it is supposed, Indians from the following tribes: Comanche, Osage, Kioway, Seminole, Creek, Quapaw, Quasauda, Delaware, Shawnee, and probably others. It is not a Council they are to meet, but rather to trade on what is called the 'Neutral Ground' where all meet friendly. The Comanches sent in word that all who wanted to trade for male Buffalo skins so [*sic*] could come, as they had enough for all."

Duval used the balance of the letter for self-promotion: "I was invited to accompany the Seminoles, which I may do, if I find I can conveniently leave home for about 4 weeks. Although it is, I am convinced, only intended as a friendly meeting, it would be highly proper for a Gov't agent to be present, if only as a spectator. This information is given, lest some one not knowing anything of Indian Affairs, hearing of it, might create an improper impression as to its objects, and occasion some uneasiness as to its results." In other words, the kind of thing Duval himself might have done behind someone's back.

It didn't matter to Wild Cat whether Duval went along or not, Miss Charles added. Even if the American brought an interpreter, there would be plenty of time to whisper to other chiefs about a possible coalition. Wild Cat made several forays west and south of Indian Territory, ostensibly to sound out other tribes about trade agreements. In fact, he was reconnoitering, studying the land for possible escape routes and locations for new, permanent settlements.

Unfortunately for Wild Cat, things didn't go entirely as he had hoped. Most of the chiefs he met from other tribes were willing to talk, Miss Charles said, but there was no formation of a grand multitribal federation. Perhaps Wild Cat wasn't persuasive enough. The Comanche in particular had never actually allied themselves with outsiders, though they sometimes entered into temporary agreements if it suited their purposes. There was also the undeniable fact that Wild Cat wasn't the principal Seminole chief. As a minor tribal leader, he couldn't speak for all his people, and the other tribes' chiefs realized it. The Comanche, Kickapoo, and others knew little if anything about the great battles against the white soldiers in

Florida. There was nothing in Wild Cat's past or present that particularly impressed them.

When Attorney General Mason ruled in June 1848 that the Seminole Negro must return to their Indian masters, Wild Cat wasn't especially concerned. He tried to help out old friend John Horse by providing him with a statement that the Seminole had set him free; John Horse knew Marcellus Duval trusted Wild Cat. But Wild Cat's focus was on Micanopy; the old man was failing fast.

On December 22, 1848, just eleven days before the Seminole went to Fort Gibson to reclaim their former slaves, Micanopy died. This was the opportunity Wild Cat had anticipated. Once elected principal Seminole chief, he would go back to the Comanche and the Osage and the other tribes and finally convince them to form a new multitribal nation, perhaps with Wild Cat as its leader.

But Wild Cat's own people rejected him, selecting Jim Jumper as their new chief. The son of old chief Jumper, who died on the way to Indian Territory from Florida, Jim Jumper favored accommodation with the Creek and acceptance of that tribe's dominance. Wild Cat was furious, and helpless to do anything about it. The Creek welcomed Jim Jumper as Seminole leader, and the whites were pleased as well.

A man with less ambition than Wild Cat might have given up. But he soon had another plan. If he couldn't bring together enough other tribes to join militant Seminole in opposing the whites and the Creek, perhaps he could create some position of power for himself outside of Indian Territory. He couldn't accomplish this to the north or east—American settlers were there, coming ever closer to the boundaries of Indian Territory and making it offensively clear that they disdained Indians every bit as much as they looked down on blacks.

To the west, the Comanche ruled, and beyond them were equally fierce legions of Sioux and Cheyenne. But there was another way to go. To the south lay a place, a country, where warriors were needed, brave men who could fight and who, in return, could receive land and gold and prestige: *Mexico.*

The massive territory once known as New Spain was in turmoil. For the first three hundred years of colonization, its hills and plains and beaches were soaked with native blood. The Spanish came first to conquer, then to leach out of the land every bit of precious metal, every crop, that could be siphoned off for Spain. They used its native people as laborers and established their colonists as the new ruling class. There was no chance for those they subjugated to successfully fight back; the Spanish had plenty of well-armed soldiers and the inclination to unleash them at the slightest provocation. Though the vagaries of world events sometimes caused Spain to abandon colonies elsewhere, New Spain was territory its leaders intended to hold.

But in the very early 1800s, Napoleon's troops overran much of Europe; for a time, his forces even occupied parts of Spain. The government there had more important concerns to occupy its attention, and its armies, than colonies far across the ocean. And even among those colonies, there were priorities. The newly independent Americans were obviously coveting Florida and Texas. The Spanish couldn't fight extended wars on two fronts, particularly if one was thousands of miles away.

So, in 1819, Spain and the United States agreed on the Adams-Onis Treaty, which ceded Florida to America for $5 million, and in which the Americans promised Spain eternal rights to Texas and other territory, which included the modern-day states of California, New Mexico, Nevada, Utah, and Arizona, as well as parts of Wyoming and Colorado. While the Seminole and Seminole Negro fought the Americans in Florida, Spain tried to hang on to the remainder of its New World empire.

That proved impossible. Beginning in 1810, there was full-scale revolution in New Spain. Eventually, Spain had neither the will or the ability to continue imposing its rule. In 1821, the Spanish capitulated, first allowing a congress to be elected, and, after one more outbreak of violence, helplessly watching a new country called "Mexico" declare itself a republic. (The name came from *Mexica,* the ancient Aztecs' word for themselves.) Later, Spain would make sporadic attempts to regain its former colony, but these were unsuccessful.

The new United States of Mexico had troubles of its own; heads of government came and went, usually overthrown, often in bloody fashion. From time to time, some leader would bring about dramatic change. In 1829, for instance, President Vincente Guerrero outlawed slavery: "I have thought it proper to decree, 1st, Slavery is abolished in the republic. 2nd, Consequently, those who have until now been considered slaves are free."

Political upheaval became traditional. The country changed leaders like shirts. Between 1833 and 1855, the Mexican presidency changed hands thirty-six times. One man, Antonio López de Santa Anna, eventually familiar to most Americans as the villain of the Alamo, was president on eleven separate occasions. During one triumphant reascension to power, Santa Anna lost part of a leg in battle. He had the leg honored with a fine parade, then buried with full honors. The next time he was driven into exile, his enemies dug up the leg and dragged it through the streets. Naturally, such lack of political stability weakened Mexico's ability to protect its northern borders. On the other side of this poorly defended boundary, Americans noticed.

Settlers from the United States—who moved into the Mexican territory of Texas at the invitation of Mexico's government—gradually resented their status as colonists. It is testament to Mexico's internal difficulties that Santa Anna himself, at the head of a numerically superior force, was eventually defeated north of the Rio Grande by Sam Houston's ragtag rebel army. Texas became first a republic, then an American state. So much for the Adams-Onis Treaty.

About the same time Marcellus Duval became the Seminole subagent in Indian Territory, American president James K. Polk offered Mexico $25 million for California and New Mexico. When that offer, ridiculously low even by the monetary standards of the time, was refused, American forces soon occupied disputed territory between Texas and Mexico. An old acquaintance of the Seminole Negro, General Zachary Taylor, led the Americans. After some skirmishing, the United States declared war in May of 1846.

Though hostilities lasted the better part of two years, the outcome was never in doubt. The invading Americans had too much firepower for Mexico. Santa Anna, leading Mexican troops during one of his innumerable political comebacks, was as useless against General Winfield Scott as he had been against Sam Houston. While the war was still underway, Mexican leaders concluded that their northern border, wherever it might be when the fighting finally was over, was too extensive for limited Mexican troops to defend. Americans weren't the only problem; roving bands of Apache and Comanche Indians also were raiding Mexican settlements, seemingly at will.

During the U.S.–Mexican War, Mexico tried to lure its own citizens north. Failing that, any warm bodies willing to risk the wrath of Americans and Indians were needed as border buffers. A law passed in December 1846 called for "military colonies, composed of Mexicans or aliens, or both, along the coasts and frontiers as the government shall designate, especially to restrain the incursions of savages." For a while, it remained a theory rather than a practice. American soldiers marched or sailed into Mexico, Mexican defenses slowly crumbled, and, finally, on February 2, 1848, Mexico capitulated. The Treaty of Guadalupe Hidalgo granted the United States all disputed territory in Texas, plus California and almost everything else. Five years later the Gadsden Purchase added final slivers of New Mexico and Arizona. In return, Mexico received $15 million, plus the American government agreed to pay about $3.25 million to U.S. citizens with claims against Mexico for land or property. It was a humiliating settlement. Many Americans wanted more, calling for further invasions until the United States captured and took for its own all of Mexico.

Mexican leaders couldn't ignore the possibility that America would be back in force. Meanwhile, Mexico's new Rio Grande northern border was regularly violated by raiding Indians and whites. The Mexican army was in disarray. Under terms of the recent treaty, American soldiers were supposed to help defend the border, but the U.S. Army failed to assign sufficient troops to the area. Mexico was on its own.

Jose Herrera assumed the Mexican presidency. In July, about six months after the war with America was over, he readdressed the concept of new military colonies that had first been raised in 1846. Mexico would accept, even welcome, "aliens" willing to settle on the Mexican side of the border and help defend it. They would be given land there, good land, with rivers and hills and plenty of room for planting crops. And there would still be more! Herrera promised that "upon the establishment of a colony, the government will advance to the colonists a six-months supply of provisions, *to be charged to the public treasury,* and tools, plows, oxen, horses, and whatever is needed to build houses for the colony." In other words, outsiders could simply show up—everything they needed to establish a settlement would be provided at Mexico's expense. There would, of course, be a resulting obligation to help fight invaders.

Wild Cat learned of Hidalgo's offer. It was exactly the opportunity he needed. From his earlier trips to Texas, he knew how to get at least partway to Mexico. Surely the Mexican government would welcome fierce warriors led by a Seminole chief who'd fought the Americans to a draw in Florida, something Mexican generals hadn't been able to accomplish in their homeland. Ben Pingenot believed Wild Cat's eventual goal was something more than working for the Mexicans. Who was to say that Wild Cat couldn't keep talking to the Comanche, to the Apache, as well as fighting them? If he were the chief of a powerful Indian colony in Mexico, he might have the status to form his envisioned federation. And if that federation was strong enough, contractual obligations to the Mexican government could eventually be, well, *forgotten.*

Sometime in 1849, after Jim Jumper was chosen to replace Micanopy, and after word of Hidalgo's decree reached Indian Terrority, Wild Cat made up his mind to go to Mexico. He probably came to that decision in the early spring, because in March he asked for permission to travel through Texas on a hunting trip, and Marcellus Duval agreed to let Wild Cat go. It's possible Wild Cat went just a bit farther, across the Rio Grande and into Mexico to inquire there whether an Indian band would be welcome as border settlers. He certainly spoke a little Spanish by then. Probably, though, he just met with chiefs of Texas tribes, asking which, if any, might want to bring warriors and join with him south of the border.

Back in Indian Territory, Wild Cat recruited as many Seminole as he could. No more than twenty-five or thirty braves were willing to follow him. That would hardly be enough fighting men to impress the Mexicans, let alone convince them to give grants of land and supplies to the newcomers in exchange for protection along the border. Wild Cat had to find more warriors, but additional Seminole braves weren't among his options. Jim Jumper was proving to be a popular chief. Most of the Seminole were happy to follow his example and kowtow to the Creek. Fortunately for Wild Cat, there was another source of manpower, and his old friend John Horse was the key.

In April 1849, John Horse led the Seminole Negro southwest from Fort Gibson, following orders from the Americans. But he only obeyed those orders for a matter of miles. Instead of meekly arriving at the Seminole camps to assume their old role of tribal slaves, under John Horse's direction most of the Seminole Negro veered off to Wewoka Creek, about thirty-five miles from the tribal agency and twenty miles from where the Seminole had planned to settle their newly reacquired human property. Some of the blacks did obediently straggle back to Seminole masters, and most of them were sold off to the Creek or to whites. "But not most," Miss Charles said proudly. "Our people had *spirit*."

With John Horse directing, the Seminole Negro defiantly built their own village in the bottomland beside Wewoka Creek. It was a good village, with its huts built better than those of the Seminole and Creek. There were a few smaller black settlements, too. The Seminole Negro plowed fields and planted crops. Those who could, acquired guns. Perhaps three hundred Seminole Negro lived in the towns; a quarter of them were warriors. That force wouldn't be sufficient to fight off an organized attack by American soldiers, or by combined Seminole and Creek forces. The blacks knew that. In part, they were gambling that capturing them would come at such a bloody cost that the whites and Indians wouldn't think an attack was worth the trouble. But the Seminole Negro were also tired of being property. Even momentary freedom was worth whatever suffering would result afterward.

Back at Fort Gibson, Colonel Loomis saw no reason why he should use his troops to make the Seminole Negro return to the Seminole. He'd been ordered to send the blacks back, and he had. Now it was the Seminole's responsibility to gather them in and reassign them to their proper owners. The American government did not have to be involved, Loomis believed, and his superior officers, Generals Arbuckle and Belknap, agreed.

Duval didn't. But he was stymied by the Seminole response, which was to let the situation resolve itself. Jim Jumper wanted his people to be in agreement concerning who owned which Seminole Negro before the drastic step was taken of surrounding the new black towns and using force to bring the Seminole Negro back if persuasion failed. The Seminole had previously agreed to let the blacks have their own separate village. They'd just moved the location farther from the Seminole camps than had originally been anticipated.

The Creek pointed out to anyone who would listen that it was against their tribal laws for negroes to own guns. The Seminole were part of the Creek tribe, subject to Creek rules. The Seminole Negro, by order of the Americans, once again belonged to the Seminole. Therefore, someone should take those guns away from the Seminole Negro—the white soldiers could do it, or the Seminole. But the Creek themselves found it inconvenient to conduct a full-scale attack on blacks who had both significant firepower and the will to use it.

Duval knew very well that Arbuckle and Belknap weren't prepared to help him. So he fell back on an old habit; Commissioner of Indian Affairs Medill received a letter from Duval slandering Arbuckle.

"It had never entered my head for a moment that a person could own property without the power of disposing of it," Duval wrote, "or that a gentleman of General Arbuckle's intelligence and experience, would have entertained for an instant so novel an idea, as that a slave is competent to make a contract."

Duval's complaints fell on sympathetic Washington ears. Arbuckle was ordered to explain himself. Why were these Seminole Negro continuing to live free after being ordered back into slavery? Arbuckle admitted that John Horse and the Seminole Negro hadn't abided by the terms of the

Fort Gibson agreement. The problem, he felt, was that the blacks had been separated from the Indians for too long and no longer felt any obligation to, let alone any affection for, their longtime masters. So, yes, the Seminole Negro were wrong: "They were counselled to conduct themselves properly when they were turned over, and assured that if they did so, they should not be cruelly or illegally treated. But it seems they have acted otherwise."

Now, Arbuckle argued, there was a more practical concern. It was obvious that the Seminole Negro would never again make useful slaves for the Indians. Using white troops to force the blacks out of Wewoka and back into Seminole camps wouldn't result in the Indians and Seminole Negro living together in peace afterward. Instead, there would be violence, perhaps an all-out shooting war. Better that the American government should broker a pragmatic agreement between the Indians and the blacks, one where the Seminole Negro would submit to some form of Seminole ownership and perhaps pay tribute in the form of crops or occasional service, while the Indians would allow the blacks to live separately and not, under any circumstances, be sold off to white or Creek slavers.

No one apparently ever considered just letting the Seminole Negro go. That would have sent too tempting a message to slaves in white towns and settlements.

Arbuckle finally told Duval the army would send an officer to Wewoka to investigate. Duval angrily responded that he'd do any investigating himself. Arbuckle ordered Belknap to send an investigator anyway. He reported back to Arbuckle via Belknap that Duval was openly consorting with slavers, and that the subagent and his brother stood to benefit financially if the Seminole Negro were forced back into Seminole clutches. Possibly Arbuckle reported these findings to Washington, but probably not. In those days, most Indian agents were assumed to be crooked. Duval would have been considered the rule, not the exception.

The tense standoff continued. The Creeks made a few limited raids on Wewoka, mostly trying to pick off solitary blacks who wandered too far from their companions. Otherwise, Duval wrote his letters and the Seminole chiefs dithered over who owned which blacks. The Seminole Negro cleaned their guns and waited, knowing that eventually they would have to fight.

And, when they fought, they would lose. There were too many Seminole and Creek, or, if it was the white army that came, there were even more of those soldiers. But, as John Horse had made clear, they were ready to die where they were rather than become slaves again. Death with honor now seemed to be their last, best option.

Miss Charles broke off the story for a while and guided me around the cemetery, pointing out various graves. She showed me her mother's and her sister's and lingered beside the markers for the tribe's four Medal of Honor winners. She tutted whenever she spied weeds growing around headstones and asked me to pick up some stray candy wrappers the hot wind blew against the fence.

"This is our good, special, place," Miss Charles said, groaning as she awkwardly bent to yank up a weed. "Without it, I think those of us left would just dry up and blow away."

Back in her darkened living room, sipping cold water and cooling off after our cemetery excursion, Miss Charles took up her story again with Wild Cat coming to visit John Horse, and what he proposed when he arrived.

Sometime in July 1849, Miss Charles said, Wild Cat rode into Wewoka. He came alone, so the Seminole Negro wouldn't jump to the conclusion that a Seminole war party was coming to attack them. While most of the blacks were suspicious of Wild Cat—to them he was simply a Seminole subchief who was openly friends with Duval—John Horse would have been glad to see his old friend. He would have invited the visitor to his cabin. A whiskey bottle would have been produced; probably Wild Cat brought one as a gift. Then the Seminole would have started talking.

Beginning here, some of Miss Charles Emily Wilson's Seminole Negro history includes snatches of conversation. Of course, she wasn't there, but her grandparents were. They told her parents what Wild Cat said, or John Horse said, or at least what they were supposed to have said, and her par-

Miss Charles in the Scout Cemetery

(PHOTO BY RON ENNIS, *FORT WORTH STAR TELEGRAM*)

ents told Miss Charles. She insisted she never made up any conversations herself, just to make her storytelling more compelling: "These are the words told to me, no more and no less." In third- and fourth-hand recounting, there is always some exaggeration, as well as some details that are left out. But when Miss Charles and Willie Warrior told the story of the

Seminole Negro exodus to Mexico in breathtaking detail, with all sorts of fascinating anecdotes and observations, they occasionally used bits of conversation as adornment, not foundation. There was no reason to doubt they were relating the gist of real conversations, if not repeating them word for word, and these occasional additions certainly made the overall story come alive in the telling.

So here, when the idea of making that historic journey is first being broached by Wild Cat to John Horse, Miss Charles could describe what they said.

Wild Cat told John Horse about Mexico, the land the Seminole Negro could have there, what they would have to do to earn that land, and how they would get from Indian Territory to Mexico. He needed the Seminole Negro's help, Wild Cat admitted, but if John Horse would be loyal to him, he would return that loyalty. And, remember: There is no slavery in Mexico. Once your people cross the Rio Grande, they are legally free.

"We're free now," John Horse replied. "We live by ourselves. We make our own rules."

"But you don't have your own land," Wild Cat argued. "Without land, there is no real freedom."

John Horse had to agree. Well, all right. He would talk to his people. He would tell them about Mexico and freedom, about a possible role of guarding the Mexican border and fighting to protect it. He'd explain how he believed Wild Cat could now be trusted, how a Seminole could be an ally. But he wanted something understood from the start. Wild Cat had to agree to the nonnegotiable reward the Seminole Negro required in return for helping him succeed in Mexico: "We want our land before we die," John Horse said, repeating it several times so there was no chance Wild Cat might misunderstand. "*Our* land. Not the right to live on *yours*."

Wild Cat swore they would have it. John Horse asked for time to talk to his people.

Almost immediately afterward, Wild Cat had an opportunity to prove he was now the Seminole Negro's friend. John Drennen, superintendent of Indian Affairs for the Western Territory, had decided to support Duval. Drennen formally requested that the army go to Wewoka and disarm the blacks, since they carried guns in defiance of the Creek tribal law to which they were legally subject. Jim Jumper and the Seminoles enthusiastically supported Drennen, as did the Creek. Arbuckle didn't want to do it; he realized that, as soon as the Seminole Negro were disarmed, Indian and white slavers would descend on Wewoka and carry off every black who wasn't killed resisting them.

In August, Duval repeated his request for the army to disarm the Seminole Negro. This time, when Arbuckle refused, the general pointed out that the individuals urging him to take away the blacks' guns were mostly white slavers, or people like Duval, who were friendly with the slavers. Duval feigned outrage, and asked Drennen, his boss, to intervene. Drennan, himself a slaveholder, wrote indignantly to Arbuckle that "I am well aware that great disturbance and much difficulty has arisen in Indian Territory by designing white men, for mercenary purposes; but I did not think for one moment that anything of the kind was intended in this case."

Wild Cat took advantage of an opportunity to ingratiate himself with the Seminole Negro. In early September he went to see Arbuckle, bringing along some other Seminole warriors. They told Arbuckle, stretching the truth, that the Seminole people didn't want the blacks disarmed; that, in fact, their tribe didn't believe John Horse was inciting his people to defy the white government. They also told Arbuckle about W. J. Duval's deal with the Seminole to receive a third of the returning slaves as his legal fee, and that, at least so far as rumor had it, Marcellus Duval was insisting his brother get even more blacks than that.

Arbuckle asked for time to decide what to do. Meanwhile, he had his aide write a letter that Wild Cat could take to Drennen. In the letter, Arbuckle suggested Duval was the one causing all the trouble: "The General believes the course adopted by the subagent is such as will probably lead to difficulty between the Seminoles and the Creeks." But Drennen wasn't deterred.

Trouble was coming; everyone knew it. Some of the Seminole Negro drifted back to Fort Gibson, which angered the Seminole and Creek. Arbuckle let them come. The Creek continued their raids on Wewoka. The Seminole dithered. Duval may have learned Wild Cat planned to take some Seminole and go to Mexico, but apparently he had no idea John Horse and the Seminole Negro were part of that plan.

In October, Wild Cat visited Marcellus Duval. He proposed to the subagent that he be allowed to take his people and live across the Rio Grande in Mexico. He no longer wanted to be near the Creek, Wild Cat added, and, as an inducement, he suggested the Seminole still in Florida might be willing to move to Mexico, too.

This intrigued Duval. The American government had long been concerned about the Seminole remaining in the Everglades. There were supposed to be about 350 of them, under the leadership of a chief named Billy Bowlegs. Duval decided to go to Florida himself and talk to Bowlegs. He immediately dismissed Wild Cat's plan for Bowlegs to join other Seminole across the Rio Grande, but what a coup for the subagent if he could successfully lure the remaining Florida Seminole back to Indian Territory! Duval arranged to go to Florida sometime in the fall. He enlisted Chief Halleck Tustenuggee to go with him. Wild Cat certainly wasn't invited; since he had gone to Arbuckle in support of the Seminole Negro, Duval no longer considered him trustworthy.

Wild Cat and John Horse met often now. They had a lot to work out. Not all the Seminole Negro were ready to run to Mexico. Besides, if they all left at once the traveling party would be unwieldy. Wild Cat had about thirty-five braves and their families who wanted to go. If the same number of Seminole Negro warriors and their families went, that would mean some two hundred men, women, old people, and children would make the trip. It was difficult to determine just the right numbers. The Mexicans would want as many fighting men as possible to be in the party, and the warriors wouldn't come without their families. Too large a party would travel too slowly. Duval would send slavers after them, Wild Cat and John Horse were certain.

The trip itself seemed impossible in so many ways. Water holes, rivers, and streams in the nine hundred miles between Indian Territory and Mexico were limited. There were few roads fugitives could follow; they had to

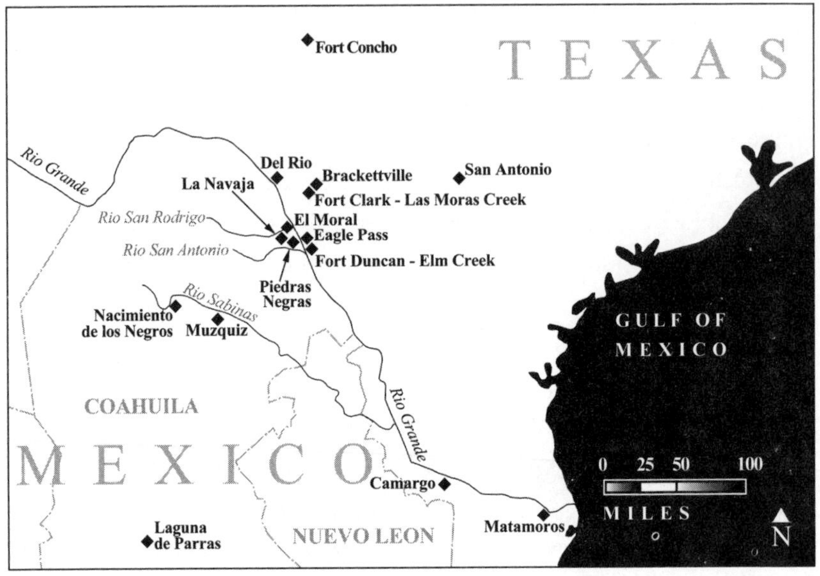

(MAP BY BROC SEARS)

avoid as many towns as possible. Texas was a slave state; blacks passing through would be considered property on the hoof, like a herd of wild ponies. There was no way the combined Seminole/Seminole Negro band could bring enough food with them to last throughout the trip, which would certainly take three months, four months, maybe more. They couldn't just go boldly in a straight line for Mexico. Duval's slavers would be looking for them, as would army patrols if Arbuckle was forced to hunt them down, and, certainly, hostile Indians. Wild Cat thought he might have forged good enough relations with some of the tribes along the way to guarantee safe passage, but the Comanche in particular were untrustworthy. Most of the men in the company would have rifles, but ammunition was limited. They wouldn't be able to fight off too many sustained attacks. For the Seminole Negro, there was the additional concern of how they would be punished if, in fact, Duval's minions did catch them and drag them back. They couldn't expect their Seminole "masters" to intercede for them if that happened.

It may have entered John Horse's mind not to go. The risks were awful, and the various consequences of failure were horrifying—starvation on the trail, massacre by the Comanche, enslavement by Texans, capture by Duval's slavers. Then, too, Willie Warrior noted the Seminole Negro had no particular reason to believe the Mexicans would keep their word about anything. It sounded fine, getting free land in return for helping protect Mexico's northern border. But John Horse had only Wild Cat's promise that the land really would be forthcoming. He chose to believe his Seminole friend.

Duval left for Florida on October 16. Besides Halleck Tustenuggee, he took with him three Seminole Negro interpreters. One, Jim Bowlegs, had been Seminole chief Billy Bowlegs's slave in Florida. No one knew how long Duval's delegation would be gone. If they met right away with the Florida Seminole, and if Billy Bowlegs was willing to move, they might be back in Indian Territory within weeks. If negotiations grew prolonged, it could take months. Wild Cat and John Horse couldn't risk waiting. It would have been better to travel in the spring, but they would simply have to shiver through the winter months instead. Wild Cat wanted to leave as soon as possible anyway; who knew how long the Mexicans would continue their offer of land in return for border protection? He urged John Horse to decide which Seminole Negro would be part of this first group heading for Mexico. Not all the blacks wanted to go; many said they would wait to hear what happened in Mexico. If land was really provided, land that belonged only to the Seminole Negro, well, they would follow right away.

The exact date is lost to memory and printed record, but sometime in late October or early November, probably in the dead of night, a ragged caravan of about 250 men, women, and children departed Indian Territory heading south. One of the bravest, most terrible journeys in American history had begun.

"Oh, the story gets good now," Miss Charles said happily, rocking back and forth a little in her chair. "My mother and daddy told me about it over and over. The story of the flight down to Mexico. I could never hear it enough."

Over the next months and years, as she and Willie Warrior described it bit by bit, I understood why.

chapter seven

SITTING IN HER darkened living room, rocking back and forth in her chair, Miss Charles provided vivid descriptions of the long, risky journey undertaken by her ancestors. I'd thought her earlier stories were extraordinary, but the variety of colors in her verbal palette expanded when she reached this point in Seminole Negro history. Miss Charles began to describe, often in astonishing detail, what people said and felt and did during the escape to Mexico. She'd learned these things from her parents, who were told the stories by participants in the nine-hundred-mile flight to freedom. When Miss Charles related them to me, her reedy old voice often gained volume, until I no longer had trouble hearing her over the groaning air conditioner. Her face glowed; she realized the magnitude of what John Horse and Wild Cat and their followers were attempting—what, in fact, they accomplished.

Willie Warrior added more. His descriptions were more basic than those of his old teacher—like the warriors on this trek, his attention was mostly given to the details of survival. Willie told how, every day, the refugees had to find water or die. He disabused my own sterile images: "When I say they loaded their things in wagons, you probably think they had those fancy wagons like in the old TV Western shows. Never. All they had were two-wheeled Mexican wagons, the kind that tip over if you go too fast." Willie knew because, as a boy, he hung on the words of the old men in Brackettville who had survived the awful trek.

Between the two, they made the story of the Seminole Negro escape from Indian Territory immediate and breathtaking. In some instances, particularly involving a Comanche attack on the refugees, their versions differed from the research of outside historians. But one thing is clear about this exodus: There isn't anything else like it in American frontier history.

Take a moment. Imagine these people as they began the journey. Thirty or thirty-five Seminole braves led by Wild Cat were joined by their families—wives, children, parents, grandparents, a mix of young and old. Almost every Seminole fighting man took along dependents. There were, perhaps, thirty Seminole Negro warriors, but half of them left their families behind, some in Wewoka, many in the clutches of Seminole or Creek masters. In most cases, the blacks who did bring along wives and children had older relatives with them, too—parents, uncles, aunts, even grandparents. The group also included a few runaway slaves from the Creek and Cherokee camps, plus one or two Creek warriors who, for one reason or another, wanted to leave Indian Territory. In all, Wild Cat and John Horse probably had about seventy grown men who were physically able to fight, plus a few teenaged boys.

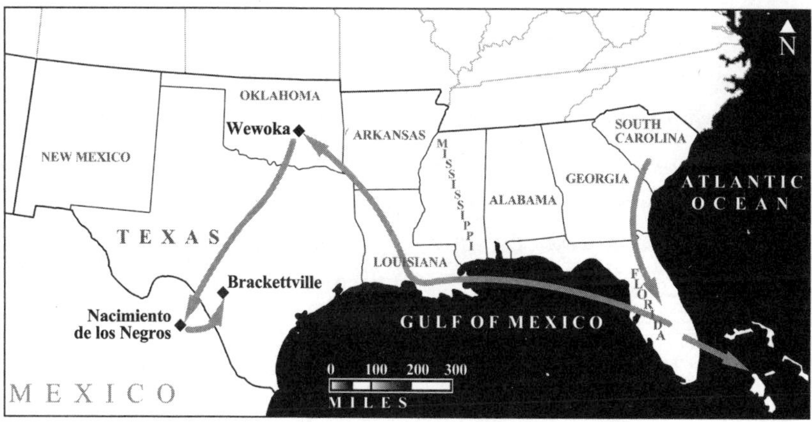

(MAP BY BROC SEARS)

It was cool so late in the year, even chilly. Those who had a sufficient wardrobe wore several layers of clothing, shirts over shirts, deerskin leggings under trousers bought from white sutlers, turbans or hats over head scarves. Those without extra clothing wrapped themselves in blankets.

There were enough horses for the men to ride. Because it was necessary to send scouts ahead and keep a rear guard behind, it would have been risky rather than chivalrous to let the old people, women, and small children ride while the men walked. Babies were carried; toddlers were encouraged to scamper along until they tired. Then they had to be carried, too. Perhaps a few sickly grandparents and one or two heavily pregnant women rode in the wagons, but there wasn't much wagon space available.

As Willie constantly reminded me, these weren't the covered "prairie schooners" familiar from old Western movies and books. The dozen or so wagons Wild Cat and John Horse had been able to scrounge were rickety two-wheelers, ones with long front shafts so mules or horses could be harnessed to pull them. At the beginning of the journey, there were enough horses for all the men and some women to ride, plus a few horses left over to pull the two-wheel wagons, which were really boxy carts. Later, Miss Charles said, as horses came up lame or died from snakebite or battle wounds or starvation, some of the wagons had to be pulled by hand.

At least, when that time came, the wagons were lighter. As the Seminole and Seminole Negro left Indian Territory, every inch of wagon space was crammed with dried meat, dried corn, sacks of weevily flour, water bags sloshing their precious contents about, frying pans and hoes and bits of bridle for repairs on the trail, packets of lead to be melted down for musket balls, a few small casks of gunpowder, wooden shafts for arrows, iron arrow points, and a modest store of medicines. When daily hunting was good, if there was meat left over, then it was smoked and taken along for sustenance when game was scarce. As the party moved south and provisions were gradually used up, there was more room in the wagons for human cargo. But, by that time, some of the weaker old people and infants no longer needed to ride, because they had already died along the way.

Privacy was nonexistent. Despite white assumptions that Indians and blacks were exhibitionist savages, both the Seminole and Seminole Negro were, in their ways, modest people. Their traditional log houses were open to the sun and wind in good weather, but even then the openings could be blocked with blankets or brush if the people inside wanted time to themselves. On this trek, though, there usually wasn't an opportunity to build temporary shelters at night, or, in many cases, materials available to build even the most primitive lean-to. Even the most personal of bodily functions had to be performed in plain sight. They were constantly aware that stalkers could pick off anyone foolish enough to separate from the main party.

The fugitives didn't have modern roads to follow that cut through hills and spanned rivers and canyons. What primitive trails there were between settlements usually had to be avoided. The fewer people who saw the raggedy refugees, the better. Not all of Oklahoma is flat red dirt, and Texas is more than desert speckled with scrubby cactus. When they came upon hills, they had to climb them. When there were gullies, they had to slide down one side and scramble up the other. Streams had to be waded; rivers had to be forded by the men, who would then gather logs to be lashed together into rafts, so the women and children and old people and wagons full of provisions could be floated across. Later, in Texas, there were craggy mesas and precipitous gorges. What they couldn't walk around, they had to somehow negotiate. Painfully, often with resulting loss of life or injury, they did. From the moment they left Indian Territory until nine months later, when the survivors reached Mexico, every mile was a challenge.

No one living knows the precise route Wild Cat led his followers along on the way from Indian Territory to Mexico. We can guess, though; the goal would have been to avoid settlements and the worst terrain, though sometimes these two objectives simply weren't compatible.

Wewoka is still in existence, a tiny Brackettville-like place in Oklahoma near the junction of country highways 56 and 270. Heading south from there, toward Texas, the land is flat and red and dry-looking. Modern roads, even the pocked, uneven ones here, are deceiving. It's one thing to drive in this area, quite another to have had to walk cross-country. Even if there aren't cliffs or canyons, there are still gullies and, sometimes, thick, prickly brush too spread out to walk around. And, just thirty miles south, the Canadian River rushes along. Two days into their journey, the refugees would have already had to stop to fashion crude log rafts, and, in this part of Oklahoma, trees were scarce. At least, on this first part of the journey, the people still felt fresh and strong.

Their pace was slow. It had to be. The children and old people couldn't march very fast or very long. They had no *remuda,* or string of extra mounts, so they were careful not to wear out the horses they did have. And so much depended on the ground they were trying to cross. It could take an entire day to build rafts and get everyone across a river, or to painstakingly traverse a series of high hills. Scouts constantly rode ahead to seek out the easiest routes through rough country, but detours could not be extreme. Wild Cat and John Horse wanted to get to Mexico before the Mexican government reconsidered its land-for-defense offer. Another practical consideration involved supplies. They didn't have much food with them. It would be used up soon, and, if hunting was bad, they would march with empty bellies and their stamina would decrease accordingly. And, of course, they wanted to get a head start on any pursuers.

That there would be pursuit was a given. What form it would take, and when it would come, was something they couldn't know. Duval was in Florida. Even if other whites or Seminole or Creek leaders telegraphed him there, he couldn't interrupt his negotiations with Chief Bowlegs to rush back home and recruit a posse. If Duval was detained in Florida through December, or, better still, until spring, then it was just possible the fugitives could make it to the Mexican border before he unleashed a pack of slavers after them.

The Creek or Seminole might follow, but John Horse in particular didn't think they would. If they'd been reluctant to attack the Seminole Negro at Wewoka, preferring to complain to Duval instead, it was likely they would wait and place the burden of pursuit on the subagent when he returned from Florida. Besides, most of the Seminole Negro were still back in Indian Territory. As for Wild Cat and his followers, Jim Jumper would probably consider his Seminole nation better off without them.

Arbuckle and Belknap had already made it clear they did not intend to use their soldiers to enforce Creek slave laws. The American army, at least in Indian Territory, didn't worry Wild Cat and John Horse at all. But the two leaders of the refugees had immediate concerns about the Comanche.

This fiercest of tribes began as a harmless race of wanderers in the American northwest, probably among the Shoshone along the Platte River in Wyoming. But by the late 1600s the Spanish had introduced the horse to North America, and these Indians took naturally to riding, and then to the kind of horseback warfare that began to distinguish them from more earthbound tribes. During most of the eighteenth century, they migrated south and east, first into what became eastern Colorado and western Kansas and finally into Oklahoma, New Mexico, and Texas. The Spanish named them Comanche, probably bastardizing the Ute term *komantcia,* which historians roughly translate as "people who want to fight all the time." The name was apt. The Comanche unquestionably took savage joy in swooping down on enemies, hanging under their horses' necks to fire bullets or arrows, happily torturing to death any men they captured, raping and enslaving women and, curiously, treating captive children tenderly and often adopting them into the tribe.

Still, according to both Miss Charles and Willie, Wild Cat hoped he had at least reached a tentative personal truce with them. The Comanche regularly dispatched hunting and war parties along the same route the Seminole and Seminole Negro wanted to follow from Indian Territory to Mexico. At some point, probably soon after the refugees fled Indian Territory, the Comanche noticed them. Then, it became a matter of Comanche whim—would they tolerate the travelers, amuse themselves by conducting small raids upon them, or decide to annihilate them altogether?

There was no way Wild Cat and John Horse could anticipate the Comanche response. They couldn't be certain when Duval would return to Indian Territory and organize some sort of pursuit. Miss Charles imagined Wild Cat was tormented by a dark fantasy—he would arrive in Mexico only to find some other chief had beaten him there and claimed all the best land along the Rio Grande border for his own followers, leaving Wild Cat a scorned minor Indian leader all over again. In light of these possibilities, he and John Horse wanted their party to travel as fast as possible.

And on good days, Willie said, they managed to go twenty miles. Even allowing for detours around white settlements and Indian camps, that average daily distance would have brought them to Mexico in two months, three at the most. But they hardly ever had good traveling days.

As Oklahoma becomes Texas, the terrain changes. It gets harder, sharper-edged. In rainy years and in winter, the Red River can run deep and fierce. North Texas still does not have many ravines or mesas, but it does have deceptively steep hills. For as far as the eye can see, everything looks the same, near-featureless and supremely uninviting.

For the refugees in 1849, the weather soon became a major problem. Just weeks out of Indian Territory, not halfway through the sprawling state called Texas, they were enveloped by winter, with cold winds and ground frost that made walking uncomfortable, and once or twice, Miss Charles noted, by sleet that froze their fingers and toes and blinded them as they tried to keep moving forward. In the upper regions of Texas, in November and December and January fierce "northers" blast out of Canada and across the Central Plains until they unleash their full stinging fury far to the south. In 1836, Santa Anna's Mexican army almost didn't reach the Alamo, because they were caught in a vicious blizzard that blew south all the way past the Rio Grande.

For the Seminole and Seminole Negro in late 1849, there were days, too many of them, when the women and children and old people simply couldn't keep going. They were literally frozen as they staggered along. Then someone would insist on stopping, Miss Charles said, usually John Horse arguing to Wild Cat that it made no sense to keep going, the Mexicans would never give land to a chief who arrived with very few followers because most died on the way. So they'd stop. If any trees or scrub brush were available, the men would build rickety shelters. The horses were hobbled; fires were lit to keep away wolves, though the flames usually blew out almost immediately. Mothers enveloped their children in tight embraces, trying to protect them from the brutal elements with their own bodies. With luck, the storms soon roared past, but sometimes they lasted for several days. In such cases, the men had to stumble about, trying to find forage for the horses. At least when there was sleet, there was a ready source of water.

But bad weather was only one obstacle to haste. Even before the winter storms, rough country slowed their pace; there were days when most of the party had to sit and wait while scouts went ahead to find ways around particularly high hills, or shallow places to ford rushing rivers. The inevitability of illness was another problem. Despite their other differences, both the Seminole and Seminole Negro were unified in devotion to family. If it became clear an elderly person or baby was dying, everyone waited until death finally came and the body could be disposed of with full ceremony, so long as scouts didn't bring back word of nearby whites or Indians. In those cases, a rough grave and a few muttered words had to do.

Though they tried to be inconspicuous, Willie said, the refugees never went unnoticed for long. Often, they would look ahead or to the side and see, on the horizon, the silhouette of an Indian warrior or white settler watching them, no doubt soon to report back to others that some strange travelers were nearby. Later on the trek, when things were desperate, Wild Cat even led his staggering followers right past farmhouses.

Because of that, we have a detailed eyewitness account. It comes from a journalist named Cora Montgomery, who saw them in July 1850, toward the end of their odyssey near Fort Duncan on the U.S.–Mexican border. Montgomery's real name was Jane Cazneau; in those days, respectable women who wrote articles and books often used a nom de plume. Even allowing for the deterioration in their condition during the nine months they had been traveling and suffering, Montgomery/Cazneau's description is helpful in visualizing what they looked like early in their journey, confirming in particular Willie Warrior's contention that the Seminole insisted on taking the lead, while the Seminole Negro had to follow along behind: "(Coming) from the broken ground in a direction that we knew was untraversed by any but the wild and hostile Indians, came forth a long procession of horsemen. The sun flashed back from a mixed array of arms and barbaric gear, but as this unexpected army, which seemed to have dropped among us from the skies, drew nearer it grew less formidable in apparent numbers, and opened upon us a more pacific aspect. Some reasonably well-mounted Indians circled round a dark nucleus of female riders, who seemed objects of special care. But the long straggling rear-guard was worth seeing . . . all ages, sexes and sizes of negroes, piled up to a most bewildering height, on and among such a promiscuous assemblage of blankets, babies, cooking utensils, and savage traps, in general, never were or could be held together on horseback by any beings on earth but themselves and their red brothers. The party began to break away and vanish into the little ravines that dip down to the river edge . . ."

Mile by painful mile, the refugees moved south. There were breaks in the bad weather; while food was still reasonably plentiful and after there was no immediate pursuit by the white army, Creek, or Seminole, sometimes there were sunny mornings or crisp, bright afternoons when optimism dominated and people sang or chanted as they walked along. Scouts returned telling of good, flat land ahead, or waterholes large enough so that everyone, animals and humans alike, would have plenty to drink. Hunters brought back fresh meat to cook over evening campfires. Scouts trailing behind reported no pursuit. It was possible to feel hopeful; Wild Cat, jolly instead of paranoid, spoke of the fine land waiting in Mexico; dark, rich land that was perfect for growing crops. Best of all—no Creek subjugating them, no crooked white Seminole subagent undermining them! But John Horse and some of the other Seminole Negro men—Dembo Factor, Hardy Factor, John Kibbetts, Cuffy, Sampson July—noticed Wild Cat's prognostications never seemed to include the Seminole Negro. It was almost as though he'd have no more use for them once Mexico had been reached and the promised land assigned. Or, worse, it was entirely possible Wild Cat wanted the blacks along so there would be slaves available to the Seminole in their new country. The fact that Mexico outlawed slavery might not mean much to Wild Cat, who recognized no higher authority than himself.

Wild Cat assured John Horse there was nothing to worry about. There would be plenty of land in Mexico for everybody. But all during the exodus, the unspoken but rigid separation between Indians and blacks remained, and most of the Seminole made it clear in even the smallest of ways, like elbowing ahead to get water from a stream first, that they still considered themselves superior to the Seminole Negro. That attitude,

John Horse knew, could only mean eventual problems. For now, he counseled his black followers to ignore all the slights. Their only chance to reach Mexico and get land of their own was to stay with the Seminole and to present a united front to the Mexicans when they arrived.

Through the last weeks of 1849, the fugitives slowly kept making their way south. For a while, they settled into the hard routine of riding and walking all day. But breakdowns were inevitable, and not just the human sort. Wagon wheels cracked on stones and had to be mended. Horses went lame. If they couldn't be healed, they had to be killed, then butchered for food. And, of course, other provisions were slowly, inexorably, used up. There were days when the hunters couldn't bring back even a few birds or scrawny rabbits. When the people were hungry, they became short-tempered. Arguments broke out between Seminole and Seminole Negro men, Miss Charles said. Wild Cat and John Horse managed to diffuse these, but resentments lingered. And, of course, as they moved into Texas, they were deep in Comanche territory.

The day finally came when Wild Cat and John Horse agreed they would have to stop and make camp for the rest of the winter. They'd been following along the Brazos River, then swung west along the Llano. The weather was a factor. So was the alarming rate that provisions brought from Indian Territory were being used up. They decided to stop while they were still strong enough to build some shelters, which might make a difference in how many old people and infants could survive. As soon as the worst of the cold was over, they'd plant corn. With luck, in a few more months they'd have a new supply that would last until they made it the rest of the way into Mexico. Wild Cat now hoped he could bring his party across the Rio Grande by June or July.

While John Horse and his Seminole Negro supervised the building of wood shelters and the planting of corn, Wild Cat left the camp. He sought out the chiefs of Indian bands who were also wintering nearby. Several tribes were there—Tonkawa, Waco, Kickapoo. Wild Cat presented his usual offer to their chiefs—join me, be part of a combined tribal force, and then the whites will have to respect us and let us be. He received the same response—no one would make a commitment to join a minor Seminole leader, especially one who had abandoned his people to go to Mexico and serve the government there. But one Kickapoo chief named Papicua was intrigued enough to let Wild Cat come back and talk again.

Wild Cat also met with John Rollins, the U.S. government's Indian agent for Texas. Rollins probably rode out to find Wild Cat after receiving reports that the Seminole and Seminole Negro were slowly traveling across Texas. Wild Cat told Rollins honestly that he was taking his people to Mexico, where they would be given land in exchange for border protection. In fact, Wild Cat added, once he'd established his first camp in Mexico, he intended to go back to Indian Territory and recruit all the rest of the Seminole and Seminole Negro there.

The winter began to abate. John Horse and his people stuck corn kernels in the ground and joyfully watched new stalks sprout. Babies were born, and their mothers were healthy enough to nurse them. Hunters brought back game. There was food for everyone; the people grew stronger.

Wild Cat decided he would go ahead into Mexico and meet with government leaders there. That way, an agreement would be in place when the main party arrived. He'd make the deal himself, then ride back to fetch everyone else. John Horse could come with him, more as an interpreter than a co-equal leader. Some historians have John Horse making the trip with Wild Cat; others have him staying behind in the Llano camp. Ben Pingenot believed, based on John Horse's concern about his people, that he stayed. Miss Charles said he went: "He wanted to hear for himself what the Mexicans had to say." But she admitted this was her own conjecture; the stories she'd been told as a child were vague on this matter.

Where all the stories agree is that the refugees' near-idyllic respite ended in the spring.

In April, for one thing, Marcellus Duval returned to Indian Territory from Florida. Predictably, he was furious about the escape, particularly where the Seminole Negro were concerned. General Arbuckle took the brunt of Duval's fury. The subagent accused him of encouraging John Horse to flee to Mexico. The Seminole wanted Duval to take responsibility for bringing the blacks back. It was in his own interest to do so. Duval's lawyer brother had died; now Duval owned those Seminole Negro originally promised to W. J. Duval for representing the Seminole tribe's slave claims in Washington.

So Duval contacted the commissioner of Indian Affairs and asked that soldiers be sent south to arrest the fugitives. Failing that, he wanted the governor of Texas and the Texas Rangers called in to capture the runaways. Duval sweetened his request to Texas officials by offering a $50 bounty on every one of *his* Seminole Negro that was returned to Indian Territory.

While Duval plotted the capture of John Horse and his followers—there was no mention of taking Wild Cat or any of the other Seminole prisoner and hauling them back north—the Creek living in Indian Territory decided it was time to raid Wewoka and the other black villages. With Duval and the Seminole so focused on getting the runaways back, the Creek could snatch the remaining Seminole Negro almost at their leisure.

They tried, and, initially, they succeeded. A party of Creek and white slavers attacked Wewoka and captured three blacks, including Jim Bowlegs. But General Belknap intervened, ordering them to release Bowlegs. The Creek obeyed, but bitterly promised to have a delegation go to Washington and demand the right to enforce their tribal laws on their land.

Belknap's action only delayed the inevitable. In June 1850, 180 Seminole Negro in Indian Territory were captured by the Seminole and turned over to the Creek. Things were bleak for blacks in Indian Territory and just as dangerous in Texas for the Seminole Negro who'd fled with John Horse and Wild Cat.

Though Arbuckle and Belknap had refused Duval's request to send troops after the refugees, the subagent's pleas hadn't fallen on deaf ears in Texas. Governor P. H. Bell was sympathetic, and the Texas Rangers were intrigued by the reward Duval offered. In 1850, the Rangers were far from the upstanding, honest law officers they have since been depicted as being, and, in fact, as they later became. Originally organized in 1823 to fight Indians, the Texas Rangers gradually evolved into a pack of lawless gunslingers-for-hire after the end of the U.S.-Mexican War in 1848. In 1874, the Rangers would be officially reformed to help police the state, but when Wild Cat and John Horse crossed Texas in 1850 with their followers, the men called Texas Rangers usually operated on the shady side of the law themselves.

I talked about the Texas Rangers with Max and Cissy Stewart Lale, both former presidents of the Texas State Historical Association. Their Fort Worth apartment is crammed with reference books. They've devoted their lives to studying the history of their beloved home state. Like their old friend Ben Pingenot, they were eager to share their knowledge.

"The Texas Rangers of that time were not people to be looked up to," Cissy Lale said. "They considered their group to be the law unto itself. They had the best arms and horses because they took what they wanted. Putting the Rangers on the track of these Indians, the Seminole and Seminole Negro, made it certain that, eventually, they would hunt them down. Oh, the Rangers were determined trackers. And they were of that popular opinion that the only good Indians were dead Indians."

"Of course, it was common knowledge concerning the general areas where Wild Cat and his people were as they made their way to Mexico," Max Lale added. "A group that large couldn't remain a secret very long. Now, you might not know exactly where they camped each night, but you could make an educated guess to within, say, twenty-five miles, and any tracker worth his salt in those days could certainly find them from there."

Duval had been told the fugitives were camped on Cow Bayou, a tributary of the Brazos River near the modern Texas city of Waco. In fact, they were some fifty miles further southwest. The Rangers began to plan a late-spring raid.

Meanwhile, probably in May, Wild Cat announced he would ride ahead south to Mexico and make an agreement with the Mexican government on behalf of his followers. There had been a great deal of grumbling in the winter camp that Mexico wouldn't trade land for border protection, Miss Charles said. Particularly among the women, there was the suspicion that Wild Cat was either mistaken or exaggerating. He knew the best way to improve morale among the Seminole and Seminole Negro was to procure official documents from Mexican officials. That way, once he returned and showed them to everyone, their enthusiasm would be renewed and the rest of the trip might go smoothly.

Wild Cat didn't ride south alone while everyone else waited back in the Llano camp. He wanted to arrive in Mexico with an entourage. A great chief had to have attendents. Then, too, Wild Cat understood the basics of diplomacy, but not well enough to hammer out any sort of complex governmental agreement. John Horse was better at such things, plus having his own translator on hand would encourage the Mexicans to consider Wild Cat an especially important leader.

How many warriors did Wild Cat take? Certainly a half dozen, probably a dozen, maybe twice that. He was more concerned about the impression he would make in Mexico than about leaving behind a sufficient force to protect the women, children, and old people at the Llano camp. The Seminole Negro warriors were staying there. There was no sign yet of pursuit from Indian Territory. Wild Cat would only be gone for a few weeks, since he and his Seminole braves could ride hard and long without women and children and creaky wagons to slow them down.

So Wild Cat and many of the Seminole men rode south. So did John Horse, if we go along with Miss Charles's version of events. They were careful to avoid white settlements and forts. They splashed across the Rio Grande at a point far from any border towns, swimming their horses against the current. They felt a certain relief. It was good to be men on their own, not burdened with dependents.

Once across the border into Mexico, they were warmly welcomed. No less a dignitary than Antonio Maria Juarequi, inspector general of Mexico's eastern military colonies, greeted them. Wild Cat grandly announced he and his people were ready to join forces with Mexico's army.

"When I was a little girl, the old people first described this meeting to me," Miss Charles said, sitting in her darkened living room, rocking back and forth as she so often did when recounting the old stories. "They recalled every word old Wild Cat said. He made such a strong impression.

'We'll fight if you give us land,' he said over and over to that Mexican. He wanted the terms of the agreement to be very clear."

Juarequi couldn't have been more agreeable. Land was something Mexico had to spare. He talked at length about the beauty and charm of the northern Mexican state of Coahuila, which also happened to be the target of many Comanche and Apache raids. There were fine rivers in Coahuila, Juarequi said, and good bottom land for farming. If the great chief Wild Cat would bring his—how many warriors, again?

Wild Cat blandly promised a few hundred. He undoubtedly was including Papicua and his Kickapoos.

Several hundred, Juarequi repeated with great satisfaction. Well, then. There would be no less than seventy thousand acres of land ("*16 sitios de ganado mayor*") waiting for the gallant newcomers. Of that mighty tract, half the property would be at the headwaters of the Rio San Antonio, and the other half along the Rio San Rodrigo. Would this be sufficient? Was the great chief satisfied?

Wild Cat agreed. Juarequi then officially named Wild Cat leader of the forces he would promptly bring to Coahuila. If there were other chiefs, other important men in the group, they still must obey all of Wild Cat's orders. This would not have entirely pleased John Horse, if he was there, but he would have realized it wasn't the right time to object. The newcomers would all be considered Mexican citizens, with the full rights and responsibilities that came with such honor. They would, of course, help fight off Indian attackers whenever required to do so—the Comanche and Apache were specifically mentioned—but they would not, could not, under any circumstances, fight with or even anger white Americans. The last thing Mexico wanted was to give Americans even the smallest excuse to invade again.

Wild Cat agreed to it all. He did wonder, though, whether the Seminole would be allowed to follow their own tribal laws in their new village, even if these laws might in some way conflict with Mexican edicts. As a result, on the official documents Juarequi had created to outline all the agreements in the meeting, there was added this peculiar clause: "Although the Kickapoos, Seminoles . . . Negroes, and other Indians who may come to

Mexico must subject themselves to the laws of the country, it is not demanded of them to change their habits and customs." Later, John Horse and the Seminole Negro would understand why Wild Cat asked his question, and why he wanted Juarequi's response in writing.

So it was done. Jaurequi promised that, when Wild Cat returned with the rest of his people, the Mexican government would be ready for them. There would be military escorts to take them to their new land, and wagons filled with food, and farm equipment and seed so they could plant crops. All that remained was for the great chief Wild Cat—no, *Capitan* Wild Cat, he would soon officially become—to go back to Texas and fetch the many other mighty warriors and their families who were waiting for his return. When everyone was finally back in Mexico, Juarequi concluded, Wild Cat should bring them to the border village of Piedras Negras, just across the Rio Grande from the Texas town of Eagle Pass. In Piedras Negras, Wild Cat was to ask for Colonel Juan Manuel Maldonado, inspector of the Colonial Militar de Guerrero. Colonel Maldonado would take care of everything else. And welcome to Mexico brave new citizens.

Afterward, Miss Charles said, Wild Cat, John Horse, and the Seminole spurred their horses back across the Rio Grande. They laughed as they rode. They'd gotten everything they wanted from the Mexicans. Even John Horse felt his concerns subside. With so much land there would be plenty of room for Indians and blacks to live adjacent but still sufficiently apart, just like the old villages in Florida.

Their joy lasted up until the last few miles before they reached the Llano camp. Many of these warriors were veterans of the Florida wars. They could sense when something was wrong. Perhaps the birds in the area had stopped singing. Maybe the air itself didn't smell right. The smiles on their faces changed to frowns of concentration and concern. Almost as one, they cocked their muskets and primed their powder. Carefully, Wild Cat and John Horse left the rest, easing over a final rise until they saw the camp before them, and—

And what? At this point, outside historians and Seminole Negro folklore aren't in complete agreement. Everyone acknowledges that when

Wild Cat returned there was panic in the Llano camp, and the refugees packed and fled immediately afterward. Why they fled, and who they were fleeing from, depends on who is telling the story.

The popular version among white historians finds the Seminole and Seminole Negro running after being warned slavers were on their way to raid the Llano camp. These slavers might actually have been Texas Rangers, searching for the blacks to earn the reward offered by Marcellus Duval. This might be true, but as an adjunct to what Seminole Negro storytellers say really happened. Today, Willie Warrior sadly shakes his head when he tells what the returning men saw as they rode into the Llano camp.

They saw smoldering ruins where wood shelters had been burned, and arrow-riddled horses beginning to rot in the warm sunlight, and, seemingly everywhere, human bodies. Grief-stricken Seminole Negro men wandered about, helplessly waving their weapons and wailing.

The Comanche had attacked, slaughtering sixty, perhaps sixty-five women, children, and old people.

It happened, probably, while most of the Seminole Negro men were hunting. They'd left as a group; there had been no sign of any danger from whites or Comanche. They'd guessed Wild Cat and his entourage would soon return, and they wanted to gather a good supply of meat to smoke and take along on the remaining three-hundred-mile journey. The camp was left guarded by a few of the older men and younger boys.

Probably, Wild Cat assured everyone he'd made a truce with the Comanche, that in recent months he'd met with their principal chiefs and promised he and his followers just wanted to travel through their territory. But Wild Cat overlooked two basic Comanche traditions. First, they lived, hunted, and fought in separate bands rather than one large tribal unit. As with the Seminole back in Florida, no individual chief spoke for every band. Wild Cat could have come to his agreements with five chiefs, but a sixth would not consider himself obligated by anything his peers had promised. Second, the Comanche habitually took advantage of opportunities to attack, kill, and burn.

Previous years had been hard on the Comanche. In the late 1830s and early 1840s, when the tribe fought Texans in full-scale battles, the firepower of the whites prevailed. Other Indians might have begged for peace, Max Lale noted. The Comanche simply bided their time and preyed on whites when the odds were more in their favor. They continued to plague the Mexicans and other Indian tribes, too. War was the celebrated part of their lives.

Certainly, several different Comanche bands had been watching the Seminole and Seminole Negro as they camped along the Llano. All it would have taken was for one chief to decide it would be pleasurable to attack them. The Comanche wouldn't have assaulted the fugitives for profit—their few horses weren't worth the attackers' trouble. In his self-published book *Black Warrior Chiefs: A History of the Seminole Negro Indian Scouts,* historian Cloyde Brown, an old friend of Willie Warrior's, speculates that a young Seminole Negro boy might have panicked at the sight of some Comanche and fired at them, giving the Indians an excuse to attack. That is certainly possible.

But attack they did, Willie Warrior insisted. The Comanche always struck swiftly, furiously. Even if the boys and old men guarding the camp heard them coming, there would have been very little time to react. The Seminole Negro men hunting a few miles away would have heard the crack of musket shots, and perhaps the shrieks of the wounded and dying carried that far, too. By the time they raced back, it was over. Not all the survivors were wounded; if the Comanche had wanted to wipe out the entire camp, they would have stayed and finished the job. The fact that many, even more than half, of the fugitives there survived is evidence that the Comanche raided for sport rather than in anger.

Even after Wild Cat, John Horse, and the Seminole warriors had returned, there was never any thought of pursuing the Comanche to seek revenge. Above all, the Seminole Negro were practical fighters, Willie Warrior said. The men would gladly risk their own lives to save their families, but in this case the damage had already been done. This was Comanche country; they knew their land like the Seminole Negro had known the Florida swamps. Continuing the fight would only result in more refugee deaths. It made more sense to run, before the Comanche decided to come back and do it again.

It was just after the Comanche attack, Willie said, that a few of the Seminole Negro who went out to scout the vicinity probably told Wild Cat and John Horse that slavers were on the way. Duval had the Texas Rangers in the area looking for the fugitives. There was just time to bury the dead, bind up the wounded, and load those who couldn't walk onto the wagons or across the backs of any remaining horses. What little corn had grown sufficiently to eat had to be picked. Wild Cat went off to find Papicua, who joined the refugees with some two or three dozen Kickapoo braves and their families. With the addition of the Kickapoo and the subtraction of the Seminole and Seminole Negro dead, the party now numbered about three hundred.

They hadn't gone far, Miss Charles said, before Wild Cat made things worse. Now more concerned with speed than secrecy, the party passed very close to the town of Fredricksburg. Wild Cat badly wanted a drink. There were several saloons in Fredricksburg, and Wild Cat went into one, taking with him John Horse and two other blacks identified by historians as John Wood and Kitty Johnson. He didn't have much money. Too soon for the Seminole leader, he'd drunk up all he could pay for, but he didn't want to stop. Loudly, he suggested the bartender buy John Wood and Kitty Johnson from him, putting the money from the sale toward the price of more whiskey. The bartender was amenable. John Horse, abstaining from liquor for once, pushed the other three out the door before the transaction was completed. He was disgusted with his old friend.

John Horse was able to get Wild Cat and the two blacks out of Fredricksburg. They rejoined the mournful party and kept moving south. Soon, John Horse knew, their white pursuers would reach Fredricksburg, and there they'd hear about Wild Cat trying to sell John Wood and Kitty Johnson. That was the kind of thing white townspeople would remember and be pleased to report. Even blind slavers could follow the path taken by the fugitives, all the hoofprints and wagon tracks and long scuffmarks left by feet dragging with fatigue.

The South Texas heat baked them. All the moisture was sweated out of their systems. They needed more water than ever, and water wasn't always available. The women were especially alarmed by the condition of the children; they'd stopped playing along the trail. None of them laughed or smiled anymore. They wobbled forward like lurching corpses, their ribs showing prominently under their skin.

The Texas Hill Country was originally a vast inland sea. Underground upheavals forced massive chunks of rock and earth up through the water, until the sea itself was sealed underneath.

Heading southwest through flat, boring country, suddenly there appears on the horizon a blue line of steep, rugged hills, which, after so much unremarkable terrain, seem like mountains. These hills are covered with thick greenery, mostly mesquite, but the soil underneath is chalky and thin. Walking through deep Hill Country underbrush often involves kicking up clouds of choking dust.

Still, the land is green, so green, and there are streams again and herds of deer and wild turkey. White settlers who discovered this part of Texas thought they'd stumbled into paradise. But all that makes the Hill Country lovely also renders speedy travel impossible. Even modern roads have to wend up and around the high hills and unexpected creeks. What usually made first-time visitors rejoice only meant additional hardships for Wild Cat, John Horse, and their frightened, exhausted people.

It was at this point, Miss Charles said, that the Seminole and Seminole Negro women began to quietly rebel—"Properly, of course. Respectfully."

"How can you rebel respectfully?" I asked.

"Listen. I'll tell you."

Some of the Seminole warriors (and, perhaps, John Horse) had gone with Wild Cat into Mexico, so they knew how far it was to their destination. But most of the Seminole Negro men didn't, and many of the Kickapoo hadn't ever traveled so far south, either. The women began to doubt Mexico existed at all. Every day they kept walking, and every day there were new hills and valleys to traverse. Snakes slithered in the sun. Bugs were everywhere. Physical discomfort and the tension of always wondering if an attack was imminent kept everyone on edge. John Horse knew the situation was grave when the women began to complain, questioning whether the journey would ever end. They didn't make comments directly to Wild Cat, or to any of the other men. That would have been too disrespectful. Instead, they spoke to each other, criticizing Wild Cat's leadership and sense of direction, making certain their voices were pitched just loud enough for the men to hear.

Wild Cat paid no attention to any of it. He continued to ride at the head of the lagging procession, back straight, eyes looking forward, talking constantly about the wonders of Mexico.

They traveled in this way for about ten days, ten terrible days. A few times, scouts reported that white men, maybe slavers, were riding in the vicinity. No one saw any sign of Comanche, which was in itself ominous. The Comanche had to be all around; if they were staying out of sight, it could mean they were planning another attack. It seemed even to the men who had accompanied Wild Cat into Mexico just weeks earlier that they must somehow have become lost, that Mexico could not have been so far away from the Llano camp. These hills, these endless, hateful hills, all looked alike and went on forever. . . .

And then the hills stopped, abruptly, and once more the flat plain stretched to the horizon. At least there had been water in the hill country. Now there seemed to be none. Water bags soon were drained. The horses got their liquids by chewing on scrub brush. Caliche dust was kicked up by the horses as they plodded along. It coated the faces of the Seminole Negro women and children who had to walk behind them. The choking particles deepened their thirst. John Horse and some of the other black warriors reminded them to place pebbles under their tongues to stimulate the flow of saliva.

Wild Cat said there would be plenty of water soon. There were springs ahead, he promised, lots of good water and even some shade from trees, a pleasant place he'd seen on earlier trips south, though not a spot on the route he'd taken for his meeting with Jaurequi. He turned the refugees a little more to the southwest, and now the women grumbled even more, for the flat vista remained unbroken by any sign of trees or water. Wild Cat was crazy, they muttered.

Then they did see trees, a cluster of them seeming to pop up out of the flat ground. They rushed toward them, or at least rushed as quickly as their weakened conditions allowed, horses straining as the scent of water reached their nostrils, humans just as eager.

Wild Cat told John Horse the place was called Las Moras. The words were Spanish for "the mulberries."

"They didn't know that, years later, they'd come back and actually live here as scouts for the army," Willie Warrior said, nodding with satisfaction as we strolled among the trees that lined the creek. "They just saw the shade and the water. But from that first moment, this place was special to our people."

"Right here where the white people built Brackettville later on was where Wild Cat and John Horse could have been caught with all their people," Miss Charles added. "It was a close thing, a very close thing. I recall an old woman who was there telling me they nearly got caught at Las Moras Creek because John Horse fell inside a whiskey bottle. I do hate to think about that."

Lightheaded with relief, the refugees flung themselves forward, not thinking to send some scouts ahead to be certain it was safe. The trees and the water—they could see a stream!—were just a few dozen yards ahead when riders pulled out in front of them.

They could have been Comanche. The Comanche had used Las Moras Springs as a gathering place ever since they drove the Spanish away from it. But these riders were American soldiers, bluecoats, though their army issue coats were so dusty with caliche that the original color hardly showed through. The soldiers had guns, but evidentally saw little danger from a staggering mob of emaciated Indians and blacks. So they kept their guns at their sides, simply watching, and Wild Cat's signal still had enough authority to make his dehydrated followers pause so close to the water they craved. Wild Cat and John Horse rode forward. John Horse asked the nearest soldier for permission to go to the water and drink. He was told to stay where he was until the officer in charge was consulted.

They could see now, around the trees, several army wagons, great lengthy four-wheeled vehicles compared to the rickety two-wheelers the fugitives still were hauling along. Obviously, these soldiers were part of an escort for a wagon train.

An officer spurred his horse ahead. Wild Cat and John Horse were delighted to recognize John Sprague, who they'd known in Florida. Sprague invited them to call their followers up and to let them drink from the river. It must have been quite a sight when more than three hundred Indians and blacks threw themselves on their bellies along the bank, sucking up as much water as they could.

Sprague observed to Wild Cat that his people seemed to be in bad shape, the women and children especially. Using John Horse to interpret, Wild Cat told about the flight from Indian Territory to Mexico, and Juarequi's promise of land waiting for them.

"We cross the river to Piedras Negras," he said. "We'll meet an officer there."

Sprague said Eagle Pass, the American town across the Rio Grande from Piedras Negras, was a bad place with plenty of greedy slavers. Gesturing toward the Seminole Negro, he said the slavers would never let the refugees cross the river unmolested.

It was late afternoon, and the fiery sun was finally beginning to set. Sprague said his detail was going to camp beside the springs for the night, and that the Rio Grande and Piedras Negras were two or three days' walk away. Not so long, not so far. Perhaps it would be best for the fugitives to take advantage of water and a long rest before the final, frantic push.

But something happened that night, as the exhausted refugees lay around their campfires. The soldiers' camp was a few hundred yards away. Because the bluecoats had sentries posted, the Seminole Negro men allowed themselves the luxury of resting, instead of posting their own guards around the perimeter of the camp.

Someone among the soldiers, probably Sprague, had produced some bottles of liquor. Uncharacteristically, Wild Cat stopped drinking before he got roaring, falling-down drunk, but John Horse didn't. He'd stayed away from whiskey during the long, bloody trek, but now with their final destination so close he abandoned himself to the bottle. Sometime while

John Horse was in a foggy place between intoxication and passing out, someone tugged at his sleeve and whispered to him to wake up. A Mexican national—a poor, ragged man—had been rescued from Indians by Sprague's troops as they rolled their wagon train east toward San Antonio. This Mexican didn't love the Americans any more than he did the Indians who'd captured him. Sprague refused to let him set out on his own for home, saying he'd only be caught by Indians again. So the man was disgruntled, considering the soldiers to be his captors, too.

While John Horse was drinking himself into a stupor and the rest of the refugees collapsed into exhausted sleep, the Mexican saw a rider quietly trot away from the army camp. He heard other soldiers whispering about sending for someone, other soldiers or Texas Rangers or slavers, he couldn't tell for certain, to come and round up all the negroes in Wild Cat's party. Sprague probably knew nothing about this; he'd been fair to the Seminole and Seminole Negro in Florida, and his offer of food and a night's hospitality would not have been a trick to hold the fugitives in one place. In fact, just before turning in he'd given Wild Cat a paper guaranteeing free passage to Eagle Pass, in case other American soldiers might try to deny him the right to travel there.

But some enterprising soldiers under Sprague's command at Las Moras Creek saw profit in turning the Seminole Negro over to those pursuing them. Duval's plea to the army and Texas governor for help would have been widely reported, along with his promised $50 reward for each Seminole Negro captured and returned to Indian Territory. Soldiers in the American army earned a few dollars a month. Fifty dollars would have seemed like a fortune, and there had to be eighty, ninety, even one hundred negroes in this travel-worn bunch.

The Mexican whispered in John Horse's ear, but the Seminole Negro leader was too drunk to fully comprehend what he was hearing. Wild Cat noticed the man, though, and came over to listen. The Mexican probably spoke a little broken English; Wild Cat understood enough to shake John Horse into reasonable consciousness, then gather Papicua and some Seminole and Seminole Negro men for discussion.

Their options were limited. They could throw themselves on Sprague's mercy, hoping he would defend them all against whoever might be coming for them. But Sprague's allegiance would be limited. Texas was a proud slave state. Most of the Seminole Negro lacked papers proving their freedom. Sprague might protect the Seminole and Kickapoo and let the blacks be taken away.

They could stand and fight themselves. The slavers or the soldiers coming for them would still have to be hours away, maybe a day or two if the rider had to go most of the way to Eagle Pass or San Antonio. Sprague would move on in the morning. They could thank him, then dig in along the creek and prepare for battle. But who knew how many white men were coming for the Seminole Negro? The women, children, and old people were still on the verge of physical collapse. Their ammunition was limited. How long could they defend themselves?

Or they could run. They were used to that. They could rouse everyone and quietly move away from Sprague's camp in these early hours before daybreak, trying to cover the last miles to the Rio Grande in two days, a desperate dash to get across the river before their pursuers caught up. That kind of urgency would take a terrible toll on the weakest members of the party. And there was, of course, no guarantee that the slavers or soldiers or Texas Rangers who were coming wouldn't catch up to them on open ground, where it would be particularly hard to fight them off.

So they talked, softly but desperately, and reached consensus: They'd run. Discreetly, the rest of the sleeping refugee camp was awakened. A few babies cried and were hushed by their mothers. If Sprague's soldiers saw the Indians and blacks leaving, they didn't try to stop them.

Whoever was coming for them was a danger. So were the invisible Comanche that must be watching nearby. And yet, as they hurried south with the sky just staining lighter blue with dawn, as Wild Cat set a brisk pace and John Horse wobbled on his mount, they knew there was great danger ahead, too. Of all the border cities where Juarequi might have asked them to cross the Rio Grande, Eagle Pass was the worst, a hellhole even well-armed white men avoided when they could. Traveling near Eagle Pass would be as dangerous as riding through a Comanche camp.

Eagle Pass didn't get its name by being built on some lofty mountain peak. In fact, it was a cluster of ramshackle buildings on a moderately steep hill along the northern bank of the Rio Grande. Mexicans had named the spot *El Paso del Aguila* because eagles frequently were seen near there. No settlement existed, or was needed, for centuries, even after Mexicans and Americans needed convenient river-crossing places. The most popular was about thirty miles north.

Then the American army established a series of forts along Texas's south and west regions. The Comanche and Apache were wreaking havoc on settlers. The forts were intended to serve both as a buffer and a base for detachments dedicated to searching out and fighting the Indians. A promising engineer, Captain Robert E. Lee, was ordered to select the best locations. Lee felt Eagle Pass was appropriate for one of the forts. It was built and opened in 1849, commanded by Captain Sidney Burbank.

Where forts were built, towns inevitably sprang up. Sutlers wanted to have stores that could sell the military convenient, overpriced supplies. Off-duty soldiers liked drinking, so saloons were necessary. Female companionship was limited for army enlistees, so whorehouses in the proximity of forts always did brisk business. And some brave soul always tried to build a church so the soldiers could attend to their spiritual well-being.

On the other side of the Rio Grande, Mexicans saw the new fort as a business opportunity for themselves as well. Cattle could be traded back and forth. Mexican goods, from tequila to silver jewelry, could be sold for American dollars. So a complementary Mexican town was constructed opposite Eagle Pass. It was only given the name Piedras Negras around the turn of the twentieth century. Originally the modest settlement was called Villa Herrera, and later, briefly, Porfirio Diaz. But most history books, and Seminole Negro storytellers as well, always call the place Piedras Negras—"the black rocks." They also refer to "Fort Duncan," even though the army camp wasn't officially given this name until 1889. Before that, it was known as "Camp Eagle Pass."

Even today, the thirty miles between Brackettville and Eagle Pass are some of the nastiest, most forlorn in all of Southwest Texas. The land stretches out like a hot, flat bed of sand and shale. Without any shade, the brutal heat makes the air shimmer, like looking at the world through a sheet of wrinkly cellophane. The brush is prickly, and snakes crawl everywhere. Every few hundred yards of State Highway 131 finds buzzards picking at roadkill—armadillos, skunks, rabbits. To the south, part of the horizon is thick with dust kicked up by construction crews and traffic around Eagle Pass and Piedras Negras on opposite sides of the Rio Grande.

Eagle Pass itself is a typical Texas border town. The shops by the river sell all sorts of cheap, gaudy clothing and household items. Mexicans legally visiting from south of the Rio Grande usually don't have many dollars to spend. There's a nervous, lawless feeling to the streets. Police are on constant lookout for drug dealers. And there are always crowds around the entrance and exit of the wide international bridge that spans the river and connects Texas and Mexico. The first bridge was built in the mid-1890s. Before that, there were ferries. It's relatively easy today for Americans to cross the bridge, if they have driver's licenses or other photo ID. The line is longer on the southern side, with Mexicans on their way to visit the United States. You can drive across the bridge, but most people seem to walk instead. The walk offers a lingering glimpse of the muddy Rio Grande, which in some places measures seventy-five yards or more from bank to bank. Trash and loose weeds float on the surface. Looking down, it's hard to imagine anyone trying to swim across. No wonder so many who try, drown.

In 1850, Eagle Pass was the kind of place Wild Cat and his refugees had every reason to avoid. But Jaurequi had instructed them to cross the river to Piedras Negras, and they couldn't refuse. How would it seem to the Mexicans if the brave warriors they were hiring to protect their border were afraid to come near an American town?

Even the way in which they would approach Eagle Pass was a delicate matter. For the two days it took to travel there from Las Moras Creek, that was what Wild Cat and John Horse debated, the latter nursing a spectacular hangover. With just over three hundred people in their party, it was unlikely they could remain near town for long without being discovered. So, should they boldly ride down its dusty main street, hoping their sheer numbers would discourage harassment by any lounging slavers? Would it be better to try to hide somewhere outside town until dark, then slip across the Rio Grande on rafts? What about the soldiers at Fort Duncan?

Finally, they hammered out a plan. The women, children, and old people were near physical collapse. These final, rushed miles had exhausted them. In case of a pitched battle on the northern side of the river, Seminole, Seminole Negro, and Kickapoo warriors would probably not be able to defend their helpless dependents. It would be necessary for someone to cross the river and find the Mexican officer Juarequi had promised would be waiting for them—Maldonado, that was his name. But the earlier mistake of leaving few men behind on guard while most rode ahead to impress the Mexicans couldn't be repeated. The best way was for their leaders—Wild Cat, certainly, and John Horse, plus Papicua—to quietly cross the river, find Maldonado, and secure his help in getting everyone else across. Maybe the Mexican would send his troops to hold off any pursuing slavers or American soldiers while the fugitives covered the few final yards into Mexico.

So they'd approach Eagle Pass, find a safe place to leave the rest of the party behind, and have the leaders seek out Maldonado. But it wasn't as simple to execute as it sounded.

They smelled Eagle Pass before they saw it. Cattle were constantly being moved through town, often from Mexican ranchers selling beef to the quartermaster at Fort Duncan. Some of the animals were slaughtered for meat; others, diseased, had to be killed and burned. Sickly mixed fumes of blood, dung, and burning animal flesh were in the air. Miss Charles said Wild Cat signaled for John Horse to ride ahead with him. They reached the crest of a low hill, and then they looked down at the town.

Eagle Pass was comprised of a few dozen buildings; a half mile or so away, Fort Duncan was visible. Among the buildings in Eagle Pass, probably a half dozen were saloons. There were some mercantiles and a jail. Very few of the buildings were designed to serve as family homes. The denizens of Eagle Pass were mostly gunslingers, slavers, and crafty hustlers. Few responsible men wanted their wives and children around such dubious sorts. Many of the women who did live in town were prostitutes, some of them as bad-tempered and dangerous as the gunfighters.

Beyond Eagle Pass, Wild Cat and John Horse could see the Rio Grande sparkling in the sun. The river was wider here than they had expected, more than fifty yards, maybe one hundred, and its rippling surface indicated an undertow. That scuttled any hopes that all the refugees might be able to wade across. Rafts would be needed, which meant trees would have to be located and cut, and then there would be time needed for lashing the newly felled logs together.

A shack on the American side and an adobe hut on the Mexican bank were obviously border checkpoints. There were some ferry boats moored on both banks. No bridge spanned the river between the two settlements. About five hundred yards past the adobe hut on the far bank was Piedras Negras, which looked practically identical to Eagle Pass, with cantinas and cattle pens and loafing men with bandoliers across their shoulders and rifles slung alongside the bandoliers.

"Bad places," John Horse muttered. To his tired eyes, both Eagle Pass and Piedras Negras seemed to glisten with evil. He wanted to get away from both as quickly as possible.

They rode to the main party and reported what they'd seen. Scouts were sent back to ascertain whether danger from pursuit was imminent. The weaker members of the group dropped where they'd stood, panting like animals. Wild Cat and John Horse announced their plan—find a place where everyone else could wait and rest while they crossed the river and met with Maldonado. Papicua announced he wanted to go, too. A few more riders were sent out to locate a place with shade near the river. At least everyone would have plenty of water while waiting. It only took a few minutes for them to report there were several spots nearby, mostly in the direction of Fort Duncan. Wild Cat still had the pass given to him by Sprague. They coaxed everyone into getting up and walking in the direction of the fort.

The nicer people of Eagle Pass lived close to Fort Duncan. That was where, from her shaded porch, Cora Montgomery/Jane Cazneau saw the refugees approaching. She and her husband had moved to town a few months earlier. They moved away within two years, eager to settle somewhere more civilized. In her book *Eagle Pass, or, Life on the Border,* Montgomery/Cazneau claimed Wild Cat interrupted his arrival in Eagle Pass to come and call on her family. While she tossed in lots of small details—she was drinking chocolate, "with every door thrown wide to welcome the breeze"—it's extremely unlikely that's what happened. Certainly, Wild Cat eventually did come to call—part of his plan was to charm local Americans in case the agreement with Mexico didn't work out—but on this July day, his focus would have been on getting his people across the river as soon as possible.

So, acting on advice from his scouts, Wild Cat herded his followers a few miles north of Eagle Pass. He called a halt near a thick patch of scrub brush. A few mesquite trees provided additional shade. The Rio Grande flowed nearby. It was a place where the women and children and old people could lay down. To every side, there was clear ground for hundreds of yards, meaning the warriors could have clear shots at anyone attacking them.

Wild Cat and John Horse conferred with the other men. There was still a bit of food loaded on some of the wagons, enough to last a day or two. Each warrior had a little ammunition left. The best plan, Wild Cat said again, was for him to cross the river, find Maldonado, and return with a squad of Mexican soldiers for additional protection as the rest of the party made their way to the south bank of the Rio Grande. John Horse would come with him, and Papicua could come, too. The remaining men could fan out to protect the weakened dependents, and maybe search out a grove of trees that could be cut down to build log rafts. If whoever was pursuing them showed up before Wild Cat and John Horse returned, they would have to do their best to fight them off.

On the Mexican side of the river, Wild Cat tried to brush the caliche dust off his clothes. John Horse did the same; he understood how important it was to make a good first impression on Colonel Maldonado. In Piedras Negras—which they could enter freely, Willie Warrior pointed out, since slavery was illegal in Mexico—they got directions to Maldonado's camp, which was several miles south of town.

Miss Charles thinks Juan Manuel Maldonado was relieved to see the three riders. It was his thankless role to try and protect hundreds of miles of border with only a few hundred soldiers. These *indios* with their *negroes* answered his prayers. Yet their appearance was perplexing. Maldonado expected mighty warriors, perhaps decked out in war paint and feathers. Wild Cat, John Horse, and Papicua wore ragged shirts and leggings and were nearly white-skinned with caliche film. Not one sported a feather. They looked like saddle tramps. But this Wild Cat, who introduced himself as a fellow officer, had an imperious way. He was obviously a leader who was used to being obeyed. The other *indio* was clearly a subordinate, but the *negro* also carried himself well.

Wild Cat promised he had many strong warriors ready to fight, all of them waiting with their families on the *yanqui* side of the river for permission to cross into Mexico. But Maldonado wasn't pleased to hear the Seminole request Mexican soldiers to guard his people as they crossed the Rio Grande. Certainly the great warriors coming to help protect Mexico could protect their loved ones on the river. Maldonado pointed this out. Wild Cat and John Horse didn't tell him about the slavers or soldiers they'd been told were coming for them. They'd agreed that sharing this information with Maldonado might give the impression that hiring the fugitives as border guards would cause more problems than their presence helped solve.

Maldonado refused to send any of his men back to the Rio Grande. Instead, he suggested that, once he got his people across, Wild Cat should return to talk to him. Then it would be time to escort the newcomers to the land set aside for them. When did the great chief think he would be back?

There was little Wild Cat could say, beyond the fact he and his companions would get the rest of the party right away. They shook hands with Maldonado—John Horse in particular always liked to shake hands at the end of meetings—and rode back toward the river.

The others were where they'd left them. It was getting dark. All night, the fugitives huddled together, afraid to light fires that might attract attention.

In the morning, there was bad news. Scouts returned to say many white riders were camped at Las Moras Springs, slavers probably, maybe some

Texas Rangers or soldiers among them, but all definitely well-armed. There was no doubt why they'd come to the area. Certainly they would have learned from Sprague or his men that the fugitives were on their way to Eagle Pass. These men would follow; riding hard, they could arrive within the day. Everyone had to get across the Rio Grande as soon as possible.

Wild Cat and John Horse conferred. Except for the warriors, almost all the rest of the travelers were still exhausted. They couldn't wade or swim across the river. Rafts would take time to construct. Wild Cat still had his pass from Sprague. Perhaps the commander of the nearby army fort would help the fugitives get to the Mexican side. Surely the army had access to boats. So Wild Cat announced he and John Horse would go to Fort Duncan. While they were gone, some of the men should find trees, cut logs, and begin building rafts, just in case. The men who didn't work on the rafts should stand guard. With luck, the white men coming from Las Moras Springs wouldn't arrive until well after their prey was across the Rio Grande.

The old West Texas army forts—Fort Griffin, Fort Concho, Fort Clark, all of them—have been preserved in various forms. Some, San Angelo's Fort Concho in particular, look much as they did in the 1850s. Tourists come to visit Fort Concho from all over the country. Every fall, there are reenactments of military drills. Docents wander about dressed in authentic old uniforms.

Fort Duncan is less of a showplace. Its few remaining whitewashed buildings squat in the shadow of a medical center. A park has been built on the old fort grounds, too. There are swingsets instead of cannon. A few original buildings are sometimes open to the public, but at odd morning and afternoon hours. There's no real sense of what Fort Duncan must have been like in 1850, when Wild Cat rode up to its headquarters building, brandishing his pass from Major Sprague.

Both Willie Warrior and Miss Charles agreed Wild Cat wasted his time visiting the fort at all. He got no help there. The commander, who was probably still Captain Sidney Burbank, didn't care if Sprague had given the Seminole and Seminole Negro a pass. They needed Burbank's permission to cross the river, and he didn't give it to them. It wasn't his job to help negroes escape from their masters. As for the Indians, well, they weren't his concern one way or the other.

It was late afternoon when Wild Cat and John Horse returned to the temporary camp north of Eagle Pass. Some of the Seminole Negro men had found a wide band of trees a few more miles north, on property identified later as Lehman's Ranch. Since no help or boats were forthcoming from the army, Wild Cat ordered everyone to get up and move into those trees, some of which had already been hacked down, and their trunks trimmed of limbs and thinner branches. Of the three hundred or so in the party, almost two-thirds were old people, women, and children who would have to be placed on rafts to get across the Rio Grande.

As they shuffled north, scouts reported the white men from Las Moras Springs had arrived in Eagle Pass. The news made everyone move a little faster.

"If we can't get enough rafts made, maybe some of the women and children can swim across," Wild Cat said, but John Horse shook his head. The Rio Grande was wide and the women and children were exhausted. If they tried to swim most would drown.

So, at a spot near the river on Lehman's Ranch—history doesn't record what Lehman might have made of three hundred Indians and blacks hacking down his trees—they set to work. Most of the men cut down trees. Women, boys, and girls trimmed the trunks. Old people cut lengths of rope, even the hackamores used by riders to guide their horses. Some of the best fighters among the warriors, mostly Seminole Negro, set up a perimeter guard.

As the sun set, the first few rafts were ready to lower into the river. In the 1920s, a University of Pennsylvania graduate student named Laurence Foster traveled to Brackettville. His thesis for a doctoral degree was on the subject of "Negro-Indian Relationships in the Southwest." In Brackettville, he interviewed Becky Simmons, who, seventy years earlier, had been one of the Seminole Negro crossing the Rio Grande. In his thesis, Foster represented her in frankly racist terms, reproducing her words in the kind of pidgen English white readers of the time would have expected from an old black woman. But if we look past that, we get a good idea of what happened:

"We felt dat we could be safe if we can git across de ribber. Our men look round wit Wild Cat fur a place to ford de ribber . . . dem hours look like ten years, for we wus so close to de American race people [the slavers or Rangers pursuing them] dat we wanted to git away across de ribber soon.

"We crossed first, den de men crossed after us. . . ."

It was, in fact, a near thing. The women, children, and old people were sent across first. Then it became complicated. No one wanted to leave the wagons behind; they might be needed in Mexico. There were various packs and bags full of helpful items like riding tack and arrow points. They wanted to ferry those across, too.

But the white men chasing them could arrive at any time. It was hard to know when the men on the north bank should swim their horses across. They didn't want one last firefight, but they did want to bring as much of their property as they could. Miss Charles said John Horse counseled hurry; forget the wagons, forget the supplies, just make sure every remaining life was saved. But Wild Cat didn't want to arrive looking like a pauper. He felt it would be more impressive to Maldonado if his people had at least some possessions with them.

On the far bank, mothers tried to hush their babies. Finally, at daybreak, the men began to ease their horses across. As they did, several dozen riders appeared on the American bank. In the near-dark, it was hard to tell if they were Rangers or slavers. They waved handkerchiefs or blankets at the fugitives and shouted to them. Thankfully, they only shouted. They didn't shoot at their quarry, probably because the refugees were now on the Mexican side of the river where, legally, the Seminole Negro were finally free.

"Come back," the pursuers yelled. "Come back here to us!" Of course, their quarry didn't.

No longer fugitives, the Seminole, Seminole Negro, and Kickapoo rested a while. On July 26, 1850, they officially met with Maldonado. True to his word, the colonel supplied the newcomers with tools, seed, and building materials. They were escorted to their homestead, though they were informed it was only granted provisionally, pending final approval by the Mexican president.

The Seminole and Kickapoo built separate villages. Almost immediately, they began to complain about their new property, from its location to its general appearance. The Seminole Negro also built a town at El Moral, some twenty miles northwest of Piedras Negras. They were ecstatic. John Horse proclaimed no Seminole Negro children would ever fight with Mexican children. His people loved their new countrymen too much to allow it.

There was a price for their new freedom and land, of course. They had to help the Mexicans defend themselves and their borders. John Horse worried about Wild Cat's plans; the Seminole chief was surely too ambitious to settle for leadership of a few hundred blacks and Indians. Then there was Duval, who would never let so insignificant a barrier as a border separate him from those Seminole Negro he considered to be his property.

So challenges would come, certainly hard times, too—but how little that mattered compared to being free.

"That could have been the end of it," Miss Charles said to me in the late afternoon. Mercifully, clouds blocked much of the sunlight. She walked me to my car without bothering to put on her massive straw bonnet. "John Horse got his people to Mexico, and they got their land there. Where some of us still live, you know."

"But there wasn't a happy ending to the story in Mexico," I said, more to indicate there was still a lot to talk about than to encourage Miss Charles to continue storytelling that day. She'd already talked to me for hours, and I knew she was weary.

"My people don't get happy endings," Miss Charles said, sounding bitter in a way I'd never heard from her before. Then she shrugged, patted my shoulder, and walked slowly back inside her house.

chapter eight

BY THE MIDDLE OF 1997, I'd spent three years gradually researching Seminole Negro history. In addition to my visits to Brackettville and phone calls to Willie Warrior and Miss Charles, I'd driven up to Oklahoma to look around and follow as much of the refugee route as I could from old Indian Territory to the Mexican border.

But in the fall of that year, another book project came up, one I had to concentrate on immediately—and, just as soon as that was done, another. It was early 2000 before I was able to get back to the Seminole Negro, and, by then, things in Brackettville were different.

My first inkling came from the Internet. Just before I planned to call Miss Charles and Willie to apologize for being out of touch so long, and to make arrangements to see them in Brackettville soon, I logged on to the Internet to see what information about the Seminole Negro might be available there. In 1994, when I started the project, the Internet was still in its infancy. But in recent years, I'd learned what a valuable resource it could be.

There were several dozen sites with at least some reference to the Seminole Negro, most of them posted by university professors. But one was labeled SISCA, an acronym for the Seminole Indian Scout Cemetery Association. Willie Warrior had told me the organization's name was the

Black Seminole Indian Scout Cemetery Association, but this obviously had to be the same group originally organized by Miss Charles.

The site touted the next Seminole Days celebration in Brackettville. There was also a message from the association president, whose name was Clarence Ward. I hadn't met him or heard his name mentioned during my previous Brackettville visits. But his Internet message was pleasant enough: He urged all tribal members everywhere to come, and to bring friends. There was also a phone number where he could be reached. I decided to call and ask if he could see me soon, whenever Miss Charles and Willie would be available, too. But when I reached him on the phone, he sounded standoffish.

"You say you're a writer? My members don't like writers much," he said. "Over the years, lots of people claiming to be writers have come down here. My members say they all ask questions, take up time, then go away and never come back."

"Well, *I'm* coming back," I said guility, thinking about how I hadn't talked to Willie or Miss Charles for so long. "Can I visit with you and your members when I'm in town?"

"I'll talk to you, 'cause that's my job as association president," Clarence said. "We've got a meeting this week and I'll ask my members if they want to see you, but I don't think they will."

"Miss Charles and Willie Warrior will vouch for me," I said. "Ask them."

"Miss Charles has the Alzheimer's," he replied. "She's with family in Kerrville now. She can't remember anybody's name, so I don't think she'd remember you."

My heart sank. This was awful news. Like everyone else, I'd taken it for granted Miss Charles would be around forever.

"Well, ask Willie Warrior," I suggested.

Clarence's voice took on an edgier tone. "Mr. Warrior is no longer very involved with the association," he said. "He just doesn't see eye-to-eye with us on some things."

I asked Clarence if we could meet in Brackettville later in the month. He said it would be all right, but that I shouldn't expect him to know much about his people's history—"I can't help you there." We also talked a little more about Miss Charles. He said that though her mind "had gone" she was still well enough to come back home for Seminole Days.

Then I called Willie Warrior in Del Rio. It was as though we'd never met.

"I've talked about our history all these years, and I've never gotten one thing out of it," he complained. "I don't know what Clarence and his people are trying to do, like ignore the black part of our history and just talk about the Seminole. Talk to Clarence if you want to talk to anybody. I'm retired from it."

"But Miss Charles is sick, and Clarence says he doesn't know anything about your history," I pleaded. "I'm trying to write this book, and there are still things you can tell me that nobody else can."

"Well, I'm sorry about that," Willie said, his tone a little kinder. "It's just that these young ones think they know how to do things better, and they're going at it all wrong."

It took another ten minutes, but Willie finally said he might see me if I showed up. I got the feeling, correctly, as it turned out, that even if he was angry with Clarence and some of the association members he still couldn't resist telling all the old stories to anyone who asked. I told him I'd be in Brackettville within a few weeks, and that I looked forward to seeing him again.

Brackettville looked about the same. The video store where Monika Cruz worked had shut down. There was a new Bubba's Beverage Barn on the side of the highway, its signage informing passing motorists they could pull up and buy a cold one without getting out of their cars. Somebody had opened a relatively upscale restaurant (salads served) in the tiny downtown district, with some outdoor seating. On subsequent visits, I never saw anyone eating there. The Krazy Chicken still had to do for most residents and visitors, or, for motel guests, there was a rudimentary restaurant on the Fort Clark grounds.

There was also a new Burger 'n' Shake. Clarence Ward, reached on his cell phone, said he'd meet me there. He arrived in a red truck. A burly forty-nine-year-old dressed in bright blue coveralls, Clarence had a friendly smile and, despite his warnings that he and his membership didn't think much of writers, greeted me warmly. Instead of going into the Burger 'n' Shake, he said, we might as well go back to his house. It was only a few blocks away. That is how far any place in Brackettville is from everything else in town. Clarence introduced me to his wife, Audrey, explaining she was a tribal descendant, too—"Her mother could tell you a lot, but she doesn't want to"—and we began talking about Miss Charles, which I thought would be a safe opening subject.

"You're her successor with the association," I said. "That must be a tremendous responsibility."

Clarence said it was and told a little about himself. A Brackettville native, he is the great-grandson of Medal of Honor–winning scout John Ward. Clarence had married into the tribe's Pompey Factor family and, after a long tour of duty overseas while working for an oil company, he'd returned to Brackettville for good with his wife and daughter in 1990. He still worked for the oil company and spent lengthy stretches each year in Nigeria and other countries. But he liked living back in his old hometown, and he'd always known about the cemetery association. His parents had been members.

"In 1998 I got real concerned that it was falling apart," he told me. We'd moved outside to sit in the shade of his carport. "Miss Charles was getting ill. Willie Warrior was always someplace else giving talks. There weren't a lot of members, and most of them were behind on dues. The cemetery needed attention. So I ran for president and got elected. My goal was to bring things up to date—get the dues paid, maybe put things on computer, just bring everybody back together."

But soon afterward, a fire destroyed the building where the association's historical materials had been stored. Almost everything—photos, government documents, diaries, letters—was burned. It was a terrible loss.

"Some of those things could be replaced, but member families who still have pictures and such mostly have them put away somewhere," Clarence observed, sipping from a sweaty bottle of beer. "What's going to happen is, the members will die and their children either won't know what the photos and things are, so they'll throw 'em away, or they'll donate 'em to some outside museum and the association will have lost out. I'm trying to help rebuild a sense of pride in ourselves, so we can present our own history. But that's hard, and I myself don't know much of it."

"What about Willie Warrior?" I asked tentatively. "He's so good at that."

Clarence sighed. He glanced quickly at his wife, who was standing in the doorway.

"We don't talk much, him and me," he finally said. "But I got to try and work with the association as I think best."

"I'm going to see Willie in Del Rio, probably tomorrow," I said, wanting to make sure Clarence knew I wasn't taking sides in whatever dispute there might be. "I'm going to keep on talking to him for this book. He's such a big part of it. Will that be a problem for you?"

Clarence said it wouldn't. He told me his members had voted not to talk to me, "but I'll work on that, see if they'll come around. You and I can talk some more while you're here, if you want. And when you see Mr. Warrior, tell him I said hello. I've got no bad feelings toward him."

Later, I spent several dollars at a pay phone by a Brackettville convenience store beside the highway, trying to track Willie Warrior down. Someone answering his phone in Del Rio said Willie and his wife, Ethel, were already in Brackettville, staying at the portion of the Fort Clark enlisted men's barracks they'd purchased as a weekend home. I walked all over the barracks area of the fort, sweating in the 100-plus degree heat, but couldn't find them. Another call to Del Rio got no answer. Neither did the third. The fourth time, Willie answered the phone, sounding distant, and told me I could come by in the morning, "though I may not want to talk much."

I drove thirty miles west of Brackettville to Del Rio, which, compared to its poor-relation neighbor, seemed like a big city. Willie's house was easy to find. When he opened the door, I saw he'd lost some weight and looked a little older. We shook hands formally—he still wasn't acting especially friendly—and then he introduced me to Ethel. I'd never been to Willie's home before, and I hadn't previously met her. She turned out to be a Seminole Negro scout descendant, too, and she was even a past president of the cemetery association.

"Now, Dub, you two go sit in the back and talk," Ethel said. She was a bright-eyed, bouncy, outgoing woman. "I know you've got a lot to discuss."

For perhaps five minutes, Willie grumbled about the association, about all the work he'd done for the group for so many years, and how he'd never gotten anything for it, and now Clarence and the others wanted to disavow their black heritage and most of the history. Then I asked my first question about the Seminole Negro in Mexico—what happened when they got there? Hadn't they moved a few times before finding a permanent place to settle?

Immediately, Willie began to grin. He and Ethel had crossed the border to Nacimiento a while back, he said, and they'd stayed with the Seminole Negro still living there.

"Dirt poor, all of them are," he added.

"Outdoor bathrooms, too," Ethel observed, popping in from the kitchen to ask if we wanted coffee. "That didn't bother us. But it just breaks your heart, the way they have to live."

Willie rummaged around looking for videocassette he'd filmed of the modern-day Seminole Negro settlement in Nacimiento. As he did, he talked about his ancestors' early experiences in their new homeland. I was pleased to be taken, through his words, back to 1850 in Mexico with the newly arrived John Horse and Wild Cat.

So now they would be Mexicans, Willie said. It had been promised that all of the refugees—Seminole, Kickapoo, and Seminole Negro—could become full-fledged citizens if they lived up to their border protection agreements and had their treaty ratified by Mexico's president. It was a heady prospect to the Seminole Negro, who had been classified in the United States as property rather than people for so many generations.

The Kickapoo had their separate village. Papicua had some contact with Wild Cat, but for the most part the Kickapoo kept their distance. Unlike the Seminole, they had no permanent stake in Wild Cat's leadership, and, unlike the Seminole Negro, they had no long history of betrayal and suffering that was assuaged by land in Mexico. From the outset, the Kickapoo commitment to Mexico was tenuous.

Soon after arriving in Mexico, Wild Cat probably made his official call on Jane Cazneau/Cora Montgomery and her family. From his first days in the area, Wild Cat and his Seminole crossed the Texas-Mexico border with impunity. He evidentally considered himself a sort of Seminole ambassador, able to pass where he pleased.

On this first visit to the Cazneaus, Wild Cat was accompanied by John Horse and a Seminole companion Cazneau/Montgomery identified as "Crazy Bear." She probably meant Nokosimala, whose name properly translated into English as "Bear Leader." He was a cousin of Wild Cat's. But Wild Cat and John Horse got most of Cazneau/Montgomery's attention.

John Horse, she wrote, "a full-blooded negro . . . marshaled" Wild Cat "with all ceremony." So, at least in white company, Wild Cat presented John Horse as a servant, not an equal.

Wild Cat himself "was dressed in fanciful Indian costume. A row of crescent-shaped silver medals, arranged in something like a breast-plate, glittered on his breast, and he had good arms . . . he saluted the ladies with a sedate and graceful bow, and accepted a chair with the grave attitude becoming a chief. He then directed his interpreter"—John Horse—"to say he thanked the Great Spirit for placing him, face to face, and in peace, with the whites, whom he now regarded as friends and brothers, in this distant country. On taking a glass with the gentlemen he gave a pledge indicative of a desire of mutual good-will, and added, afterwards, that once when he met the white men, blood flowed, but now he had no thought in his heart but friendship and a desire for peace."

Actually, Wild Cat's heart had plenty of thoughts. In a subsequent visit, he would tell the Cazneaus that his alliance with Mexico was temporary. What he really wanted to do was resettle his people in Texas. Whether that was entirely true, or whether Wild Cat was just trying to develop another option if the Mexican treaty didn't work out as planned, is something only he knew. Certainly John Horse and the Seminole Negro believed they had come to Mexico to stay.

Accordingly, at El Moral the blacks began building a permanent village. They couldn't construct their beloved houses thatched with fronds, so they built "chink" homes, using mud to plug gaps between logs. Later, as they learned Mexican methods of construction, they switched to adobe. At least initially, their Mexican neighbors liked them and informally christened the industrious black newcomers *Mascogos*. The term may be a variation on "Muskogee." Almost immediately, other black refugees who had fled to Mexico came to join them. A small settlement of about two dozen blacks who'd run from the Creek had already been established nearby. These families' surnames were mostly Wilson and Warrior. They were welcomed into the Seminole Negro community. Hundreds of acres needed to be cleared and plowed, so extra hands were a blessing. While Wild Cat pressed Maldonado for guns, John Horse and the Seminole Negro gladly accepted seed corn and began planting. They preferred lives devoted to farming, not fighting. Providing border protection was the price they were willing to pay for their own land to live on and cultivate.

The mood in the neighboring Seminole village was less domesticated. Most of the Indians were unhappy that the blacks seemed independent of them. Once in Mexico, they had expected a resumption of old roles, with the blacks held in benevolent servitude, pleased to simply be far away from the tougher slave laws of the Creek. Then, too, the Seminole weren't satisfied with the land they'd been assigned. Yes, it had good water. Yes, it provided decent hunting. But no, it wasn't exactly what they wanted. Twice before, in Florida and in Indian Territory, they'd been ordered onto land they'd considered unfit for habitation. There was, obviously, plenty of other land in Coahuila, and, as about-to-be Mexican citizens, they felt they had the right to choose their own part of it. Later, Wild Cat would press this argument on Maldonado, but for now, having reached Mexico with his first party and worked out a treaty, his principal objective was to lure even more fighting men to his new stronghold. So, while the Seminole Negro farmed and the Seminole fumed, Wild Cat took a few warriors and returned to Indian Territory. Even traveling light and without the burden of dependents who couldn't keep up a brisk pace, the trip took over a month. Longtime Seminole Negro historian Kenneth Porter, who actually came to live for a while with them in Brackettville in the 1940s, notes Wild

Cat made several stops along the way in fruitless attempts to recruit "the Comanche, Caddo and Waco, urging them to join him in Mexico, where he said they would fight not the 'wild Indians' but the Texans, and threatening punishment to those who refused." So much for Wild Cat telling the Cazneaus he wanted to live in peace with the white man.

What Wild Cat didn't realize, as he rode north and was frustrated in efforts to persuade other Indians to join him, was that, at the same time, hundreds of would-be recruits were trying desperately to make their way from Indian Territory to Mexico. They were Seminole Negro, and, for many of them, the way south was marred by suffering, blood, and death.

"John Horse and his bunch had a hard time on that first trip, but there were others who tried and had it even worse," Willie Warrior said. Not an hour into my Del Rio visit, he was already comfortably back in his storyteller's mode. Coffee mug in one hand, he sat back on a couch in his den and waved his free hand as he spoke. "You can't just talk about that first bunch. Jim Bowlegs, some others, they caught hell, too."

With John Horse gone, Jim Bowlegs had assumed command of the Seminole Negro still in Wewoka back in Indian Territory. He and most of the other blacks knew their position was shaky. The Creek were determined to re-enslave them; the Seminole were willing to go along with that. Marcellus Duval was back, dedicated to subjugating every negro under his authority, and the various army officers were trying not to get caught in the middle of a potentially explosive situation. John Horse and the Seminole Negro who'd gone with him, on the other hand, were probably already settled happily in Mexico, where no black man or woman was a slave. Texas was a nasty, forbidding place to cross, but the Seminole Negro had survived under dangerous conditions before. It seemed simple enough to Jim Bowlegs: He would take as many of his people as he could and run south to join their old leader. So, in early July—about the time John Horse, Wild Cat, and the first refugees were splashing across the Rio Grande just ahead of pursuing slavers or Texas Rangers—Jim Bowlegs led another 180 Seminole Negro away from Wewoka toward Mexico. They were armed with a makeshift arsenal of battered muskets, knives, and bows and arrows. Like John Horse's group, the men were hampered by the presence of wives, children, and old people. They held few illusions about how safe their journey would be; unlike the first refugees, they expected to be pursued immediately. Also, there was no Wild Cat with them to assure that he'd made temporary peace with the Comanche who stood between them and Mexico. It was not a question of *if* they'd have to fight for their lives and freedom, but *when.*

Accordingly, Jim Bowlegs decided that it would be best to split his party into several smaller groups. These might have a better chance to pass undetected by the Comanche. As for whoever might chase them from Indian Territory, well, at least they'd have to pick one group or another to follow.

None of the smaller groups got away clean. The Creek sent a large mounted troop after the runaways. They picked up the trail of one ninety-member band and followed it south, gaining rapidly because they didn't stop at night. After only a few days, they closed in. The thirty or so Seminole Negro men told the women, children, and old people to run ahead as fast as they could, giving up their own horses so their dependents could ride. Then the warriors turned to fight the Creek on foot. It was an awful mismatch. There were three or four Creek braves to each Seminole Negro, and the Indians were on horseback. The Creek were in no mood to spare their opponents. When they'd slaughtered the men, they followed the other blacks and easily recaptured them. All sixty black survivors were herded back to Indian Territory.

In some ways, they were the lucky ones. In Texas, the Comanche were lurking.

The Comanche, though too independent to form permanent alliances with other tribes, kept well-informed. They were aware the Creek considered the Seminole Negro to be slaves, and that any Seminole Negro crossing Comanche territory heading south was on the run. Besides being great fighters, the Comanche were shrewd businessmen. Parties of Seminole Negro were fair game for either sport or commerce. They used the fragmented followers of Jim Bowlegs for both.

First came the group led by Jim Bowlegs himself. The Comanche surrounded and captured them. They took them from ambush; even the fabled scouting skills of the black warriors didn't detect the presence of the Indians until it was too late. The Seminole Negro expected the worst—at least the slaughter of the men and the rape of the women—but the Comanche had other ideas. They tied everyone up and herded their prisoners back north. Soon, they encountered an armed party of Creek and sold the Seminole Negro back to them. The Creek unceremoniously forced the blacks back toward Indian Territory, punctuating blows to stragglers with promises of complete subjugation to future Indian masters. It was a terrible prospect, and, somewhere along the way, the Seminole Negro men decided they couldn't face it. They fought the Creek. Since they were unarmed, it was an unequal struggle and some died, but others, including Jim Bowlegs, managed to escape. They fled south again, this time successfully. Eventually they reached Mexico, and Jim Bowlegs became one of John Horse's most trusted lieutenants.

But there was still another band of Seminole Negro trying to flee south, and the Comanche found this one, too. They used them for targets. About sixty black men, women, and children were in the party, and all but two died horribly, the men probably tortured and the women raped before they were killed, for this was the Comanche way. Two young girls were spared death, but little else. The Comanche used them like modern scientists experiment with laboratory rats. What the Indians wanted to know was whether, in negroes, black skin extended all the way down to the bone. So they tested the girls, first burning them with coals and then skinning parts of their bodies with hunting knives. When their curiosity was satisfied, they sold the bleeding children to a passing Delaware, who in turn sold them in a white slave market. A soldier saw them there, inquired what had happened, and wrote about it in his journal. Scarred, undoubtedly emotionally as well as physically, the girls weren't heard of again.

It is possible that this massacre is the same one Willie Warrior said occurred during the exodus of Wild Cat and John Horse. Certainly, over the decades tribal tales may have occasionally combined separate events for storytelling convenience. Willie told the story the way his parents and uncles had told it to him. Either way, eagerness to kill or torture the Seminole Negro was a pattern the Comanche were happy to repeat. In later years, historians wondered why the tribe was always so anxious to assault these blacks. What they gleaned from various Comanche sources was that the tribe never believed Wild Cat's promise not to fight them, which was wise. Any Seminole Negro who passed through Comanche Territory could later form part of the Mexican border guard. Why should the Comanche let future foes go in peace?

Of the 180 Seminole Negro who left Indian Territory with Jim Bowlegs, about seventy actually reached Mexico. The rest died or were taken back to Indian Territory as slaves. That didn't prevent others from wanting to risk the journey. For the next decade, Seminole Negro and other Indian Territory blacks, including slaves from white farms and settlements, attempted the same danger-frought flight. But they went in smaller groups. After Jim Bowlegs, there was no large, organized escape attempt.

Duval had much to do with that. He stirred up Creek and Seminole indignation by taunting them about their lost property. At the same time, he warned his superiors in Washington that the Seminole Negro settlement in Mexico would tempt white men's slaves to run away, too—in October 1850 he wrote that the black Indian Territory refugees "would constitute a formidable band in Texas where they would secrete, protect, and guide all runaway slaves who made their way to the Texas plains."

It was crafty of Duval to present the runaways in Texas rather than Mexico. That gave him a reason to inundate the Texas governor with pleas to catch and return the Seminole Negro with John Horse. The governor wouldn't do that; those blacks were across the Mexican border, and it was at least technically illegal for him to send soldiers or Rangers to capture them there. What could be done, and was, involved orders to the commander of Fort Duncan. He was not to allow any blacks to cross the Rio Grande without first proving they were freemen, not escaped slaves. Those blacks who had no papers were to be arrested and held in military custody until their rightful owners could be determined.

"Old Duval got his pretty soon after this," Willie Warrior said, chuckling. "But he still had a bad turn or two for Wild Cat and John Horse first."

"Was he waiting when Wild Cat got back to Indian Territory?" I asked.

" 'Course he was. Just because Duval was bad didn't mean he was dumb, too. He got Wild Cat pretty good."

Wild Cat knew nothing of the governor's edict as he rode north toward Indian Territory. He had to be in a terrible mood. Except for the Kickapoo, his efforts to recruit more Indian warriors had been soundly rebuffed by the Comanche and other Texas tribes. Wild Cat was returning to Indian Territory not to enlist more Seminole Negro, but to talk a substantial portion of the Seminole into returning south with him. It was still Wild Cat's dream to be principal chief of his own people. Jim Jumper and Marcellus Duval, of course, had other ideas.

He wasn't arrested immediately upon his arrival, though Duval was tempted. He could, at least, have charged Wild Cat with fomenting a slave rebellion and illegally leading the Seminole Negro away. But the agent shrewdly let Wild Cat make his own bad impression. For one thing, the Seminole was drunk when he arrived.

The Creek, expecting Wild Cat to head for Wewoka as soon as he sobered up, sent several hundred men to surround the town and prevent any of the remaining blacks from leaving. Roley Macintosh, the Creek chief, began to plan Wild Cat's arrest if the white authorities wouldn't cooperate and capture him themselves. Wild Cat eventually met with some Seminole warriors and tried to talk them into following him back to Mexico. Duval later claimed Wild Cat even promised the Indians that, once in Mexico, they could have the Seminole Negro living there as their slaves. The reason the Seminole didn't join Wild Cat and head south, Duval said, was because he personally informed the Indians that slavery was illegal in Mexico, and that Wild Cat was making a promise he couldn't keep.

Did Wild Cat really promise that the Seminole Negro in Mexico would become tribal slaves again? Probably. That would explain why he insisted the agreement made with Maldonado include a clause that the Seminole could keep their traditional tribal customs. Certainly, slavery was illegal in Mexico, but Wild Cat hoped the Mexican government would overlook subjugation of a few hundred blacks. Whether they would have is something no one will ever know. Because of Duval's alleged intervention, or because they weren't impressed by a drunken braggart, most of the Seminole in Indian Territory disdained Wild Cat's proposal.

Marcellus Duval hated Wild Cat, but the agent went to the Indian anyway and warned him that Roley Macintosh had ordered his arrest. Wild Cat fled, taking with him a few Seminole who'd decided to try life in Mexico—maybe a few dozen in all—and probably one or two blacks who'd sneaked out of Wewoka or run away from Creek or Cherokee masters. The Creek pursued him, but not for very long. Historian Kevin Mulroy postulates that the riders chasing Wild Cat were intercepted by the Comanche trying to sell Jim Bowlegs and his escapees and gave up the pursuit of the Seminole to buy back the captured Seminole Negro.

Wild Cat got back to Mexico sometime in early November. By then, John Horse and the Seminole Negro had already begun earning their land by defending the border.

"I need a minute here," Willie Warrior said. "Bathroom break." While he was out of the room, I glanced at my watch and saw it was nearly noon. When Willie came back, I said I'd like to take him and Ethel out to lunch.

"Not necessary," he said, and nodded in the direction of the kitchen. While we'd been talking, even though she'd never met me (and, it turned out, hadn't even known I was coming), Ethel Warrior had fixed lunch, a big meal of roast beef and gravy and vegetables.

"You didn't have to go to this trouble," I protested to her. "I would have been glad to take you out to eat," but on that day and every other that I was in her home around mealtime, Ethel cooked. As I spent more time visiting Clarence and some of his association members, I learned that this was the Seminole Negro custom. Guests were fed. Even when I met Clarence for quick snacks at the Burger 'n' Shake, he always wanted to pay because he was the host. Miss Charles had never offered drinks or snacks in her home, but she was much older. There was an additional reason. When I mentioned to Ethel that Miss Charles had never fixed a meal for me in her home, Ethel said that "Charles was always church." After I thought about it a while, I understood. As a devout Christian maiden lady, an unchaperoned Miss Charles simply would not entertain a male caller in her home for anything other than conversation in the formal parlor. It didn't matter if she was very old, and her visitor was half her age. Decency recognized no age limits.

While we ate, Willie and Ethel talked about their children and grandchildren, asked about my family, and treated me like a special friend. Later on, Ethel would prove almost as gifted a storyteller as her husband. But on this visit, after our meal it was Willie who picked up the story of the Seminole Negro in Mexico.

Though John Horse and his followers were thrilled to be accepted in Mexico, living conditions there weren't perfect. The biggest problem lay just across the Rio Grande in Eagle Pass. The thriving community of slavers there earned their money by capturing runaway blacks and returning them to their white masters. To these slavers, the Seminole Negro village at El Moral became an instant target. They didn't organize and attack en masse, which the Mexican government could have taken as a provocation. Instead, they slipped across the rivers alone or in pairs and lay in wait outside the black settlement, hoping individual *mascogos* might be foolish enough to wander away from the village. For the first few weeks after they arrived, no one did, but eventually a small girl toddled away and was snatched. Fortunately, an adult Seminole Negro saw what was happening and rescued her. After that, everyone was careful to stay near the main camp, and John Horse sometimes ordered guards posted around the area. But the constant threat of slaver incursions was an unpleasant reminder that, even in Mexico, Americans were nearby to threaten them.

Food was a problem, too. It would take a while for the corn they planted to grow. The *mascogo* women had to learn the Mexican arts of creating meals with tortillas and other area staples. John Horse appealed to Maldonado, and the Mexican government supplied some food. The Seminole Negro warriors hunted, and they also hired themselves out as farmhands and day laborers. It was anticipated that the food shortage would be temporary. The tribesmen were good farmers. Here, for the first time, they had land of their own, and they skillfully cultivated it. In their settlements, the Seminole and Kickapoo weren't as industrious. They, too, begged food from the government, but the Indian men spent far less time planting and nurturing crops than their black counterparts. The Indian warriors had come to Mexico to fight, not farm.

In early fall, while Wild Cat was still in Indian Territory, they got their chance. Willie said he didn't know how Maldonado felt when Wild Cat was absent the first time he called the newcomers to help repulse Apache raiders. Mexico had, so far, kept its word. The newcomers had their land, they had their seed corn, they'd been given guns and food. Now they were required to earn their keep, and their great chief was not present to lead them. It probably surprised Maldonado when John Horse assumed command. Certainly, Papicua had nominal charge of the Kickapoo, and some Seminole or other rounded up his tribesmen. But when the fifty or sixty riders joined Maldonado in Piedras Negras, John Horse was the one who reported to the colonel and asked for orders.

Twice, before Wild Cat returned, the Indians and Seminole Negro fought alongside Mexican troops, and they acquitted themselves well. Maldonado saw that the black men in particular seemed fearless; they were crack shots who never panicked. Both times, raiding Indians were driven off before they could steal many cattle or do much damage to Mexican property. This was what Maldonado had anticipated. If there weren't as many Seminole, Seminole Negro, and Kickapoo as he had hoped Wild Cat would provide as a fighting force, at least the ones who had arrived were up to the tasks assigned to them.

Maldonado made favorable reports back to his superiors. On October 16, 1850, as Wild Cat fled Indian Territory, Mexico's president formally confirmed his country's contract with Wild Cat's people. The blacks and Indians were now Mexican citizens.

A month later, Maldonado met formally with Seminole Negro and Seminole leaders. The Mexican government wanted no possible misunderstanding; did Wild Cat and his people realize the land was only theirs in return for perpetual military service? That theirs was not a limited commitment of five or ten years, but for eternity?

Wild Cat, just back from his humiliating foray, said he understood. He mentioned that his people and Papicua's were not especially pleased about the land they currently occupied. He hoped—no, he expected—that in the spring there could be discussion about relocating.

Then John Horse had something to say. He wanted to assure the colonel that his people, the *mascogos,* were very happy with their land at El Moral. Though their Seminole and Kickapoo friends might want to be elsewhere, the Seminole Negro wanted and intended to stay put. Yes, they understood they had to fight to earn their keep, and they would be glad to take up arms against encroaching Indians or even Americans if it came to that. But John Horse and his people had come to Mexico to stay. They realized there was constant turmoil within the Mexican government. It was hard to remember who was the country's president from one day to the next. The Seminole Negro would always be ready to protect their new homeland from foreign invaders. But never—*never*—would they align themselves with one side or the other during internal strife. In all governmental matters, the Seminole Negro must and would remain neutral. Was that acceptable? Maldonado said it was.

So, on behalf of their respective people, Wild Cat, John Horse, and Papicua swore oaths of fidelity to the Mexican government. Hands were shaken; gifts were distributed. As winter approached, the cold weather shut down Indian raids into Mexico, and the newest Mexican citizens had time to reflect. Though Wild Cat was dissatisfied and the Kickapoo were grumbling in their camp, the Seminole Negro relaxed for perhaps the first time in centuries. They had land. They were full-fledged citizens. They were happy.

But events in early 1851 reminded them this happiness came with a price. Both the Seminole and Kickapoo reiterated dissatisfaction with their current locations and asked to move. The Seminole Negro had no desire to leave El Moral. So the two Indian bands shuffled about to new areas around Piedras Negras, while the blacks continued to expand their fields and plant spring crops. There was some grumbling about this, mostly from the Seminole. The Indians still expected their black allies to till Seminole fields, too. Obviously, that was not going to happen.

In March 1851, the first Apache and Comanche full-scale spring raids began. Maldonado ordered Wild Cat to bring his warriors into Piedras Negras, where they would join with Mexican troops to track the intruders. Wild Cat arrived with about one hundred men, two-thirds Seminole and Kickapoo and the other third black. He had overall command, but the Seminole Negro looked to John Horse for orders. The combined Mexican/Indian/black force chased after the raiders and eventually found and routed them. They returned to Piedras Negras in sweaty triumph—and Wild Cat found American army officers Samuel Cooper and Robert Temple waiting for him there.

Officials of the U.S. War Department were worried. Duval continued to hound Washington bureaucrats about his "stolen" slaves. His latest rant was that Wild Cat, far from organizing a negro fighting force for the Mexicans, was actually accumulating blacks for the purpose of selling them himself to Texas slavers, meaning runaways joining the Seminole Negro in El Moral might end up illegally owned by other Americans—a terrible mess to sort out. The army had a different concern. If Wild Cat built a formidable Indian force just across the border, what was to prevent him from attacking settlers on the north side of the Rio Grande, then escaping back into Mexico and claiming sanctuary there as citizen and employee of the Mexican government? Already, some residents in and around Eagle Pass were complaining that Wild Cat and his Seminole routinely crossed back and forth across the river as they hunted—and that, sometimes, their cattle disappeared while these Indians were in the vicinity.

So Cooper and Temple were sent to interrogate Wild Cat. The Mexican government granted permission as a courtesy to the United States. Significantly, there is no record that John Horse translated for Wild Cat during this meeting. Maybe the American officers brought their own interpreter, or Wild Cat used one of his people who spoke English. According to U.S. Army records, what Wild Cat told Temple and Cooper would have appalled John Horse.

He had no intention of staying in Mexico, Wild Cat said. He'd been driven out of Indian Territory against his will—the Creek had forced their laws on his people. So he led some of his followers to Mexico. What Wild Cat really wanted was to have his people's land in Indian Territory swapped for property in Texas. That way, they'd be away from the hateful Creek, and could live peacefully under their own laws and customs. If the American government could arrange such a transfer of property, Wild Cat and his people would leave Mexico immediately.

Cooper and Temple were surprised. They promised Wild Cat they'd deliver his message to their superiors, but, added that, in the meantime, he ought to stay in Mexico.

Later, Wild Cat mentioned the same plan to the Cazneaus, who themselves would soon leave Eagle Pass. Crossing the border as apparently had become his custom, he, a few "followers," and an interpreter, not John Horse, called on the Cazneaus.

"Wild Cat drew up unexpectedly at our door," Cazneau/Montgomery wrote, "It was a quiet business call. . . . He wishes to become the accepted soldier and agent of the United States, and win renown and influence by taming down the hostile and troublesome border Indians to keep peace with the whites."

If Wild Cat hoped the Americans would jump at the opportunity to acquire his services, he was disappointed. Cooper and Temple never returned to tell him his land-swap plan was acceptable. If the Cazneaus passed along his unsubtle suggestion to military officers at Fort Duncan, no one there responded. Wild Cat had been rejected by his own people in Indian Territory. Now, the Americans didn't want him, either.

At least the Mexican government did. Indian raids in Coahuila were especially frequent during 1851. Perhaps the Comanche and Apache felt challenged by the presence of the new border guards there. In *Freedom on the Border,* Kevin Mulroy writes there were "ninety-four incursions by more than three thousand Comanches and Lipans [Apache] resulting in sixty-three deaths, many wounded and captured and many livestock losses." Wild Cat and his followers were kept busy. Alarmed by the frequency of the raids, the Mexicans sweetened the defense pot. Besides the land they lived on and some farming supplies and weaponry, the Indians and blacks would also receive bounties for each raider captured or killed—as much as $250 for a live male Indian, or $200 for his hair.

In mid-June, Wild Cat led about 120 Indians and blacks on a prolonged, seven-week chase punctuated by occasional battles. These were rarely all-out confrontations; the main purpose of the border guards was to act as a deterrent. Their presence was supposed to encourage the raiding parties to attack elsewhere, preferably on the American side of the Rio Grande where the U.S. Army was assigned to protect settlers.

But there were some battles, and, when there was fighting, the Seminole Negro continued to distinguish themselves. They fought, always, with the attitude of businessmen earning their salaries. They were less interested in bragging about various exploits than in completing their excursions and returning safely home to El Moral. In particular, they worried about their corn crop. They'd been counting on a good harvest to provide food for the winter. Now, with only women, children, and old people left to tend the fields, they worried about the corn surviving the blistering summer heat. This didn't escape notice by the Seminole and Kickapoo. The Kickapoo in particular complained bitterly about everything, from the unmanliness of the blacks to the orders they were given by the Mexicans via Wild Cat and Papicua.

So the mission was successful, but not particularly happy. In the end, the Indians and blacks had recaptured hundreds of horses stolen by the raiders. Most would have to be returned to their Mexican owners, but, as provided in the treaty with Mexico, Indian mounts captured became Seminole, Seminole Negro, and Kickapoo property. Dozens of good horses fell into this category. All the animals were kept in one large herd as the party headed south for home.

They camped one last night near the Texas border. Probably some of the Kickapoo braves volunteered for guard duty while everyone else slept. They should have stayed awake. In the morning, many of the Kickapoo were gone, along with most of the livestock. Their tracks led to the Rio Grande, and, on the north side of the river, deep into Texas. Wild Cat had been humiliated again. His fighting force was reduced to about 150 men, more than half of them Seminole Negro.

In El Moral, the corn crop failed. Despite all their hard work, the Seminole Negro had no grain to store for the winter. It was a bitter lesson. Eager to satisfy his people's obligation to the Mexican government, John Horse had ordered almost every able-bodied warrior to go on the mission, leaving behind just a skeleton guard for the village. Yes, the Mexican government would undoubtedly provide the Seminole Negro with enough food to get them through the winter, but it was always John Horse's goal for his tribe to be self-sufficient. Requiring subsistence from the Mexicans was the same as having to beg food from the Americans back in Indian Territory. It was better for the Seminole Negro to depend on no one other than themselves.

As bad as things seemed, they soon got worse.

"You think those white people back in the States had forgotten about us?" Willie Warrior asked sarcastically. "No way."

White settlers throughout Texas had learned of and resented the Seminole Negro community in El Moral. Like early colonists in Georgia, they believed a free black community would tempt their slaves to run away. Since outlawing slavery, Mexico had already been a lure to runaways. The Seminole Negro only exacerbated the problem. Texas newspapers editorialized about the threat El Moral represented. Pressure was brought on the state government to do something.

Some private Texas citizens decided to force the issue. A Mexican revolutionary provided an opportunity. It was almost routine in Mexico for an insurrection to be in progress. In the fall of 1851, Jose Maria Carvajal tried to take over portions of northern Mexico. He proposed an alliance to rich Texans—they should give him the money he needed to buy guns and hire mercenaries. In return, once he controlled Coahuila and other former Mexican northern states, he'd return every last black man, woman, and child to the United States. Slaves would stop running away from Texas farms and ranches, because "free" Mexico would be separated from the United States by Carvajal's new, runaway-extraditing country. It sounded good to businessmen in San Antonio and Houston. They pulled out their wallets and encouraged Carvajal to act quickly.

As soon as Carvajal had their money, he approached John S. "Rip"

Ford, who informally headed a footloose contingent of several hundred former Texas Rangers. They were, essentially, gunslingers for hire, and Carvajal had a special incentive to offer them. True, many of the blacks he expected to capture would be legal property of U.S. slave owners and would have to be returned to them, hopefully for a reward. But some of the blacks would have no papers; there would be no proof of prior ownership. Those could be taken by Ford's militia and sold for whatever they would bring in American slave markets—clear profit for the mercenaries.

Carvajal had his own contigent of Mexican fighters. On September 18, he joined them with Ford's men and charged across the Rio Grande, attacking and capturing the small Mexican town of Camargo. From there, they surrounded Matamoros.

Wild Cat was ordered to gather his fighting men and march with Mexican soldiers to Matamoros. The timing was terrible for the Seminole Negro. Winter was on its way and the men needed to hunt, since dried meat was a staple of their cold-weather diets. But they had to go with Wild Cat. They had far more to lose than the Seminole if Carvajal succeeded in separating Mexico's northern states from the rest of the country. The Indians would only be defeated; the blacks would be marched back into American slavery.

So they went, and, when the combined forces of the Mexican government met Carvajal's mercenaries outside of Matamoros, the Seminole Negro fought brilliantly. It was close, brutal combat; don't imagine relatively pristine sniping back and forth using repeating rifles. The weapons of the day were still single-shot muskets, inaccurate from anything other than short range. Much of the fighting was hand-to-hand with knives, hatchets, and fists. Carvajal's forces were equal in number to the troops sent by the Mexican government. But the invaders were driven back. The Seminole Negro fought like men possessed. Their desperation to win quickly and decisively was based on something more than fear of being returned to slavery. Their dependents back at El Moral had been left nearly defenseless, and they were concerned about what might happen to them.

Unfortunately, they were right to feel that way. While Carvajal had been organizing his raid, Duval was busy, too. He'd given up on getting help from the army, but there were other avenues to explore. One involved hiring a thug from Texas. Though the Creek and Seminole had urged Duval to go to Texas himself to direct efforts to recapture the Seminole Negro, the subagent's official Indian Territory duties kept him from doing that. So, in April 1851, Duval hired notorious slave hunter Warren Adams, whose reputation in proslavery circles was sterling. He was brutally efficient in tracking slaves and returning them to their masters, though often in battered condition.

Adams took a small advance force over the border. His opportunity was unequaled. Almost all the Seminole Negro men were away fighting Carvajal. Since the location of the Seminole Negro settlement was no secret, all Adams had to do was summon his main force from San Antonio and overwhelm the few black warriors left behind to guard all the dependents. By the time the rest of the Seminole Negro warriors could ride back from Matamoros, they would find only smoking ruins.

But a curious thing happened. The U.S. Army had no particular reason to love the Seminole Negro; in fact, their presence on the border was a constant concern, since area slave owners constantly badgered the army about runaway slaves heading to El Moral. Yet, when the commander at Fort Duncan learned Adams had plans to march on the Seminole Negro village he sent word to the Mexican authorities, stressing it was a message from one friendly government to another.

Mexicans around Piedras Negras had come to appreciate their new black neighbors. Certainly, they were safer because of the Seminole Negro presence. Alerted by the United States, they mobilized. About 150 armed men set out to intercept Adams before he could reach El Moral. Adams was in it for the money. When his scouts reported that a large Mexican contingent was protecting El Moral, he ordered his own forces to withdraw. Adams retreated to Eagle Pass and awaited another opportunity.

The Seminole Negro were thrilled when Mexicans protected El Moral. Honest service had earned loyalty back, something unique in tribal history. But their pleasure soon turned to dismay. They were informed that their Mexican hosts now considered their presence near the border to be too dangerous. So long as the Seminole Negro were within easy riding distance of Texas, slavers would keep coming for them. Too many ambitious men like Carvajal could earn American support by promising to make northern Mexico a slave-free zone. The blacks had to move from El Moral to someplace farther south in Coahuila where they wouldn't attract such constant interest from the wrong elements. The very relationship between Mexico and the United States was at stake.

The Seminole Negro didn't want to go. They loved their new village and accepted the risks of living there. But their appeals did no good; besides, the Seminole wanted to leave the area anyway. They complained that their camp at nearby La Navaja didn't have sufficient water. The Seminole Negro believed the poor farming there was due to Indian negligence rather than arid land. The Seminole men preferred lying around bragging about exploits in battle to sweating behind a plow. But Wild Cat was still leader of the combined tribes, and he wanted to move. Only a few remaining Kickapoo stayed at the original site.

The new land grant was some eighty-five miles south of Piedras Negras. Hacienda de Nacimiento nestled near the Santa Rosa mountains. There was ample water; streams cut through most of the area, eliminating Seminole complaints from their earlier property. Hopefully, the new location would keep the Seminole Negro out of the Americans' way. Besides, Nacimiento was squarely in the center of a region Indian raiders loved to attack. The Mexicans living in the area were thrilled to have the Seminole and Seminole Negro there to protect them. They welcomed the newcomers with gifts of food, farm implements, and seed.

"Ethel and I were just down in Nacimiento," Willie Warrior said. "I took some movies." He inserted a cassette into his VCR. The images on the TV screen jumped and flickered, then steadied. A number of rickety shacks appeared. A few ragged, skinny children raced by them. Somewhere, goats were baa-ing.

"Nacimiento today," Willie said. "Poorest people you've ever seen. Hear those goats? That's how they make their livings. They milk the goats, get that milk into cans, and some company truck comes by every day and buys the milk."

Then a rushing, shallow stream appeared onscreen.

"They got a better road in now, but before you had to get across this water," Willie said. "It's still the way a lot of people come. A chief runs the village, a headman. But mostly everybody milks their goats and sits out of the sun. Sometimes they get hired for different labor-type work."

"These are the Seminole Negro descendants?" I asked, just to make certain. "This is how they live?"

"Yep," Willie replied sadly. "Lots of 'em want to come here to the States, just to visit, but they don't have papers, and they don't have what it costs to get the papers. Ethel and I are going to a meeting with the border people in Eagle Pass. We got to help them figure out a way to get border cards for these people. Border cards, see, let Mexican citizens come into the States to visit, though not to stay."

"Do they hate Nacimiento, or Mexico?"

"No," Willie said. "It's their life, where they're from, you know? Back when we first got there, the land wasn't all that bad, and we were excited because it was *ours*."

The Seminole Negro missed El Moral, but they were pragmatic enough to accept the Mexican government's decision. Nacimiento had its charms. The nearby mountains were beautiful, and, this far from Eagle Pass, the threat from slavers was diminished. Piedras Negras and its saloons were still well within riding range for a few of the Seminole Negro men who wanted to enjoy a little of the high life.

The main drawback to Nacimiento was its continuing attraction to Apache and Comanche raiders. At El Moral, the Seminole Negro were threatened by white Americans. In their new home, they had to be constantly on the alert for Indian attacks. Their agreement with the Mexican government required them to provide armed service when requested. They were not expected to constantly patrol the region, looking for invading Indians instead of responding to them. But two early raids on Nacimiento that resulted in the loss of their own livestock encouraged the Seminole

Negro and Seminole to be particularly aggressive when they did find themselves summoned for duty. The Mexican government's scalp bounty was still in effect, and in the first months of 1852 they collected almost $18,000.

In Nacimiento, the Seminole Negro found enough leisure time to revel in their freedom. With no skulking slavers to threaten them, they began to leave their village alone or in small groups, just to ride or hunt or enjoy a drink in the local cantinas. While their new Mexican neighbors initially welcomed them, there was never any chance the Seminole Negro would gradually blend into their community. As in America, black skin invited blanket accusations. If, for instance, a runaway American slave with no attachment to the Seminole Negro stole from a Mexican, the Seminole Negro often would be blamed.

And runaway slaves did keep coming. More often than not, Nacimiento was their intended destination. The black population grew, and, as it did, so did its problems. It was hard for John Horse and his lieutenants like Cuffy, John Kibbetts, Jim Bowlegs, and Sampson July to exert authority over those who had no knowledge of, or interest in, tribal traditions.

In late 1852, Duval finally came to Texas himself. By that time, he had served as Indian Territory Seminole subagent for seven years. All his attempts to control, and eventually own, the Seminole Negro had failed, from making his brother the Indian Territory Seminole tribe's legal spokesman in Washington to hiring Warren Adams to raid the black village in El Moral. The army had rebuffed Duval's pleas for help. The Seminole Negro—many of them his *property*—still enjoyed the protection of the Mexican government. It finally became too much for Duval to stand. Though his duties as subagent required him to stay in Indian Territory, he headed south to meet Adams.

Duval didn't arrive empty-handed. The Seminole in Indian Territory had given him various documents that supposedly proved which Seminole Negro in Mexico actually belonged to them. If only Adams could round these blacks up and haul them back across the Rio Grande, Duval believed, U.S. courts would uphold Seminole ownership—and, in some cases, his own.

But Marcellus Duval finally pushed his superiors too far. Several highly placed army officials, in particular, had always questioned his motives in becoming so obsessed with the Seminole Negro. Now they learned Duval owned a plantation in Louisiana, and there was reason to believe he had covertly moved some of the remaining Seminole Negro there from Wewoka. It wasn't necessary to prove; by deserting his post to go to Texas, Duval had provided his bosses with all the excuse they needed to fire him.

No one seems quite sure what happened afterward to Marcellus Duval. The Civil War was still a decade away, so presumably he went back to his Louisiana plantation and lived there. Certainly, his removal from government office relieved the Seminole Negro of one of their oldest, most hated enemies. But Duval's influence, at least, would haunt them just a little longer.

Warren Adams had remained in the Eagle Pass–San Antonio area, hoping for another chance to go after the Seminole Negro. Even though he'd been fired as subagent, Duval's offer to Adams remained in effect. Adams's pride was involved, too. His reputation as a great slave hunter had been tarnished when he backed off his attack on El Moral. About the same time Duff Green was confronted by Wild Cat, John Horse gave Warren Adams his opportunity.

In many of the Seminole Negro tribal legends told by Miss Charles and Willie Warrior, John Horse is a shining hero, and rightfully so. More than anyone, he led his people from Indian Territory to Mexico and held them together during the bad times. His skill as a negotiator was legendary, and, in battle, he was a cool, decisive leader. But he was prone to occasional lapses, which usually involved drinking. Now, in late 1852, he stumbled again. Nacimiento had its charms, but the undisputed leader of the Seminole Negro missed the bigger cantinas of Piedras Negras. Winter was approaching; the Comanche and Apache were taking their traditional break from raiding. There was, in John Horse's mind, no reason why he couldn't ride north to Piedras Negras for some hard-earned fun.

There was a *fandango* in progress. John Horse began drinking. At some point, he got into an argument with a white American. Insults were exchanged. Some witnesses claimed John Horse drew his knife. Another white man pulled his gun and shot John Horse, in the chest or the shoulder. He fell to the floor, badly wounded.

Warren Adams had friends in Piedras Negras. They hurried across the river to inform him that the leader of those uppity runaway slaves was lying helpless nearby. Adams rushed into the Mexican town, placed the bleeding John Horse in handcuffs, and dragged him back to Eagle Pass.

It was Adams's greed that saved John Horse. Adams could have contacted Marcellus Duval. John Horse wasn't one of the Seminole Negro that the ex-agent claimed as his own, but certainly Duval would have been pleased to have the wounded man in his clutches. Still, there might be another source of more money, someone else who would want John Horse back at any cost.

"I think sometimes that the Seminole Negro storytellers have a tendency to present John Horse as all good and Wild Cat as mostly bad," Ben Pingenot said in 1994. "When Willie Warrior starts telling you about the Black Seminole time in Mexico, make sure he tells about when Wild Cat ransomed back John Horse. That tells a lot about both of those men."

"Wasn't it Wild Cat who Adams contacted, asking for a ransom?" I asked Willie six years later.

"Oh, yes, the money dipped in blood," he replied, smiling.

It's too easy to think of Wild Cat as a failure. He didn't become principal chief of the Seminole in Indian Territory. He never convinced the Comanche to join his proposed grand tribal alliance, and most of the Kickapoo he'd recruited not only left Mexico to return to Texas, but stole Wild Cat's horses to compound the insult. Stymied in everything else, he made it clear to the U. S. Army that he'd be glad to come back to America and settle with his people in Texas, but the Americans didn't want him. Even in his personal dealings, Wild Cat was often less than honorable. He'd promised the Seminole in Indian Territory that, if they'd come back with him to Mexico, they could re-enslave the Seminole Negro there, even though he'd encouraged the Seminole Negro to join him by promising them their freedom.

Despite all this, Wild Cat had his good points. He was a fierce fighter. In the face of overwhelming odds, he bravely battled the Americans in

Florida. In Indian Territory, he had the vision to imagine an Indian union strong enough to make the white soldiers leave them alone. He did strike a long-lasting treaty with the Mexican government that brought both his Seminole followers and the Seminole Negro their own land, and the blacks their freedom.

And now, with John Horse hurt and a captive, he also proved himself a true friend. Realistically, Wild Cat was better off with John Horse gone. That would have given him an opportunity to take control of the Seminole Negro. He was shrewd enough to realize this. But two days after John Horse was taken by Adams, Wild Cat rode into Eagle Pass. He was risking his own life. Many of the people there hated him. He met with Adams, probably in a saloon, and he kept his wits about him. Ben Pingenot thought that John Horse, weak and bandaged, might have served as translator. The conversation was blunt. Wild Cat wanted John Horse back. Adams said it would cost $500—in gold. He also wanted Wild Cat to turn over at least some of the Seminole Negro, who Adams could then return to various masters for a reward, or else sell in one of the ubiquitous slave markets. Wild Cat agreed to everything. He rode back into Mexico, but wasn't gone long. When he returned to Eagle Pass, he didn't have any Seminole Negro with him. But he did have a bag of gold. Wild Cat told Adams that it would take time to round up some blacks, but here was the money. He wanted John Horse back *now*. Adams may or may not have believed Wild Cat would ever come back with the Seminole Negro, but at least the money was there. He took the gold and handed John Horse over. Wild Cat immediately took his friend back to Nacimiento.

When he was gone, Adams examined the gold. It was the real thing; Wild Cat hadn't tried to trick him. It was probably gold the Seminole had earned from the Mexican bounty on Comanche and Apache scalps. Adams didn't care where the Indian got it. He was puzzled, though, by a dried film on the coins. It was dark and flaked off when touched. Adams took the gold over to Fort Duncan. The post surgeon looked at the coins and announced they'd been dipped in blood. Human blood, if he was any judge.

Even arrogant Warren Adams couldn't mistake the message being sent.

He didn't linger in Eagle Pass to see if Wild Cat returned with the Seminole Negro that had been promised. Instead, Adams fled, and the Seminole Negro never were bothered by him again.

Willie added a postscript to the story. In the weeks immediately after John Horse's rescue, he said, ranchers around Eagle Pass on the north side of the Rio Grande began complaining that their cattle were being rustled. On the Mexican side of the river, Wild Cat suddenly had cattle to sell. Abruptly, the rustling stopped, just about the time American ranchers decided they'd collectively been robbed of $500 worth of cows.

"Old Wild Cat was getting his money back," Willie said, grinning and slapping his own thigh with glee.

In Nacimiento, John Horse recovered from his wound. Presumably, he was grateful to Wild Cat for rescuing him. But, almost immediately, that gratitude was tested. The final split between the Seminole and Seminole Negro, which would take several years to play out, was brought about, at least in the beginning, by a series of small incidents.

Both the Indians and blacks continued to serve the Mexican government whenever requested, usually conducting wide sweeps of Coahuila in the spring—general searches for signs of raiders—and then responding to specific attacks. For the first time, there were more black warriors available for duty than Indians. The Seminole population was static, but the Seminole Negro ranks continued to be swelled by the addition of runaway slaves. It was accepted as fact among white Texans that most, if not all, fleeing blacks ran to Nacimiento. In fact, most didn't. Though about four thousand escaped slaves were supposed to be living in Mexico, John Horse's followers never numbered more than four or five hundred, including noncombatants. But Texans *believed* their slaves were joining John Horse and Wild Cat, and they were resentful.

The Seminole also were unhappy with their black partners for much the same reason. The Indians knew, of course, that there weren't thousands of blacks at Nacimiento. But they also knew there were now more Seminole Negro than Seminole, and they didn't like being in the minority. It especially affected the amount of water used for their fields. The Seminole thought the more numerous Seminole Negro were hogging the water supply. Several Indian leaders complained about it to the Mexican authorities, who asked the blacks to be more considerate.

Then, in June 1853, Wild Cat himself was accused of slave trafficking.

Cuffy had been a prominent Seminole Negro even before they fled from Indian Territory. On the long flight to Mexico, he'd served John Horse well, scouting ahead for water and behind for pursuers, encouraging tired old people and women to keep moving forward, making exhausted children smile with small jokes and stories. In El Moral and later in Nacimiento, he was perhaps second only to John Horse and John Kibbetts as a village leader. He fought bravely against raiding Indians and never shirked chores tending crops.

So it was devastating to the Seminole Negro when, after a long, unexplained absence, Cuffy returned to their village claiming Wild Cat had sold him into slavery. The Seminole chief had tricked him, Cuffy insisted, by asking him to cross the Rio Grande and help out in America as an interpreter. But, on the north side of the river, Wild Cat instead took his surprised companion into the camp of a slaver and sold the Seminole Negro for eighty or a hundred pesos. Eventually, Cuffy escaped and made his way back to Nacimiento. Now he wanted Wild Cat punished.

The Seminole chief wasn't punished, of course. Wild Cat never denied Cuffy's story, instead treating it as something beneath his dignity to discuss. It would have made no sense for the Seminole Negro to demand Wild Cat pay Cuffy some sort of indemnity, or even apologize. He wouldn't do either, and his refusal would only have split the Indian and black communities further.

But there was one lingering, negative effect besides increased ill will between the two camps. On at least two occasions, when the Seminole came to fetch Seminole Negro warriors for expeditions, they were told that no black men were available. Wild Cat had to carry out the missions with only Indian braves. Since he was successful in driving off the raiders, the Mexicans didn't care whether his troops included Seminole Negro or not.

Wild Cat's behavior grew more erractic. In February 1854, citizens of

Eagle Pass charged that the Seminole had stolen dozens of their horses and mules. Confronted by area Mexican authorities, Wild Cat cheerfully admitted he had. But he wouldn't return the stolen property because he'd planned the raid in partnership with the governor of Coahuila. That made the local Mexicans back off, and, apparently, U.S. officials didn't consider the theft important enough to risk an international incident.

Soon, local officials were annoyed with their "border patrol" again. This time, John Horse was the object of their wrath.

In May, the state's governor called for fifty Indians and blacks; they were to follow him somewhere, but he wouldn't give more details. John Horse learned that the warriors were to be used against other Mexicans from Nuevo Leon. The Seminole Negro leader had sworn his people would never participate in Mexican internecine conflicts. Now, he told officials in Coahuila, "We all live in one house. I won't take up my gun and kill you, because you're my brother. And I won't kill someone for you who is also my brother." The clash between the Mexicans went on without participation from the Seminole or Seminole Negro.

At the same time, there were new stirrings on the Texas side of the Rio Grande. Once again, prominent citizen-businessmen were concerned about runaway slaves. In meetings throughout the southern regions of the state, it was decided that the Seminole Negro presence at Nacimiento was chiefly to blame—forgetting that slaves had been fleeing to Mexico and freedom long before the Seminole Negro arrived in 1850.

Hotheads called for another armed expedition to wipe the Seminole Negro out, but peaceful means were explored first. Civic leaders in San Antonio wrote a long, friendly letter to Colonel Emilio Langberg, inspector of northern Mexico's military colonies. What would entice Mexico, the letter writers wondered, to return all runaway slaves to their American masters? Would some amount of money be appropriate? Were there other friendly gestures by concerned Texans that could help resolve the situation? After all, no one wanted to see this unfortunate problem resolved through the use of force.

After the recent problems with Wild Cat and the Seminole Negro,

Langberg wasn't feeling charitable toward the Indians and blacks under his command. Like most Mexicans, he still considered Wild Cat the principal leader of both groups. Perhaps depriving the Seminole chief of some of his black troops would send a useful message about who really was in charge. Langberg wrote back to the Texans that he would consider some sort of new arrangement, perhaps one where Americans would exchange illegally emigrated Mexicans for blacks.

There was a new governor to whom Langberg had to report. General Santiago Vidaurri was gradually wresting Coahuila from the central Mexican government, combining it with Nuevo Leon, which he already administered. Langberg passed along the Texans' request, adding his own enthusiastic endorsement. But Vidaurri was a canny military tactician. He considered the Seminole Negro subservient to the Seminole, but he also realized what good fighters the black warriors were. Escaped slaves formed a useful portion of Nuevo Leon y Coahuila's population. He ordered Langberg to tell the Texans there would be no extradition treaty. Only the respective governments of Nuevo Leon y Coahuila and Texas could conclude such an agreement, Vidaurri stated. A mere Mexican colonel and some self-important Texas ranchers lacked the authority. In fact, the next time Texans or any other Americans crossed into Mexico without permission to chase runaway slaves, Langberg was to use force to repel them.

That wasn't what Langberg or the Texans wanted to hear, but the Americans had another option. Texas governor Elisha M. Pease had just the solution to the problem. A few months earlier, he'd organized a group of Texas Rangers whose sole responsibility was to pursue raiding parties of Comanche and Apache. There were a lot of Indian raids in Texas during 1855. The leader of the Rangers—a legitimate group of battle-toughened state employees, not ex-Ranger mercenaries—was Captain James H. Callahan, who had a considerable reputation as a cold-blooded enforcer of frontier justice. He hated blacks and Indians equally and was known as someone who obeyed orders without question or concern about the rights of others.

Callahan's crack troops were all well-armed with the best modern rifles. They were far more accurate than the lesser models carried by Mexican troops and their Seminole and Seminole Negro allies. The Rangers rode the finest horses and didn't lack for trail supplies. Just over one hundred men served under Callahan's command.

Pease gave Callahan permission to pursue Indian raiders wherever they might flee, including over the Texas border into Mexico. This violated agreements between Mexico and the United States. The Mexican government occasionally allowed American forces to come south of the Rio Grande, but only after receiving prior approval. This time, that wouldn't be the case, and Callahan's Rangers wouldn't even be coming on their own. William R. Henry, a celebrated Indian fighter and slave speculator, got wind of the plan. He and several of his men joined forces with Callahan.

"Now, this was a big fight," Willie Warrior said, sounding excited even though it was a tale he must have told hundreds of times before to school classes and civic groups. "Big, tough Texas Rangers were going to come into Mexico and handle the blacks and Indians. We lose this one, we might as well give up. But we weren't going to lose, no way, because a few of us could always whip up on plenty of them."

Around midnight on October 1, Callahan's force crossed the Rio Grande just a few miles outside of Eagle Pass. They had a flimsy excuse; some Lipan had snatched horses from a nearby Texas ranch. Governor Pease could, and later did, swear that—so far as he knew—the Rangers were only chasing the Indians.

As soon as they were in Mexico, though, Callahan split his troops. The Ranger captain proposed sending his gunslingers to draw out the Seminole and Seminole Negro men near Nacimiento. Henry would then use his forces to capture all the black dependents left behind in the village. They could be sold back in Texas at considerable profit. With most of the black men killed in battle by the Rangers and all the black women and children returned to slavery, the Seminole Negro town would, essentially, no longer exist. That meant slaves in Texas wouldn't be tempted to run there.

But the Seminole Negro weren't taken by surprise. John Horse convinced his warriors to put aside hard feelings and work together with Wild

Cat's braves. A combined force of blacks and Indians ambushed and destroyed Henry's men long before they neared Nacimiento.

Meanwhile, Langberg gathered a formidable army of Mexicans. It was one thing for the Texans to propose a businesslike, peaceful solution to their slave problem. It was quite another for them to send Texas Rangers into Coahuila without permission. Apparently, Langberg never considered whether attacking Callahan might somehow precipitate another all-out war between America and Mexico. That could have happened—the United States had little regard for Mexico's ability to defend itself, but perhaps what happened to Callahan convinced American leaders otherwise.

Callahan sent another pack of gunmen to attack Wild Cat's camp, but he was thwarted again. A combined Seminole–Seminole Negro force fought off the intruders. But Callahan still had the bulk of his men, and, whatever bad qualities he possessed, he wasn't a coward. He'd started a fight, and he intended to finish it with a flourish, so he and his men fell on Piedras Negras. The citizens there weren't prepared for an attack. On October 4, Callahan and his troops occupied the town. Callahan sent a message back across the Rio Grande exaggerating his exploits: He had defeated 750 Mexicans, blacks, and Indians, but was now in great peril. He called on all Texans to rush into Mexico and join him. But no one felt compelled to rescue Callahan, whose own written words about fighting "Mexicans" proved he and his Rangers weren't on an Indian-hunting expedition.

The next day, Callahan's Rangers looked out over the muzzles of their rifles to see more than seven hundred Mexican soldiers and Seminole and Seminole Negro warriors gathered outside Piedras Negras. Outnumbered seven to one, the Rangers were ready to run back to Texas. But recent rains had swollen the Rio Grande, and they couldn't swim their horses across. Grimly, the Mexicans, Indians, and blacks prepared to attack.

Perhaps responding to a request by Pease, soldiers from Fort Duncan suddenly appeared on the northern river bank. Their presence sent a message: If and when the Rangers were forced out of Piedras Negras, their pursuers should not think about crossing the Rio Grande after them.

On October 6, Callahan and his men escaped back to Texas. How they escaped is open to debate. American historians generally disagree with Seminole Negro tribal legend. Somehow, the town of Piedras Negras erupted in flames. The Rangers used the cover of smoke to make their way across the Rio Grande. Callahan later bragged he'd ordered his men to set fire to the town, figuring the enemies all around him would concentrate on putting out the flames and saving as many of the Piedras Negras citizens and buildings as they could, instead of chasing after the Rangers. It was, Callahan implied, a heroic act, punctuation of a successful attempt to teach the Mexicans a lesson about welcoming escaped slaves.

Tribal storytellers who were there related a different story to Miss Charles and Willie Warrior. Along with the Mexican soldiers and the Seminole warriors, the Seminole Negro in this version were ready on October 6 to overrun Callahan's men in Piedras Negras. Like Santa Anna storming the Alamo, they had enough numerical superiority to overwhelm the defenders, though, since they were facing crack Ranger troops, there would be a heavy cost to their inevitable victory. It had always been the Seminole Negro custom to try to win at the least risk to their own warriors. So, while their Mexican and Indian allies prepared for a costly onslaught, the Seminole Negro lit fire arrows and shot them onto the roofs of the buildings where the Rangers had taken cover. Panic-stricken, the white men ran, and the men surrounding the town quickly extinguished the flames. Callahan was routed, and none of the Seminole Negro—or the Mexicans or Seminole—were lost.

Callahan wasn't quite finished. Back in Texas, he boasted about his triumph in Piedras Negras and began organizing a second invasion. Langberg heard about it and ordered Wild Cat to assemble Seminole and Seminole Negro troops near the place Callahan was expected to cross the Rio Grande. Wild Cat was happy to follow orders; fighting was always more interesting to him than farming. John Horse wasn't available among the blacks—he was away on some other business—so John Kibbetts was asked to put together the Seminole Negro contingent. A few men agreed to come, but more refused. Among the Seminole Negro, Langberg was blamed for Callahan's expedition. If he hadn't encouraged the Texans, they believed, the Rangers would never have come across the Rio Grande.

So Wild Cat took his own men and the few John Kibbetts could muster and rode out to face Callahan. Callahan never came. Apparently, one defeat was enough.

The Seminole Negro refusal to serve troubled Langberg, but Vidaurri generally appreciated what they and the Seminole did for his wartorn province. Toward the end of 1855 and during the early months of 1856, Vidaurri sent staff to Nacimiento. Their instructions were to tutor both the Indians and blacks on the latest farming methods, to instruct them in religion, and to teach those who wanted to learn how to read and write. The Seminole were less interested in these new opportunities than the Seminole Negro, who were particularly pleased to have the opportunity to become literate.

Vidaurri ingratiated himself at Nacimiento in other ways. Once, when he requested warriors to repel invading Indians, he arranged for the families they left behind to be taken to a nearby ranch so they'd be protected while their men were away.

But what Vidaurri would not do was give complete ownership of the Nacimiento property to the Seminole and Seminole Negro. Their right to live there had originally been certified by the Mexican president, but they still remained as guests of the government, employees essentially earning long-term squatting rights. It was a situation that especially troubled John Horse. Though there was never any indication the Mexicans might someday evict the Seminole Negro, it was clear that they could.

Then, in 1856, things in Nacimiento turned bad, and quickly. Many Seminole Negro men began to refuse to go on government-assigned missions. They would say they were needed in the fields. The Seminole kept going to fight, and they resented the blacks' absence. Certainly, the Seminole Negro knew they were endangering their position with the Mexicans. If they didn't help protect the border, why would Mexico give them land? John Horse was no fool. Ben Pingenot suggested that they were perhaps conducting an unofficial strike until Vidaurri gave them their land outright. But, probably, the crux of the problem was that the Seminole Negro no longer wanted to associate with, let along fight alongside, most of the Seminole.

The Indians had never stopped treating the blacks as subordinates. They made it clear every day that they still wanted, even if they no longer expected, the Seminole Negro to plow Indian fields and pay tribute to the Seminole by donating portions of their own crops to the Indian tribe. Another element was the continued influx of escaped slaves and a few free blacks into the Seminole Negro community. These men and women had never lived under Seminole rule. Lacking that tradition, they also lacked respect for the Indians. Their refusal to kowtow in even the smallest ways inspired the other Seminole Negro to act the same. Only John Horse's friendship with Wild Cat was left to keep the two tribes even marginally allied.

Even that friendship was fated to end. The Indians had always been susceptible to diseases carried by other races. A smallpox epidemic struck northern Mexico late in 1856. It devastated native villages, and eventually reached Nacimiento. The Seminole camp was infected first. The Seminole Negro seemed to suffer less; historians believe their better diets may have strengthened their immune systems. Only two Seminole Negro died of smallpox during the outbreak. In the Seminole camp, though, bodies stacked up like firewood. Someone set up a primitive vaccination program to try to save as many of the Indians as possible. About one-fourth of the Seminole died. These included twenty-eight women, twenty-five warriors, and Coyote, a subchief who had challenged Wild Cat for tribal leadership.

But the smallpox killed Wild Cat, too. With him died any hope that the Seminole–Seminole Negro alliance would hold together much longer.

chapter nine

ON A FREEZING Saturday morning in March 2001, Clarence Ward addressed a few dozen SISCA members huddled together for warmth in the scout association's tiny Brackettville park. Someone had built a small fire, but its flames were no match for the howling wind. It doesn't get cold too often in Brackettville, but when the northers do come howling in there are no buffering trees or hills to stop them from venting their full fury on the drab little town.

But Clarence had called people out anyway for a short ceremony. Ground was being broken for two outdoor toilets, so that association members and guests gathering in the park for programs wouldn't have to hustle to nearby gas stations every time their kidneys grew cramped. "This is a big thing for us," he told me on the phone a few weeks earlier, when he'd called to invite me down. "I want you to see for yourself that we're moving forward, getting things done."

Now, in the park, his teeth chattering a little, Clarence made a few formal remarks. He told the small crowd that they should feel proud of this important accomplishment, which proved the association was looking to the future. The bathrooms would be finished in time for Seminole Days in September, he promised, and then he named area businesses that promised to donate materials—one company was to give concrete mix, another some of the pipes: "We appreciate their help in accomplishing our important goals. Now, let's get to it—who remembered to bring a camera?"

Two hands went up. Clarence sidled over to me and whispered, "The newspaper here will run a picture if we take one and give it to them. Very important to my members." He pointed to a pile of shovels and said loudly, "Now, somebody pick those up and get ready to put 'em in the ground. Then we'll take the pictures."

"You be in it, Clarence," somebody suggested, and Clarence beamed.

"If you insist," he replied, and took one of the shovels. He and some of the others posed with the edges of their shovel blades just touching the hard-packed frozen dirt. The two Instamatics clicked, and Clarence asked his photographers to "quick snap off the rest of those rolls" so he could take them to a drugstore to be developed. After a few parting words, reminding everyone that the Brackettville paper would certainly run its story by the next weekend, Clarence hollered for everybody to go home

Clarence Ward, president of the Scout Association, at Seminole Days 2000

(PHOTO BY RALPH LAUER)

and get warm. While they scattered to the pickup trucks parked outside the park's chain-link fence, Clarence kicked dirt on the fire and thanked me for coming.

"This is what we're needing to do," he said. "Activities, growth things. I got critics telling me it's all the history, the history, the history, and I don't dispute that. But the fact is, the years have gone by and nothing new ever got done. You got the old members dying off, and the younger ones just standing around. I'm sorry Mr. Warrior and some of his people don't agree with me all the time, but their history won't mean anything if there's no association left to carry it on. I'm just trying my best, you know?"

"Why don't you and Willie sit down and talk it out?" I asked. "It shouldn't be that hard."

"I hope we will," Clarence said noncommitally. "I'd always be ready to do that, if he asked."

Later on that day, I visited with Willie. He was disdainful of the new park restrooms: "You can't put toilets so close to the barbecue pits," he jeered. "It's unsanitary. Typical Clarence. Decides what he wants to do and does it whether it makes sense or not."

"He'd like to talk to you, I think. Would you sit down with him?"

"Who knows, but what good would it do? He wouldn't listen, anyway."

Willie and I spent the rest of the day talking about the Seminole Negro in Mexico and what happened after Wild Cat died. I couldn't help but compare the life-or-death drama there in 1856 with the apparently trivial spat currently dividing the modern-day Seminole Negro. The bitter estrangement between the Seminole and Seminole Negro in Nacimiento had an understandable, if regrettable, dimension. But as with Willie and Clarence, such estrangements could only be remedied if both sides wanted reconciliation, and after Wild Cat's death there was no Seminole leader left for John Horse to consider a friend and ally.

"When Wild Cat died, that was the beginning of the end for the Seminole Negro in Mexico," Ben Pingenot said in 1994. "Wild Cat was the one who'd worked out the original deal with the Mexican government. Without him in charge of the Seminole, it was only a matter of time before relations between the Indians and blacks were going to get untenable. And, of course, the young chief the Seminole selected to succeed Wild Cat as their leader had nothing but contempt for John Horse and the Seminole Negro. They were sending a clear message when they picked Lion as their leader."

John Horse mourned Wild Cat. He had loved him in a pragmatic way, by recognizing and acknowledging his flaws while still appreciating his better qualities. But he desperately missed Wild Cat for more than personal reasons. Though the Seminole Negro were no longer enthusiastic about fighting for the Mexicans, they didn't want to move on, either. To the north, there were the slavers and Rangers of Texas; to the south, a Mexico that placed little value on black immigrants who weren't in their country to fight Indians. John Horse was wise enough to know the Seminole Negro still needed a relationship, if not friendship, with the Seminole Wild Cat had led.

So he was greatly concerned about the new chief elected by the Seminole to replace Wild Cat. John Horse and most of the Seminole Negro had expected them to choose Bear Leader, who, even if he lacked the charisma of his deceased kinsman, at least was sympathetic to the blacks. Instead, the Seminole turned to a younger warrior named Lion. No one knew much about him, except that he didn't care for the Seminole Negro.

In early 1857, not long after Wild Cat's death, Lion organized an expedition against Apache raiders. He didn't lead the Seminole himself, trusting that duty to another Indian named Juan Flores. John Horse, no doubt hoping to mend relationships, brought along several Seminole Negro. He and Juan Flores jointly commanded the warriors. Working together, the Indians and blacks managed to recapture seven horses—not a particularly distinguished haul, but still something. If the Seminole Negro had continued to join the Seminole on missions, perhaps Lion and his lieutenants might have warmed to them, at least a little. But even John Horse couldn't convince the black warriors to go out again. They had farming chores. They didn't like the Seminole. They knew the Seminole didn't like them. So they stayed in Nacimiento.

In 1858, Lion requested a meeting with Vidaurri. He told the governor the relationship between the Seminole and Seminole Negro had to change. For one thing, the blacks no longer went out to fight, which was bad enough. Worse, though, was the way their farmlands increased in size and fertility. Seminole men were often away, fighting, and so the Indians' untended farms suffered while the Seminole Negro men and their families grew fat after abundant harvests. The larger Seminole Negro farms needed—and *used*—much more water than those of the poor, suffering Seminole. Lion also related charges from an area *alcalde* that black newcomers were stealing Mexican cattle. What the new Seminole chief wanted from Vidaurri was an order that "the Negroes subject themselves to the care and command of the Seminole chiefs as they were previously under the command of the (Wild) Cat."

Vidaurri listened, then issued a new edict. From now on, the Seminole Negro must fight when requested to do so. They were to expel any bad runaways from their ranks. If they couldn't keep their own people in line, Vidaurri would. From now on, any Seminole Negro shirking duty on expeditions or committing crimes would be hauled off to Monterrey as prisoners sentenced to hard labor. In the future, a Mexican judge would arbitrate disputes between the Seminole and Seminole Negro regarding land and water rights.

"You can't blame the Mexicans for laying down those rules like that," Willie Warrior said in the summer of 2000. "They figured they had a contract with us, and we weren't living up to it. But those Seminole had it in for us all the time, just all the time. Still do. You know what's going on in Oklahoma right now?"

I didn't.

"Those Seminole are throwing our people out of their tribe," Willie snapped. "After the Civil War, the blacks still up in Indian Territory got taken into the Seminole as full members of the tribe. You knew that part, right? Okay. Couple years ago, the government admitted the first Florida treaty was a crock and gave more than $50 million to the Seminole to make up for it. Those Seminole didn't want our people to get a cent of it.

So they said the money would only go to descendants of tribe members in 1823, and in 1823 the blacks were still slaves, not members. They're screwing black descendants out of a share."

"That sounds pretty bad," I said, thinking he might be exaggerating, or least inadvertantly have some of the story wrong.

"Pretty bad's the way we always get treated." Willie said. "That mess up in Oklahoma has nothing to do with us in Texas, except for it's part of our family getting screwed. Our people up there are fighting it. Who knows?"

Six months later, the front page of *The New York Times* carried a long story under the headline "Who Is a Seminole, and Who Gets to Decide?" The story noted that the Seminole's fifteen thousand full-blooded Indian members had voted two thousand Seminole Negro out of the tribe completely and were keeping every cent of the government's $56 million settlement for themselves. The Seminole Negro who'd been booted out had brought suit. The case was dragging through the U.S. courts. When I told Willie about the story, he shook his head

"You'd think we'd been kicked around enough already," he said sadly.

Back in Mexico in 1857, the Seminole also decided to separate themselves from the Seminole Negro. It happened about a year after Vidaurri's ruling. At first, the Seminole Negro joined the Seminole on one or two minor expeditions, but mostly they stayed on their farms. This infuriated the Seminole, but, for a while at least, Vidaurri was too busy elsewhere to monitor problems between his hired Indians and blacks. The Mexican War of Reform was tearing the country apart as liberals and conservatives battled for control of the central government. The Seminole were chasing Indian raiders and the Seminole Negro never interfered in internal Mexican strife, so Vidaurri didn't call on them for help. While his attention was diverted, the Seminole looked north for relief.

Word had reached Nacimiento that things were dramatically different back in Indian Territory. About five years after Wild Cat moved south, commissioner of Indian Affairs George W. Moneypenny studied the situation and concluded that "the Seminoles of the West have been denationalized, and in a manner degraded, by being placed among the Creeks and made subject to their laws. They felt the humiliation of their position, which not only discouraged them but engendered a recklessness of disposition and conduct."

If the Seminole in Indian Territory were spared any obligation to the Creek, Moneypenny believed, then the few hundred Seminole left in Florida might finally be willing to move west. That would please white Florida citizens who had railed for years about the savages in their midst. So in August 1856, the Seminole in Indian Territory were legally separated from the Creek. They were given new land in Indian Territory and allowed to live under their own tribal laws.

The news took a long time to trickle down to Nacimiento, but when it did, the Seminole there were intrigued. In the fall of 1858, when problems between his people and the Seminole Negro were at their most pronounced, Lion sent three braves north to Indian Territory. They met with Seminole leaders there, who assured them that, yes, their tribe was now completely independent. Why didn't the Seminole down in Mexico come back home?

The Seminole in Nacimiento had no particular reason to stay. Mexico was being shattered by civil war. Who knew which side would win, and, afterward, how would whoever was in power feel about hired Indian border guards? Besides, the Seminole Negro were proving themselves useless in battle and greedy in matters of land and water. Lion made discreet inquiries; by September, his people received permission from the American government to return to the United States.

The citizens of Musquiz, the region in which the Seminole and Seminole Negro lived, didn't want their Indian protectors to leave. They promised all sorts of inducements, including extra guns and other supplies, but Lion declared he was leaving, taking with him any of his people who wanted to go.

Did John Horse plead with Lion to stay? Seminole Negro tribal legend makes no mention of it if he did. Miss Charles said she had no idea. Certainly John Horse knew the Seminole departure would put new pressure on the Seminole Negro. Now, if the Mexicans required protection from raiders, they'd send their orders directly to the blacks instead of the Indians. That situation would test John Horse's strength as a leader. If he ordered his reluctant men to fight, would they obey? And, if they didn't, how would the Mexicans react?

But John Horse also realized the relationship between the Seminole and Seminole Negro was beyond repair. Ever since General Jesup first split the allies in Florida by promising freedom to whichever blacks voluntarily left their Indian masters and surrendered to the army, things had never been the same. Wild Cat, for all his faults, had generally recognized the advantages of keeping the factions together, but Lion didn't and never would. Perhaps it was better for everyone if the Seminole went back to America, while the Seminole Negro worked out whatever their new status was to be with the eventual winner of the Mexican civil war.

When, in February 1859, Lion and the first four dozen Seminole set out on the return trip to Indian Territory—it would take almost two years for all but a few of the Indians to leave—none of the Seminole Negro came out to wish them well on their journey.

Only a few weeks later, the Seminole Negro learned about another, unexpected consequence of the Seminole departure from Nacimiento. An officer from Fort Duncan crossed the Rio Grande to meet with Mexican officials in Piedras Negras. Texas slavers were organizing another raid on Nacimiento, he told them. These Texans believed that, with many of the Seminole warriors already gone and the rest rumored to be leaving, the Seminole Negro would be easier pickings than they'd proven for James H. Callahan. Vidaurri was infuriated by this news. He already had his hands full in the Mexican civil war—he was backing the liberals and Benito Juarez. It was a particularly bad time for the liberals. The conservatives had gained control of Mexico City. Vidaurri's troops were needed further south than Nacimiento. If the slavers attacked, he would either be forced to use some of his soldiers to defend the blacks, or else let the Seminole Negro fend for themselves and possibly be wiped out.

The slaver attack, if one was ever actually planned instead of only rumored, never happened. But Vidaurri still decided that Nacimiento was too close to the Rio Grande for the Seminole Negro to ever be safe from slavers there, particularly now that the Seminole were leaving. So John Horse's people, he decreed, must pack and move three hundred miles south to Laguna de Parras, a province still in Coahuila but far removed from the Rio Grande. There were plenty of Indian attacks to be beaten off in Parras, Vidaurri said, and there was no shortage of land and water for the Seminole Negro.

Vidaurri had more than Seminole Negro safety in mind. Their years of toil in the fields had made their Nacimiento farmlands especially fertile. Several wealthy Mexican families were interested in acquiring the property. Not much earlier, one of them had even come forward with a claim to much of the Seminole Negro land, initiating an argument that was only settled by Vidaurri promising John Horse his people would never have to leave unless it was of their own free will.

Now, they weren't really being given a choice. Vidaurri claimed he was acting in their best interests, and, in some ways, it was hard to argue. Without the Seminole, the Seminole Negro were more vulnerable to slaver raids. Certainly, their Mexican neighbors near Nacimiento disliked them. But they'd also worked long and hard on "their" land, which they now were reminded wasn't really theirs at all. They'd have to start all over again in Laguna de Parras. Eventually, they deferred to Vidaurri. It was better to have some land somewhere in Mexico, where they were free, than to risk losing land and freedom entirely.

The Seminole Negro and their wagons had hardly disappeared over the horizon when Vidaurri turned the bulk of Nacimiento's fertile land over to a powerful local family. The new owners immediately declared that the remaining Seminole had to either get out or make do with less property. Combined with several Indian raids on their village, the Seminole found this final insult to be enough. By August 1861, they had all gone back to America, where their people in Indian Territory made an agreement to support the Confederacy. The last straggling Seminole to cross the Rio Grande back into Texas were escorted the rest of the way to Indian Territory by Confederate soldiers. The Seminole, to the last, condoned slavery.

Down in Laguna de Parras, the Seminole Negro were homesick for Nacimiento. About four hundred of them had been moved south, with those from Nacimiento soon joined in Parras by a much smaller group of runaway Creek blacks led by Elijah Daniels. Daniels, like John Horse, was exceptionally intelligent. He spoke several languages—probably English, Spanish, Creek, Seminole, and perhaps some Gullah—and soon became one of John Horse's most trusted lieutenants. John Horse needed all the help he could get. While the Seminole and Seminole Negro had offered some deterrent around Nacimiento, Apache and Comanche were used to raiding Laguna de Parras with relative impunity. Now the Seminole Negro had to go out and fight by themselves, instead of relying on the Seminole to do most of that bloody work.

Their struggles with invading Indians, principally Apache, weren't confined to chasing after them. The Indians now attacked the Seminole Negro village and farmlands at Parras on a regular basis. Thomas Factor, a prominent Seminole Negro warrior, was killed during one of these raids. Several women and children were murdered or kidnapped. When the Seminole Negro men went after their attackers, they often suffered as many casualties as they inflicted. It was a bad time, made worse by national Mexican turmoil.

The civil war, or the War of the Reform, split the country from 1858 through 1861. Benito Juarez and his liberals eventually won, but they took over a government riddled by debt. Desperate, Juarez suspended debt repayments to foreign powers. He intended a two-year moratorium, but Spain, England, and France weren't willing to wait. They formed the so-called "Triple Alliance" and, in December 1861, sent troops into Mexico with orders to collect whatever money they could. There were 6,000 soldiers from Spain, 700 from England and 2,000 from France—enough to get Juarez's attention. He offered to negotiate; Spain and England came to relatively quick repayment agreements, but the French were after more than money. In the spring of 1862, just as Spanish and British troops pulled out, another 4,500 French soldiers landed in Mexico in a full-scale attempt to conquer the country. With its own civil war raging, America kept out of the Mexican fray.

Within a year, the French occupied Mexico City and Juarez was forced to flee. For the next five years, he presided over a government in exile. Austrian archduke Ferdinand Maximilian von Hapsburg, brother of the

Austro-Hungarian emperor, was installed as emperor of Mexico. He apparently meant to be a benevolent ruler. He ardently supported freedom of the press and separation of church and state. But Juarez remained at large to oppose him, and Maximilian's French troops were merciless in putting down even suspected revolts among the Mexican people. By some accounts, as many as fifty thousand Mexicans were executed for treason during Maximilian's three-year reign.

In Parras, the Seminole Negro soon had to make their peace with Mexico's new rulers. Saltillo, the Coahuila province that included Laguna de Parras, was occupied by the French in August 1864. Juarez fled through the area just before the French arrived. Seminole Negro tribal legend, at least as related by Miss Charles, has Juarez stopping off to chat with John Horse, who asked for the old Nacimiento land back and was promised it would be returned if Juarez ever controlled Mexico again. This may be more fable than fact. Juarez had more important things on his mind than the welfare of four hundred marginal blacks. But John Horse could no longer turn to Vidaurri for help; the governor of Nuevo Leon–Coahuila had fled from the French to Texas.

"Like always, we had nobody to help us but ourselves," Willie Warrior said. "The Mexicans were running and the French were coming. So old John Horse goes out to meet 'em, and sets 'em straight."

The invading French began systematically burning farms in the Laguna area, apparently in retaliation for the region's support of Juarez. Eventually, they came to the Seminole Negro settlement at Parras. Over the course of four years, the blacks had made the best of their water-limited circumstances there. Their new farmlands were far less developed than the ones they'd left behind in Nacimiento, but they still didn't want them destroyed by the French. John Horse, accompanied by his son Joe Coon and at least one other Seminole Negro warrior, rode out to meet the French commander. They explained the Seminole Negro policy of not getting involved in Mexican politics or internal warfare. They weren't fighting for Juarez against the French. Instead, they were protecting Mexicans from the Indians. All they wanted was for their current property to be spared.

The French commander agreed; in fact, since Maximilian had turned Nacimiento over to one of his own supporters, it seemed that if France kept control of Mexico the Seminole Negro might be permitted to return there. If anything could have tempted John Horse to throw in with the French, it would have been that inducement.

He didn't. His people remained neutral. Juarez continued to oppose Maximilian, and the Seminole Negro tended their farms in Parras and fought off Indians. By late 1866, the French had enough. The American Civil War was over, and the United States began pressuring France to get out of Mexico. As soon as the French troops were called home, Juarez counterattacked Maximilian. By May 1867, Juarez was back in power and Maximilian had been executed. On behalf of the restored Mexican government, John Horse was presented with a silver saddle, spurring later conjecture that he actually fought on behalf of Juarez against the French. In fact, the gift was probably meant to reinforce the longstanding agreement between the Mexican government and the Seminole Negro. Though the Mexican and American civil wars were over, the Apache were still raiding across the Rio Grande on a regular basis. Without the Seminole, the Seminole Negro were the Mexican government's best option for curtailing the raids, though it was obviously going to be impossible to shut them down completely.

But now the Seminole Negro had internal problems of their own. For the first time, the tribe had a significant geographic split. While John Horse and about two hundred blacks stayed at Parras, John Kibbetts and some one hundred followers moved back north to Nacimiento.

It was inevitable that, sometime or another, John Horse would be challenged for leadership of the Seminole Negro. In 1866, when John Kibbetts's followers moved to Nacimiento, John Horse was in his mid-fifties. He'd led his people for more than twenty years, going all the way back to Florida when he encouraged Seminole Negro to accept Jesup's flawed offer of freedom. During John Horse's tenure, his people had suffered a great deal, though through no fault of his. With the French gone—Juarez had regained control of Parras before Maximilian's flight and subsequent execution—Mexico was more or less internally at peace. The American

Civil War was over. There was no longer slavery in the United States. That ended the threat in Nacimiento of slavers sneaking over the border looking for Seminole Negro to catch and sell back across the Rio Grande. The land in Nacimiento was far better for farming than the property occupied by the Seminole Negro in Parras. So, even if John Horse was reluctant to move back north, at least for the time being, John Kibbetts was glad to lead those who wanted to go. It wasn't an unpleasant parting. John Horse and John Kibbetts remained on good terms. John Horse, though, would never be undisputed leader of the Seminole Negro again.

We know a few things about John Kibbetts, mostly from Seminole Negro legends related by Willie Warrior and Miss Charles, and from American military records. By all accounts he was shrewd, a gifted leader who was not above challenging authority. But he also exemplifies how history is inexact—for one thing, there isn't complete agreement on how he spelled his name. Historians choose between "Kibbetts" and "Kibbitts." He was eventually sworn into U.S. military service as "John Kibbitt." He may have identified himself all three ways. "Kibbetts" is how Miss Charles said his name should be spelled.

The Kibbetts group wasn't the only one to leave Parras. Elijah Daniels and his people moved back into Texas just as soon as the threat of slavers was gone. They settled in Uvalde County, fifty or sixty miles from Del Rio, the nearest town of any significance. A half-dozen other Seminole Negro families relocated to Matamoros, a Mexican village just across the Rio Grande from the Texas town of Brownsville.

Still, John Kibbetts's followers were the most significant defectors. Reclaiming the former Seminole Negro land in Nacimiento would have been an important step in luring even more blacks north from Parras and John Horse. But things in Nacimiento weren't the way John Kibbetts had expected.

There were Indians, a lot of them, living on or near the land claimed by the Seminole Negro as their own. A year earlier, almost one thousand Kickapoo had come south from Kansas, fleeing the last violence of the Civil War. They were welcomed by the people of Musquiz, who hoped the Kickapoo presence might serve as a deterrent to raiding Apache. The newcomers were given nine thousand acres for farming and hunting. They weren't willing to hand it over to the returning Seminole Negro.

There were black families living in Nacimiento, too. The forced departure of the Seminole Negro seven years earlier hadn't stopped runaway American slaves from arriving, then staying. About sixty of them now lived in Nacimiento, paying rent by sharing their crops with the Mexicans.

Though he'd just left his old leader, John Kibbetts immediately turned to John Horse for help. Together, they petitioned the Mexican government for the return of the Nacimiento land, or at least acreage equivalent to that given to the Kickapoo. Their argument was that the Seminole Negro had bought the land with their blood, only to have it taken from them by Vidaurri. Representatives of Juarez were sympathetic. Terms of the old 1852 agreement were reestablished. The Seminole Negro would again be granted land in Nacimiento; in return, they would provide border protection. Things would be as they had been.

Almost immediately, they weren't. The Seminole Negro in Nacimiento weren't pleased with their new property; it didn't seem as fertile as the nearby area they'd previously occupied. Much of the problem was that they didn't want to have to start over, clearing and planting land. It seemed that every time they did try to settle in and begin planting, the Mexicans expected them to drop their hoes and rush off to track raiding Apache. Now, for the first time, the Seminole Negro began accusing Mexicans of stealing their livestock. It might have been true; the native farmers in the area were trying to recover from the war, too. Their stock needed replenishment and Seminole Negro horses and cattle were tempting.

Within months, it became clear that most of the remaining Seminole Negro weren't going to ever be happy in Mexico. In Parras, families still considered the settlement there to be a temporary place to live, but Nacimiento no longer seemed welcoming, either. John Kibbetts and his people in Nacimiento wanted to farm, not fight, but fighting was required of them if they stayed.

So . . . what about America?

In 1850, the Seminole Negro had fled south to escape slavery—to the Seminole, to the Creek, to white Americans. After the Civil War, that was no longer a problem. Back in Indian Territory, they believed, blacks formerly owned by Indians now lived among them as equals. And, despite its recent internecine conflict, America was certainly more politically stable than Mexico. South of the Rio Grande, the Seminole Negro had been able to avoid throwing in on one side or the other in every civil dispute, but as long as the Mexican government kept changing there was always the chance some president or other would decide the Seminole Negro services were no longer needed and throw them out of Nacimiento or Parras.

John Kibbetts in particular was intrigued by a possible move back to Indian Territory. He sent his son Bob north to investigate. Bob's report was positive. There were black communities adjacent to, but separate from, Seminole camps. Blacks had the same rights as Indians; the relationship between the races seemed strong.

At the same time, the U.S. government began encouraging the Seminole Negro to return. After the Civil War, American military concerns focused on Indians. In particular, the southwest was a trouble spot. Many of the raiders who plagued settlers used the Rio Grande as a buffer, attacking Americans and then fleeing south across the river to hide in Mexico. As far as the United States was concerned, the Kickapoo in Nacimiento were a potential threat. So were these Seminole Negro, who supposedly helped the Mexicans protect their border but who, in the near-twenty years they'd been in Mexico, had constantly been accused of sneaking across the river to steal American stock. Following the Civil War, U.S. military ranks had been depleted as soldiers who'd fought on both sides left to return home. America didn't have enough soldiers to adequately defend its southwestern borders and fight off Indians preying on Texans. Somehow, the threat had to be reduced.

A committee of Texas businessmen lent its services to the effort. The Texans asked S. S. Brown to go to Nacimiento and tell the Seminole Negro and Kickapoo they were welcome back in America, though the Texans hoped the blacks would go back to Indian Territory instead of resettling in Texas. The Kickapoo could return to Kansas, or wherever it was they originally came from. Brown met with John Kibbetts and other Seminole Negro leaders in July 1868. There is no record of what was discussed, but

Brown undoubtedly stressed the abolition of slavery and the continued inability of Mexico to develop a stable, long-term government. If he was smart, he also emphasized that Seminole Negro living in America wouldn't be required to earn their keep by fighting Indians. Instead, the blacks could live out their longtime dream of living free and farming.

Certainly, the Seminole Negro wanted to know about land. Would they be given any? Would it be theirs forever, not just a place on which they lived until someone decided to take it from them? Brown represented Texas business interests, not the U.S. government. He couldn't promise anything.

So nothing could be resolved. Kibbetts and his people said they'd consider moving back. Brown returned to Texas. Seminole Negro life in Mexico went on. Relations between the blacks and Kickapoo in Nacimiento turned poisonous. Each resented the presence of the other. Then another smallpox epidemic struck. Many Kickapoo died, and this time the disease killed quite a few Seminole Negro, too. By early 1870, more and more of John Kibbetts's people told him that they wanted to leave Mexico and move back to Indian Territory.

In the next weeks and months, Kibbetts met with army officers and negotiated his people's return. The agreement under which they came back to Texas is still argued about; it will be as long as anyone remembers the Seminole Negro. Subsequent years of honorable, often glorious service eventually ended disastrously for the tribe, all because of either misunderstandings or deliberate misrepresentations during the spring and summer of 1870. Seminole Negro storytellers and modern-day U.S. historians have radically different versions of what happened. No one can be entirely certain.

What we do know is that, after twenty years in Mexico, the Seminole Negro were eager, not just willing, to return to the United States. They'd tested and discovered the limits of their "freedom" south of the Rio Grande. Yes, they were allotted land and allowed to cultivate it. They'd known from the outset they were expected to regularly take up arms on behalf of their hosts. From their first negotiations with Wild Cat and John

Horse, Inspector General Jaurequi and Colonel Maldonado made that clear.

They hadn't expected to be moved so often—from El Moral, where they were content, to Nacimiento, where they were happy with the land if not their neighbors, and to Parras. The Seminole Negro had come to Mexico for freedom—and for land of their own, which to these descendants of slaves, was the one undisputable symbol of freedom. Denied that security, they could never be satisfied.

So, obviously, their desire to move back to America wasn't motivated only by the new absence of U.S. slavery. They wanted what everyone else—the white Americans, the Mexicans, the Creek and Seminole in Indian Territory—had: land. Property to live on and cultivate in perpetuity for their own benefit. Freedom without land translated into ongoing servitude, always working for someone else, slavery in practice if not in name. Despite their increasing reluctance to chase raiding Indians on behalf of the Mexican government, the Seminole Negro had never been adverse to earning their keep. They would approach their new alliance with the Americans as a business deal.

Business deals of any era are subject to misunderstandings. In his negotiations with the Americans, John Kibbetts didn't have a staff of lawyers at his side advising him. No one, apparently, wrote anything down. Men sat and talked and probably drank while they bargained. Trying to discern what was promised to John Kibbetts and what was merely assumed by him, we can only rely on Seminole Negro legend and scattered American military correspondence, some of which indicates officials in Washington didn't even realize their representatives in Texas were negotiating with blacks instead of Indians.

Still, no moment in Seminole Negro history is more critical. It began in the spring of 1870, when Captain Jacob DeGress, commander of Fort Duncan in Eagle Pass, decided to approach the Seminole Negro again about leaving Mexico to return to Indian Territory.

chapter ten

SAN ANGELO is a medium-sized city on the edge of the dusty West Texas plains, about two hundred miles north and slightly west of Brackettville. When the United States built a series of forts as a line of defense against the Apache and Comanche, San Angelo was a logical location for one. Fort Concho became famous as the base of the Buffalo Soldiers, black post–Civil War recruits who earned their famous nickname from the Indians, when their foes likened their hair to the curly topknots found between a buffalo's horns.

Most of the forts have been preserved in some form or another. Fort Concho is the jewel. Unlike Fort Duncan, which is an out-of-the-way afterthought in modern-day Eagle Pass, or Fort Clark, which has morphed into a sprawling golf course/residential community, Fort Concho is mostly preserved as it was—the long barracks, the immaculate parade ground, the dispensary, the schoolhouse. Knowledgeable docents, wearing authentic uniforms, guide visitors around. The official name now is the Fort Concho Museum and Historical Grounds. Director Robert Bluthardt is a walking encyclopedia on all things having to do with the frontier military. He'd invited me to meet with him and Ross McSwain, an eminent Texas historian living in San Angelo, to talk about the Seminole Negro scouts and the agreement they'd made to serve the American army.

"Certainly there has been controversy attached to that situation," Bluthardt said. He, McSwain, and I sat in his Fort Concho office. "There is, of course, the Seminole Negro version. There are rumors of some sort of army documentation, though none has been discovered. And we know, too, what the army in those days usually would and wouldn't offer in return for scouting services."

Miss Charles and Willie Warrior were always adamant about what was offered—permanent title to land, probably back in Indian Territory but acceptable almost anywhere, in return for a period of enlistment as Indian scouts for the Seminole Negro men. Their older relatives, who'd been part of the tribe at that time, swore to them there was never any question about it.

Outside historians—Bluthardt, McSwain, Ben Pingenot, Max and Cissy Lale—had their own ideas, which involved elements of outright U.S. duplicity, wrongly assumed powers of negotiation on the part of certain army officers, or misunderstandings by John Kibbetts and other Seminole Negro leaders.

"The one truth of it is, the Seminole Negro thought something had been agreed to, and they acted on that belief," Ross McSwain said. "Now, I know Miss Charles. We've talked about this. She's got her ideas about it. But on this misunderstanding, if that's what it was, the fate of those black Seminoles turned. We're never going to know exactly what happened, what was said, what was promised."

Bluthardt opened up the Fort Concho library to me, which contained copies of some military documents and many, many articles about the Seminole Negro that had appeared in obscure military publications and civilian magazines. Along with material from Ben Pingenot's library, a few scholarly books about the Seminole Negro, and Max and Cissy Lale's voluminous collection, there was enough marginal documentation to provide a picture of what happened from the army perspective. Miss Charles and Willie Warrior filled in the Seminole Negro side, repeating what they'd been told by their parents and other older relatives who were privy to John Kibbetts's version of the negotiating process.

In the end, it becomes a matter of who and what we want to believe.

On March 17, 1870, Captain Jacob DeGress, commanding officer of Fort Duncan in Eagle Pass, sent a letter to General Clay Wood, assistant adjutant general of the army's Fifth Military District headquarters in San Antonio.

"Sir," wrote DeGress, who liked to adorn his correspondence with extraneous capital letters, "I have the honor to inform you that the Chief of the remaining Seminoles in Mexico, John Kibbett, came to this Post this morning for the purpose of getting permission to move to the Seminole Reservation in Arkansas, and to receive subsistence and forage for his people and horses while in transit. He states that his Tribe, consisting of about one hundred people, is poor, but willing to work.

"They are mostly blacks and moved to Mexico under the Seminole Chief Wild Cat . . . I most respectfully ask the approval of the Major General Commanding of my action so far, and instructions as to what shall be done in case of Seminoles com(ing) over agreeably to my promise."

DeGress added that the Kickapoo in Mexico wanted to move back to the United States, too.

On March 25, Wood wrote back: "I have the honor to acknowledge the receipt of your communication of the 17th instant in relation to the 'Seminole' and Kickapoo Indians, reporting your action in granting permission to the Seminole tribe to cross the Rio Grande and camp on . . . Fort Duncan until their request to move to Arkansas, on the Reservation of the Seminoles can be considered and decided upon by the Major General Commanding, and to inform you that your action in the premises is approved."

These letters are early indications that negotiations were in progress, and that higher-ups in the army may not have realized the Seminole Negro were more black than Indian. DeGress certainly points out that they are ("mostly Blacks"), but Wood's response labels them simply as "Seminole." That sort of vagueness characterizes the whole agreement between the Americans and the tribe. It's all bothersome, yet critical; whatever was offered by the United States and accepted by the Seminole Negro became the genesis for disaster forty-four years later—disaster for the tribe, of course, not for the American government. To fully comprehend the awful fate of the Seminole Negro in 1914, we have to try and understand events of 1870.

Miss Charles's version begins with either U.S. Army Captain Frank Perry or Major Zenas Bliss (she didn't know who it was for certain) going to Nacimiento and actively recruiting the Seminole Negro to sign on with the American military as scouts against the Apache, who were now raiding West Texas ranches with particular abandon. According to her, John Kibbetts was intrigued enough to go to Fort Duncan and discuss the possibility. Others believe the Seminole Negro chief approached Captain DeGress. All of them find some area of disagreement, from the spelling of John Kibbetts's name to DeGress's rank, which is variously reported as colonel, lieutenant colonel, and captain.

We do know that the Seminole Negro weren't happy in Nacimiento in 1870. The families following John Kibbetts had returned to their northern Coahuila village only to find Kickapoo ensconced there. Instead of reclaiming fertile farmland, they were being treated like squatters. Many Seminole Negro believed Mexican thieves were stealing their livestock. The Mexican government was in a constant state of upheaval; the tribe had been forced to move twice during twenty years of reasonably faithful service.

For two years, since S. S. Brown's visit in 1868, the Seminole Negro of Nacimiento knew the U.S. government wanted them back on the north side of the Rio Grande. Robert Kibbetts reported after his visit back to Indian Territory that blacks living there among the Seminole were now treated as full citizens. That made a return to Indian Territory appealing—*if* the expatriate tribe was allocated its own land, instead of being placed on the property of someone else.

So it seems only logical that, sometime around March 1870, John Kibbetts saddled his horse and rode to Fort Duncan. He'd been John Horse's second in command for a long time; surely he'd absorbed negotiating tactics by watching such a master at work. Captain DeGress (he was careful, in signing letters, to note he was a brevet, or temporary, lieutenant colonel, which accounts for some historian confusion) would certainly have been pleased to talk with him. Carrying out army policy—in this case, luring south-of-the-border Indians back to the United States—could only have helped an ambitious junior officer's career.

Unlike everyone else involved in the process, DeGress was a thorough chronicler of events. In his March 17 letter to Wood, he goes into some detail. John Kibbetts came to Fort Duncan "for the purpose of getting permission to move." Perry and Bliss succeeded DeGress as commanders of Fort Duncan. They wouldn't have negotiated with John Kibbetts without DeGress's knowledge, and he doesn't mention them in his letter to Wood. That probably means this visit by John Kibbetts was the Seminole Negro chief's idea.

He'd obviously thought carefully about what to ask, undoubtedly after consulting John Horse in Parras. The two weren't enemies, after all. DeGress told Wood that the Seminole Negro wanted permission to come back to Indian Territory and "subsistence and forage for his people and horses while in transit."

At the beginning of negotiations, it was obvious John Kibbetts and the rest of the Nacimiento Seminole Negro hoped to go back to Indian Territory. They weren't asking for, or expecting to be given, property around Fort Duncan in Texas. They had no intention of becoming homeless nomads; their planned destination was clearly stated. Rather than live among Mexicans and Kickapoo in Nacimiento, they wanted to return to Seminole Negro villages in Indian Territory.

DeGress's letter gives us another clue why the Seminole Negro wanted to go. He tells Wood that John Kibbetts "states that his tribe, consisting of about one hundred people, is poor." If the Seminole Negro had enjoyed even adequate farming conditions after their return to Nacimiento, they would at least have been able to provide much of their own food for what would have been about a four- or five-week trip under reasonably good conditions. Instead, they were coming back to America with their hands out. Though they weren't starving in Nacimiento, they weren't eating all that well, either.

So John Kibbetts approached Captain DeGress in March, and DeGress initiated some necessary red-tape snipping. Things seemed fairly clear-cut. The Seminole Negro would cross back into the United States. They'd camp at Fort Duncan until the government approved DeGress giving them supplies and perhaps an armed escort back to Indian Territory. Then they'd ride north, resettle among the people they'd left in 1850, and live as happily ever after as would be possible for black Indians in racially charged post–Civil War America. The extent of their desperation for land to call their own is evidenced by their willingness to go back among the Seminole, with whom they'd just split so bitterly in Mexico.

Things quickly—predictably—became complicated. Around the end of March, Captain Frank Perry replaced DeGress as commander of Fort Duncan. There is no question Perry was also enthusiastic about bringing the Seminole Negro back to the United States. Unlike DeGress, he wanted them for reasons beyond simply carrying out a general policy.

The Seminole Negro's demonstrated ability as trackers during their service to Mexico had greatly impressed Perry. Perhaps some of the Seminole Negro men could be persuaded to stay on at Fort Duncan for a while and hire out to the U.S. Army in much the same way they'd worked for Mexico. Sometime between late March and the end of June, Perry probably went into Nacimiento himself to meet with John Kibbetts and discuss the possibility.

We know bureaucratic haggling ruined any chance that the Seminole Negro relocation to Indian Territory would happen quickly, if at all. The army wanted Indian Affairs officials to pay trip expenses. Staff there responded that the military had to get the Seminole Negro to Indian Territory, after which Indian Affairs would help the returnees get settled. Called in to arbitrate, the secretary of war "declined to give any order in the case of these Indians." Obviously, one hundred impoverished Seminole Negro weren't considered important enough for any government department to go out of its way to help, general policy for bringing tribes in Mexico back to America notwithstanding.

Perry may have known this when he went to talk to John Kibbetts. He probably did. All he could offer the Seminole Negro chief was a chance for the Nacimiento band to camp at Fort Duncan while red tape got unsnarled, if it ever did. It would have been hard for John Kibbetts to give up even a marginal existence at Nacimiento for so meager a guarantee. But if Perry raised the possibility of staying on in Texas to work for the American government—well, that would certainly have been something to consider.

For so many generations, the Seminole Negro had fought the United States, and then suffered at governmental hands after laying down their arms. They'd believed Jesup's promise of freedom, only to have it taken away from them in Indian Territory. Now Perry was offering a deal, but, unlike Jesup, he represented an American government that mandated complete freedom for blacks. That would mean, *must* mean, that all American promises would be kept this time.

The mystery that has never been solved is, what promises were made?

"The army always wrote everything down," Willie Warrior insisted, sounding a little angry as he always did whenever the subject of the 1870 negotiations came up. "You know that somebody somewhere had a paper where the army agreed to give us land for being scouts. And when we called them on it, they said they couldn't find it."

"Wouldn't John Kibbetts have been given a copy?" I asked. "Did the Seminole Negro lose theirs, too?"

Willie waved an impatient hand at me.

"I'm telling you what happened," he said.

But there are so many plausible versions.

We don't know if it was Perry or Major Zenas Bliss, who succeeded him as Fort Duncan commander (probably Perry's was a temporary posting between the commands of DeGress and Bliss), who sat down with John Kibbetts to hammer out details. Bliss came to Fort Duncan well aware of the value of black troops; he had commanded Buffalo Soldiers at Fort Concho. We do know that sometime in July, probably between the fourth and tenth, John Kibbetts led his people back across the Rio Grande and onto the grounds of Fort Duncan, where, on August 16, he and nine other Seminole Negro men were sworn in as Indian scouts. The original "muster in roll" lists John Kibbetts, Joe Dixie, Dindy Factor, Hardy Factor, Pompey Factor, Adam Fay, Bobby Kibbetts, John Thompson, John Ward, and George

Washington. John Kibbetts and Hardy Factor are listed as age sixty; the others are much younger, from sixteen to twenty-one years old.

Part of the proposed deal has never been in question: The Scouts would be paid at the same rate as other soldiers of their rank, about $12 a month for privates. John Kibbetts, sworn in as a sergeant, would get $25. They and their families would receive military rations. That the army misjudged how many members each new scout would claim as part of his family caused almost immediate trouble; the military anticipated feeding a few dozen Seminole Negro at Fort Duncan. All one hundred who showed up expected to eat army food. As part of a government bureaucracy that counted every block of hardtack and scrap of beef, Fort Duncan commissary officers faced a near-impossible situation from the beginning.

But food wasn't the most important initial issue. Given the opportunity, the Seminole Negro men could feed their families. What the tribe wanted to know was, what land they would be given to hunt on and farm?

Perhaps, if Perry or Bliss thought about it at all, they envisioned the Seminole Negro scouts serving honorably for a short period and then, using the money they saved, moving back with their families to Indian Territory, where the Seminole would make room for them on land already allocated to the tribe by the government. They considered the Seminole Negro men to be government employees, not government wards.

The Seminole Negro expected more. They were contracting with the United States to provide the same sort of service they'd given in Mexico, where the Mexican government had provided them with land (provisionally, perhaps, but thousands of acres all the same) as well as pay, rations, farming supplies, and military titles in return for border protection. If John Horse wasn't happy about something in Mexico, he could petition state governor-generals or even ride to the national capitial to request an audience with the president. When he negotiated, often with John Kibbetts at his side, the government representatives he talked with had the authority to give whatever it was that they promised.

Whether it was Perry or Bliss who worked out a deal with John Kibbetts in 1870, neither had the clout to promise too much. Yes, they had

Drawing of a Seminole Negro scout that appeared in Century *magazine, 1889* (COURTESY OF THE INSTITUTE OF TEXAN CULTURES SAN ANTONIO)

been given the authority to bring the Seminole Negro over to Fort Duncan and to enlist some of the men as scouts. The scouts would receive the same compensation as any other soldiers of similar rank. That was all Perry or Bliss had the power to guarantee.

It is possible John Kibbetts didn't realize this. It is also possible, even probable, that he and whoever he negotiated with both assumed there would later be land for the tribe back in Indian Territory, forgetting that only so many acres had been allocated to the Seminole, and that this tribe had never been generous with the Seminole Negro.

So, the first question: When he met with DeGress, and later Perry and/or Bliss, did John Kibbetts specify his people must be given land entirely their own in return for service in the army? And the second: If so, was John Kibbetts promised his people would get that land?

Right up to the moment that Alzheimer's disease claimed her memory, Miss Charles Emily Wilson was definite on the subject. From the time she was a child, Miss Charles insisted, it was passed down as fact that the original agreement between the Seminole Negro and the army included land for the tribe.

"They had land in Mexico," Miss Charles pointed out, trying to make her whispery voice heard above the groaning window air conditioner. "Whyever would they give up land they already had to come back to Texas, and then not have land of their own anymore? There is no question. Don't try to tell me there is. They wouldn't have come back to Texas otherwise."

In San Angelo, Ross McSwain agreed, though he thought the Seminole Negro might have asked for land in Texas rather than in Indian Territory.

"My best guess is they were promised plots, not a lot of land, a few acres (in Texas)," he said. "They wanted to stay there. A lot of the scouts left family in Mexico, and during slow periods when they weren't working, would go back there to see them. Yes, I think some sort of promise was made, and it wasn't kept."

If there was such a promise, Perry or Bliss had no authority to make it. In a July 14 letter to General Wood, Bliss spelled out the terms John Kibbetts was seeking: "Kibbett's [*sic*] men will not enlist in the army, but are willing and anxious to be employed as scouts. They (are) good trailers and understand the habits of Indians perfectly, and would make excellent scouts. Kibbett [*sic*] and his party are very anxious to get work of some kind, and are perfectly content to remain here on the Reservation, provided they can have land to cultivate, with permission to hunt and labor in the vicinity, and act as Scouts when required by the proper authorities."

This may be the crux of any misunderstanding. In every important way but one, the conditions Bliss describes in his letter parallel the Seminole Negro arrangement with the Mexican government. The men of the tribe would, essentially, be part-time help, working for the army when asked to do so and otherwise staying home to tend crops and hunt. In the United States, as in Mexico, they would have "land to cultivate." But Bliss does not say, at least in his letter, that the Seminole Negro would *own* the Texas land they were allowed to farm.

Later in his letter, Bliss does use the term *given:* "I would therefore respectfully recommend that they be given as much ground as they can cultivate on the U.S. Military Reservation on Elm Creek." In this context, "Reservation" doesn't mean land like Indian Territory that was assigned in supposed perpetuity to Indians. "Reservation" means the fort property. Further, if Bliss really was giving away army land, he would have had to be more specific than "as much ground as they can cultivate." An army that demanded accounting for each can of beans would hardly have condoned such an open-ended offer.

That doesn't mean Bliss went out of his way to explain such details to

John Kibbetts. Bliss was a true military hero—besides his command of the Buffalo Soldiers, he was also a Medal of Honor winner in the Civil War. But he was pragmatic. If John Kibbetts was insisting on land, well, he and his people could have some to use on Fort Duncan. Scouts were needed, and the Seminole Negro had the necessary skills. The whole land situation could be cleared up later. No one was talking about Indian Territory for the moment, but that was perhaps the right place for these black Indians to eventually end up. The concern now was to get the Seminole Negro to Fort Duncan and the men of the tribe signed up as scouts.

Or Bliss could have deliberately misled John Kibbetts. Fort Concho's Robert Bluthardt, who has studied frontier army history, says lying—inadvertant or otherwise—could have been part of the negotiating process.

"Perhaps the officer dealing with [the Seminole Negro] promised them things he did not have the authority to deliver," Bluthardt said. "That happened all the time."

Cissy Lale offered another possible explanation that puts Bliss in a better light. The army never traded land for scouting services, she points out: "Land in Texas, at that juncture, was not as prized as pay. The agreement the army had with all its scouts was to pay them, give them housing, and feed them. If the Seminole Negro were actually promised land on top of all that, well, it would certainly have been a unique arrangement."

Instead, she speculates, John Kibbetts may have misunderstood what Bliss and/or Perry was offering.

"It is quite possible they believed they were promised land because that was what they wanted to believe," she says. "But it also must be said that the army then, as now, had its way of doing things and did not often deviate. There would have been some communication back and forth between whoever was negotiating with [the Seminole Negro] and Washington. But that documentation has never been found, at least so far as I'm aware."

Willie Warrior and Miss Charles believe that documentation once did exist—a written agreement between the United States and the tribe, signed by some American representative, probably Bliss, and John Kibbetts. They insist "the treaty" spelled out land in exchange for scouting services. But, like rumored lost books of the New Testament, if this treaty ever existed no one has seen it for a long time.

There is a good chance any official written agreement that obligated the United States to give land to the Seminole Negro is apocryphal. John Kibbetts may have made notes about what he thought was promised. Perhaps that is the "treaty" Willie Warrior and Miss Charles tell about. And, as Cissy Lale points out, people usually hear what they want to hear, even Seminole Negro leaders negotiating with army officers.

But there is one inescapable conclusion, as we imagine one hundred Seminole Negro men, women, and children in July 1870 wading north across the Rio Grande, or perhaps easing from one bank to the other on rafts. They have packs and bundles with them, each full of household items, clothing, and blankets. They're leaving Mexico for good. Perhaps the U.S. government hasn't promised them land of their own—but they believe it has. That belief has brought them back to America. That belief will eventually lead to their near destruction.

chapter eleven

WILLIE WARRIOR and Clarence Ward disagreed over the official name of the scout cemetery group. At times, it seemed to be the basis for their estrangement.

"From the beginning it's been the Black Seminole Indian Scouts Association," Willie insisted. That's what he had printed on the business cards he handed out. "Clarence and his bunch, for some reason they want to take *black* out of it, and that's just wrong. Denying the black part is like denying our whole history."

But Clarence was just as convinced that Seminole Indian Scouts Cemetery Association is the proper name. "It's right on the charter," he said. "All I'm doing is calling us by the right name again. I'm not denying the black part. Anybody who looks at me knows I'm black. Same with the rest of us. I don't know why the black thing is even an issue."

There was definitely confusion in 1870 as the Seminole Negro prepared to assume scouting responsibilities for the army. From the beginning, most military reports concerning the tribe identified them only as "Seminole." DeGress was careful, in his first queries to superiors, to emphasize the Seminole Negro were "mostly blacks." But return correspondence referred only to "Seminoles." In 1870, the army had provisions for Indian scouts, but not black scouts. The all-black Buffalo Soldiers were full-fledged enlistees who fell into a more general category. The Seminole Negro were classified from the beginning as "Indian scouts." It became painfully clear, within a few years, that authorities in Washington hadn't realized at the time of their enlistment that these new Texas scouts were black instead. Because of that misconception, some promises made to the tribe would eventually be ruled invalid.

Even the names of the first scouts were mangled. It didn't matter to the army whether the new men were called by their correct names or not. John Kibbetts was alternately listed as "Kibbett," "Kibbitt," and "Kibbitts." Pompey Factor was enrolled as "Pompie." John Warrior had even worse luck. For some reason, it was one of Willie Warrior's favorite stories. He said his ancestor had a bad stutter. When a white army sergeant at Fort Duncan mustered the ten Seminole Negro scouts for the first time, Warrior had to give his name. "John War-War-War," the nervous recruit stammered. The impatient sergeant listed him as "John Ward," and there have been Wards among the Seminole Negro ever since.

The newcomers and their families were given land around Elm Creek, flat land near the muddy Rio Grande that offered little in the way of trees or shade. They built their chink houses there and began to plant gardens. Unlike the old village in Nacimiento, there wasn't enough land to properly farm. The gardens provided some crops—corn, squash, different kinds of beans—but certainly not enough to feed so many people. That meant everyone depended on additional rations from the Fort Duncan commissary. These were provided for a while, but the fort quartermaster made it clear the arrangement was only temporary. At some point, either the army would authorize full rations for every Seminole Negro, or else they would only be supplied to the actual scouts and their immediate families. No one was clear on the definition of "immediate family"—did that only include husband, wife, and children, or could it also encompass parents, in-laws, aunts, and uncles? The tribespeople weren't certain whether they should be concerned. The Mexican government had always seen they'd received whatever supplies they needed. Wouldn't the Americans do the same? Still, some of the old men found part-time work on nearby ranches. Several women of the tribe helped with the post laundry. Just about everyone learned some English, though they still spoke Gullah around their campfires. They found comfort in using the old language.

During their first months back in America, the scouts didn't face much active duty tracking Indians. They didn't have to fight at all. Comanche and Apache raids came mostly to the north and west. The army had built a series of West Texas forts, not so much to form an impenetrable boundary as to give cavalry units bases from which to operate. Fort Clark, for instance, was built about forty miles north of Eagle Pass. Soon the town of Brackettville sprang up around it.

As part-time army employees, the scouts were expected to report for duty when requested. They were thrilled to be issued Spencer carbines in place of their outmoded Mexican muskets. It would be years before they were required to wear official uniforms.

John Horse arrived in December of 1870. After Kibbetts and his group left Nacimiento, John Horse visited Mexico City to clarify the Mexican government's agreement with the Seminole Negro. The Mexicans didn't want their border guards to leave. Finally, they agreed to give the tribal members who left five years to return to Nacimiento before losing rights to the land there. The Seminole Negro who remained south of the Rio Grande would, of course, continue to have property in Nacimiento.

When John Horse and his contingent arrived to swell the numbers living along Elm Creek at Fort Duncan, Bliss was able to swear in more Black Seminole men as scouts. Within a year, Elijah Daniels and his followers would come, too. Even so, there were never more than about fifty scouts enlisted at any time. The majority of the Seminole Negro at Fort Duncan were noncombatants.

In all, Bliss was pleased with the scouts. In early dispatches, he praised them as fine trackers. Captain Orsemus Boyd went into great detail in another report, citing an unnamed Seminole Negro who "brought me intelligence that six hours previously six horses, four lodges, one sick Indian, five squaws and several children had descended into the canyon one mile above us. . . ." Simply by studying signs on the ground, the scout told Boyd what the Indians had been eating (corn and buffalo meat), why he knew one of the Indians was sick (they were pulling a travois), and even that one of the horses was blind in an eye (all the other horses grazed on both sides of the trail, but this horse only ate grass on one side). Two hours later, Boyd caught up to a group of Indians who exactly matched the scout's description.

Despite this, Boyd remained contemptuous of the black scout, saying he'd provided the information "with no ray of intelligence upon his stolid face." That attitude was typical among white officers.

It's not surprising that the Seminole Negro felt less than respected. John Horse never even signed on as a scout. Despite his advanced age—he was about sixty, roughly the same age as John Kibbetts and Hardy Factor—he would have been a welcome addition to the enlistees. But John Horse preferred to stay in the Elm Creek village, occasionally lending a hand with interpreting duties. When Elijah Daniels and his people arrived, they weren't made welcome by the Seminole Negro, who felt they were being crowded out of their limited property. There was some squabbling. John Horse and other men of the tribe soon looked for solace in the Eagle Pass saloons, where the white drinkers were openly hostile. The scouts considered themselves to be proud, free men. To many of the white townspeople in Eagle Pass, they were nothing more than uppity blacks. Eagle Pass was still a rough, relatively lawless place. Fort Duncan officers soon tired of having to rush into town to intervene in scuffles between scouts and white detractors.

"The way it worked, nobody wanted us unless there was Indian trouble," Willie Warrior explained. "Down in Nacimiento, the Mexicans always claimed we stole their cattle and chickens. Then when Indians really did come to steal, these same people who'd lied on us expected us to jump up and help get their property back. The white people in Eagle Pass, and later on in Brackettville, acted the same. Didn't want us in their towns, insulted us all the time, started fights, but let the Apache get close and all of a sudden we're all right for a little while."

In 1872, when the commander of Fort Clark requested that some of the scouts be reassigned to him there, many were eager to go. Elijah Daniels and his people made the move, building a new village along Las Moras Creek where, twenty-two years earlier, Wild Cat and John Horse had met with Major John T. Sprague just days before crossing the Rio Grande into Mexico. Their departure eased tensions in the Elm Creek camp.

Except for problems with white residents of Eagle Pass, the scouts' first two years of U.S. Army service were relatively uneventful. They tracked raiding Indians, but never fought them. They guided some official government parties and helped interpret in meetings between the army and various Indian chiefs, primarily among the Kickapoo. Certainly, the army considered their service to be worth something; the scouts were always urged to reenlist for additional six-month terms, and the Fort Clark commander had been sufficiently impressed with the Fort Duncan scout contingent to want Seminole Negro scouts of his own. It was, for the Seminole Negro, a relatively safe, dull existence. Then everything changed.

"Our people's feeling was, a bargain is a bargain," Miss Charles said firmly. We were back in her living room after a hot, sweaty visit to the Scout Cemetery. I'd asked her, on the ride back, how long it had taken the Seminole Negro to begin asking what land they would get and when they'd get it after their initial army enlistment. "We were serving in return for something, for land, and after a year or two with the army it was natural for the question to come up. Of course, the army said it had a different problem. We wanted to talk about land, the army wanted to talk about food."

This was the time, Ben Pingenot added later, "where the first misunderstanding about being black, rather than Indian, came up."

Around 1872, Kibbetts and other Seminole Negro leaders began wondering aloud when their people would be allowed to go back to Indian Territory. After all, it had been two years since they'd originally committed to six-month terms as scouts, with the plan that after a brief, helpful service they could move north to a permanent home. Major Henry Merriam, the current Fort Duncan commander, promised to look into the matter. Meanwhile, he had another problem involving the Seminole Negro.

Their stores gradually drained as more tribes surrendered and needed food while being moved to reservations, the army's Office of the Adjutant General ordered that rations no longer be given to any Indians on a regular basis. Because the Seminole Negro were classified as Indian rather than black scouts, the army's Department of Texas ruled that they couldn't be issued regular rations, either. Merriam did what he could for his scouts. He argued that the Seminole Negro hadn't permanently settled in at Fort Duncan, since they expected to leave soon for Indian Territory. Accordingly, they hadn't found means of completely feeding themselves. If the army didn't help out with additional food, Merriam warned, the men of the tribe would have no choice but to begin stealing from the herds and gardens of white settlers. He received permission to temporarily supply the scouts and their families with rations. But within weeks, Secretary of War W. W. Belknap notified officials at the Department of the Interior that the army would cut off food supplies to the Seminole Negro soon. Interior Secretary B. R. Cowan would just have to order the Indian bureau to provide the food. Cowan, who seemed to be the only official in Washington to recognize the scouts' actual race, replied that it wasn't his department's job to feed negroes. He suggested that the commissioner of Indian Affairs, Francis A. Walker, could do something for the tribe. Walker wanted to know if the Seminole Negro were prepared to leave Texas for Indian Territory. If so, perhaps money was "available for relieving their present necessities."

John Kibbetts made it clear the Seminole Negro were ready to go. All they wanted were supplies for the trip and permission to leave. Merriam sent word to General Philip Sheridan, commander of the Military Division of the Missouri, that the scouts and their extended families were about to be sent on to his region, which included Indian Territory. Sheridan invited them to come.

Then Walker reconsidered. No one from the Indian bureau, he decided, had ever invited the Seminole Negro back to Texas from Mexico. The army had done that. So let the army pay to return them to Indian Territory.

Merriam protested on behalf of the tribe. Belknap asked Sheridan to investigate. The Seminole Negro spent the cold winter months on the

Scout Ben July and his family in the Las Moras Creek Village about 1890
(COURTESY OF THE MUSEUM OF THE BIG BEND, SUL ROSS UNIVERSITY)

banks of the Rio Grande, waiting impatiently for permission to leave. In January 1873, Sheridan made his report to Belknap. In every way, it was sympathetic to the Seminole Negro. Both the army and the Indian bureau, Sheridan declared, had been part of the agreement bringing the scouts and their families to Fort Duncan. So both departments should take some responsibility for them now. Since there seemed to be no money to send them back to Indian Territory, why not simply give them ample land on Fort Duncan for a village and reasonably extensive farms? Then they could grow enough crops to feed themselves, freeing the army and bureau from having to continue providing extra rations. Would the Seminole Negro accept that?

They would. John Kibbetts informed Merriam that his people wanted land somewhere, almost anywhere. Fort Duncan wasn't as pleasant as Nacimiento, let alone Indian Territory, but it would do. They would make it do.

Belknap sent Sheridan's report on to Columbus Delano, who was the new secretary of the Interior. Delano's response was that Sheridan's information contradicted whatever reports the Indian bureau had provided. Everyone should wait while he looked into the matter himself, which he would do as soon as he conveniently could.

They waited. Resolving the fate of the Seminole Negro wasn't a high priority for Delano. As the first months of 1873 passed, no word came to Fort Duncan from the Department of the Interior. But on March 6, one of the best friends the Seminole Negro would ever have arrived to command them. His name was John Lapham Bullis, and, coming from an assignment at Fort Concho commanding the Buffalo Soldiers, he was very comfortable working with blacks.

In 1866, Congress had authorized formation of black cavalry and infantry units, with army officials making certain that these new soldiers were stationed as far away from large cities as possible. West Texas, where there were wide-open spaces and particularly savage Indians to be fought, seemed ideal. There was never any real thought of mixing black and white troops, though the black units were led by white officers. It was possible for black soldiers to rise in rank from private to corporal or sergeant. Unlike Seminole Negro scouts, the black troops enlisted for five-year hitches. There were even pensions for those who lasted through several terms of enlistment. Along with regular pay, meals—even if the food was usually pretty bad—and uniforms provided by the government, the possibility of a guaranteed pension was the sort of job perk most blacks of the era couldn't otherwise hope to receive.

These black troops, soon popularly known as the Buffalo Soldiers, fought hard and well. One of their commanders in Texas was Lieutenant Bullis, who served with distinction in the Civil War, temporarily left the military, then reenlisted. Bullis was an exemplary officer. As a commander of black troops, he proved himself willing to fight by their side on the battlefield and to treat them decently in camp. His assignment to command the Seminole Negro scouts completely changed the nature of their military service. While the government dithered about whether to feed them and where they could eventually live, Bullis led the scouts for the first time into combat. The country that didn't care enough to feed Seminole Negro dependents still expected the scouts to risk their lives defending it. At least, in Bullis, they felt they had a caring white leader.

The arrival of Bullis was the beginning of a remarkable eight-year period. During that time, the Seminole Negro scouts would engage in more than two dozen extended missions tracking and fighting Indians. They would always be outnumbered. Usually, they fought after exhausting themselves on long, brutal chases. Yet, taking the field against the fiercest Indians, not one Seminole Negro scout was killed or even seriously wounded. Between 1873 and 1881, the army used thousands of "Indian scouts." Only sixteen were awarded the Medal of Honor, the army's ultimate recognition of battlefield distinction. Four of those medals were won by Seminole Negro scouts. In all, their record of service was exceptional, and their scouting glory days began with the arrivals of Bullis and Colonel Ranald S. Mackenzie.

Mackenzie was sent to Fort Clark about the same time Bullis arrived at Fort Duncan. Mackenzie's presence was significant. The army was tired of reacting to raids on Texas settlers by Indian bands who had permanent camps south of the border. Mexico had tenuous relations with the United States; it was not considered appropriate for troops from one country to cross into the other while pursuing Indians. The Indians, of course, soon realized this and were happy to take advantage of the situation. With most of the Seminole Negro back on the north side of the Rio Grande, it was easier for Apache and Kickapoo to operate out of villages in Mexico, mostly ones located a few dozen miles northwest of Nacimiento. So long as they terrorized Americans instead of Mexicans, the Mexican government was glad to let them alone. Besides, with most of the Seminole Negro gone, it was harder for the Mexican army to fight the Indians.

Mackenzie, who'd established himself as a particular Indian scourge, arrived in South Texas with a specific mission. He was to eliminate the problem of Indians residing south of the Rio Grande and raiding north of it. When he got to Fort Clark on April 1, 1873, Mackenzie immediately ordered that all troops begin training for extended expeditions. Bullis was told to prepare the Seminole Negro scouts for combat.

On April 11, Secretary Belknap and General Sheridan arrived at Fort Clark themselves. They wanted to be certain Mackenzie knew exactly what was expected of him. Weeks earlier, Mexico-based Indians had raided into Texas, massacring civilians, killing a Ninth Cavalry officer, and making off with stolen stock. The army knew very well where these Indians were camped—near Remolino, close to the old Seminole Negro village in Nacimiento. Belknap and Sheridan directed Mackenzie to "immediately commence preparations for an expedition against them . . . punish them for the past, and check their raids in the future . . . [undertake] a campaign of annihilation, obliteration and complete destruction." It was not an insignificant assignment. Besides the danger of fighting the Indians, Mackenzie would also be risking a border incident that could result in war between the United States and Mexico.

Bullis met with the Seminole Negro scouts to explain the mission. They would be gone from their village for at least a few days, he warned. There would be fighting, hard fighting. He knew of the scouts' fine service in Mexico, how they had defeated Indians again and again. He believed they would be glad to fight some more. It was just the right approach.

"Our people have always had, you see, great pride," Miss Charles said. "Old Bullis didn't say to them, 'Get up and don't be lazy.' He said, 'I honor you for your past service, and you are badly needed again.' I was told as a child that until Bullis got there, lots of us were about ready to tell the army enough was enough, give us our land or else we're gone. But Bullis said all the right things. And that first time our men went out with him, they had a great, great battle."

The Seminole Negro men may have briefly considered how the army was threatening not to feed their dependents anymore. They may have wondered why, after two years, they still weren't being allowed to go back to Indian Territory. But they were members of the U.S. Army, after all. If they were being ordered into a fight, they would go. Besides, everyone liked Bullis. He ate and drank with them, danced with them around their campfires, made a point of respectfully greeting their wives and older relatives. They had no great love for the Apache, who Bullis identified as the tribe they were going to fight. Two kinds of Apache, he promised, both Lipan and Mescalero. And maybe some Kickapoo.

So the scouts hefted their shiny new rifles, hugged their wives and children, and rode off with Mackenzie and Bullis into Mexico. They did regret that the Americans wouldn't pay scalp bounties like the Mexican government had.

Mackenzie, six companies of cavalry, sixteen Seminole Negro scouts from Fort Duncan under Bullis, and eighteen more scouts from Fort Clark under another officer—about 425 men in all—left camp on May 17. It was typical sweltering weather. Because the Apache would have lookouts posted, and because such a large party was too easy to spot, Mackenzie ordered a near-killing pace. They rode all day and all through the night, eighty miles in one twenty-four-hour stretch, driving their horses until froth from the animals' mouths flew up into their riders' eyes. Everyone ate while still riding. Many of the cavalrymen dozed in their saddles. The Seminole Negro scouts rode proudly upright, enjoying the honor of following directly behind Mackenzie.

Just before dawn, Mackenzie sent some of the scouts ahead to reconnoitor. They knew the country well, having lived in it themselves for so many years. Soon, they reported back. Yes, the Indians were ahead. But they were in three separate, though adjacent, villages along the San Rodrigo River—Lipan and Mescalero and Kickapoo. There were about fifty lodges in each camp. These were substantial settlements.

There is some disagreement about Mackenzie's subsequent orders. Several historians have written he ordered attacks only on the Apache camps. The Kickapoo were relatively peaceful; these may have been some of the same Kickapoo who'd moved into Nacimiento while the Seminole Negro had been moved south to Parras by the Mexican government. But it's also possible that the Kickapoo, along with the Apache, were among Mackenzie's targets all along—they'd begun raiding north of the Rio Grande, too.

Certainly, the Seminole Negro still held a grudge against the Kickapoo. They remembered how, in 1851, most of the Kickapoo who'd been recruited by Wild Cat left Mexico with stolen Seminole Negro horses. So it's entirely possible that even if Mackenzie did order his troops to confine their attacks to the Lipan and Mescalero, the Seminole Negro scouts deliberately fired on the Kickapoo camp.

In any event, Mackenzie issued his orders, and at about one in the afternoon he commanded the troops to charge. They'd been able to conceal themselves behind low bluffs; now they swept down on the Indian villages, catching their enemies completely by surprise. The Mescalero, whose camp was farthest from the point of attack, tried to run. The Lipan men dug in and fought. Many of them died. The Kickapoo defended themselves briefly, then surrendered. Within an hour, the final shots were fired. Nineteen Indian braves were dead. Forty women and children were captured. Mackenzie lost just one soldier. The Seminole Negro scouts fought with particular distinction—one even lassoed Costilietos, the Lipan chief. He made a particularly significant prisoner.

The U.S. troops also captured Teresita, the daughter of Costilietos. Biting, snarling, she had to be dragged back to Texas. Once there, though, her attitude softened, at least toward the scouts. Eventually she took the American name of Marcia and married Seminole Negro scout James Perryman. It probably wasn't a legal marriage under white law. Miss Charles said Bullis officiated.

Mackenzie had nothing but praise for his troops, Bullis and the scouts especially. Bullis got a promotion to first lieutenant. Miss Charles said he celebrated in the Seminole Negro camp at Fort Duncan instead of an Eagle Pass saloon. The scouts celebrated, too—it was good to have fought and won. But when their hangovers subsided, they were still in Texas, and their people were still hungry.

chapter twelve

ONE AFTERNOON I sat with Willie and Ethel Warrior on the porch of their barracks-turned-residence on Fort Clark. We'd just finished another huge meal, and I was pleased Ethel was joining us for conversation instead of washing pots and dishes. She always deferred to Willie when we talked about tribal history, though she was a native of Brackettville and also served a term as president of the Scout Association. This time the conversation turned to the plight of the Seminole Negro who'd been voted out of the Seminole tribe in Oklahoma, and Ethel felt indignant enough about it to speak for herself.

"That is dirty business," she declared. "Telling people they were part of the same tribe, the same family, so to speak, and then turning them out over a few dollars. The Seminole should have been grateful the government gave any settlement at all."

"It seems so petty with the Seminole," I interjected. "Even with $56 million divided thirteen thousand ways instead of fifteen thousand, they only get about $4,300 instead of $3,700."

"Listen," Willie snapped, "lots of people living up there are dirt poor, ours more than the Indians. They'd screw us over $5, let alone a couple hundred."

"Are you surprised this happened?"

Scout Billy July sometime in the 1890s

(COURTESY OF THE INSTITUTE OF TEXAN CULTURES SAN ANTONIO)

"Hell, no. It's just one more time somebody's doing this. Think about the army when the scouts in Texas wanted the land they'd been promised," Willie said, scowling. "They got put off and put off, and, finally, got nothing. This Oklahoma thing is part of a pattern."

"Miss Charles told me back in 1994 that she'd given up hope your people here in Brackettville would ever get something from the government," I said. "Do you feel that way, too?"

I thought Willie would answer, but Ethel spoke before he could.

"I don't care if, eventually, we just get $50 each," she said. "I'll go to my grave thinking we should get something, anything, just as a sign that the army was wrong and we were right. Even if we never got the land, I want our people to know we at least got a little bit of justice."

Willie began talking about when the scouts first decided they'd provided sufficient service, and the time had come for the army to satisfy its part of the bargain. It was in June 1873, he said, that Seminole Negro scout Elijah Daniels presented a formal written request to Mackenzie. Like many Seminole Negro adults, Daniels had a halting grasp of spoken English and a reasonable ability to present thoughts in that language on paper. The colonel was feeling kindly toward the scouts after the successful raid on Remolino, and Daniels felt it might be a good time to press once again the Seminole Negro request for land back in Indian Territory.

Specifically, Daniels asked for a "track of land" in "Arkansaw," which was one name the Seminole Negro used for Indian Territory. They wanted the land for "a home for Life Time." The scouts had long since fulfilled any obligation they'd had to the army, Daniels and the rest of the Seminole Negro believed. The action at Remolino was a good way to conclude their service. Surely Colonel Mackenzie would agree that the scouts had fought honorably and well.

There was a new urgency to Daniels's request. It was clear, after Remolino, that Mackenzie and Bullis planned to use the scouts on lengthy expeditions against hostile Indians. The men could be gone from their villages for weeks, or even longer. The army's decision not to feed most Seminole Negro noncombatants put extra pressure on the able-bodied men of the tribe to stay close to home. It was time for the scouts to take care of their own dependents, instead of riding off to protect the interests of white ranchers and farmers.

Mackenzie didn't want to lose the services of the scouts, but he appreciated their plight. A survey of the Seminole Negro camps at Forts Clark and Duncan reported "twenty seven enlisted men and eighty two old men, women and children [at Fort Clark], and about the same number at Duncan." Actually, there were probably fewer enlisted men and more dependents at both posts. Rations provided for two dozen scouts at each village, plus what crops could be gleaned from gardens, simply weren't enough to feed everyone.

So Mackenzie did what he could by kicking Daniels's request up the military ladder. Sheridan forwarded the new plan to Washington and waited to hear back. No reply was forthcoming. The Seminole Negro remained stranded in Texas.

Out of pity, commissary officers at both forts found ways to feed them. It was only a matter of time before inspectors from regional headquarters ordered them to stop. Though there were still tensions between the two scout groups, they came together late in the year to try to conceive a strategy to make the Americans honor their 1870 agreement.

At first, they couldn't even agree among themselves. John Kibbetts led the Fort Duncan Seminole Negro. Elijah Daniels spoke for the Fort Clark scouts. But John Horse still considered himself the official Seminole Negro spokesman. In December, he and John Kibbetts rode to San Antonio, where they spoke directly to General Christopher Augur, commander of the army's Department of Texas. The scouts and their families wanted to live in Indian Territory, they said, but, if that wasn't possible, their people would be happy to go back to Florida. They knew there was plenty of available land there.

That request, both Seminole Negro leaders knew, was one Augur wouldn't have the authority to grant. They were asking as a matter of record. They had really come to San Antonio to ask for help in another way.

When the Seminole Negro scouts were off duty, some army officers had been ordering them to cut wood and do other time-consuming chores around the forts. John Kibbetts wanted Augur to let the scouts use all their spare time to provide for their families. That was something Augur was glad to do. Then John Horse asked for full rations for every Seminole Negro on Fort Duncan and Fort Clark. It wasn't a matter of tribal laziness, he argued. Every able-bodied man, woman, and child was willing to work for even the smallest wage. But there was very little work available to them; the white ranchers usually didn't want their help. So they couldn't earn money for food; they couldn't grow enough vegetables in their tiny village gardens to feed everyone; and, with the scouts apparently to be gone for long periods of time, they wouldn't be able to hunt and bring back game for their hungry families. Augur had to order all the Seminole Negro fed, or people would starve.

Augur tried to help. He wrote to army officials in Washington, saying the

Seminole Negro would soon have to resort to stealing food, which would only cause trouble in Eagle Pass and Brackettville: "It [would] cost vastly more to restore peace than . . . to give them the desired support." If approval was obtained to send the tribe back to Indian Territory, Augur added, he'd even provide wagons and drivers to transport them there. Mackenzie and Bullis, his subordinates, added their enthusiastic endorsement.

In Washington, officials in the War and Interior Departments began investigating. The wheels of bureaucracy moved slowly. There wouldn't be a response for almost a year. Meanwhile, the scouts were called in again.

"Now, Adam Payne was a big, mean man," Willie Warrior cautioned. "I'm not going to tell you he was a saint. He drank and he ended up running with some bad outlaws, but what he did to earn his medal ought to be a movie, except nobody'd believe it could be true."

In December 1873, Lieutenant Charles Hudson led forty men on an expedition against the Kiowa-Comanche raiders. The party included six Seminole Negro scouts, among them George Washington and three members of the Payne family—Titus, Aaron, and Adam. Adam Payne was perhaps the most exotically dressed of all the scouts. They still weren't required to wear official uniforms, so they wore what they pleased. It pleased Adam Payne to wear a spectacular buffalo headdress complete with horns. It was almost too much for even his fellow scouts to accept. But Payne was a hulking, nasty fellow who armed himself with a pistol, shotgun, and huge-bladed knife. He liked to drink, and he liked to fight. When white citizens complained about thugs among the Seminole Negro, Adam Payne was often who they were talking about. Like the hostile Indians he scouted, he was happiest in battle. If he wanted to wear his buffalo headgear, even John Horse was unlikely to tell him he shouldn't.

Hudson and his troops found the raiders; the Seminole Negro scouts picked up their trail as easily as an off-duty Adam Payne would have found a saloon. The ensuing firefight was a mismatch. The soldiers and scouts had better weapons and numerical superiority. Nine of the Indians died; only one soldier was wounded. Dozens of horses were recaptured. But this was only an early skirmish in what was about to become an extended fight.

During the first months of 1874, many Cheyenne, Comanche, and Kiowa fled from their Indian Territory reservations. This wasn't a matter of small bands of hotheads chasing off on recreational raids; rather, hundreds of Indians at a time escaped on mass exoduses to rejoin tribes who still hadn't been subdued by the army. That meant there were now large bands of hostile Indians moving throughout the midwest and southwest.

Sheridan was ordered to muster as many troops as he required and to corner the hostiles wherever they could be found. First, General Nelson Miles led an expedition out of Kansas. The flat midwestern plains offered little refuge for the Indians, and they fled south. Eventually the Indians used West Texas, specifically a canyon-riddled area along the westernmost extremities of the Red River, as a base of operations. It was an obvious choice; the rugged terrain would make it difficult for the army to attack there, even if they had a general idea of where the hostiles might be camped.

In late August, Mackenzie took troops into the field. He hoped to locate and destroy the Indians before the onset of winter prevented further tracking. Bullis was ill and didn't go, but his scouts did. The Seminole Negro were sent to look for sign of the hostiles. They moved ahead of the main party, fanning out in all directions. It was hard, hot work. In August, the heat in West Texas is particularly brutal. But the scouts reported back to Mackenzie that a large group of the Indians was camped along the Pease River, a tributary of the main Red River. The hostile camp was about two hundred miles north of Fort Clark.

Mackenzie began marching his troops north. Needing to know the exact location of the camp, he sent Seminole Negro scouts ahead—James Bruner, George Washington, and Adam Payne. A few Tonkawa Indians had been recruited as scouts, too, though they never lived among the Seminole Negro. Two of these went with the black scouts. Mackenzie stressed that they were only to find the Indian camp. There was to be no fighting if at all possible, to retain the element of surprise when the army attacked. Each of the five scouts took along an extra mount; the heat and rough, broken ground wore out horses quickly.

Adam Payne was probably hoping for a fight. Certainly the tension was palpable as the three Seminole Negro and two Tonkawa slowly rode forward, eyes alternately glued to the ground in search of tracks and to the horizon looking for enemies. Bruner was in charge; he was a sergeant. Washington had been given the rank of corporal. Adam Payne, undisciplined and sometimes foolhardy, was only a private. He was the least gifted tracker among the three and knew it. When darkness made it impossible to keep searching for signs, the five men made a cold camp. Lighting a fire would have signalled any hostiles in the area that enemies were nearby.

They were up and moving again at dawn, still riding their original mounts. Their fresh horses were being saved for emergencies. Soon, there was one.

A large band of Comanche—two or three dozen, perhaps—suddenly overflowed a nearby hill and descended on the scouts. It was a sudden, unexpected attack, and probably a complete accident. The Indians were out on a hunt, or else on their way to join the main hostile camp another dozen miles to the north. But they'd seen the scouts, and with the odds so much in their favor, they cocked their rifles, kicked the sides of their horses, and charged.

The scouts' only hope was to run. Hurriedly, they tried to switch from their tired horses to their fresh mounts. Adam Payne was able to transfer his saddle from one horse to the other. Bruner, Washington, and the two Tonkawa had to ride bareback. They moved quickly, but their attackers were quicker. Within minutes, the scouts were surrounded. They knew there would be no mercy if they were captured. Instead, the Comanche would undoubtedly amuse themselves with ingenious methods of torture. Together, each trying to hang on to the bridle of his spare horse, the five charged toward the south, and were able to break through. Firing his shotgun, blasting his pistol in the faces of his enemies, Adam Payne was in his awful element.

But the Comanche were wily warriors. The temporary breakout of the scouts only meant that the sport would be prolonged. They chased after their quarry, screeching war cries. Willie Warrior said the distance between the pursued and their pursuers was often no more than a few dozen yards. They weren't racing along flat, easily negotiable prairie, either. The ground was pitted with gullies and festooned with cactus and scrub brush. The scouts had to worry almost as much about the terrain ahead of them as the Comanche behind them.

The chase lasted for more than a dozen miles. All the horses were being pushed to the brink of exhaustion, Adam Payne's especially. He was a big man, described by Willie Warrior as more than six feet tall and weighing two hundred pounds. His was the only horse hauling a saddle; he wanted it for the ammunition in the saddlebags and to hold his shotgun while he rode. At some point, George Washington tried to switch mounts and ride on a saddle, too. It was a mistake. Both Washington's horses bucked in confusion, and the Comanche thundered toward him.

Adam Payne could have ridden on; if the Comanche stopped to kill or capture George Washington, that would have given him, Bruner, and the Tonkawa several invaluable minutes to race ahead. But the giant in the buffalo headdress instead wheeled and rode back toward the Comanche, yanking out his shotgun and firing at them. It was a fearsome sight. Just for a moment, the Comanche reined up. Washington calmed his horses, switched from one to the other, and started riding south again. But Adam Payne couldn't. As the Comanche fired back, one of their bullets killed his horse. Unlike Washington, he no longer had a spare mount. The other two Seminole Negro and the two Tonkawa were still running south. Probably, they didn't realize their giant companion was on foot behind them.

So Adam Payne did the only thing he could. He dove behind the body of his horse and fired his shotgun at the Comanche as, whooping with delight, they charged forward to capture him. It wasn't as easy as they'd expected. When the first Indian was close enough, the huge scout knocked him from his horse, killed him—probably with his knife—and jumped up on the Indian's pony. Firing his pistol into the astonished faces of the rest of the Comanche, he began riding south again.

Now the chase settled into a grim pattern. The Tonkawa were slightly ahead of Bruner and Washington. Adam Payne lagged behind, with the quickest Comanche hard on his heels. Periodically, the Seminole Negro private wheeled his horse and fired at the Comanche, who prudently slowed up for a moment. They'd already seen what Adam Payne could do in hand-to-hand combat.

It was almost two o'clock in the afternoon when the two frightened Tonkawa scouts raced their wild-eyed, exhausted horses into the army camp. George Washington and James Bruner soon followed, their horses in equally poor condition. Then came Adam Payne.

The Comanche were still right behind him. When they saw the main party of soldiers, they stopped, shook their rifles to signal disdain, and raced back north. Mackenzie knew he now had little chance of surprising the hostiles when he finally found their main camp.

But the five scouts were alive, mostly because of Adam Payne. His valor was an example Mackenzie wanted to encourage among all his troops, white and black alike. So Mackenzie recommended the Seminole Negro for the prestigious Medal of Honor. In his report, Mackenzie said that "This man has, I believe, more cool daring than any other scout I have known."

The army might not have been willing to feed Adam Payne's extended family, but it officially recognized his bravery. His Medal of Honor was approved. But even in this, governmental disrespect for, or at least lack of interest in, the Seminole Negro surfaced. Modern-day records still indicate a Medal of Honor for conspicuous battlefield gallantry in 1874 was awarded to Adam *Paine*.

Willie Warrior is not a profane man. Sometimes, if ladies aren't present, he utters an occasional "damn." But telling his story about Adam Payne, he couldn't help himself.

"Shit," he said softly, drawing out the single syllable as a token of admiration. "*Shee-it.* You think that Adam Payne wasn't something?"

The scouts' safe return to camp didn't conclude the expedition. Mackenzie was still charged with finding the main hostile camp and destroying it. Now the Indians knew exactly where the soldiers were. Less experienced officers might simply have blundered on ahead, but Mackenzie knew better. He ordered his troops forward, but at a cautious pace. At night, he ordered that every horse be hobbled, which would make it harder for Indians to sneak in close and steal them. The Seminole Negro scouts spread out ahead and to the side of the main column each day, looking for tracks. Gradually, the whole force entered the infamous Llano Estacado, the so-called "Staked Plains." It was, and is, one of the largest tablelands on the North American continent, approximately 32,000 square miles in all, or approximately the size of New England. Except for the Red River cutting through its northern boundary via the Palo Duro Canyon, there was little water anywhere.

Mackenzie decided to establish a base, then send out scouts from there. A week after the scouts had escaped from the Comanche, he selected a spot with a little shade and water. The troops pitched tents and rested. That night, the Indians attacked.

It was a massive raid, and well-planned. Some two hundred shooting, whooping warriors descended on the soldiers, but the hostiles were less interested in killing white men than in stealing their horses. That would offer double benefits; the soldiers would be stranded far from their forts. Many would undoubtedly die of exposure or thirst. The stolen horses would also provide the raiders with transportation and wealth. Army horses were usually much better fed, and, as a result, healthier, than Indian ponies.

But Mackenzie wasn't entirely taken by surprise. The Seminole Negro scouts had told him they'd found some sign of hostiles in the area. All the horses in camp were carefully tethered, so the attacking Indians weren't able to simply chase them off into the darkness. Mackenzie had even ordered that his men sleep fully clothed, with their weapons by their sides, so within seconds of the attack the troopers were firing back.

The two sides exchanged shots through the night. For the hostiles, it was more a matter of saving face. They were outnumbered and outgunned by the soldiers. Around dawn, Mackenzie sent Lieutenant William Thompson, a company of cavalry, and the scouts to chase the Indians off. The hostiles didn't put up much resistance, riding away to the east and trying to hide in a series of small canyons, or *arroyos*. The scouts pursued them there and killed two Indians. No one in Mackenzie's party, though, thought they'd won any sort of significant battle. If and when they finally found the main Indian camp, where families lived side by side with warriors, they expected the hostile braves to fight to the death.

Even in the vast llano, it was only a matter of time before the Seminole Negro tracked their quarry down. The hostiles didn't want to flee north—General Miles and his troops were waiting there, and, besides, it was Indian Territory they were escaping from. Mackenzie and his men were between them and Mexico. A full-scale battle in Texas was inevitable.

It came three days later. The scouts found many signs of the hostiles. They learned the big camp was in Palo Duro Canyon, perhaps the wildest territory in all of the llano.

The canyon walls are precipitous. In those days, the only trails down them were narrow goat paths. The canyon floor was spacious, and, when the scouts first peered over it, they could count hundreds of tents in the extended Indian camp, which consisted of five separate villages. Just two years later, Colonel George Custer and the Seventh Cavalry would find a similarly sized camp hundreds of miles north along the Little Big Horn River, and the army troops would be wiped out by the Indians there. Mackenzie was a more cautious officer than Custer. He took the time to carefully think through his options, staring down into a canyon so vast that one observer later recalled the Indians in it looked no larger than chickens.

While Mackenzie cogitated, the scouts kept busy. Eventually, they reported finding a fair-sized trail down to the canyon floor that probably would accomodate enough troops at one time to mount a serious attack on the hostiles. Thirteen of the scouts were ordered to lead the troops down the path. It took almost an hour for them to descend. The Indians had lookouts posted, but the scouts led so silently that the white troops were advancing on the nearest village before the first shouts of warning alerted the Indians they were under attack.

Most of the Indians were sufficiently caught off guard to run rather than fight back. Mackenzie chose to destroy their supplies rather than pursue them. He burned their supplies of dried corn and meat and destroyed all the rifles, bows, and spears they'd left behind. As a token of respect for their fine efforts, he allowed the Seminole Negro scouts to choose horses from among the fifteen hundred in the captured hostile herd. Then, because it would have been too difficult to drive the remaining horses back to the far-off forts, and because he didn't want to risk the routed Indians regaining them, Mackenzie ordered his troops to kill every other horse. As the troops moved out, buzzards swooped down behind them and began to feast.

The destruction of their horse herd effectively broke the band of hostiles. Mackenzie kept his troops in the field. There were smaller groups of Indians yet to be tracked down. Twice in November the scouts led successful attacks on hostile camps. Both times, the army prevailed with little loss of life. With winter coming on, most of the Comanche, Cheyenne, and Kiowa bowed to the inevitable and skulked back north, where they were taken onto Indian Territory reservations and guarded closely. By year's end, it was clear what historians later called "The Red River War" was over, thanks mostly to Mackenzie and his men.

The scouts arrived back at their camps in Fort Duncan and Fort Clark to learn that the government once again had decided not to do anything to help the Seminole Negro. For months, special agents for the commissioner of Indian Affairs had been studying the tribe's case, undoubtedly in response to General Augur's report. During the summer of 1874, officers at Fort Duncan had simply defied orders to stop providing extra rations to Seminole Negro dependents. That ended in August; the region's commissary general announced there was no extra food to hand out. Secretary of War Belknap, or, more likely, one of his staff minions, sent a message to the Indian bureau that it would have to begin providing the food needed. The bureau's reply was succinct: If the Seminole Negro were in Texas instead of Indian Territory, then responsibility for them fell to the army, not the bureau. If the army wanted to send the tribe north at military expense, the matter might be worth reconsidering. The army wanted the dependent Seminole Negro fed, but didn't want to pay to move them to Indian Territory. It was a governmental stalemate.

In November, about the same time the scouts were distinguishing themselves in the Red River War, the commissioner of Indian Affairs received the report on the Seminole Negro that he'd requested. It, too, was succinct. The military and the bureau should share responsibility for the tribe. The Seminole Negro had been promised the chance to make a homeland for themselves. Indian Territory was where that homeland should be; the two departments should jointly help them get there, then provide for them until such time as they could completely fend for themselves.

No one in Washington liked that suggestion. A month later, the same agent who'd written the initial report added a coda. Conditions among the Seminole Negro at Fort Clark and Fort Duncan had grown even worse. While the scouts had been gone on Mackenzie's expedition, the families they'd left behind had begun to starve. It was not a matter of being a little hungry on occasion. Old people and infants were wasting away. Winter weather meant game was scarce, and the tribe's gardens wouldn't produce even a few scrubby vegetables again until spring. Desperate, the men and boys were openly stealing from nearby farms and ranches. The white population around Forts Duncan and Clark was outraged. Mackenzie and Bullis deluged their superiors with written pleas for help. None was forthcoming. It was a cold, miserable winter for the Seminole Negro.

Around Christmas Day in 1874, Corporal George Washington felt like having a drink in Eagle Pass. That the few cents whiskey would cost might have been better used for food for his tribe probably never crossed his mind. Seminole Negro men drank because it was their privilege. It was part of being male, like giving women orders and expecting to be instantly obeyed.

The saloon where George Washington slaked his thirst proved to be a bad choice. Outlaw King Fisher and his men were already there. They may have been drunk; moderation wasn't an outlaw trait, either. They certainly weren't pleased to be joined at the bar by an uppity black man acting as though he had the same right to prompt service as they did. Words were exchanged. The Seminole Negro could have swallowed his pride and left. He was outnumbered; none of the other saloon patrons were going to risk angering King Fisher by taking a black man's side against him.

"But we had pride," Miss Charles said firmly. "Our men served their country—*their* country, just as it was the white people's country—with honor and distinction. There was no reason for them not to walk the streets of any city like the proud citizens they were." In particular, the scouts who'd been in recent combat saw no reason why they shouldn't patronize saloons and shops with the same aplomb as white customers. So George Washington and the other scouts refused to kowtow in the way more pliant blacks in Texas did, often by meekly accepting any verbal insults tossed their way. When offended, the scouts were ready to fight, and, in this case, George Washington did. Punches were followed by gunshots. George Washington was able to fire his pistol at least once; King Fisher staggered back with a wound across his scalp. But the Seminole Negro scout ended up on the filthy floor of the bar, bleeding profusely from a bullet wound in his stomach. He lay there, suffering, until someone finally summoned help for him from Fort Duncan. George Washington was taken back to the Seminole Negro village by Elm Creek. He lived for a short time, suffering greatly, then he died. His death didn't lessen King Fisher's newfound enmity for the tribe. Army officials saw to it that the notorious outlaw was indicted for murder, but the charges were eventually dropped. No Eagle Pass jury was going to find a white man, even one as evil as King Fisher, guilty of murdering a black man. Mackenzie and Bullis told the rest of the Seminole Negro men to stay out of Eagle Pass saloons—in fact, they should stay out of Eagle Pass altogether. But, if they stayed on the Fort Duncan grounds, the scouts were surrounded by proof of their inability to care for their people.

A few found it all to be untenable. There began to be occasional desertions. Some other scouts, Adam Payne among them, refused to reenlist. These men drifted back into Mexico, or else wandered away from Eagle Pass and Brackettville to look for work as wranglers for ranchers who would hire blacks. But most of the able-bodied Seminole Negro men stayed, and it's fair to wonder why. It had to be obvious that the Americans were in no hurry to honor promises the tribe believed had been made in 1870, if the Americans meant to honor them at all. The Seminole Negro were no nearer going back to Indian Territory than they'd been when they'd arrived at Fort Duncan. Their old people were starving in Texas. The scouts were being ordered into dangerous duty. The tribe was hated by the white people living around them. They could even be murdered—the white law apparently offered no protection for the Seminole Negro. At the very least, all the scouts and their immediate families could have survived by returning to Mexico, where they would have been guaranteed some land and food.

But most of them didn't. One reason was a traditional sense of responsibility for weaker tribal members. Old men and women without younger relatives weren't strong enough to return to Mexico from Texas. Left behind in the fort camps, they would soon either starve there or be turned out by the army onto the filthy streets of Brackettville and Eagle Pass. Leaders like John Kibbetts, John Horse, and Elijah Daniels would never have considered this. It simply was not the Seminole Negro way to abandon their old people.

Also, the tribe was determined that, eventually, the Americans would do what they had promised. The scouts had tracked and fought for the army. Adam Payne had a Medal of Honor. Bullis, who they loved and respected, was talking about new spring campaigns. The Seminole Negro side of the bargain had been kept, was still being kept. Leaving Texas on their own would let the Americans get away with not keeping theirs. Somewhere—in Indian Territory, in Florida, in Texas—the United States could surely find a few acres of its vast territory to give to the Seminole Negro.

A few sympathetic army officers kept trying. In early 1875, General Edward Ord became the latest commander of the Department of Texas. He approved a new study—the Seminole Negro should be counted again and asked about their preferences. Did they still want to go to Indian Territory? Would they prefer staying in Texas? Patiently, the people answered everything that was asked. While Ord evaluated the information, he risked his own career by issuing an order for rations to be given to hungry Seminole Negro at Fort Duncan whenever officers there believed they were suffering. Ord didn't ask his superiors for permission before issuing the order, which is probably why it remained in effect for several months.

While Ord counted, Bullis took his scouts back into the field. Within weeks, the Seminole Negro proved their value to the army again. What happened on April 25, 1875, is unquestionably the best-known event in tribal history.

"I don't see why so many of these magazine writers get the facts wrong," Willie Warrior groused, waving the Xeroxed pages of some article as he spoke. "This one's about John Ward, Isaac Payne, and Pompey Factor getting their medals. But it's got all these mistakes in it. Big ones."

"Like what?" I asked.

"I'll tell it all to you myself, and show where this writer got it wrong. He should have asked me. I don't know who he talked to, or what he thought he read. There's bad information out there about us, and I'm tired of trying to correct it."

Bullis had heard of Comanche or Apache raiders in the lower Pecos, miles above Fort Clark, Willie said. He set out to track them; at one point, Bullis separated from the rest of the troops, taking with him three Seminole Negro scouts—Sergeant John Ward, Private Pompey Factor, and trumpeter Isaac Payne. The four headed west, looking for spoor. The scouts found signs that a large body of Indians, twenty-five or even thirty of them, was driving a herd of about eighty horses ahead of them, heading for the Pecos River with the apparent intention of moving further west. It was probably Bullis's intent to follow the hostiles until they camped, then return to get the rest of his troops. Anything else would have been foolhardy. Four men could hardly fight thirty.

It was hard going for Bullis and his men. Even in April, it was brutally hot, and there was little water to be had. The few springs in the area were known as well to the hostiles as to the army. When the Indians felt they might be pursued—as was the case here—they would fill up their own water bags and then foul the springs to ruin the water for whoever came along next. Sometimes they would kill an animal and dump its body in the water, or else they would relieve themselves in the water, anything to render it undrinkable for men or horses. Bullis and his three scouts had to drink to keep from becoming dehydrated; their horses, at least, had been well-watered before they left. So, coming on a fouled spring, Willie said, they put their handkerchiefs over their mouths and sucked water through the cloth, trying to keep out the maggots that already crawled on the water's surface. The liquid that they sucked in tasted horrible, but at least it was wet. Afterward, they put pebbles under their tongues to stimulate saliva flow and kept on riding.

Eventually they breasted a crest near the Pecos and saw below them the Indian war party preparing to drive the horses across. Maybe Bullis and the scouts were too used to Indians running away when attacked. After all, most of the hostiles they fought had come to Texas to steal, not to fight. So the officer and three scouts tethered their horses, grabbed their rifles, crawled to within seventy-five yards of the Indians, and opened fire.

It was a terrible mistake. Besides having a huge advantage in numbers, these hostiles were well-armed. For almost an hour, they stood their ground and returned fire. Bullis, Ward, Payne, and Factor spread out, trying to give the impression there were more than four men on their side. At least twice, their attack was effective enough to drive the hostiles away from the horse herd.

But the Indians fought back. Finally, they figured out there were only a few soldiers shooting at them. Now it was the hostiles' turn to try to cut their enemies off from their horses. Realizing what was happening, Bullis and the three scouts gave up their attack and tried to run back to their mounts. In Bullis's words in a later report, "We were at last compelled to give way, as they were about to get around us and cut us off from our horses."

"Now, I've walked this place," Willie said. "What I tell you is fact. I saw the place with my own eyes and heard these stories from men who were part of it all. This next part I'll tell you is the exact truth."

The four men had all they could do to put up fire to cover their retreat. Momentarily, each lost sight of the others. The three scouts made it to their horses, mounted up, and began spurring their animals away. But the Indians got between Bullis and his horse. The white lieutenant was as good as dead.

John Ward yanked his horse to a halt; he realized that Bullis was missing.

Looking back, he saw what was happening. He called to Pompey Factor and Isaac Payne. Experienced fighters all, they knew instinctively what to do.

John Ward rode straight to Bullis. The other two Seminole Negro fired at the Indians as fast as they could pull their triggers. The hostiles didn't turn and run; they fired back, and several bullets smashed John Ward's rifle to bits. It was a miracle he wasn't hit, except for a few flying splinters from the stock of his gun. Bullis saw his sergeant coming; the white officer and Seminole Negro scout clasped hands, and John Ward pulled Bullis behind him on his horse. Pompey Factor and Isaac Payne kept up a covering fire until the other two were beyond the range of the Indians' rifles. With at least four of their own number dead, the hostiles didn't pursue them.

In his subsequent report, Bullis admitted, "The truth is, there were some twenty-five or thirty Indians in all, and mostly armed with Winchester guns, and they were too much for us." Far from faulting Bullis for extremely questionable judgment in attacking the hostiles at all, on May 12 his superiors issued General Order No. 10, which read in part "words commendatory of the energy, gallantry and good judgement displayed by Lieutenant Bullis, and the courageous and soldierly conduct of the three scouts who composed his party are not needed. The simple narrative given by himself explains fully the difficulties and dangers of his expedition. His own conduct as well as that of his men, is well worthy of imitation, and shows us what an officer can do who means business."

So Bullis was officially commended for something that could very well have been cause for criticism, if not disciplinary action. It says a lot about him, though, that afterward he was unstinting in his praise for the three Seminole Negro scouts who saved his life. Bullis took the necessary steps, and, on May 28, John Ward, Pompey Factor, and Isaac Payne were each awarded the Medal of Honor. The army even spelled "Payne" correctly this time.

When Willie was finished telling the story, he handed me the offending article and told me to read it. I did and didn't see much difference between its version of events and his. I said so.

"Wrong!" he snorted. "Look at this here!" He pointed to a paragraph describing the fight.

"It says John Ward got his rifle shot to bits, but that he still saved Bullis," I said. "What's wrong with that?"

"What's *wrong*? I'll tell you. It says here John Ward's rifle was shattered during the main fight. It wasn't. It got shot up near the end, while he was riding to Bullis. That's a big mistake."

"It doesn't seem like one to me. It's just a little detail."

Willie glared. "You think so because it's not a lie told on *your* people. We never got respect, never got our land. Can't we at least get our story told right?"

chapter thirteen

WILLIE AND ETHEL WARRIOR occasionally had other guests when I went over to their home in the old Fort Clark barracks. Sometimes they were relatives—there always seemed to be a grandchild clattering around—and once in a while Willie might say I should sit down and talk to someone because he or she was a scout descendant and had heard good stories from an older relative. These people were wonderful to meet; if there's a consistent trait among modern-day Seminole Negro, it must be friendliness. After accepting coffee and some sort of snack from Ethel, they would tell me about the adventures of a grandfather or great-uncle, but their tales often weren't coherent enough for me to include in my notes. Names might be garbled, or the name of a place might change three or four times in a single story. This made it all the more evident how rare a true gift for storytelling is. Miss Charles had that gift; so did Willie Warrior. But most people, no matter how well-meaning, don't.

So I was pleased but not overly excited one hot July day—there are no other kind of July days in Brackettville—when Willie greeted me on his back porch by saying he had two special people for me to meet.

"One's got a story about Bullis and the scouts you need to hear," he said. "It's never been written up before, to my knowledge. Girl's name is Cynthia Ventura, and she's come down here from Illinois trying to get some information on her family."

"Is she related to a scout?"

"You bet, and otherwise related, too. I'll let her explain what I mean. And she's got an auntie with her, older lady, and this one's got great stories about the old fort camp that her granddaddy passed down to her. You'll want to write these down. Get on in and meet 'em."

Thirty-something Cynthia Ventura and Odilia Menchaca, her elderly aunt, both had plenty to tell about. Odilia needed little urging. I'd barely shaken her hand and pulled out my notebook before she started. Like Miss Charles, she was bent with age, and her voice was fluttery. And as with Miss Charles, there was the immediate sense that she was repeating something exactly as she had heard it herself many years earlier.

"My grandfather used to tell us about when his father was a scout," she began. "Grandfather's name was Everado. His father was Victoriano Frausto, one of the scouts. When my grandfather was twelve, living with his family in the village at Fort Clark, he decided he wanted to be a scout, too. He heard his father and some of the other men telling about chasing Indians with Bullis. He wanted to do this, too. He kept insisting he had to join. Finally his father took him to Bullis, who told him he was still too young, he had to wait until he was sixteen or seventeen. But at least Everado was given a rifle for his twelfth birthday."

It was a battered old gun, Odilia explained, too dented with battlefield use to be very accurate anymore. But it thrilled the boy, who took it with him on his daily assignment of keeping an eye on the camp's small flock of sheep and goats, which grazed out of sight of the main village. The flock had to be guarded; occasionally, though not often, hostiles came sneaking into the area. Everado had spent many happy hours daydreaming about how he might someday thwart an attack single-handed. His new weapon helped make those daydreams more specific.

"He was real proud of that rifle," Odilia said. "As Everado watched the goats he kept praying, 'God, send me an Indian to kill.' Then late one afternoon he looked across a little rise and saw an Indian coming up, then another, then another, until there were about twelve in all."

The Indians spotted Everado, too, and raced their ponies toward him. The boy dropped his rifle and ran. Everado was able to dive into a ditch just before the hostiles caught up to him. There was enough cover there for him to hide. The Indians knew he had to be near. They eased their horses around the brush, quietly calling, "Muchacho." They couldn't launch a full-scale search, because crackling branches and the child's screams, if he survived the first seconds of capture, would have alerted the rest of the Seminole Negro.

"To Everado, it seemed like the longest time before they went on, and then he realized they were heading for the camp where his mother and sisters were," Odilia recounted, waving her hands a little as her own story got her excited. "He got out of the ditch and ran in that direction, and when he got to the camp it was deserted. He heard horses coming again. That's when he realized he didn't have his rifle. But when the horses came into camp he saw it was his father and some of the soldiers. After Everado had left to watch the goats and sheep, word came from the fort that there were renegades in the area. Everyone in camp had been rounded up and moved to the main part of the fort, and in the excitement his mother had forgotten about him. She remembered, told his father, and his father got some soldiers and they went back to find him. So you see, it wasn't safe all the time in the camp."

Sadly, even when the scouts were back from their expeditions they still weren't safe. In Eagle Pass and in Brackettville, white townspeople continued to resent their presence. It still wasn't clear if they were soon to be given land in Indian Territory, which would please them and their unfriendly Texas neighbors. Before Cynthia Ventura told her story, Willie said he needed to set the stage by explaining how the scouts at Fort Duncan were all transferred to Fort Clark, where the citizens of Brackettville were unhappy to see them arrive.

"We'd won those Medals of Honor," Willie began, leaning forward on the hard metal chair he'd taken while leaving the more comfortable chairs and sofas for his guests. "But the army at Fort Duncan and here at Fort Clark still weren't set on what they were supposed to do with us. They kept taking these damn surveys, like that was going to solve anything, and our people still couldn't get government food and their babies were *hungry*."

In May of 1875, the tribe waited in the camps at Fort Duncan and Fort

Clark while information gathered at General Ord's command was tallied and evaluated. First came results from Fort Duncan: The Elm Creek camp was inhabited by 107 Seminole Negro. Nineteen men were enlisted as scouts. Two more men "weren't suitable." Fifty-five women and children were part of the scouts' immediate families. That left seven old people who couldn't fend for themselves at all, and seventeen assorted men, women, and children who needed some assistance. John Horse was described as "decrepit." The report identified John Kibbetts, now at least in his mid-sixties, as the undisputed camp leader.

There was something more that the report compilers found disturbing. Except for John Kibbetts, none of the Seminole Negro at Elm Creek wanted to go back to Indian Territory. They were settled in Texas, they said. It was their home now. Many of the younger people had never even lived in Indian Territory—they'd been born in Mexico or at Fort Duncan. To them, "Indian Territory" was simply a name, not a longed-for promised land. The consensus of the Elm Creek tribe was that the Americans should honor their promise by giving the Seminole Negro land around Fort Duncan.

Colonel William Shafter, the current commander of Fort Duncan, was less than delighted by this news. Perhaps he wanted the scouts and their families to leave, a curious wish in light of the great military service the scouts were providing. At any rate, Shafter responded with an order that only enlisted scouts and their immediate families could have army rations. He softened the edict slightly by adding it might be permissable to occasionally give extra food to sick Seminole Negro, and to women and children who had no man to provide for them.

At Fort Clark, the count indicated 151 Seminole Negro, twenty-nine of them scouts. It was reported about one-third of the rest had no means of supporting themselves. Further, most of the older Seminole Negro in the Las Moras Creek band wanted to go back to Indian Territory. There were a lot of them—fifty, at least—who were ready to leave.

Bullis emphasized in his reports that the Fort Clark band was stealing livestock from white ranchers. They had to steal or starve, he noted, but that didn't mean their white neighbors appreciated the tribe's dire situation. Many of the younger Fort Clark scouts were threatening to go back to Mexico, and the U.S. Army still needed them in Texas.

Various officials in Washington returned their rulings: The Seminole Negro at Fort Duncan didn't want to return to Indian Territory, and the Indian bureau couldn't do anything for them in Texas. The older Seminole Negro at Fort Clark wanted to return to Indian Territory, but the bureau didn't have the money to get them there, so they were out of luck, too. Secretary of War Belknap ruled that no more food was to be given to Seminole Negro dependents, period.

Elijah Daniels didn't give up. In August, he was back with a new proposal. He asked Colonel Edward Hatch, the current commander of Fort Clark, to make another request of the government. Daniels recognized that most of the nonfort property in the area was owned by white men, so there wasn't much hope there. But in Florida, where the Seminole Negro had originally lived, it was different. There was plenty of uncultivated land. What about an arrangement where the tribe went back to Florida and rented land for farms? If things went well, they could make enough profit from their harvests to eventually buy the land outright. Failing that, Daniels warned, the tribe was ready to give up on the Americans and return to Mexico.

Hatch forwarded the plan to Belknap. The war secretary liked it; sending the pesky Seminole Negro back to Florida would get them out of his hair once and for all. The Daniels plan was passed along to Edward P. Smith, the commissioner of Indian Affairs.

As Smith and his staff began to deliberate, someone else inserted himself into the debate. Charles Jones, a U.S. senator from Florida, got wind of the proposal and immediately opposed it. While Jones had never personally met a Seminole Negro, he somehow divined that they were shiftless border thugs. Black thugs, at that. If they came to Florida, the white people there wouldn't tolerate their presence. There would be violence, maybe outright riots. It was a case of government interference in states' rights, Jones added. These black Indians were poor people, downright beggars, and once they came to Florida, it would be the taxpayers of the state who had to support them. Forget their promises to plant crops and support themselves. Who believed that? And don't try and make out that because the tribe had once lived in Florida, the people of Florida had any obligation to them. Those original Seminole Negro had been slaves, not real citizens. Those living in Florida prior to the Civil War had no rights. Those born after the tribe had left the state were foreigners. None of these "semi-barbarous people" was owed anything by the good citizens of Florida, and the government would just have to inflict them on some other state.

Commissioner Smith thanked Jones for his comments and continued deliberating. Back in Texas, Bullis expected another Indian bureau mandate that it was someone else's responsibility to help the Seminole Negro. But, on September 20, Smith shocked everyone by ruling in the tribe's favor.

There were several reasons why it was the government's responsibility to help the Seminole Negro, Smith concluded. The United States had initially moved them from Florida to Indian Territory, but didn't protect them in their new home. John Horse led his people to Mexico out of desperation, not any attempt to disavow ties to the American government. The problems the tribe now faced in Texas were the direct result of the earlier U.S. decision to uproot them from their original homeland. Second, if the Seminole Negro were left to starve in Texas, they might easily become bandits themselves. It was already hard enough for the army to protect white citizens on the border. Third, the tribe had shown ample evidence that, given enough land for farming, they were capable of raising sufficient crops to feed themselves—that meant they would no longer have to rely on government handouts. So they must be helped—immediately.

But sending the Seminole Negro to Florida obviously wasn't the best option. Senator Jones had made it clear they weren't wanted there, and it would be wrong to impose them on such inhospitable hosts. In 1866, the Seminole Nation had formally adopted all the Seminole Negro still living in Indian Territory. These blacks were made full citizens among the Seminole and given places on the tribal council (no one knew, of course, that 130 years later they would be voted out again). Smith requested a $40,000 governmental supplement to pay to move the rest of the Seminole Negro from Texas back to Indian Territory. And, miracle of miracles, Interior Department officials agreed.

It wasn't what all the Seminole Negro wanted—the old people at Fort Duncan were especially disgruntled—but it was something. To expedite the plan, the Elm Creek Seminole Negroes were told to move over to Fort Clark, so all members of the tribe would be together when it came time to leave. That, at least, was the public explanation.

"Thing was, the white outlaws in Eagle Pass were out to kill all the scouts at Fort Duncan," Willie continued. "They hated 'em, just *hated* 'em. So the army had to move the scouts out."

In January and February of 1876, the Fort Duncan Seminole Negro moved themselves and their meager belongings to the other scout camp along Las Moras Creek on the Fort Clark grounds. The spot, perhaps a mile long and a half-mile wide, was, and still remains, astonishingly lovely. The main post, which was about three miles from the Seminole Negro village, stood on what passed for a high bluff in that part of West Texas. A deep creek and natural pool of spring water offered a sort of oasislike effect for the officers and enlisted men stationed there. A few hundred yards away were the stores and saloons of Brackettville.

But the Seminole Negro lived in an area shaded by massive oak trees; the creek bubbled near the wood huts they built. There were fish in that creek—unlike many Indians, the Seminole Negro were happy to eat fish—and the water was convenient for washing clothes and watering the gardens planted by each family. There were deer and wild turkey in the surrounding woods. The land seemed more like lush Florida territory than something to be found and enjoyed in arid West Texas. In that sense, the Seminole Negro were lucky to live there. Their surroundings were certainly less oppressive than the dusty ranches of most of their white neighbors.

But such advantages were largely offset by new or continuing problems. With some 260 men, women, and children in the combined group, there wasn't enough room on the land allocated to the scouts for any families to have extended gardens. There were also pride-of-place issues. Elijah Daniels had been headman of the Fort Clark village since its inception, and his followers had, naturally, claimed all the best land for themselves. But the Fort Duncan group was more senior in army service. John Kibbetts had always understood himself to be the head Seminole Negro scout. He insisted that Elijah Daniels answer to him, not vice versa. Old John Horse still had his pride, too; he expected to be consulted on everything. Many of the older arrivals from Fort Duncan constantly grumbled about the promised permanent relocation back to Indian Territory. They didn't want to go and often commented they simply might refuse to leave, which made the Fort Clark contingent nervous. After all this time, they'd finally extracted a promise by the Americans to fulfill old promises and send everyone back home to Indian Territory. What if these grumpy ingrates complained so much that the Americans reneged? It seemed, so often, that Americans were ready to capitalize on the slightest excuse to back out of agreements. Gradually, the two sides split geographically as well as philosophically. Most of the Daniels group lived above Las Moras Creek; the Fort Duncan families lived below it.

Such in-family fussing was only part of the tribe's problem. Though they argued among themselves, they seldom resorted to physical violence. But they had other enemies with no qualms about attacking Seminole Negro. Eagle Pass had been dangerous for the Seminole Negro. Brackettville turned out to be worse.

The town existed because of the fort. In 1852, Oscar B. Brackett opened a dry goods store near newly built Fort Clark. The soldiers often needed sundries not available at the fort commissary. Where there were soldiers, saloons would inevitably follow. The village soon known as Brackett or Brackett City almost instantly had several. It was another twenty years before the place had its first church.

The town officially became Brackettville in 1873, when it received a post office. There was already another Texas city calling itself Brackett. But by any name, Brackettville itself was a squalid, nasty place.

Part of that couldn't be helped. The fort was built on the best land. A few civilians had the money necessary to purchase sprawling tracts north of town, where at least there were some hills, but many Brackettville citizens found themselves limited to harsh, rattlesnake-riddled property that defied efforts to grow crops at all. They ranched rather than farmed, raising cattle and goats. These people worked hard, hot hours just to survive. Then, too, towns near the border always attracted a criminal element. Limited law enforcement meant poor, honest citizens often had to defer to gunslingers. People stayed in Brackettville because they didn't have the means or the gumption to go anywhere better.

What they all seemed to have was a seething resentment for two races—Indians and blacks. Few settlers in these parts escaped hostile raids. If some of their cattle weren't run off by raiders, or if members of their immediate families didn't die at Indian hands, they probably had friends who'd suffered such terrible fates. The philosophy of the only good Indians being dead ones was never more prevalent than in this region. Indian scouts, to these people, weren't much different from the hostiles. They hated them all.

They also hated blacks. Southern whites living hand-to-mouth existences had at least, prior to the Civil War, been able to style themselves superior to negroes and had that whole race to order around and otherwise denigrate. Now a forcibly reunified national government decreed that blacks were equal to whites. This was impossible for hardscrabble West Texas settlers to stomach.

So the vast majority of Brackettville's white citizenry couldn't decide which race they hated more, Indians or blacks. The Seminole Negro, of course, were something of both. If that wasn't guarantee enough that white townspeople would despise and resent them, from the first days that Elijah Daniels's people settled in at Las Moras Creek they began to supplement their inadequate army rations with chickens and cattle pilfered from small area ranches. The Seminole Negro were stealing to avoid starvation, but the impoverished whites they were stealing from weren't much beyond near-starvation themselves. There was constant tension because of the ongoing thefts. Delegations of Brackettville citizens would call on the various commanders at Fort Clark. Promises would be made that the tribespeople would stop raiding chicken coops and corrals. For a while, things might be better. Then there would be another governmental decree cutting tribal rations, and the stealing would start again.

The Seminole Negro always believed that, about 1876, some Brackettville citizens hired their old enemy King Fisher to move north from Eagle Pass and do whatever he could to terrorize the tribe into leaving Fort Clark. There certainly was never any written contract, and the matter is clouded further by the alleged presence in the area of two King Fishers, one black and one white. Supposedly the black King Fisher later claimed he'd been hired for that purpose, but it would be odd for angry white Brackettville citizens to turn to a black gunslinger for help. Still, there is no question the townspeople wanted the Seminole Negro gone—if not to Indian Territory, then back to Mexico. Anywhere but Brackettville.

There's also no question that on Friday, May 19, matters exploded in violence. John Horse was still spry enough, on warm late spring days, to ride gently from the Las Moras Creek camp to the Brackettville saloons. He had to love his liquor to frequent such dangerous places. One was named the Bloody Bucket. All of them were frequented by angry drunks looking for fights. But on this particular day, John Horse came, drank for a while, and then began the ride back to the Seminole Negro camp. Just back on fort grounds, he met retired scout Titus Payne, who was carrying a sack of rations. Food was scarce back at the Las Moras Creek camp, and someone in the commissary had felt generous. Titus Payne was armed; we don't know if John Horse had a gun. They began taking the dusty trail that led from the main fort area to the Seminole Negro camp, and, as they moved away from the last buildings and white soldiers, they were ambushed. Titus Payne was killed instantly; his body dropped to the dusty ground. Sixty-four-year-old John Horse was hit several times; his horse was shot twice. Incredibly, the old man wasn't knocked out of the saddle. His wounded horse lurched back toward the Seminole Negro camp, with John Horse bleeding badly and doing his best to hang on.

The bushwhackers didn't follow; when John Horse reached the camp and fell to the ground there, he was conscious and gasped out what had happened. The men in camp snatched up their rifles and raced back toward the main fort. It was easy for them to spot where the ambush had taken place—there were scuff marks in the dirt, not to mention pools of blood—but Titus Payne's body was missing. Whoever murdered him had also mastered the art of stealth. The scouts, among the finest trackers in the history of the American West, couldn't find their old comrade's body for three days. Finally, on Monday, it was discovered when buzzards began circling over a nearby spot. Payne's body was laid out in the dirt, his gun laid prominently across his chest. This menacing gesture proved to the scouts that ordinary Brackettville citizens hadn't made the attack. The army investigated; none of Brackettville's residents claimed to know anything about the incident. At the Las Moras Creek camp, tribal leaders fumed. There was much discussion about everyone leaving at once, with the enlisted scouts simply deserting. They could all go back to Mexico, or up to Indian Territory. They'd made their own way before with no help from the Americans.

Kibbetts, Daniels, and other community elders argued that things were different now. Yes, Titus Payne was dead. John Horse was seriously hurt, but the tough old man would survive. The Americans had promised to send everyone back to Indian Territory soon. Yes, they'd promised this before, but now they had moved everyone to Fort Clark because the move north was imminent. Bullis probably helped emphasize this point. Why risk leaving on their own, he told them, when, in a matter of weeks, or, at most, a few months, the government would provide them with everything they needed to make the trip to Indian Territory in relative comfort?

Angry as they were, the tribespeople saw the sense in waiting just a little longer. John Horse rested, recovering from his wounds. There were no more ambushes. There wasn't much food, either. Everyone seemed to be marking time.

That lasted for about three weeks, until a new commissioner of Indian Affairs reversed his predecessor's decision to help the Seminole Negro go back to Indian Territory.

John Q. Smith shared only a last name with Edward P. Smith. Their attitudes toward the scouts were radically different. Edward P. Smith spoke of government obligation to the Seminole Negro. John Q. Smith said there was no obligation at all. The Indian bureau, the new commissioner ruled, had never invited the tribe to come back to America from Mexico. Maybe their presence in Texas was helpful to the army, but it meant nothing to the Indian bureau. Further, it was the *Indian* bureau, and *Indian* Territory. These people were black, not Indians. How could anyone believe they were entitled to land in Indian Territory, or help from the commissioner of Indian Affairs?

The Seminole Negro didn't accept this edict. They kept trying. But Smith's decision had the effect of fragmenting the tribe. A few wanted to go back to Mexico immediately. Others wanted to make their way north to Indian Territory, where they were certain they'd be welcomed by both their Seminole Negro friends and relatives and the Seminole who had once considered them nothing more than slaves. Most, though, saw no particular sense in wandering somewhere else. They'd lived in Indian Territory, they'd lived in Mexico, and neither place had proven safe or permanent. The camp on Las Moras Creek was home. Enemies seemed to be everywhere, not just in Brackettville. At least in Texas there was Bullis.

The Seminole Negro loved John Lapham Bullis. Usually, when history books mention the scouts at all, it is as an adjunct to describing Bullis's exceptional army career. In every one of his assignments—leading the scouts was only one of these—he always succeeded in inspiring troops to achieve more than most observers would have considered possible. Just before Bullis retired in 1904, President Theodore Roosevelt promoted him from major to brigadier general, one of the greatest leaps in permanent rank in American military history. That wasn't all; a decade later, when the army built a new training base near San Antonio, it was named for Bullis.

But in all his service, during the Civil War and with the Buffalo Soldiers and in the Philippines and Cuba, perhaps Bullis's greatest, if entirely unnoted, achievement came in 1876, when he was able to convince the Seminole Negro scouts to continue their own dedicated service to the army even though their fabled leader had been shot from ambush and the commissioner of Indian Affairs had reneged on the promise of his predecessor. In part, certainly, they stayed because many among them had given up hope they would ever be given land of their own. But they also stayed because Bullis said he needed them.

Certain scholars, Kenneth Porter especially, have written about Bullis's knack for making each scout feel he was important to his white commander. Bullis not only knew every scout's name, he made a point of knowing the names of their wives and children, too. If a Seminole Negro at Fort Clark was sick, Bullis would call on his or her family, offering best wishes for a full recovery and, sometimes, a dollar or two for extra medicine or special treats. (Though Bullis's army pay was negligible, his father was a doctor and his wife came from a wealthy family.) In the field, Bullis fought side by side with his men. The decision in 1875 by John Ward, Pompey Factor, and Isaac Payne to risk their own lives to save Bullis was indictative of the loyalty he inspired.

"There's another thing about Bullis, though," Willie Warrior said, his eyes twinkling. "I asked Cynthia to show you something."

Cynthia pulled out a plastic-covered notebook. Inside were old photos, letters, and a Xeroxed copy of an ancient birth certificate.

"Everybody talks and writes about how good he was to the scouts, how he cared about them," she said. "Of course he did. He was part of the family, of my aunt's and my family, the Fraustos."

"I've never heard this," I said.

"You're hearing it now," Cynthia replied. "Bullis was my great-great grandfather. You need to hear all about Bullis and Gomacinda."

An exceptionally beautiful young woman, at least according to Cynthia Ventura, Gomacinda was the daughter of Victoriano Frausto and Nicomedes Rodrigues. When her father joined the scouts, he moved from Mexico to Fort Clark and brought his family with him. Gomacinda was about nineteen when she arrived in Texas.

In 1872, Bullis, then assigned to the Twenty-fourth Infantry on the lower Rio Grande border, married Alice Rodriguez of San Antonio. It was not common for army officers, especially those of junior grade—Bullis

Lieutenant John L. Bullis, army commander of the Seminole Negro scouts at Fort Clark
(COURTESY OF THE FORT CLARK HISTORICAL SOCIETY)

was still a lieutenant—to bring their wives to primitive forts in dangerous territory. Alice remained in San Antonio; Bullis would visit her on leave.

When Bullis was transferred to command the Seminole Negro scouts in 1873, he didn't tell Alice to pack up and move to Fort Clark or Brackettville. Instead, he rode off to his new assignment, met Gomacinda, and, apparently, took up with her. Though he was assigned a bed in Fort Clark's officer's barracks, Bullis actually moved to the Las Moras Springs camp. He lived openly with Gomacinda there.

"It's always been common knowledge among the descendants," Willie Warrior said. "Everybody knew about it. We never talked about it other times because nobody ever asked."

If it happened, Bullis's relationship with Gomacinda would not have been unusual, either for military officers with scouts under their commands or among the Seminole Negro themselves. On the so-called "Indian Frontiers," officers often took tribal mistresses. Some helped themselves to women who had been captured, which, even if not overt rape, certainly seems morally questionable. George Custer is rumored to have done this.

"Officers were allowed a certain license in such things," observed Ross McSwain when I talked with him a few days later in San Angelo. "I don't doubt there's a basis to this Cynthia Ventura's story."

In the case of Bullis and Gomacinda, the Seminole Negro were probably proud to have their commander take one of the group's women as his lover. Seminole Negro men were often not monogamous themselves. Bullis hadn't forced himself on the young woman.

On July 27, 1876, just about the time John Q. Smith was squelching Seminole Negro hopes of returning to Indian Territory, Gomacinda gave birth to a son named Jose Frausto. The birth certificate, which Cynthia Ventura found and copied, includes information about the mother, but not the father. Baby Jose had blue eyes. His tribespeople nicknamed him "El Boleo," Spanish slang for "white man."

So, after Gomacinda's son was born and John Horse and Titus Payne were ambushed, Bullis argued from the position of a tribal member that the Seminole Negro should remain in Brackettville. Because of this, his opinion carried even more weight than that of a beloved commander. In any case, with the exception of a few deserters, they decided to stay.

Staying, of course, would require more fighting by the scouts. Despite their disappointment and anger, they followed Bullis back out into West Texas to serve the government that had rejected them and the white settlers who despised them.

chapter fourteen

IT WAS ALWAYS BEST to visit the old scout village site on Fort Clark in the very early morning, around six or seven A.M. when the heat wasn't as oppressive. Usually, there were grazing deer to watch, or waddling flocks of wild turkey. Everything was shady and peaceful. It was a special place to be.

After my three-year absence, I was anxious to go there again. Besides the pleasure of Willie and Ethel Warrior's company, and getting to know Clarence Ward, there wasn't much else that was enjoyable about Brackettville. I deliberately didn't go to my favorite spot along Las Moras Creek when I arrived at Fort Clark in the middle of the afternoon. Instead, I put the pleasure off until the next morning, so I could enjoy the old village place at its optimum moment.

The slow ride south along Fort Clark's narrow main road wasn't much different. There were still trailer parks and houses along the way, with many of the latter's front yards sporting FOR SALE signs. The golf course was as flat and burned-looking as ever. Even at a little past six A.M., there were people out on its fairways and greens. Then I was past most of the course and approaching the clubhouse. A left turn, a short slow drive down the rock-and-dirt road, and I would be there.

Then I made the turn, and felt sick.

On the northern boundary of the area, close to where the first Seminole

Negro huts had once stood, two new houses had been built, big and sprawling, one with a wide, terraced garden. They were fine houses, much nicer than any others I'd seen on the Fort Clark property, but seeing them intruding on what had been near-pristine, bucolic grounds was like discovering a McDonald's and Burger King snuggled up to the Vatican.

It made sad sense. Affluent people wanting to live in Brackettville, on Fort Clark, would want to build on the choicest land, where they could lounge on their patios in the shade and maybe see a deer ease out from the adjacent woods. The surprise was probably that there hadn't been any houses built here earlier.

"Are they going to build houses all the way through where the old village was?" I asked Willie Warrior a few hours later. He'd driven in from Del Rio.

"'Cause I'm a member of the residents' association here with my place back in the old barracks, I get to vote about things like that," he said. "I hope they don't, I'll try to see that they don't, but who knows? They might take a little bit at a time, and I'm getting old. After me, who's gonna argue?"

"Do the people living at Fort Clark know anything about the scout history at all? Do they care?"

"Some do, though since Ben Pingenot died there isn't anyone I'd call an expert," Willie said. "Miss Charles and me put together a display about the scouts in their little museum here, and they've always been nice about it. Thing is, that old village when it was still standing was ours, and yet it wasn't. Army could come, tell us what to do. Damn sheriff came one time with a posse and murdered Adam Payne. You know about that? Right after John Horse got ambushed, right after we'd run some more damn Apache off for 'em. Still, they came onto our home, our *home,* and did us badly that way. It happened like this . . ."

In 1876, two main bands of Apache were preying on Texas settlers. The Mescalero swooped east from New Mexico, where, at least in theory, most of them lived on reservations. The Lipan still based themselves in Mexico; torn by internal civil strife, and without the services of the Seminole Negro, the government there simply couldn't keep the hostiles under control.

That was bad for the Mexicans, and not good for the Americans, who were also the objects of frequent Lipan raids. Even as John Horse lay in the Las Moras Creek camp recuperating from his wounds, Colonel Shafter was ordered to clean out Lipan villages in Mexico. He ordered Bullis to assemble the scouts, and in July a large company of troops marched south across the Rio Grande, risking a confrontation with Mexican soldiers to surprise the Lipan in their home territory.

On July 29 the scouts struck signs of a large Lipan camp, and soon Shafter ordered an attack. Though it lasted less than half an hour, this fight was no rout. Besides gunfire, there was hand-to-hand fighting. Several U.S. soldiers were hurt. One or two scouts had serious injuries, though they maintained their record of not suffering a single death. After the Indians finally retreated, the expedition had captured over one hundred horses along with four women. Driving the horses before them, the Americans headed north. They ran into a much smaller Mexican patrol, which threatened the larger U.S. contingent and then proved sensible enough to let it pass. As usual, the scouts had performed sterling work.

They'd barely returned to the Las Moras Creek camp when there was more trouble. Two scouts were accused of horse theft. One was Medal of Honor–winner Isaac Payne. He and Dallas Griner, the other scout included in the accusation, fled south to Nacimiento, where they joined the Seminole Negro still living there. Back in Brackettville, a white Kinney County jury indicted them for "the theft of a prize gelding," which belonged to Brackettville deputy sheriff Claron Windus. Stealing the deputy's horse was a particularly foolish thing to do; afterward, certainly, it gave Windus a grudge against the Seminole Negro remaining at Fort Clark.

But the Seminole Negro outlaw who became most notorious was Adam Payne, who'd left the scouts after winning his Medal of Honor—"One of the ones who just couldn't take all the army rules," Willie Warrior explained. The giant Seminole Negro had never really fit in as a scout, except for his ability as a fighter. Most of the tribesmen drank, but Adam Payne was a mean drunk. Sometime around Christmas 1875, he fought in Brownsville with a black Buffalo Soldier, John Bradley, and stabbed him to death. A plea of self-defense was never considered. The authorities weren't willing to grant Adam Payne much benefit of the doubt. Since he'd been discharged from the army in February, he'd prowled border towns getting drunk and, in rumor at least, stealing American livestock and selling it in Mexico. There wasn't a jail in Brownsville, so he was locked up in the town bull ring.

Imagine this hulking man pacing around, his boots kicking up dirt on the arena floor. Probably an armed guard was watching him. Like most of the Seminole Negro, Adam Payne combined mainstream Christian beliefs with Seminole tribal religion. Did he pray for help to the white or the Indian god? Some deity seemed to respond. A tornado raged into Brownsville and decimated the bull ring without injuring Adam Payne so badly that he couldn't escape in the confusion.

"You think God heard Adam Payne praying and sent a tornado?" I asked Willie tentatively. This was an element of almost biblical overtone I hadn't heard in his stories before.

"I don't say how that tornado came, just that it did."

"But you think it could have been some kind of miracle?"

"I think the spirits like to have their way. Whoever he had to thank, old Adam Payne ran out of there as fast as he could."

The Rio Grande offered the most convenient escape route. Adam Payne stayed in Matamoros for a while, but within months he was spotted riding in the gang of Frank Enoch, an outlaw whose reputation rivaled King Fisher's. Only the baddest of men rode with Enoch. Adam Payne qualified.

Maybe, if the Seminole Negro at Fort Clark hadn't been so bitter about the government reneging on its promise to send them back to Indian Territory, and if there hadn't been such anger about the ambush of Titus Payne and John Horse, the tribe would have been less willing to let Adam Payne and Frank Enoch occasionally come into Las Moras Creek and stay there. The outlaws were bold about their presence. Sometimes they rode into Brackettville and drank in the saloons there. At least once, Sheriff L. C. Crowell and Claron Windus tried to capture them. They found the two outlaws in a saloon. Crowell came through one door and Windus through the other. They demanded that the pair surrender.

In interviews separated by three years, Miss Charles and Willie described Adam Payne's reaction the same way. Not even bothering to put down his whiskey and go for his gun, the ex-scout snarled, "If you want to drink, do it. If you don't, get away from the doors!" Claron Windus was a brave man. He, too, had won a Medal of Honor, for battlefield gallantry in the Civil War. But Windus and Crowell moved away from the doors, and Adam Payne and Frank Enoch walked out.

Word of the confrontation got around. Both the sheriff and his deputy had been publicly humiliated, and they seethed about it. The next time, they agreed, there would be shooting instead of talking, and they would shoot first. The nature of the Seminole Negro guaranteed there would be a next time.

"Custom has been both the strength and the weakness of my people," Miss Charles commented during my first Brackettville visit in 1994. "We draw comfort from doing familiar, traditional things. Speaking Gullah at our old village. Greeting family and friends warmly, and never letting anyone go hungry in our homes. Coming home at any time of celebration. But this means we are also predictable, and I believe at times that offered an advantage to our enemies. This was the case with the death of Adam Payne. I'll tell you about that part of it soon."

She never did, but six years later Willie Warrior provided details.

It was easy enough for the white lawmen to guess when Adam Payne would be in Brackettville again. The Seminole Negro traditionally celebrated American holidays. For those who'd left Indian Territory with John Horse more than a quarter-century earlier, it was fitting to return to either Nacimiento or the Las Moras Creek camp to sing and dance with family and friends. There was limited feasting in both places; food was scarce, no matter what the occasion. Most of Adam Payne's family was at the Fort Clark camp, so that was where he went for Christmas and New Year's.

Sometime during the afternoon of December 31, Crowell was informed that Adam Payne was at the Las Moras Creek village. Frank Enoch was with him. Isaac Payne and Dallas Griner, those other two horse thieves, were also in the Seminole Negro camp. Crowell and Windus recruited a couple of local teamsters and started cleaning and loading their guns. It would be better to take the four after dark, they decided. With luck, all four would be drunk. They might not even be armed themselves.

That night there was dancing and singing at Las Moras Creek. The Seminole Negro men had whiskey bottles to pass around. There was music; perhaps someone was playing guitar. Adam Payne was dancing "in the Bowlegs yard," which makes the location sound more formal than it really was. Each Seminole Negro hut was separated from the others by as much distance as restricted space allowed. Crowell, Windus, James Thomas, and Jonathan May crept close under cover of darkness. Apparently, they hadn't announced themselves to the troops at the main fort. Windus cocked his shotgun; someone—probably Crowell—called out Adam Payne's name, and the deputy sheriff jumped up from hiding, pushed his shotgun against the ex-scout's back, and pulled the trigger. It was point-blank range; Adam Payne's shirt caught fire. He died instantly. Later, the white posse members claimed Adam Payne was shot in self-defense after he struggled while being handcuffed. But every Seminole Negro eyewitness denied it.

Robert Kibbetts was standing nearby. He leaped on Windus. Crowell and Thomas attacked Kibbetts. More shots were fired. In the confusion, Isaac Payne and Dallas Griner got away. Frank Enoch writhed on the ground, mortally wounded. He would die several days later.

Holding the rest of the Seminole Negro at bay with his gun, Crowell sent Windus back to town to fetch a justice of the peace and a wagon to haul off Adam Payne's body. But when the wagon arrived, the Seminole Negro wouldn't let their kinsman's remains be put in it. They said they would bury him themselves. Crowell, sensing the potential for a full-scale riot, agreed to leave the body. Enoch was loaded onto the wagon instead.

Not long afterward, Robert Kibbetts was indicted for interfering with Windus while the deputy sheriff was attempting to arrest a wanted criminal. Worse, Crowell tacked on a charge of attempted murder. He wasn't going to let anyone get away with attacking his deputy sheriff. This was too ludicrous for even a Brackettville jury. Five months later, when the case came to trial, the Seminole Negro was found not guilty.

But there were still repercussions. As morning broke on January 1, 1877, Medal of Honor winner Pompey Factor rode away from Fort Clark and headed back to Mexico. The army declared him a deserter. Within a week, there were two more—Pleasant McCallip and Joe Philips, the latter among the most gregarious of all the scouts, and the one who told the most tales of tribal history to the village children. Ex-scout Dindy Factor also returned to Nacimiento, but since he had no longer been on active duty he was not listed as deserting too. Isaac Payne and Dallas Griner joined the other four. They were all hired by the Mexican government to fight Indians there.

One more member of the tribe rode south. Old John Horse, still aching from the wounds he'd suffered months earlier, swung stiffly onto his saddle and went back to Mexico. Though his service to his people wasn't quite over—he was immediately proclaimed chief of the Mexican *Mascogos*—he never set foot in the United States again.

"John Horse would not have left, I think, if he held any further hope the government was going to give land to the scouts," Ben Pingenot said. "I will say it's hard not to believe that, most of the time, the Seminole Negro were just too trusting of a people. They should have realized years earlier that no land was coming to them, at least not from the Americans, even if the scouts did believe there was a binding treaty. But they chose to stay anyway, and it took some of them being killed in brutal ways to get the message across."

Bullis now had a near-rebellion to quell. Somehow, he convinced the remaining scouts to join in an expedition against raiding Lipans. The chase was unsuccessful; this time, at least, the scouts didn't track down their quarry. But by getting the Seminole Negro men out of camp and keeping them busy, Bullis probably averted more immediate trouble.

But when the scouts returned to Fort Clark in late January, they found everyone else in camp to be depressed. For so many years, the Seminole Negro had expected that sometime soon they'd be given their own land—

in Texas, in Florida, in Indian Territory. That hadn't happened. In recent months, they'd seen two of their people murdered. Who would be next?

It took an extended mission in June and July to force the scouts to shake their lethargy. The high summer months were always prime for Apache raids. This time Bullis and his men trailed a substantial band of hostiles. The Indians moved quickly, always staying ahead of their pursuers. As usual, they poisoned water holes after filling up their own water bags. For almost two days, the trailing scouts and their commander had no water. They were afraid that their horses would die. Finally, they stumbled upon water. The men and animals were saved from dying of thirst, but some of the scouts had to be left behind with sick horses while the rest of the party continued the pursuit. When signs indicated the Apache had somehow crossed a deep portion of the Rio Grande, the scouts built log rafts to ferry across. Some of the old-timers remarked how, in 1850, they'd done the same thing to cross from the north to the south bank. Soon afterward, they caught up to the Lipan and engaged in an hour-long gunfight. Some of the hostiles died, but none of the scouts. They recaptured many stolen horses, and Bullis rode ahead on the trail back to Fort Clark to write his report praising the Seminole Negro.

By this time, the scouts weren't fighting in the belief that their service would be ended soon and that they'd then be given land for a permanent home. Along Las Moras Creek, their tribe's old people were still hungry. Their own wives and children needed food and clothing. At least the army salaries were paid as promised. Tension between the Seminole Negro and white citizens of Brackettville had eased somewhat. After Adam Payne's death and the white jury's vote to acquit Robert Kibbetts, the Seminole Negro and townspeople gradually entered into an uneasy truce. Each side disliked the other, but there was no more gunplay. Some of the area ranchers still complained that their chickens, goats, and cattle were being stolen. If so, tribal members weren't stealing enough. When Seminole Negro old people died, it was often from diseases that claimed them while they were weakened by hunger. In 1872, the army had allowed the tribe to utilize a small tract of land as a cemetery. Later, a little more land was added to that by a sympathetic white rancher. The Seminole Negro buried their people there with love and elaborate ceremony. Many of them had studied or even adopted Catholicism in Mexico. Various threads of Protestantism were assimilated in America. There was also some adherence to earlier Seminole religion. This spiritual stew was always in evidence at the cemetery. There would be prayers and hymns during burial services. At other times, just as earnestly, men and women would gather to commune with spirits and talk seriously of shape-shifters. But, as they became convinced that land to permanently live on might never be coming from the American government, the cemetery itself began to mean more and more to the tribe. It was the only land they had anywhere that was clearly their own. Many families with relatives buried there would have been reluctant to leave the graves of their loved ones behind by moving back to Indian Territory or Florida. The army and Brackettville townspeople seemed to respect the Seminole Negro attachment to the cemetery with its scrubby mesquite brush and flinty, pebble-strewn ground. And, even during the summer of 1877 when the people of the Las Moras Creek camp were at their most discouraged, they still kept the grounds well-weeded and clean. It was *theirs*.

On the afternoon of the same day I discovered the new houses on the edge of the old village site, Brackettville was struck by a violent thunderstorm. There was no surprise to it. The boiling black clouds were clearly visible along the flat western horizon for several hours before the first lightning flashed. But the immediate result of the pounding rain was amazing.

Brackettville and all the country around it began to flood, instantly and extensively. The scrawny brush outside the greener fort grounds was always anchored by shallow roots in a shallow layer of dirt and dust covering hard, nonporous shale underneath. In typical weather, Brackettville is parched. But anything heavier than a soft shower drops too much water for the thin dirt to absorb. Every bridge, every ravine crossing for a hundred miles in any direction has by it a highway sign warning of flash floods. Drivers are urged to immediately get to higher ground. Often animals, and occasionally people, drown in flash floods.

The storm lasted about two hours before raging past Brackettville and on to the east toward Uvalde. The sun reappeared. Some of the water ran off; more steamed away. The moment the clouds were gone, the sun was back in full summer force, and the moisture added to the normal heat made conditions brutal. By late afternoon there were still huge pools of water standing everywhere. I tried to drive to the old village site to see what damage might have been done there, but the final back road of rock and dirt that seemed so solid before was a muddy mess and I had to turn around. Curious, I drove instead to the scout cemetery outside of town. The road there was littered with brush uprooted by the storm. Steam rose from the pavement.

The cemetery was a mess. Many of the newer graves, rising up from the ground where dirt, rock, and clay had been heaped over coffins, were suddenly lopsided. No casket edges seemed to be poking out anywhere, but it had to be a near thing. Everywhere, artificial flowers were strewn in dripping bunches, blown away from the headstones where they'd been lovingly placed. Even the nicest graves had been marked by the storm—glops of mud, kicked up by the pounding raindrops, freckled every headstone. I didn't stay long. It was so hot and damp that even the breeze felt oily.

The next morning, I went back to the old village site, noting with relief that, except for the two houses, it looked all right. There were even a few deer grazing there. I drove on to the cemetery, intending a closer look at the damage and was shocked for the second morning in a row.

The battered fresh graves had been remolded. All the artificial flowers were back in place. Most of the headstones, though not all, had been cleaned. All this had to have been done in the broiling, steambath conditions of yesterday in the late afternoon and evening. But who?

"I guess some of my members got out," Clarence Ward said as we sipped iced tea at the Burger 'n' Shake. "We *are* the cemetery association, you know."

"That must have been brutal work yesterday, though," I said. "It was so hot and sticky. Why didn't they wait until the next morning?"

"That cemetery is all some of them have got. I expect that during the whole storm, they were just waiting to go out there and fix things back up."

In fall 1877, when their cemetery was still relatively new, the scouts were called back for active duty. Their original part-time arrangement with the army was still in place. When Bullis needed scouts, the enlisted Seminole Negro were expected to report and obey his commands. Otherwise, their time was their own. There is every indication that, for the first nine months of 1877, Bullis sometimes set out with the scouts on expeditions that weren't initiated by hostile raids. Probably, he just wanted to keep his charges busy and away from Brackettville, where so much off-duty trouble had occurred. But, beginning in September 1877, the Apache intensified their attacks in the area, and the scouts were unquestionably needed.

On September 26, Bullis and the scouts were again deep in Mexico. There were also some troops along on the mission. The Seminole Negro told Bullis they'd found tracks of Lipan hunting or war parties. After following the tracks for three days, the entire force stumbled on the Lipan village. The hostiles were caught by surprise and ran while their village and all their supplies were destroyed. Some of the U.S. troops chased after the Lipan; a small guard of Mexican cavalry intervened. There was no fighting between the American and Mexican soldiers, but the Mexicans made a point of following the U.S. troops as Bullis led them back north to the border. Later, the Mexican government filed a protest about the unauthorized invasion of their country by American troops. In Washington, officials were concerned enough to ask Bullis and Shafter to testify about the incident. But, at the time, the Lipan encounter seemed to be nothing more than an easy victory. Perhaps it lulled Bullis and his scouts into a false sense of complacency.

So it was, in mid-October, that when Bullis and the scouts went Apache-hunting again, they took along a Mexican guide, a surgeon, and even Teresita, the captive Lipan woman who'd married a scout. This time they went west instead of south; the Mescalero had frequently been sending raiders into Texas from their base in New Mexico.

The scouts found plenty of Mescalero signs; the hostiles had embarked on a series of raids along both sides of the Rio Grande. Following them on a direct line required the U.S. party to keep crossing the river, so they were sometimes in Texas and sometimes in Mexico. Eventually, Bullis, the scouts, and their civilian companions found themselves picking their way through the deep canyons of Texas's Big Bend country. This area was the antithesis of Brackettville's flat environs. Moving from one place to the next in the Big Bend required careful maneuvering up and down narrow, rocky paths carved along canyon walls. Just walking along these paths was dangerous: People and animals fell to their deaths all the time.

Still, Bullis and his scouts could manage them nimbly enough. Teresita was a surefooted Apache herself; the path held no particular risk for her. The American party began working its way across. The ledge was only a few feet wide. A mountain towered above them. Below, after a long dropoff, was the river. Bullis and the Seminole Negro knew all that. But they didn't realize the hostiles were waiting for them.

In most of the Seminole Negro scout battles with hostiles, the Indians were less interested in fighting than in escaping. While it is a testimony to the skill of the scouts that they'd never suffered a single combat death, that statistic also reflects the fact the Comanche, Kickapoo, and Apache hadn't been the aggressors. On the afternoon of November 1, it all changed. The Mescalero had realized they were being followed. There were enough of them to put the odds in the hostiles' favor against Bullis and about thirty-five scouts. The Mescaleros set their ambush in the perfect place. Their enemies, tottering on a narrow ledge, would be facing gunfire from both sides of the canyon rim. They had no place to take cover. If they tried to run, they very likely would fall to their deaths. If they stood and fought, the Mescalero could cut them down. It was a perfect trap, and the Indians sprang it.

Later, Bullis admitted he and his beloved scouts had been "severely handled." Wounds abounded. The expedition staggered away with most of its pack animals and all of its supplies gone, the majority having fallen precipitously to the bottom of the canyon. The Mescalero who set the ambush all got away, free to ride into Texas and raid again.

But none of the scouts died. With literally no cover available to them, they squirmed on their bellies along the narrow ledge and wormed their way behind rocks large enough to afford some protection from the Mescalero bullets. They managed to return fire until the hostiles decided it was better to leave and fight another day, rather than press the current battle any further. A few days later, another army officer passed by the ambush site. He wrote that "the sides of the mountain were very precipitous; we passed the place where Bullis had been [and it] was a narrow ledge not more than ten or twelve feet wide, with a mountain towering above and the river hundreds of feet below. How he ever got his men out of there, with Indians on both sides, was a mystery to us all."

Bullis sent for reinforcements; he and the scouts then picked up the Mescalero trail and followed the hostiles again. Shafter sent additional troops. By mid-November, Bullis's force totaled 162 men. They found the Mescalero camp in the Mexican region known as Sierra del Carmen, and they obliterated it. Pitiliessly, either at Bullis's command or through their own initiative, after gorging themselves on the dried deer and horse meat that they found, the scouts burned every other bit of food camp inhabitants had set aside to see themselves through the winter. Women and children, as well as warriors, had been driven off during the attack. Many of them undoubtedly starved during the next few days and weeks. But the Seminole Negro had exacted revenge for the ambush that could have decimated the scouts. If they'd all been killed in that battle at Big Bend, their own wives and children might have starved to death back in Texas.

It appeared, for a while, that the battle of Sierra del Carmen might have ended hostile raids into Texas. The Apache seemed to have had enough, at least in terms of large-scale fighting. In all of 1878, even though they went on numerous trips searching for hostile sign, Bullis and the scouts did not engage in a single recorded fight. This might have comforted West Texas settlers, but it unnerved the Seminole Negro. They realized that, once there were no more hostiles to be tracked, the army would have no further use for them. Under terms of the 1870 agreement as they understood them, the tribe believed the U.S. government was still obligated to give them the land they had craved for so long. But the Americans obviously weren't planning to fulfill the agreement. So what was to become of the Seminole Negro? The men and women at the Las Moras Creek camp debated the topic endlessly around their campfires. Bullis offered what comfort he could, but there was little he could say. Because John Horse had gone back to Mexico, and because John Kibbetts died in 1878, there was no single leader among the Seminole Negro at Fort Clark who might have been able to rally the entire tribe behind some plan—to go back to Mexico, to go north to Indian Territory, to try to meet again with army officials and demand a tract of land—anything involving some sort of unified action. Instead, the people dithered, unable to reach consensus.

Perhaps by its own design, or at Bullis's suggestion, or even just by coincidence, the army did find other uses for the scouts during the lull in fighting throughout 1878. They were assigned to guide surveyors who mapped parts of West Texas. They helped build roads to a new army post and then constructed buildings on the site.

In January 1879, there was word that the Mescalero were raiding again. A sense of relief washed over the inhabitants of the Fort Clark village. The scouts were still needed! Bullis had no trouble summoning every able-bodied enlisted Seminole Negro. On January 31 he led about forty scouts, a dozen cavalrymen, and several dozen civilians off in pursuit of Mescalero who had raided in Fredricksburg, some fifty miles northeast of Brackettville. It was a big band of hostiles; they were quick and smart. They raced west with their stolen horses, heading for sanctuary on their reservation at Fort Stanton in New Mexico, but they didn't flee directly there. Instead, they led their pursuers along a zigzag path that cut through the most barren desert in West Texas. As always, the hostiles being pursued had the advantage of reaching scattered springs and trickling creeks first. After drinking themselves and watering their animals, the Mescalero fouled the water, leaving Bullis, the scouts, and the rest of the Fort Clark party to drain their canteens and then go thirsty.

West Texas is cold in the first weeks of February. Biting winds sweep out of the north, swirling icy dust. Dehydration exacerbated discomfort from the weather. The Mescalero angled west and south, making it impossible for the scouts to determine whether they were eventually heading for New Mexico or across the Rio Grande and deeper into Mexico.

Bullis and his scouts trailed the Mescalero for twenty-seven days. On February 28, in the desert that spanned West Texas and the eastern portions of New Mexico, they couldn't go on. Their horses were dying of thirst, and so were they. It was going to be a sad end to glorious service. Grimly, the scouts pulled kerchiefs over their mouths and noses so they wouldn't inhale dust, and fanned out, looking for some source of water the Mescalero might have missed. After many dreadful minutes that seemed like hours, scout David Bowlegs grunted with joy. He couldn't shout, Willie Warrior said, because his throat was too raw from thirst. Beneath some innocuous-looking rocks, the Mescalero had plugged a tiny, seeping spring. Obviously, they meant to use this route again sometime during raids. Carefully, David Bowlegs unstopped the water flow. Each man took a few tiny sips, then exercised rigid self-discipline, letting enough water accumulate to take care of the horses before any humans drank again. Bullis named the spot Salvation Spring.

Refreshed, Bullis and the scouts pressed on. They tracked the Mescalero to the boundary of the Fort Stanton reservation and called on the Indian agent there to ask for permission to find and arrest the raiders they'd trailed so far and so long. The agent said he'd make his own inquiries. Soon, too soon for any careful investigation, he reported to Bullis that it was impossible to tell which, if any, of his Mescalero were the culprits. And no, Bullis and his men couldn't enter the reservation themselves. Frustrated, Bullis gave the command to head back to Fort Clark. In all, he and the scouts had covered 1,266 miles in eighty days, only to return empty-handed.

For the rest of 1879 and all of 1880, the scouts occasionally rode into the field to hunt for hostiles. But any raiding was sporadic, mostly minor thefts from small ranches and farms. Rumors reached Fort Clark that the army soon would have other plans for Bullis. Such an experienced Indian fighter would certainly be more useful in other territories where hostiles still were active in large numbers. So, in June of 1880, David Bowlegs,

Sampson July, Pompey Perryman, and Bob Kibbetts met with Bullis and asked for permission to go as a delegation back to Indian Territory, where they would meet with the Seminole Negro still living there and find out what, if any, rights they might have if they rejoined them.

Colonel David Stanley now commanded Fort Clark. He joined Bullis in recommending that, if the scouts liked what they saw and heard in Indian Territory, the tribe be assisted in moving there. In a rare, generous gesture, the army would pay to transport them if the Interior Department would be responsible for them once they arrived. Yet another acting commissioner of Indian Affairs, E. J. Brooks, promised that if the army got the Seminole Negro to Indian Territory, his people would "find them suitable homes on the Seminole Reservation."

This was, of course, a plan that had been suggested and approved before. But it sounded good and seemed contingent on a few of the scouts visiting their kinsmen in Indian Territory and finding some basis for permanently rejoining them. It was agreed that the visit would take place very soon.

First, there were Apache to track and fight. In April 1881, some Lipan sneaked from Mexico into Texas, attacking a ranch on the Rio Frio and killing two white people living there. Perhaps it would not be fair to say Bullis and the scouts were pleased to hear this news, but they were certainly happy to swing back into their saddles and ride out for real action again. If nothing else, the Seminole Negro could hope this violent raid would cause enough military concern for the army to want to keep the scouts around at least a little while longer.

These Lipan were crafty. Before driving their stolen horses away, they killed one, and used its hide to wrap around the hooves of the rest of the animals and their own mounts. That way, there would be few, if any, tracks left behind in the Texas dust. They even had a two-week head start. Word of the attack hadn't reached Fort Clark very quickly.

But Bullis and thirty scouts came after them anyway, and the scouts picked up the Lipan trail. One of the Seminole Negro on the expedition was Teresita. She could track as well as any of the men—perhaps a little too well. Somehow, from minute scuffmarks in the dirt, she realized the hostiles they trailed were part of the same Lipan band she'd belonged to before being captured by the Seminole Negro. Cunningly, Teresita pretended that the signs she found indicated the Lipan were now heading west instead of south into Mexico. Bullis might have been fooled, but the scouts weren't. They suspected Teresita was lying and confronted her. Caught, she screamed and tried to run, but she was captured and tied to her horse. Keeping their prisoner under control was an extra task during the additional two or three days it took the Seminole Negro to catch up to the Lipan.

When they did, they fought magnificently, creeping up on the Lipan camp in the Sierra del Burro (Burro Mountains) after dark and attacking. The hostiles were caught completely off guard. Five Apache were killed and several wounded, including their chief, San De Va. When the last ringing echoes of the gunfire faded, Bullis and his scouts rounded up the horses the Lipan had stolen, retied Teresita in her saddle, and began the long ride back to Fort Clark.

The firefight at Sierra del Burro was the last major Indian battle in Texas, and the last full-scale battlefield action of the Seminole Negro scouts. They didn't know this, of course, but they soon suspected it. During 1882, army records indicate the scouts engaged in twelve expeditions covering more than 3,500 miles, all trips looking for signs of hostiles rather than reacting to raids. But there were no more raiding Lipan or Mescalero to be found.

"We have only mattered to other people whenever they found our help to be necessary," Miss Charles said one evening. "Otherwise, no one has ever wanted us. It's hurtful to say, but certainly true. We should feel perpetual gratitude toward our Seminole kinsmen, who took us in early on down in Florida. But they never really considered us anything but helpers, slaves in Florida or, later on, in Indian Territory. We could go from them to the Mexicans, because the Mexicans wanted us to fight the Indians for them. They told us they would treat us as equals, but they did not. Then we came to the Americans, who promised us land for our help against the Indians. They did promise us that. And we gave devoted service. But when the Indians were no longer a threat, and there was no longer a need for our scouts, no one felt any obligation to deal with us further. Everyone just wanted to be rid of us, really."

The inaction gave David Bowlegs his chance to head north to inspect conditions in Indian Territory. He probably brought a few other scouts with him, but it was David Bowlegs who reported back to the army in Texas that he and his tribe were ready to leave. The Seminole Negro living in Indian Territory, who now called themselves "Black Seminole," said they were ready to welcome their Texas relatives.

"If I had no one but myself and my wife," David Bowlegs wrote the Fort Clark commander, "I would rather soldier than do anything else I know of. But I have a large family growing up, and we are here where we own nothing, and can get no work. My children will grow up idle, and become criminals on this frontier. I have been raised like an Indian, but want to go to my people and settle in a home and teach my children to work, and most of my people are like me."

It was an eloquent request. Bullis endorsed it. Farther up the army line of command, so did General Philip Sheridan, who added, "I have known these Indians for many years, and they are in every way worthy of having their wish complied with. They should long since have been sent to the Indian Territory to join their people." Sheridan, of course, could afford to be so magnanimous. There was no further Indian threat in Texas. If the Seminole Negro stayed on at Fort Clark, soon they would either have to be dismissed completely from service or else employed to do odd jobs instead of scout and fight.

It had seemed, earlier, that the army and Department of the Interior were in agreement that the Seminole Negro could and should go, with the army absorbing the expenses for the move and the Indian bureau taking responsibility for resettling the Texas Seminole Negro among the Indian Territory Black Seminole. Bureaucratic wheels turn slowly, though, so the scouts settled in at the Las Moras Creek camp and waited. But the news that reached them in June sent someone else to Indian Territory instead. Bullis was assigned there.

There were tears among the scouts and their families. Bullis shed some, too. It was a good assignment for him. He'd have more responsibility in his new position, supervising disbursement of supplies and generally spending his time behind a desk instead of on a horse. With Apache raids virtually nonexistent in West Texas now, there was no need for him to remain stationed at Fort Clark. Before he left, the citizens of Kinney County honored Bullis by presenting him with not one but two ceremonial swords and naming him "The Friend of the Frontier."

According to Cynthia Ventura, Bullis did not abandon Gomacinda and his blue-eyed son. Quietly, he deeded some land to the Frausto family and kept in touch after he left. After six years in Indian Territory, Bullis was transferred again to Arizona, where he was the Apache agent on the San Carlos Reservation. Alice Bullis died in 1887, while her husband was still assigned to Indian Territory. Cynthia says that eventually Bullis asked Gomacinda to join him "as his mistress," but she had already married someone else. In 1891 Bullis remarried, too; he and his second wife had three daughters. Gomacinda's marriage failed. She found another husband, who made her move back to Mexico with him. Apparently, she and Bullis never saw each other again after he left Fort Clark.

The scouts missed Bullis terribly. Many of the Seminole Negro were apprehensive as they waited for permission to move north to Indian Territory, where, at least, Bullis would presumably be waiting to greet them. Once again, though, the next news they received was not the hoped-for permission to go. It involved the death of the most famous Seminole Negro of all.

chapter fifteen

AS I GOT TO KNOW Clarence Ward, I couldn't help liking him. He was so friendly I always looked forward to our meetings. My respect for Willie Warrior was such that I sometimes felt guilty liking someone he didn't, and his disdain for Clarence was pronounced. Willie said Clarence had no respect for older association members, and that he was trying to deny black tribal heritage by insisting the official name of the group was Seminole Indian Scouts Cemetery Association.

Clarence emphatically disagreed. The association had been falling apart, he insisted, and he'd run for president to try and kick start the group rather than ignoring the history so beloved by its founders. He called his organization the Seminole Indian Scout Cemetery Association because that was its name on the original charter.

"If Mr. Warrior had actually spent much time in Brackettville around ninety-eight, ninety-nine, he would have seen for himself that nobody was doing anything, and I can show him the charter with the right name anytime he wants," Clarence said. He always referred to "Mr. Warrior" rather than "Willie." "I respect Mr. Warrior, I do. But he mostly sits in Del Rio with some of the other older people who used to be active, and they just talk down anything I try. We've got to move forward, got to get the younger people excited and involved. You can't tell me there's anything wrong with me thinking we have to do that."

It initially seemed as though the problem between Willie and Clarence was the predictable, petty one: An older leader resented the emergence of a younger association president who wanted to do things in his own, different way. But I knew Willie quite well. He could certainly be arbitrary, and where his interpretation of tribal history was concerned he did not tolerate disagreement. But he wasn't petty. He did realize he was getting on in years, and that younger Seminole Negro had to step up and lead. Much of the real disagreement between them centered on designating the scouts as Seminole or Black Seminole. And, on this issue, Clarence and Willie would not—could not—reconcile.

Willie and the older Seminole Negro were children in the Jim Crow era, when separate but *un*equal was the order of the day. Blackness had been their people's unfair stigma from the beginning—black slaves of the white people, black slaves of the Indians, black employees of the Mexican government, black employees of the U.S. Army. Being black prevented them from ever having control over their own lives; always, they took orders from others. This was what made Seminole Negro ownership of land so crucial to John Horse and John Kibbetts and other tribal leaders. Only then would they be able to make their own decisions as free people who could not be uprooted at the whim of masters or employers.

After being thrown out of their beloved Las Moras Creek village on Fort Clark, the Seminole Negro were once again limited by their blackness. The only available employment was as menials serving white bosses. Their children went to school in a shack, and white children jeered at their funny accents and ragged clothes. Willie Warrior and his boyhood peers responded to near-smothering prejudice by developing pride in their ethnicity, thanks in large part to the tales related to them by the old scouts. These men told the youngsters to hold their heads high, that they were descended from great black fighters, great black *people* who had survived every sort of adversity, including hateful treatment by the Indian tribe that had once taken them in. For Willie and his generation, *black* was more important to their identity than *Seminole*. Like whites, the Seminole were their oppressors.

Clarence Ward knew about prejudice, too, but he'd been in junior high when civil rights legislation mandated the end of segregation. In post-integration school settings, he and the other Seminole Negro kids not only learned about the outside world, they finally had the opportunity to go out and succeed in it. For them, being black gradually became less socially and professionally limiting. They still took pride in the heritage of their people, even if they didn't soak up every scrap of historical information. There was also, I eventually learned, a lengthy lapse in the tribe's storytelling tradition. Clarence's generation grew up without constantly hearing about Seminole treachery, so by the 1980s and '90s, being black seemed far less pleasantly self-defining than being related somewhat by blood and completely by name to the Seminole, to *Indians*. Accordingly, Clarence didn't feel the same bitterness toward the tribe that Willie did. Even the modern-day Seminole vote to disenfranchise the Oklahoma Black Seminole didn't seem critical to Clarence. He was more focused on the best interests of his scout cemetery group in Brackettville. For Clarence, Seminole Negro history was pretty much confined to the scouts at Fort Clark—who were always incorrectly designated by the army as *Seminole* scouts—and the plight of the modern-day Seminole Negro in Nacimiento. To Clarence, whatever happened to his people before they came to Texas was background, rather than vital, information. This became an unbridgeable gulf between Willie Warrior and Clarence Ward. It seemed to me that, for Willie, the most important part of tribal history was *black*, and, for Clarence, it was *Seminole*. He was just as proud of his heritage as Willie—it was just a differently interpreted heritage. That was something Willie couldn't bring himself to accept. The circumstances under which he and Clarence had grown up were so radically different that neither man seemed able to appreciate, let alone accept, the motivation and concerns of the other.

"I really would like to know the history," Clarence said to me, and he meant it, but usually regarding the Texas history that he thought mattered most. He never seemed curious about Florida or Indian Territory. "I want to know what happened up on the fort. John Horse, all that."

"Are you the modern-day John Horse?" I asked. "Are you going to lead your people on to better things?"

"I wish I knew more about John Horse," he said. "John Horse was a great man, and I'm just me."

That afternoon when Willie Warrior told what he knew about John Horse's death, I wished Clarence was listening, too. I took careful notes, deciding which parts of the tale I'd pass along to Clarence later on.

"Old John Horse was a tough one," Willie began. "He should have already died so many times, 'specially after he got ambushed here at Fort Clark. They got him from hiding right over there—see where I'm pointing? But after he was able to ride again, he went on back to Mexico, and that was the beginning of the end for him."

John Horse never physically recovered from the gunshot wounds he suffered in the Fort Clark ambush. Dolly July, one of the Seminole Negro living at Las Moras Creek, later said "John Horse always walked straight until he was shot. Then he was bent over and his feet all broke out." It was a sick old man who left Fort Clark and rode to Nacimiento in 1877.

He found conditions there appalling. Because the Mexican government had virtually given up attempting to protect villages in the northern states, hostile raids were frequent and deadly. Even when the Seminole Negro in Mexico negotiated temporary truces, particularly with the Lipan, Apache still made raids on the tribe's horse herd. John Horse organized retaliatory raids, and drove the Apache away.

But there was another threat to the Seminole Negro at Nacimiento. There had been, since the early 1850s, occasional efforts by Mexican families to reacquire some or all the land granted to the tribe by their government. Periodically, attorneys would wave deeds and other legal documents. There would be heated discussions. Sometimes the Seminole Negro were left as they were. Other times, part of their property was whittled away. In 1866, the tribe supposedly had its title to the land upheld for good, but when most of the Seminole Negro left Mexico for Texas, new claims against the Nacimiento property once again began to be filed in Coahuila courts.

In 1879, two years after John Horse returned to Nacimiento and resumed leadership of the Seminole Negro there, A. E. Noble declared he had purchased all the tribe's property from Sanchez Navarro, who he identified as the rightful owner. (Some historians believe the purchaser was John Willett, but Kenneth Porter said Willett was the agent representing Noble in the deal. Ben Pingenot agreed. Willie Warrior and Miss Charles had no opinion.) The Seminole Negro ignored him. In 1881, Noble announced he was evicting them. The tribe responded that they would fight anyone who tried to make them leave. But the people of Nacimiento were tired, worn down by these repeated attempts to make them give up land they believed to be unquestionably their own, and when Evaristo Madero, the governor of Coahuila, took Noble's side, it seemed the Seminole Negro would be thrown off the property they had received from the Mexican government in return for their unquestionably brilliant work defending Coahuila against Apache and Comanche.

Not everyone in the area had forgotten the tribe's fine service. Francisco de Paula Andres, a priest, helped John Horse draft a rebuttal to Noble's claim. Madero then suggested the matter should be decided by a court. Noble, who had money to spend on lawyers, agreed. But it seemed to John Horse that a hearing before a judge shouldn't be necessary. The Mexican government had officially given the Nacimiento land to his people in 1852; a lengthy investigation had confirmed their ownership in 1866. Enough of this negotiating with state governors and greedy lawyers! In August 1882, John Horse left Nacimiento for Mexico City. He would put the matter before President Manuel González and have it decided once and for all.

Miss Charles said she thought everyone in Nacimiento donned their finest clothes and sang and made speeches in the old man's honor before he left. Supposedly a delegation of Kickapoos came to pay their respects, noting that they did not expect John Horse to ever return from Mexico City. Miss Charles said "the old folks" told her all about it, and the tale of the Kickapoo prognostication would be accurate.

But John Horse had been to Mexico City to see a president several times before. He was seventy years old and physically weakened by his old wounds, yet still capable of mounting a horse and making a trip. Though his mission to Mexico City was critical, there was no reason for anyone to suspect that he wouldn't be back in Nacimiento in a matter of weeks. His son Joe Coon may have gone with him; there could even have been a few more Seminole Negro men along. No one is certain.

Miss Charles and Willie Warrior agree that John Horse and his party, if he had one, arrived in Mexico City, and that John Horse was granted an audience with the president (who they identify as Porfirio Díaz rather than Manuel González; Porter also believed John Horse met Díaz rather than González "because Díaz was controlling the government at that time," which could explain the apparent contradiction between Seminole Negro legend and recorded Mexican governmental history). González and/or Díaz emphatically endorsed the tribe's right to its Nacimiento land. Word eventually reached Coahuila that *el presidente*, at least for now, wanted the tribe and its property left alone—not that, in 1882 Mexico, state officials always paid attention to edicts from the national government. Perhaps John Horse was given some sort of document conferring absolute title to the property. If he was, no one back in Nacimiento ever saw it.

And no one there ever saw John Horse again. He died in Mexico City on August 9. It was whispered in Nacimiento and north of the Rio Grande at the Las Moras Creek camp that the old man had been murdered by his enemies, perhaps thugs hired by Noble. There had been assassination attempts before; it was easy to believe that a final one succeeded. Outside the tribe, it was reported and accepted that John Horse contracted pneumonia and died quickly in a Mexico City military hospital. His remains were never returned to Nacimiento. Most likely he was buried as a pauper, his nameless body interred in a public cemetery's unmarked grave.

John Horse's death did not signal the end of the Seminole Negro struggle to retain their Nacimiento land. For ten more years, the *Mascogos* argued back and forth with Coahuila authorities about it. Governor Galan eventually turned on them. Much of the land in question was particularly fertile and considered too good to remain in the possession of people Galan now described as "vicious, indolent and disobedient." Most of the men of the tribe, Galan charged, were deserters from the American army. An 1891 census listed 123 males in Nacimiento. Probably a dozen or so were ex-scouts, some of whom had left Fort Clark before their enlistments were up.

In 1919, Mexican president Venustiano Carranza seemed to end the controversy, ruling on behalf of the Seminole Negro that "these lands belong to the descendants of the original families, to whom the government donated these lands." It still wasn't enough for the citizens of Coahuila, or for the tribe whose land they coveted. In 1938, fifty-six years after John Horse died, Mexican president Lázaro Cárdenas ratified the original Seminole Negro claim and added a few thousand more acres of pastureland. By that time, though, the tribal members in Mexico had other worries.

While modern conveniences like functioning sewer systems and, later on, electricity, gradually became commonplace in most of Mexico, conditions in the northern states remained relatively primitive, especially in isolated areas like Nacimiento. Gradually, the green fields of the Seminole Negro became overgrazed and overplanted. The land was exhausted. It became harder for the tribe to support itself in what was now known as Nacimiento de los Negros.

"Last summer, I was asked to meet with some immigration people down in Eagle Pass," Clarence Ward said in 2001. "Our people back in Mexico, in Nacimiento, need help bad. They want to be able to come to the states and see their relatives here, but they don't have the right papers to get out of Mexico. For that they need birth certificates, and there aren't any in the village. So they need a few dollars to get those, then it's a few more dollars to get the papers to cross legally. Say $100 a family, but that's out of reach for most of them."

"What did the immigration people want you to do?" I asked, chewing on a fish sandwich. Clarence had insisted on buying me something to eat. He kept apologizing about not having me over for a meal at his house, but his daughter wasn't well and his wife was busy with her, so we were back at the Burger 'n' Shake. I'd offered to pay for my own food and Clarence's, too, but he said I was his guest, period.

"They wanted the association to be aware of the problem, and to see if we could help any," Clarence told me. "What I want is, the association could have programs and raise money to send to Nacimiento, not a lot of money because we don't have much ourselves, but a few hundred dollars here and there. We could do that. So I'm talking about this with my members. Things like toilets in our park are important, too. If we fix up the park, make it more comfortable, we can do more out there. Getting members involved, that's the thing."

"Are you in touch with the people in Nacimiento? You know Willie and Ethel Warrior have been down there."

"Mr. and Mrs. Warrior were at the Eagle Pass meeting, too. I guess the immigration people invited them. If Mr. Warrior wants to help the association in this, we'll be glad to hear from him. Me, I haven't been there in Nacimiento, though I hope to go. Meanwhile, I can at least make sure my members are aware of them needing our help, though right now our big concern has to be helping ourselves."

That was just as true in 1882. With John Horse dead and everyone in Nacimiento preoccupied with feeding their families, the *Mascogos* lacked the resources to help themselves. There was no use appealing to the Seminole Negro at Fort Clark, either. Immediately after Bullis's transfer, things at the Las Moras Creek camp deteriorated, too. And, not for the last time, the Seminole in Indian Territory were proving to be far more terrible enemies to the scouts and their families than the Comanche and Apache had ever been.

chapter sixteen

JUST BEFORE SEMINOLE DAYS in September 2000, I spoke to a Brackettville high school student history club. Its sponsor, teacher Kathy Bader, had asked Clarence Ward to come and tell her seniors and juniors all about the Seminole Negro, with the aim of intriguing them enough to convince them to attend the Seminole Day programs and maybe learn a little more "about the history of their town and some of their classmates." But Clarence never pretended he knew much about Seminole Negro history. Willie Warrior had been telling everyone that he was through giving presentations about his people. So Clarence asked me to do it.

"I can't, Clarence," I protested. "I'm not Seminole Negro. The kids will just think it's stupid."

"I don't know the history, Miss Charles is ill, and Mr. Warrior isn't available," Clarence said. "You're the only one who's going to be here that I know to ask." I went, reluctantly, thinking how sad it was, after so many colorful centuries, that the president of the Seminole Indian Scouts Cemetery Association couldn't find anyone better to tell about their people's rich heritage.

Kathy Bader, a no-nonsense type who spoke as briskly to her adult guests as to her pupils, greeted me at her classroom door. I arrived laden with copies of documents, reference books, and a few photos.

"How long did you want me to speak?" I asked, anticipating at least half an hour, maybe more. I thought I'd begin by talking about meeting Miss Charles, and her opening tale of the six unidentified runaway slaves in Florida, and then go on to hit as many high points as possible with particular emphasis on the exodus from Indian Territory to Mexico and the wonderful scout service to the U.S. Army.

"About ten minutes," Bader said. "We've only got this little bit of club time, and then the bell will ring and the kids have to go on to their regular classes. See if you can get them to ask questions. That gets them more involved."

Ten minutes to tell about five centuries! Bader called the club to order, introduced me ("He's going to share with you the fascinating history of the Seminole scouts from right here in Brackettville!"), and nodded for me to begin. The two dozen students in the classroom watched me with varying degrees of interest. Even before I began, a few were obviously bored and whispered quietly to each other near the back of the room. It was a mixed-race group, mostly whites and Hispanics, but there was one black girl in a cheerleader's uniform—the Brackettville High Tigers had a big game that night in the adjacent school stadium—who, from her facial features, had to be Seminole Negro. She was one of the bored kids who was talking instead of looking at me.

I did my best. I started with the slaves arriving in the old Seminole village in Florida, frantically thinking all the while what else I might include or edit. What I decided to emphasize to the kids was the long, drawn-out, sad end to the scouts' army service, because events in their hometown might seem more immediate to them. Even skipping all but the most important moments, it was tough to get quickly to 1882, particularly when, once I did get there, so much had to be explained about that year and the next thirty-two, the final years the Seminole Negro spent in their Las Moras Creek camp. It certainly made me appreciate, if I hadn't before, the rare talent of gifted storyteller-historians like Willie and Miss Charles.

If only, I thought, there was time to tell the kids the full version. It would surely shock them, maybe outrage them, certainly encourage them to want to know more about these unique and wonderful people who suffered so

A formal portrait of the Seminole Negro scouts in the late 1880s
(COURTESY OF THE MUSEUM OF THE BIG BEND, SUL ROSS UNIVERSITY)

much. Because, in 1882, the awful conclusion to the Seminole Negro service to the U.S. Army began.

John Bullis had been transferred. John Horse was about to leave Nacimiento for Mexico City, never to return. Hostile raids in West Texas were virtually nonexistent. It was clearly just a matter of time before the army decided the Seminole Negro scouts were no longer worth employing. And David Bowlegs was tired of waiting for permission to relocate to Indian Territory.

He'd received his discharge papers in May. He could have reenlisted, but why bother? He meant to leave soon, he'd been promised he would be allowed to leave, and, further, had been assured the army would pay for the trip, and that the Indian bureau would help with resettlement in Indian Territory. What, David Bowlegs frequently asked Fort Clark commander David Stanley during the spring and summer of 1882, was taking so long?

Stanley did what he could to expedite the process. He proposed lending the fifty or so impatient Seminole Negro who still wanted to leave (some had changed their minds and wanted to settle permanently in Texas) four army wagons to help transport their belongings, along with enough rations to last throughout the trip. Arrangements were made with commanders of other forts along the route to supply fresh teams of mules to pull the wagons. Sheridan remained committed to helping David Bowlegs, too; he endorsed Stanley's new plan and had it forwarded to the secretary of war, who in turn passed it along to the Indian bureau. From there it ended up in the hands of agent John Q. Tufts, who decided it would only be right to ask the Seminole tribal council what they thought of adding a few dozen Seminole Negro to their Indian Territory community.

They hated it. Despite the formal adoption of Indian Territory Seminole Negro into the full Seminole tribe in 1866, the self-styled "Black Seminole" had places on, but not control of, the Seminole council. Power there still belonged to the Jumper clan, which had never wavered in its disdain of the Seminole Negro.

So, in the late summer of 1882 when Tufts asked whether the Seminole would be willing to accept Texas newcomers, principal chief John Jumper emphatically refused to consider the plan. "The Council are unanimously opposed to the coming of said Bowlegs and his party," Jumper responded. "[There] is no foundation in fact for the assertion that the Seminole here were willing for them to come among them to settle."

Jumper was a clever man. He did not base his response on simple dislike of the Seminole Negro. Instead, he argued that the members of that group who left with John Horse in 1849 had voluntarily surrendered any claim to membership in the full Seminole tribe. They were living in Mexico in 1866 when the "blood" Seminole agreed to adopt the Black Seminole left in Indian Territory. If a few sympathetic relatives in Indian Territory had told these Texas refugees they would be welcome to come back, well, they had done so without permission from the tribal council, and only the council had the power to decide the issue.

"You see," Willie Warrior said to me balefully when he came to this part of his story, "those bastards were already cutting us up with their rules and things way back then." It was the only time, in the years I knew him, that I ever heard Willie use the term *bastards*. "The Seminole did it to us, are doing it to us, everybody did it and does it. Always some rule for why we can't have what we earned, what we deserve. Always some damned rule."

Tufts reported back to his bosses that it would be a bad idea for David Bowlegs and the rest of his party to return to Indian Territory. Who knew how the *real* Seminole would react if these relatively unimportant people—did the army even *need* these so-called scouts anymore?—were forced upon them? Hiram Price, the latest commissioner of Indian Affairs, didn't need to hear any more. He informed Stanley via Sheridan that there would be no action taken to move David Bowlegs and the other Seminole Negro to Indian Territory. If earlier promises were broken in the process, well, that was too bad. He was acting for the greater good, and the Fort Clark Seminole Negro were simply out of luck.

This wasn't welcome news back in the village beside Las Moras Creek. The scouts' predicament worsened when the town of Brackettville got its own bad news. For years, citizens there expected the long-promised railroad line would come right through town, bringing with it all sorts of economic benefits. In anticipation, the population had increased dramatically, from a few hundred in the 1870s to about fifteen hundred by 1882. Just as the Seminole Negro were being informed they were persona non grata among the Seminole in Indian Territory, their old adversaries in Brackettville got an equivalent message from the railroad company. The new track would run at least ten miles south of town. It was an awful economic blow; a rail depot would have meant customers for mercantile outlets, travelers using Brackettville as a hub, many more visitors stopping off on their way to San Antonio or Del Rio. Some Brackettville businessmen simply uprooted their families and moved south to the spot where the railroad would run, shrinking the town population. That meant fewer jobs in Brackettville for its white residents, let alone the despised Seminole Negro.

In light of this unwelcome news, David Bowlegs was more determined than ever to go north. Family members lived there; they promised he and his wife, along with their nine children, would be welcome in their homes. What right did John Jumper and the Seminole council have to say they couldn't come? So, in November, David Bowlegs and his family simply left Fort Clark. A few other Seminole Negro may have gone with them. It took them weeks, perhaps a month, to make the trip. They reached Indian Territory sometime in December 1882 and were quietly absorbed into the Black Seminole community. No one bothered to inform the Seminole council or the white authorities that they had come. It would be months before these outsiders were aware of it.

But the friends they'd left behind at Fort Clark knew, and many of them were anxious to go north, too. In the spring of 1883, some of the scouts, probably led by Robert Kibbetts, again requested help in relocating themselves and their families to Indian Territory. They presented their case to General Christopher Augur, who commanded the army's Department of Texas. The Seminole Negro request touched on two points. First, and most obviously, the army wouldn't need their services much longer. Yet those services had been distinguished—so many successful expeditions, plus four Medals of Honor. Assistance in moving back to Indian Territory was surely a small enough reward. Then, too, the scouts raised the issue of the original treaty they believed had been negotiated back in 1870 between John Kibbetts and Captain Frank Perry, perhaps with input from Major Zenas Bliss. Things had been written down, the scouts insisted, including the promise that, when the scouts were no longer needed, they and their people would be given land to live on. Now it was time for the army to produce the treaty and honor it.

But this treaty, if it had ever existed at all, was still nowhere to be found. Frank Perry, the best authority on whether there had ever been any promise of land in exchange for service, let alone a written record of that pledge, had been dead for seven years. Bliss, who remained sympathetic to the Seminole Negro, was careful not to commit himself on the treaty issue. The tribal members at Las Moras Creek were "in almost helpless condition," he noted, and certainly the government had a moral responsibility to assist them. On the other hand, he hadn't been part of negotiations between Perry and John Kibbetts. As to whatever incentives Perry offered, Bliss said carefully, "I presume he had the authority for what he promised."

Tired of being hungry, unwilling to wait around at Fort Clark until the army released the scouts from service and evicted the tribe from its Las Moras Creek camp, about fifty Seminole Negro announced in May 1883 that they were returning to Indian Territory. They asked the army for help getting there, and Augur again recommended to Indian Affairs commissioner Price that they be allowed to move and helped to settle in once they arrived. Once more, Price ordered Tufts to talk to John Jumper about it.

Predictably, Jumper remained adamantly against an influx of Seminole Negro. In lawyerly fashion—perhaps he was coached by Tufts—Jumper outlined a specific objection. These shiftless Seminole Negro left Indian Territory of their own volition in 1849. It was only in 1856 that the Seminole were granted their own land in Indian Territory separate from the Creek. In 1866, the tribe had agreed to adopt as full members the Black Seminole still in Indian Territory, but nothing was said about this bastard offshoot group residing in Mexico. *Residing.* They had never declared any intention, at least then, of wanting to return to America and Indian Territory. Jumper didn't care what any supposed agreement between the army and John Kibbetts might have promised insofar as there was no obligation by "blood, tribal organization or treaty" for the Seminole to take the unwanted interlopers in.

Jumper did make one undeniable point: Land among the Seminole and Seminole Negro already living in Indian Territory was limited. Much of the land wasn't even good for farming. If its present inhabitants were hard-pressed to eke livings out of it, how could this property be further divided to include tracts for more families?

"To sum it all up," Jumper reported to Tufts, "they have no rights here, we have no room for them, and we protest against their being sent here as we have done before." By mid-October, Price pronounced his usual verdict: It would be better for the Seminole Negro scouts and their people to stay in Texas. Without the evidence of a written treaty, and without the testimony of Frank Perry and John Kibbetts available, Augur gave up.

But some of the scouts didn't. In October 1883, another twenty-seven Seminole Negro left Fort Clark and made their slow, painful way north to

Indian Territory, where they, too, joined the community of Black Seminole that still lived separately from the "blood" tribal members. David Bowlegs and his family were able to quietly ease themselves among the Black Seminole without Jumper noticing, but this new group immediately came to the chief's attention. He was outraged.

Jumper spent much of 1884 demanding that the Seminole Negro from Texas be summarily evicted from Indian Territory. Tufts, to his credit, wanted to listen to the Seminole Negro side of the story before making a decision. While deliberations proceeded, Tufts infuriated Jumper by allowing the newcomers to stay on Seminole Nation land and even grow some crops there. Despite grudging, conditional permission to remain, the relocated Seminole Negro faced hard times. There was at least food for them in Indian Territory, and the friendly faces of Black Seminole relatives, but the hostility they encountered from "blood" Seminole was easily equal to the poisonous disdain they'd encountered from the white citizens of Brackettville.

Back in Texas, the two hundred or so Seminole Negro left at Fort Clark were still troubled. In mid-1884, there were still forty adult male Seminole Negro enlisted as scouts, earning a monthly wage and extra rations for themselves and their families. Outside of these men, the tribe had little other income. A few women did the fort laundry. Some of the boys and men too old for military service occasionally found work on area ranches. Each family in the Las Moras Creek village had a garden, which yielded some food. Hunters sporadically brought in game, and, in times of particular hunger, a cow or goat might be filched from a white neighbor. But survival was day to day. People were still hungry, still desperate.

Imagine, then, the general reaction in the village when, in August 1884, the army announced that, in two weeks, it would reduce the number of active scouts from forty to six. Because the hostiles in the area had been subdued, the scouts were now mostly idle. A few needed to be kept on hand to serve as occasional guides, but otherwise their presence was superfluous. Implicit in the order to reduce the scouts' ranks was that the tribe would, eventually, have to leave its village at Las Moras Creek, since most of the people living there would no longer have any official affiliation to the military.

General Stanley, the Fort Clark commander, tried to temper army pragmatism with compassion. Though he could not refuse the order to reduce the number of scouts, he could, and did, ask to do it gradually. His request to army headquarters in San Antonio took into consideration the scouts' service, their tribal customs, and the grinding poverty of Brackettville itself.

"Thirty-four men—all with wives and children—who have served as soldiers for an average of thirteen years; without any trades or property; and with habits essentially Indian, are thrown upon a community itself poor, and hostile to these harmless vagabonds," Stanley wrote. "What is to become of them, I cannot imagine."

Neither could the "harmless vagabonds." Stanley reported 234 tribal members of all ages were living beside Las Moras Creek. How could they possibly survive on the income and rations of only six scouts? The easy answer, of course, was that they couldn't. Probably army higher-ups hoped the Seminole Negro would realize the hopelessness of their situation and, some day or evening, simply leave Fort Clark as a group, going to Indian Territory or back to Mexico or to squat on some local rancher's hot, inhospitable acreage, anywhere the army would no longer be responsible for them.

Instead, the Fort Clark village inhabitants responded as they always did. They supplemented what the half-dozen active scouts could bring in with vegetables they grew, with animals they shot and trapped and, undoubtedly, with stock stolen from their white neighbors. After a few months, their lot was considerably improved when the army partially relented and allowed twenty scouts to remain on active duty.

Sensing that eviction was imminent, the scouts made a new request. They asked that the army give them until the spring of 1885 to find some other place to live and work. Permission was quickly granted; Stanley himself was in the process of transferring to San Antonio, and Bliss was returning to command Fort Clark. Approving the scouts' request at least postponed the painful, inevitable moment when they would be ordered off fort property.

After discussions with Robert Kibbetts and Sampson July, now the acknowledged leaders of the Seminole Negro community, Bliss resurrected an old plan. Why not find some unoccupied land in Texas, acreage no white settlers wanted, and give it to the scouts? Yes, Bliss acknowledged, the people in question were black and would be resented by any white community in the state, but they were still "better than the same class of their color now living in Texas." Given the opportunity, Bliss promised, the Seminole Negro would plant crops, raise cattle, obey all white laws and, in general, not be of any further trouble to anyone. Stanley still supported the concept of the scouts getting land for their service; so did Major General John Schofield, whose command of the Military Division of the Missouri encompassed Indian Territory. But both Stanley and Schofield believed the Seminole Negro place was in Indian Territory, not Texas. In any case, it was not for the army to decide where they could go, but the Department of the Interior's Bureau of Indian Affairs.

In May 1885, Indian Affairs commissioner Price bowed to pressure from the Seminole council and ordered agent Tufts to get the Seminole Negro off Seminole tribal land. Force could be used, Price added bleakly. Tufts rode out, found David Bowlegs and some of the other Seminole Negro living among the Black Seminole, and delivered the edict. But the former scouts had enough experience to recognize an empty threat. No one was leaving, Tufts was informed. Any attempt to use force would be met with force. Tufts had to report back to Price that the Seminole Negro wouldn't go. Was he *really* supposed to use force to drive them out, and, if so, who would supply it? The army? The Seminole council? Price didn't want the responsibility of making such a decision. He quickly established a new policy: The Seminole Negro who had already joined the Indian Territory community of Black Seminole, or "freedmen," would not be forced to leave. But no more of them were going to come without the full agreement and cooperation of the Indian bureau and the Seminole council.

Eighteen eighty-five dragged into 1886. The Seminole Negro at Fort

Clark still waited for word of their eventual fate. Robert Kibbetts decided waiting was too painful; he paid his own way to Washington to plead his tribe's case directly to the Indian commissioner and anyone else who would give him a hearing. He brought with him letters of support from several army officers. His specific request was for Seminole Negro land in "Seminole country." Over a period of weeks, Robert Kibbetts met with various Indian bureau officials and finally testified before the Senate Committee on Indian Affairs. The senators were impressed with him. They asked the secretary of the interior to investigate the Seminole Negro situation and report back to them.

Someone in that department drafted a letter to John Jumper. It was, essentially, a plea for flexibility and compassion. Perhaps the Seminole–U.S. treaty of 1866 didn't specifically apply to the Seminole Negro in Texas, but certainly they were "a portion of the people whose rights were intended to be secured by it." Accepting the Seminole Negro into the full Seminole community would be "an act of justice as well as generosity." Jumper ignored the letter.

Then John DeWitt Clinton Atkins, the latest commissioner of Indian Affairs, got involved. He came up with an entirely new reason to deny the Seminole Negro any right to land in Indian Territory. When John Horse led his followers into Mexico, Atkins ruled, they had effectively relinquished their American citizenship. Because these black people left the United States before slavery was abolished, and returned afterward, they could not in any sense be classified as "freedmen." They were not in Indian Territory in 1866 when the Seminole adopted the Black Seminole. During all these events, they were in Mexico, enjoying the rights of citizens there.

So, in Atkins's opinion, the Seminole Negro were neither Seminole nor negro. They were Mexican. If the Senate committee wanted to give Indian Territory land to Mexicans, some new legislation would be required. Meanwhile, John Jumper had every right to refuse the Seminole Negro entry onto Seminole tribal land. The Indian bureau would have no more to do with them, either.

"Mexicans. How do you like that?" Willie Warrior snorted when he talked about Atkins's pronouncement. "We've had some real stupid reasons given for people not treating us right, but I think that had to be the craziest one. Look at this black skin. Does it look *Mexican*?"

Several of Kathy Bader's students were incredulous when they heard about Atkins.

"How could they be Mexicans?" one boy wanted to know. "Hadn't they been back in Texas for a long time? This whole thing is crazy."

"It gets crazier, and sadder," I said, and then, doing my best to mimic the storytelling rhythms of Miss Charles and Willie Warrior, I hurried on.

The Seminole Negro had long experience with new Indian commissioners. Some had been sympathetic and some hadn't. Atkins would surely be replaced, probably sooner rather than later. But they'd been seeking justice for so long. It was obvious that, even when some government official or another did agree land ought to be forthcoming for the Seminole Negro, there would always be some other higher-up who would keep it from happening.

So they gave up on Indian Territory, at least for the time being. The Indian bureau controlled Indian Territory, but the army had jurisdiction over Fort Clark. From Sheridan to Stanley, army officials had always seemed to side with the Seminole Negro cause. Perhaps a permanent solution, a satisfactory if not completely happy ending , could come from them.

So, in 1888, another formal petition was prepared, this one addressed to President Grover Cleveland. It requested a Seminole Negro reservation that included the Las Moras Creek village plus enough other adjoining property to total fifteen thousand acres, as well as seed, cattle, farm equipment, and money to build a school. (The Las Moras Creek village took up about 235 acres.) Given that support, the petition promised, the Seminole Negro would create a law-abiding, self-sustaining community. All they wanted was what they had originally been promised in 1870. They had fulfilled their part of the agreement with long and honorable service. But there was no response to the letter.

During this time, and in the years since 1882 when the threat of hostile

The Seminole Negro scouts sometime near the end of their active cavalry service
(COURTESY OF THE FORT CLARK HISTORICAL SOCIETY)

raids no longer existed, the scouts occasionally were put to work by the army. They were still being paid, after all, and there is no record of any scout refusing an order out of anger or frustration that the Seminole Negro pleas to the government for land were refused. Some of the work still involved physical danger. In 1884, Seminole Negro scouts were part of an expedition chasing Mexican raiders. In 1885, the scouts were commanded to patrol the border area because Geronimo had left his reservation and was expected to rally some Apache. After Geronimo surrendered hundreds of miles away, the scouts were ordered to stand down.

They did construction work for the army, too, helping to build two new forts in West Texas and, later, Fort Ringgold to the south. In 1892, when civil war in Mexico threatened the U.S. border, all the active scouts—a sergeant, two corporals, and twelve privates—were sent to Fort Ringgold, which was much farther south along the Rio Grande than Fort Duncan. It was a combat assignment. The scouts had to leave their families back at Fort Clark, and no one was certain how long they'd be assigned to Fort Ringgold. They imagined, as they scoured the hot South Texas plains, that their loved ones were dying of hunger back at the Las Moras Creek camp. Miss Charles suggested, though she said she had no proof, that the commissary officers at Fort Clark took pity on the hungry women, children, and old people, sneaking them extra rations while the men were away.

The scouts were gone until 1903, making occasional visits home on leave. It was an awful time for them. They could never be certain that, while they were at Fort Ringgold, the army wouldn't simply put their families off Fort Clark grounds. By this time, there was no reason for the Seminole Negro to expect anything but bad news.

That didn't mean the scouts in any way shirked their duty. In February 1893, Corporal Billy July and Private Sam Gordon helped lead lawmen to the hideout of Eusebio Martinez, one of the most notorious Mexican bandits. There was a gunfight, and Martinez was killed. By 1894, General Frank Wheaton, commander of Fort Ringgold, had nothing but praise for the scouts: "Little or nothing was accomplished until they were utilized," he wrote in one report.

"That Martinez was a bad ass," Willie Warrior said as we sipped soft drinks one hot summer afternoon on the porch of his Fort Clark home. "What he'd do was, he'd catch a whole bunch of people and burn 'em, shoot 'em, and stack 'em up like firewood and set fire to 'em. Those were the kinds of bad men that were still out here in those days. This Mexican bad guy was running wild down around Fort Ringgold, so who do they look to for help catching him? Us."

Willie swallowed some Coke and added reflectively, "It was like they didn't think we were really people, that the scouts wouldn't miss their wives and children. The army took those scouts away from their families for years, sending them down to Fort Ringgold hundreds of miles from here. They weren't gone from home for a few months or anything."

In fact, it was nine years before the army considered the southern U.S.–Mexican border safe enough to return the scouts to Fort Clark. They were thrilled to go, but, once there, found themselves in the familiar position of waiting helplessly for more bad things to happen. The quartermaster there found things for them to do—mending fences, fending off poachers on fort grounds—but it was clearly busy work.

Sometimes, word reached the Las Moras Creek camp from the scouts and their families who had moved uninvited to Indian Territory and defied efforts by John Jumper and the American agent to make them leave. In the late 1890s, the U.S. government took steps to gradually allow reservation Indians to become American citizens. Then, as citizens, each could be allocated some reservation land. As landowners, the Indians could then sell their new property to white speculators anxious to pay as little as possible for land that might produce rich fields of grain or deposits of oil. It was good politics and pleased influential businessmen.

In 1897, agents began to divide land among the Seminole. The Oklahoma Black Seminole were included; the Texas Seminole Negro were not. In all, about 347,000 acres were divided between three thousand adult "blood" Seminole and Black Seminole. In 1906, the land was completely allocated, and on March 4, 1907, the government officially "closed" the Seminole rolls. No one could be added to the list of tribal members owed land or any other compensation by the United States. The Seminole Negro in Texas were now separate from the Seminole tribe for all time.

For the scouts and their dependents at Fort Clark, it became a matter of waiting, like delinquent renters dreading the arrival of a landlord with eviction papers. For years, they had fastened onto any faint hope the army might just let them stay. In 1902, for example, an official military survey map of the fort clearly indicated a 225-acre "Seminole camp" that, at least on paper, seemed listed as permanently as any of the other fort buildings. The survey map was astonishing in its detail. Each individual Seminole Negro family's cabin area was indicated—Bob Kibbetts's near the center of the village on the very bank of Las Moras Creek, the Wilson brothers side by side a quarter mile away, John Ward for some reason alone on the east bank of the Creek, Kelly Warrior also isolated, closer to the main fort compound than his own people.

They kept building new cabins and adding other improvements. It was something to do, and they were excellent carpenters. In 1909, General James Bell tried to provide the army with a complete description of the camp. He got most of the details right, though his estimate that it covered 150 acres erred on the low side.

Scout Fay July and his wife pose in the Las Moras Creek Village about 1909

(COURTESY OF THE FORT CLARK HISTORICAL SOCIETY)

"A settlement or village in which these people live has been permitted to grow up on the military reservation of Fort Clark without any evidence of protest or interference on the part of the Government," Bell wrote, apparently surprised the construction had been condoned at all. "This village now contains 93 buildings, including a church. The buildings are for the most part constructed of logs or pickets with chinks stopped with mud and with grass roof (s). Some have shingle roofs, but all are one story. The village, including the yards, occupies about 150 acres, of which but little is cultivated. The inhabitants of the village seem to own about 5 farm wagons, 9 buggies and 2 spring carts, also the following live stock: 93 horses, 10 mules, 18 burros, 10 cattle, 790 goats and 18 pigs, all of which live stock is fed upon the military reservation."

From the tone of Bell's report, even the presence of the Seminole Negro animals seemed to be considered an inconvenience to the military. Had Bell bothered to count the human inhabitants of the camp, he would have added 113 adults and 94 children lived there, plus, most of the time, some families making lengthy visits from Nacimiento. It speaks to the ongoing poverty among the tribe in Mexico that the near-starving Seminole Negro in Texas were still considered their rich relations.

The tribe never let its village deteriorate. Some families even made a point of adding wood floors to the front rooms of their cabins, "for visitors," according to Miss Charles, who was born in 1910 and now in this narrative becomes a participant as well as a storyteller. "There seemed to be no sense that we would really have to leave," she said. "It was our home, the only one many had known, since some of us had lived there for more than thirty years. Wooden floors in front rooms were meant to make things nice for guests. Good manners were important! The other rooms just had dirt floors. Those were for the family."

Miss Charles had another vivid memory—the Seminole Negro people's last day in the Las Moras Creek camp. Her voice always shook a little as she told her tales, but in describing this day, tears came to her eyes. The pain she'd felt eighty years earlier had never lessened.

"I was four years old and I had a new doll, a stick doll," Miss Charles said. "Someone had carved it for me. My father, an uncle, some adult. All the grown-ups treated each child as his or her own."

It was early fall in 1914. It was clear, and the sun was warm. The camp was a particularly pleasant place to be. The towering oak trees provided shade. Chirping crickets and baa-ing goats contributed soothing background noise. Some of the children were running about, playing chase and tag. Their hoots and screeches blended into the gentle chorus from the insects and livestock.

Suddenly, there was another noise, coming from the north, on the road between the camp and the main fort grounds. Wagon wheels were bouncing along the rutted trail; the wagon beds creaked on their frames. Four empty wagons, six, finally a dozen pulled by horses swept into the center of the camp. Soldiers moving at double-quick pace seemed to materialize out of nowhere. They were armed with rifles. An officer stepped forward, pulled out a piece of paper, and began reading aloud. After the first few words, wails from the women began to drown him out. Some of the men yelled, their voices shaking with anger. But the white officer read on. Except for a few of the very oldest and most helpless members of the tribe, all the Seminole Negro were to leave Fort Clark right away, taking with them all of their personal property. Such items were to be loaded in the wagons. Do it *now*. And, to be certain no one tried to sneak back and re-occupy the cabins, every building except those lived in by the old people allowed to remain would be demolished immediately. As they heard this, the people noticed some of the soldiers held crowbars and sledgehammers instead of rifles.

"When I heard the soldiers, I dropped my doll somewhere and never saw it again," Miss Charles said. "I guess the soldiers threw it away if they found it."

For the little girl and her people, a lost doll was the least of their concerns. As the Seminole Negro realized that the time had finally come when they were being evicted, many responded with tears.

"I cried and cried," recalled Miss Charles. "Everyone seemed to weep. We had to hurry and load our things in the wagons, and then they rushed us down away from the fort and into town."

On the dirty streets of Brackettville, the soldiers dumped everything that had been put in the wagons. The dispossessed Seminole Negro stood crowded around the piles of their meager personal possessions—some raggedy bedding, handmade chairs, dented pots and cracked plates, and other bits of near-effluvia. Soon white town residents began to congregate nearby, first muttering imprecations and then shouting commands for the injun-niggers to get the hell out of the street, get lost, go somewhere, anywhere else. Miss Charles said she remembered some of the bad language, but could not, as a decent woman, ever repeat it.

Above the curses and the shouts, there was another sound, carried faintly down to the town by the warm wind. Looking past the guarded entrance to the fort, the Seminole Negro could just hear the sound of logs breaking under heavy hammers, of boards screeching as they were pried apart. The Las Moras Creek village was being obliterated, its former inhabitants were standing in the streets of a redneck town where everyone hated them, and they truly had no idea of what to do next, or where to go.

I finished talking to the Brackettville High history club with seconds to spare. As the kids began gathering up books and backpacks in anticipation of moving on to their next classes, Kathy Bader asked, "How many of you have been to any of the Seminole Days programs? Raise your hands." Not one hand went up. "All right, how many of you will go tomorrow?" A half-dozen hands were raised. After the bell rang, some of the students stayed behind, asking questions about the Seminole Negro. They'd heard a little, they said, but there weren't books about them in the school library.

"Shauntee is a Seminole," one girl said, gesturing at the black cheerleader. But Shauntee didn't stay to talk. She gathered her books and backpack and hurried out of the room.

"Actually, I think Shauntee was listening when you talked," Bader told me months afterward. "A few days later she brought in this video, one I guess her family had, about Seminole Days, and told me I might want to look at it. I don't think it's true that she and the other Seminole kids here don't care about their history. It's just the age they are. Kids don't want to act like they're too interested."

Kathy Bader intrigued Willie Warrior. When I told him about her history club and how I'd talked to the kids at her request, he said wonderingly, "A teacher in Brackettville asked you to do that? A white teacher?"

"Sure did."

"A white teacher," Willie mused. "Well, I know they got a new superintendent, so maybe that makes a difference. I always offered to come talk about the scouts, but they kept on turning me down. Sounds like it's different now."

"You could call Kathy Bader," I suggested hopefully. "We'll get her phone number. I'll bet she'd ask you to come talk to her kids. She says she thinks they all ought to know the scout history."

Willie wouldn't call. It was somebody else's turn to tell the stories, he insisted. But he agreed, since he and I had been talking about it for so many years, to finish telling about the Seminole Negro struggle to survive in Brackettville.

"This is the last time I talk about this, I swear," Willie said. "See, there all the people were in the street, thrown off the fort, out of the place they'd been living, the scouts and the women and the babies and the old people, and everyone around them just hating them so much . . ."

chapter seventeen

MEMORIES MOST often consist of fact, hearsay, and personal preference. Willie Warrior wasn't born until 1927, thirteen years after the Seminole Negro were forcibly evicted from their Las Moras Creek village. Unlike Miss Charles, he wasn't there when it happened. But he did spend much of his childhood listening to the reminisences of those who were, and his version differs from hers.

"The scouts knew what was coming down," Willie said as we strolled around the old village site. At least a dozen deer were grazing nearby. They raised their heads as we walked slowly toward them, then delicately picked their way across the clearing and into the deeper woods. "The order to kick 'em out came in the summer of 1914," Willie continued. "They got notified a couple months ahead of time that they would have to leave. Now, some of 'em probably didn't believe those orders would get carried out. I guess they figured the army would back off, like it did when, for a while, they were supposed to be cut back to six scouts. I know Miss Charles said nobody knew, but she was just a little child. I don't think the grown-ups talked about it with the children, so probably for the little ones it was a surprise."

Army records bear Willie out. On July 10, 1914, official orders reached Fort Clark commanding that "The Seminole Negro Indian Scouts . . . be

HEADQUARTERS
14TH U.S. CAVALRY REGIMENT
FORT CLARK, TEXAS

To Whom It May Concern

In compliance with orders contained in the 3rd Indorsement Headquarters Southern Department, May 7th, 1914, and the 5th

Indorsement War Department, June 29th, 1914, on communications 2128018-A.A.G.O., April 16, 1914- Subject Seminole Negro Indian Scouts. The Seminole Negro Indian Scouts will be disbanded and cease to exist as an organizatikon after September 30, 1914. They will be discharged from Serviceg of the United States in three detachents as follows: Privates, Curly Jefferson, Fay July, Sam Washington, and Charles J. July on July 31st, 1914. One third in the Scout camp on the reservation including the families of the scouts discharged July 31st, 1914 will move from the Fort Clark Military Reservation between August 1st and August 15th, 1914 with all of their stock anb belongings.

The following named scouts will be discharged from the Service of United States, September 30th, 1914, - 1st Sgt. John Shields, Privates; Antonio Sanchez, Isaac Wilson and William Wilson. The remainder of the people including the Scouts discharged September 30th, 1914, and their families withthe exception of those named in the following paragraph will move from Fort Clark Military Reservation between October 1st and October 15th, 1914 with all of their effects.

The following named members of the Scout Camp will be permitted to remain and live on the Fort Clark Military Reservatioon until the older people pass away in the course of nature. or until such time as the War Department may see fit to order their removal. After the removal of the people from the Scout Camp, the buildings not in use by those permitted to stay, will be demolished.

LIST OF FAMILES AND INDIVIDUALS OF THE SEMINOLE CAMP WHO ARE AUTHORIZED TO REMAIN AND RESIDE ON THE FORT CLARK MILITARY RESERVATION.

Joseph Phillips and 1 child....................2
Renty Grueon...................................1
Eva Payne and 3 children.......................4
Dolly Bowlegs White and 1 daughter.............2
Pompey Perryman and 1 son......................2
Jim Perryman and son, son to remain during
the life of the father.........................2
Phyllis Kibbets and adopted child..............2
Ann Williams and 4 children....................5
Julie Ward and 1 son. The latter to remain as
means of support during the life of the mother.2
Adam Smith 1
Joe Thompson...................................1

By Order of Colonel Sibley
STERLING P ADAMS
Captain & Adjutant 14th Cavalry
Adjutant

Fort Clark, Texas, July 10th, 1914

The official army command to disband the camp

(COURTESY OF FORT CLARK HISTORICAL SOCIETY)

disbanded and cease to exist as an organization after September 30, 1914. They will be discharged from Service of the United States in three detachments as follows: Privates Curly Jefferson, Fay July, Sam Washington and Charles J. July on July 31st, 1914. One-third in the Scout camp on the reservation including the families discharged July 31st, 1914 will move from the Fort Clark Military Reservation between August 1st and August 15th, 1914 with all their stock and belongings."

The order continued, mandating in excruciating detail how several more scouts and their families would have to leave by September 30, and then everyone else between October 1 and 15—with a few exceptions. Demonstrating just the barest hint of compassion, the order concluded with the ambiguous concession that "(a few) members of the Scout Camp will be permitted to remain and live on the Fort Clark Military Reservation until the older people pass away in the course of nature, or until such time as the War Department may see fit to order their removal. After the removal of the people from the Scout Camp, the buildings not in use by those permitted to stay will be demolished." Then came the brief list of those authorized to stay on, mostly widows and children, twenty-seven names in all. That meant over the next several months 180 men, women, and children were officially to be turned out into the Brackettville streets.

Certainly, the scouts learned about the order almost as soon as it was received by the Fort Clark commander. They begged army officials to plead again with Department of Interior and Indian bureau staff to let them go back to Oklahoma and what had been known as Indian Territory. An official bureau missive soon arrived at Fort Clark. It noted Seminole tribal rolls had closed seven years earlier. Accordingly, the letter concluded, "no allotments can be made to them as Seminoles and, of course, there is no provision of law for making allotments to them as Negroes."

So far as the army was concerned, that ended the matter. The scouts and their families would have to pack and leave. It appears, though, that the order mandating them to be dismissed from service and evicted from the Las Moras Creek camp by thirds might have been temporarily ignored. Meanwhile, Willie says, the scouts who could afford it began moving their families away from the fort as soon as it became clear the disbandment edict would stand. A few, most of whom had Mexican wives, chose to return to the poverty of Nacimiento. One or two drifted to Del Rio or San Antonio, and several made new, cramped living arrangements with relatives in Oklahoma. By the time the soldiers and wagons arrived at the scout village, less than half the scout families were left to evict, and they were all removed at once rather than on three separate occasions.

"The people they moved out didn't like it, but there wasn't anything they could do about it," Willie said. "I guess Miss Charles's family was still there, one of the last. But it, the eviction, wasn't really a surprise."

Surprised or not, the Seminole Negro unceremoniously dumped on the streets of Brackettville still felt dazed and uncertain about what to do next. It never occurred to the younger and stronger among them to abandon the others. They considered one another, in the most basic sense, *family.* The strong would not leave the weak to fend for themselves.

There were other black families in Brackettville, living in shacks on the periphery of town, but the Seminole Negro would not go to them for help. There was tension between the two groups, Miss Charles said. The Brackettville blacks felt the arrogance of the Seminole Negro inflamed racist whites and made it harder on everyone in town who had dark skin.

Instead, some displaced members of the tribe found friendship and temporary shelter among Brackettville's sizable Mexican population. The Seminole Negro were used to Mexicans as neighbors, and as mates. Most of the tribe spoke fluent Spanish. There was no sense of class or racial separation between the two groups.

Neither Willie Warrior nor Miss Charles knew for certain where most of the forlorn Seminole Negro slept that first night after eviction, or the next, or in the first few weeks after being thrown off Fort Clark. Probably a few of them already had some sort of shack in Brackettville. They were hardy sorts; certainly they were capable of rigging temporary shelters. Their greatest danger was from surly townspeople who would have welcomed the chance to drive them away from Brackettville. Where they would have, or could have, gone from there is impossible to guess. They didn't have the money to go to Oklahoma, the option of returning to Nacimiento—the people already there had troubles enough of their own—or the inclination to stumble east to Uvalde or west to Del Rio. Those places were just as inhospitable as Brackettville. Besides, some of the very oldest and weakest

Seminole still lived at the Las Moras Creek camp. They couldn't be left behind. Then there was the scout cemetery. In all their orders about getting off fort property, the army never mentioned that. Either through oversight or someone in authority deciding two or three grubby acres full of dead black Indians weren't worth mentioning, the cemetery remained under tribal control. The spirits of their ancestors could not be abandoned.

So Brackettville, by default, was where they stayed. Ben Pingenot believed the remaining tribal members pooled money they earned and acquired a small tract of land that most could live on. It's certainly possible they did—Miss Charles never mentioned it, but she had so much history to try to repeat to anyone interested that she might have simply forgotten. And, not long after they were forced off Fort Clark, some of the Seminole Negro families really did have a little money for buying land. It came about because white Brackettville ranchers, as much as they disdained the Seminole Negro, also had a grudging appreciation for the abilities of the scouts.

"Most of the men went to work on the ranches," Willie Warrior explained. "The scouts were great riders and handlers of horses, and they were needed. See, back in those days, 1914, '15, in there, most horses used on ranches were built for hard work. They were lanky, big old hammerheads with funny eyes. A man riding one of those horses hated to get down, because the horse would just bite him and run. They were wild. You'd see horses out there with parts of a bridle—it'd thrown the rider and then gone on. Probably bit him or kicked him to hell first."

Civilian employers of the scouts discovered the same qualities to admire in them that the army had. If they were paid to do a job, they did it, thoroughly and without complaint. They rode those crazy horses well enough to herd cattle, goats, and sheep. They repaired fencing, dug wells, and did the branding and castrating, all for the same few dollars a month they'd been paid by the army. Meanwhile, those women of the tribe who were able got work as laundresses or cooks or maids. Rebecca July Wilson, Miss Charles's mother, worked for a while in a cafe. Mothers who couldn't leave infants cared for the children of women who were able to go out to work. Old men earned a few cents splicing ropes and patching bridles. Everyone worked together to survive, despite their acceptance of the fact there would not be now, and, probably, never would be, any substantial tract of land for the Seminole Negro to call their own.

"Even if we didn't have the land we were promised, we still had our pride, still had our dignity," said Willie. "The old people at night told the stories about John Horse and Abraham, slaves running away to Florida, about going from Indian Territory to Mexico, about the great battles the scouts fought in Texas. That was our evening entertainment, not radio or anything like that."

Not that the Seminole Negro were sanguine about what they considered betrayal on the part of the army and the American government. "Oh, there was bitterness," Miss Charles remembered. "But there was no way to seek satisfaction. What could we do, write a letter to the president? We had already tried that. It was a very hard time, particularly in having to live among some people who made it very clear they did not enjoy our company, and never would."

Though their menfolk were useful on the ranches, the Seminole Negro as a people were simply not accepted by whites in Brackettville. Their early years living in town were, to be sure, hard times for residents of every race. The Depression blasted big-city economies to smithereens, but Brackettville had been impoverished long before the stock market took its near-fatal plunge in 1929. There were a few relatively wealthy ranchers, but most were working hardscrabble properties and struggling to survive. Many of these whites treated the Seminole Negro badly because they simply felt they could. Kicked hard by life themselves, they wanted someone else they could kick around.

It happened physically and in other even crueler ways, particularly to the Seminole Negro children. Now that they lived in Brackettville, they were sent to school there. Of course, there was one school for white children and another for nonwhites. Teachers in the "colored" school immediately shamed the Seminole Negro children "because we mostly spoke Gullah," Miss Charles recalled. "They said that was primitive talk. We were supposed to only speak English. But at home everyone spoke Gullah, which was a comfort to the old people and a way of retaining our heritage. We children who also spoke English had sort of funny accents, because Gullah was the language with which we'd been raised. And the teachers would make a fuss over that, telling us to talk like Americans. We would wait until we got home to cry. Children, you know, can be so easily embarrassed."

Social humiliation at school would often be followed by physical attacks afterward. Packs of older white boys would wait outside the colored school for the Seminole Negro boys to leave for home. "But when they did that, they got whipped up on," Willie said, grinning at the memory more than sixty years later and, perhaps, allowing himself some nostalgic exaggeration. "We had some fights, maybe twenty of us against a hundred of them, and we won. Damn, that made it rough when I was growing up."

It wasn't all bad. Ethel Warrior said she was raised "in a mixed neighborhood. Whites, Mexicans, blacks. People could get along. Mostly they did, especially after enough time passed for everybody else to get used to us living in town with them instead of on the fort."

In Oklahoma, the Black Seminole coexisted uneasily with the self-styled "blood" Seminole. At least in Black Seminole opinion, tribal leaders there were determined to keep their adoptive relatives restricted to unofficial second-class citizenship. Seminole councils were dominated by the bloods. Seminole Negro visiting from Texas often left thinking their uneasy lot in Brackettville was still preferable to the unspoken class divisiveness to the north.

"Those Oklahoma Seminole kept trying to take from us all along," Willie Warrior said. "Hell, after a while they even tried to get our Nacimiento land. They'd've grabbed our wallets if they could have."

Willie Warrior and his generation of Seminole Negro in Texas saw constant examples of the Seminole Indians trying to take land away from their former slaves and allies. Around 1900, and then well into the twentieth century, Seminole leaders made periodic requests of the Mexican government to give them either the Nacimiento land occupied by the *Mascogos* or comparable land in the same vicinity. The Seminole justification was that, when the Mexican government originally gave the land to its Indian protectors, the bequest was actually made to the leader of the group—Wild Cat, a full-blood Seminole, not one of those rascally Seminole Negro. True, the *real* Seminole had eventually returned to Indian Territory while the Seminole Negro stayed in Mexico, but that was a technicality. At one point, a Seminole delegation to Mexico was led by Ahalakochee, one of Wild Cat's grandsons. But the plan seemed better to the Seminole in theory rather than practice. Once they came to Mexico and inspected the Nacimiento area for themselves, they found it "wild and desolate territory infested with bandits and laid waste by revolution." By the late 1930s, when the Mexican government seemed willing to give the Seminole some sort of land parcel in Coahuila, the tribe's leaders didn't think it was worth having.

Still, the audacity of the Seminole land-grab scheme permanently alienated the Brackettville Seminole Negro from that tribe. They stayed in close contact with their family and friends in Oklahoma, but communication between the Texas Seminole Negro and the Oklahoma Seminole would, in the future, be infrequent and icy. Willie and his peers would never like, let alone trust, the Seminole again—and their strongly held convictions later made it impossible for them to understand why Clarence Ward and younger Seminole Negro were comfortable designating themselves simply as "Seminole."

A dozen years after they'd been turned out of their Las Moras Creek village, it seemed the Seminole Negro in Brackettville had reached a sad cultural dead end. They lived mostly in near-hovels. Adults worked in poorly paid jobs for autocratic white bosses—not much of a step up from the old master-slave relationships their ancestors had originally fled. Their children received substandard educations in colored schools, until such time as family finances forced them to drop out and take jobs, or else they worked their way through a very rudimentary high school curriculum and graduated to join the lowest ranks of the local workforce. There was no longer any expectation of a miracle happening and the U.S. government deciding, however belatedly, to award the tribe the land the Seminole Negro still passionately believed they'd earned. The harsh day-to-day existence they now endured appeared to be all they could expect in the future, too.

"There was no thought life for any of us would be anything but hard work and staying poor," Ethel Warrior said. "You might say we lived, but we didn't dream."

But the Seminole Negro had one more hero to add to the line that began with Miss Charles's anonymous runaway slaves and extended through Abraham and John Horse and John Kibbetts and, more or less collectively, Robert Kibbetts and David Bowlegs and all four Medal of Honor winners—even Adam Payne, whose subsequent rascality and violent death didn't negate, at least to his people, the heroism he demonstrated in battle on behalf of the American government. The same four-year-old girl who cried when the soldiers forced her family off Fort Clark grounds eventually stepped up to lead her people in Brackettville.

"I felt, from an early age when it was impressed upon me by my mother, that our tool for future success would have to be education," Miss Charles recalled. "So long as our children learned very little in school, they would have very little to offer the world after graduation besides the ability to do physical labor—mending fence or washing clothes. But if they had the opportunity to get better educations, perhaps even go to college, then they might eventually acquire the skills to be the bosses rather than the bossed. It was all a matter of someone leading the way."

In the colored school, young Charles endured it when teachers corrected her pronunciation, and the little girl memorized every textbook she was issued. After receiving a certificate of high school completion—"degree" is too complimentary a word to describe the paper issued in those days to "colored school" graduates—teenaged Charles took the unprecedented step among her people of applying to Huston-Tillotson College in Austin, one of a few "black" colleges in the state.

"Charles and her sister, Dorothy, were the lucky girls," Ethel Warrior said, sounding a bit envious. "Their mother, Rebecca, was the reason, I believe. She was a hardworking woman everyone admired. While all the other girls had to leave school and go to work, she said her daughters were getting a college education and making something of themselves. She drove them to do better than the rest of us."

Admittance to Huston-Tillotson was only a beginning for Charles Emily Wilson, rather than sufficient achievement in itself. Austin was a huge, frightening city to a young woman whose experience in the world previously extended only to the Brackettville town limits. Unsophisticated Charles knew nothing about taking notes from class lectures or how to socially interact with strangers. There was also the matter of paying her expenses with the kinds of odd jobs—waitressing, dishwashing—that were available to respectable young black women in those days.

"But I was determined to become a teacher, as was my sister, Dorothy," Miss Charles said. "I took an undergraduate teaching degree, then a master's degree in bilingual education so I could speak to each student in the language he or she found most comfortable." At Huston-Tillotson, and later at Prairie View A&M College in Houston, another Texas college for blacks, Miss Charles memorized textbooks as she had in high school, determined to master every fact available to her. It was brave, but, after being awarded her graduate degree—such an achievement was virtually unimaginable among the Seminole Negro—she did something far braver. A young black woman with these glittering college credentials could have taught anywhere, though, in the 1920s, she would of course have been restricted to teaching in schools for minority students. Life in New York or Chicago or Los Angeles was there for Charles Emily Wilson's taking, culture and excitement far beyond the shoddy confines of Jim Crow Brackettville. But she came back to her hometown anyway and began teaching in the colored school herself. That this limited the possibilities for her own life mattered less than the opportunity to make better things possible for younger Seminole Negro—and for the Mexican and "American" black pupils she prized equally.

"If they were in my school, I loved them," Miss Charles said, smiling. "We talked and talked in my classes, and we found something for each child to feel proud about. We discussed how honest effort can make almost anything possible. We talked, even in hard times, about the blessings of freedom and the personal responsibility to help not just yourself, but your neighbor."

At least initially, Miss Charles didn't fit in well with some of the other Seminole Negro after she returned to Brackettville. She hinted, though never said outright, that many were jealous of her education and professional success. But Ethel Warrior remembers that Miss Charles came back home with a high opinion of herself.

"I love Charles dearly, but for a while she was not one who was too friendly," Ethel said. "I can remember, after she got back, that sometimes her mother, Rebecca, would drive over to our house to visit with my mother, bringing Charles and Dorothy with her. Rebecca and Dorothy would get out of the car and come in to visit, but Charles would sit out in the car all by herself. It was only after her mother died, and after it was plain somebody had to do something to keep us together, that Charles stepped forward."

In the 1930s, Miss Charles began to take it on herself to rally the rest of the Brackettville Seminole Negro. As the scouts themselves began to die off, it was even more important, she insisted, to talk to those who still survived and have them repeat the stories of their adventures, in fact to have them repeated over and over until every word was burned into the memories of those listening. And, more than that, the scouts and old people must be asked to repeat the tales they'd heard from their own parents and grandparents. Miss Charles wanted it all preserved, in oral history and, hopefully, someday in writing. All this knowledge would give her people pride, Miss Charles insisted, and that pride could translate into the Seminole Negro children considering themselves not different in bad ways, but special in good ones.

And it worked, to a limited extent. Some of the children picked up on the new oral tradition, drinking in the words of the old people and committing them to memory. Willie Warrior became one of Miss Charles's favorite youngsters. He trailed after the old scouts, asking as many questions as they would answer. As he grew older, he began appearing in area churches and schools as a guest speaker, telling the story of the Seminole Negro and their long quest for land and freedom. A barrel-chested man with a commanding voice, Willie Warrior could mesmerize audiences.

"All I did was repeat the stories that had been told to me," he said. "I tried to use all the same words, or as close to them as I could remember. Afterward, sometimes, people would come up to me and ask if all that, about John Horse and the rest coming down to Mexico, and the scouts' fights with the Indians, could possibly true. And I would tell them that it was."

But just as Miss Charles became established as the leader of her people, and Willie Warrior began to emerge as a first-class storyteller, the army brought new trouble to the Seminole Negro in an unexpected way. Fort Clark had always been essentially a cavalry and mounted scout outpost. But as the 1930s gave way to the forties, the army phased out its mounted troops. It was becoming a world of cars and jeeps and other motorized transportation. World War I had already demonstrated that mounted troops were outmoded. World War II drove the point home. The Seminole Negro had no idea that, as the conflict ended, so too would the existence of Fort Clark as a military base. The fort was deactivated in 1946; trying to make money out of the deal, the government sold the property to Brown and Root Company, a massive engineering firm that had plans to turn the old fort into some sort of ritzy guest ranch.

The elderly Seminole Negro who'd been allowed to stay on at the Las Moras Creek village were all gone by 1946, but when the army controlled the premises it was still possible for tribal members living in Brackettville to at least come onto the post and wander several miles south to their old camp. Not all the old buildings had been torn down. There were bits and pieces still there. Along with the scout cemetery—which remained under Seminole Negro control even after the fort was shut down and sold—the village ruins had incalculable value to the tribe. That was where they'd lived the longest; in the years before their eviction, it was where most of them believed, or at least hoped, they would be allowed to live permanently. A few old folks, Miss Charles said, still held some hope that, miraculously, their old campsite would be officially restored to them. Now, with Brown and Root as owners, there was a barred gate at the entrance to the fort, and even the most hopeful Seminole Negro had to accept that the Las Moras Creek village area would never be theirs. The new proprietors envisioned the springs near the north edge of the fort as natural pools teeming with swimsuited, wealthy clientele. The shady woods to the south where the Seminole Negro had lived could be marketed to prospective clients as near-elysian picnic grounds. In both instances, the last thing Brown and Root wanted was a bunch of raggedy black Indians hanging around. The last vestiges of the old village disappeared. Not a stone or plank of it was spared.

That made the cemetery even more precious. Many of its graves were primitive, with lashed-together sticks serving as rudimentary crosses, but it was still a place for the Seminole Negro to gather. Often, death became an occasion for reunions and celebration. "Any descendants and their husbands or wives can be buried there," Willie Warrior explained. "We have no restrictions on that, and not too many years ago it was even our custom to dig the graves together. There would be a wake, then at three or four in the morning maybe five or six guys would go over and dig the grave. The tradition was, there were a couple of bottles of whiskey for the gravediggers. They'd have that to drink, go dig the grave, and afterward the family of the dead person would feed them breakfast. That stopped because, after a while, guys would sign up, drink the whiskey, get drunk, and never go dig the grave."

Members of the tribe who moved away tried to return for funeral services in the cemetery. "When I first got in touch with Willie Warrior to learn more about my family's history, he said I ought to come right over because somebody had died and all the people at the funeral could tell me about our ancestors," Cynthia Ventura said. "When my daughter and I went to the cemetery for the first time, we felt like people were watching us from the graves. We thought we heard them whispering to each other. I told Willie, 'We need a ceremony to let these people go back to sleep.' He laughed and said, 'We have ceremonies to wake them up.' Afterward, Ethel Warrior explained that somebody among the spirits knew who I was and started explaining that to the other spirits. That was the whispering."

Almost universally, the Seminole believed—and still do—that the spirits of their ancestors inhabit the cemetery. They're offended, though, by the use of the term *haunted.*

"See, the wind always blows out in the cemetery, even if it's not blowing anywhere else," Willie explained. "Don't say the cemetery's haunted. It's just that the spirits are still there."

To preserve the resting place of those spirits, in the 1950s Miss Charles, along with her uncle, Tony Wilson, proposed a group be formally organized to keep the grounds in pristine condition. Members of the same group, she suggested, could also serve as informal tribe historians. Its official name was Seminole Indian Scouts Cemetery Association, probably selected to reflect the ethnically incorrect army designation for the scout unit. It didn't seem especially important, back then, if Willie and others chose to refer to the "Black Seminole" cemetery association instead.

Government-mandated integration brought the next great change to the lives of the tribe. The "colored school," by law, merged with the white one. Miss Charles was among the first black teachers in Texas to have white students. Thrown in with white kids, the Seminole Negro youngsters were treated as inferiors. Skin color was only one issue; when speaking English, many still had traces of Gullah accents, and their new white teachers were quick to correct and criticize. Still, the quality of education they now received from first through twelfth grades was better overall than what had been available in the colored school. They had better textbooks, and guest speakers talked about a world outside Brackettville that few of the Seminole Negro children had previously imagined. Television, even primitive black-and-white broadcasts, also made it clear that there were far more exciting places to live. Soon, most Seminole Negro teenagers had something in common with the majority of their white classmates—they wanted to get out of town as soon as they graduated. Young adults felt the urge to go out and do better, too. Even Willie Warrior moved to Del Rio, where he became a truck driver, though he still spent much of his spare time making speeches about the tribe to any organization that invited him.

The exodus of the younger Seminole Negro didn't sit well with some of the older members of the tribe, who'd expected their offspring to stay and care for them in their old age as they had done for their parents. But the tug of tribal history was lessening for its new generations. In 1959, Curly Jefferson died; he had been the last living scout. There were now middle-aged Seminole Negro who'd never even lived in the Las Moras Creek camp. To their children, the stories often took on the aspect of fairy tales. John Horse and Abraham and Wild Cat weren't in the history books they read in school.

Television took the biggest toll, Miss Charles always insisted. Evenings in most Seminole Negro homes were no longer spent with elders reciting tribal history to youngsters hanging on every word. The Seminole Negro kids preferred *The Mickey Mouse Club,* she said, and later *The Beverly Hillbillies* and *Happy Days,* all seeming more exciting, more tantalizing with possibilities, than tales of flight from Indian Territory to Mexico. TV shows were a lot more entertaining. You could talk about them the next day with your friends at school. Who wanted to hear those boring old grandparents' stories over and over?

"Television about did our history in," Miss Charles said sadly, shaking her head. "That, and those video-game things."

But Clarence Ward, choosing his words carefully, said there was another reason Seminole Negro youngsters in the sixties and seventies lost interest in the old stories.

"For a while there, Miss Charles and Mr. Warrior and the others who knew all the stories started getting asked to talk to outside groups, rather than staying around with the rest of us," Clarence said. "So they would be gone, and while there would still be association meetings, they got to be more social than anything else. I remember going with my mother, and the adults would always play cake bingo—you know, where cakes would be the prizes. We kids were told to play outside, and the idea at those meetings was that we shouldn't speak unless we were spoken to. So you can't blame us completely for not listening to the old stories, because there weren't grown-ups telling them to us."

Besides John Wayne coming to town to film his epic, if less than historically accurate, movie called *The Alamo,* not much happened in Brackettville in the late fifties and early sixties. Other filmmakers followed. Many of the "desert" scenes in old Western movies now shown on late-night cable TV were filmed around Brackettville. Then, in 1971, old Fort Clark was purchased by a company called North American Towns of Texas, which envisioned using its 2,700 acres as a private recreation/retirement community. Fields and parade grounds were turned into flat, sun-baked golf courses. Old barracks were modestly spiffed up and offered for sale as separate housing units; the nicer stone homes of officers were also sold as private homes. Two administration buildings were turned into motel rooms; another became a restaurant. Ironically, it subsequently became easier for many of the Seminole to go back onto the property where their parents and grandparents had lived; they were part of construction and cleanup crews.

They were needed for another purpose, too. Brackettville civic leaders now began to stake their town's economic future on attracting visitors, people stopping off on their way to San Antonio or Del Rio to play golf on the new Fort Clark course, to visit the old Alamo set, or even the Old Fort Clark Guardhouse Museum. Suddenly, the presence of the scouts' descendants was a plus for Brackettville. These colorful people were, in their quaint way, a civic asset. They were encouraged to donate family photographs to the museum. Miss Charles and Willie were glad to oblige. The Whitehead Museum in Del Rio and the Institute of Texan Cultures in San Antonio also developed extensive Seminole Negro exhibits. Visiting journalists, writing stories about the renovated fort, were directed to Miss Charles, who would patiently tell them about her tribe's fabulous history. In the mid-1970s, Miss Charles was even named the Brackettville Chamber of Commerce Woman of the Year.

Miss Charles was pleased that white Brackettville finally seemed ready to assimilate its Seminole neighbors, but she continued to feel concerned about the tribe's young people losing interest in their rich heritage. Once again, something had to be done. Around 1984, about the same time she retired from teaching, Miss Charles had a new idea: Each fall, there should be a special celebration, perhaps a weekend crammed with events commemorating tribal history from the swamps of Florida to the shady camp at Las Moras Creek. Seminole Days, the celebration could be called, and there could be a parade and everyone could dress up in traditional cloaks and turbans, and old-time dishes like stewed goat could be prepared. All the farflung scout descendants would be invited to come back home to Brackettville, from Oklahoma and Nacimiento and any other place they'd strayed since 1914. Brackettville's non-Seminole citizens would be very welcome to attend; it would be a way for them to learn about their long-estranged fellow residents. Best of all, the Seminole teenagers would turn off their TVs and video games, because what child could resist a party?

Miss Charles, Willie Warrior, and a few others went to the Brackettville Chamber of Commerce. It was easy to get a parade permit for a weekend in September, and the cemetery association had its own park property on the west side of town. Vendors supplied food (Miss Charles and the ladies

Seminole Days 2000

(PHOTO BY RALPH LAUER)

Miss Charles rides in the Seminole Days 2000 parade

(PHOTO BY RALPH LAUER)

of the tribe did some cooking, too) and a local beer distributor made certain nobody went away thirsty. Hundreds of people turned out for the first Seminole Days in 1985, many of them coming from Oklahoma. It was harder for the Nacimiento *Mascogos* to get across the border; few had the birth certificates necessary to be issued passports by the Mexican government. Only a few of Brackettville's white citizens turned out, though that was all right. Surely they'd turn out in greater force the next year, or the next. But there was also some evidence that Miss Charles's eyesight was beginning to fail. She swore to everyone that the Seminole Negro teenagers, the kids, were swarming all over the association park having fun and learning about their heritage. Nobody else saw many youngsters there. No one, though, was about to contradict Miss Charles.

"Charles was already slowing up at that point," Ethel Warrior said. "Sometimes she would forget dates, get names wrong, and she was not someone who liked making mistakes. At one point she went to a Washington, D.C., program with Dub and me, and when we were there she kept telling him he should be the one to do the talking. It was because, we figured out later, she was already losing track here and there."

But there was never any thought of supplanting Miss Charles as leader of the Brackettville tribe.

"We all loved her, and, besides me, there wasn't anybody else anyway who knew much of the history anymore," Willie said. "Though, thinking back about it, I should have known that sometime somebody unqualified was going to push his way in and take over the association."

Subsequent Seminole Days drew journalists from San Antonio and Houston and Fort Worth. Miss Charles and the Seminole—only occasionally identified in subsequent stories as Seminole Negro—were the subjects of several long stories. Miss Charles carefully cut out copies of each and pasted them in scrapbooks, which were then turned over to the cemetery association for safekeeping. She always made herself available for interviews, sent visitors to Del Rio to talk to Willie Warrior, and was glad to escort interested journalists to the cemetery herself.

Miss Charles and Willie Warrior remained the principal members of the tribe who still told the stories to anyone willing to listen. By the late eighties and early nineties, it sometimes seemed they were the only ones who cared, unless it was time for the Seminole Days festivities. Even the cemetery grounds grew periodically unkempt. It became too hard for Miss Charles and a few other tribal elders to mow and weed it, and younger Seminole had their own jobs and families to occupy their spare time and attention.

At least, in the eighties and nineties, Miss Charles and the rest of the Seminole were accepted into the general Brackettville population. The town settled into a sort of dusty torpor. Seminole Days were celebrated each September, but more and more participants were visitors rather than Brackettville residents. As the first generation of tribal teenagers who'd attended integrated Brackettville schools graduated and began their lives as adults, few stayed in town.

In Brackettville, Miss Charles held things together as well as she could, until the time came in the late nineties when she began routinely forgetting names as the Alzheimer's fog descended on her mind. Her remaining family decided it was time for her to go live with relatives in Kerrville, about

Miss Charles Emily Wilson in late 1994,
before she became afflicted with Alzheimer's disease
(PHOTO BY RON ENNIS)

an hour's drive from Brackettville. Her absence was keenly felt in the ever-dwindling Seminole Negro community.

Willie Warrior spent most of his time in Del Rio, though he and his wife, Ethel, did purchase part of the old Fort Clark enlisted mens' barracks to use as a getaway home. In 1998 Clarence Ward, a descendant of Medal of Honor winner John Ward, successfully ran for association president. He knew very little about tribal history, but he set up a web page on the Internet, hoping to use new technology to reach out to old association members who'd somehow lost touch. By Clarence's best estimate, the association in fall 2000 had about 150 members, "but just thirty or forty actually have their dues paid up. Dues are one dollar a month."

By the summer of 2001, the long and honorable history of the Seminole Negro had come to this: Near-destitution in Nacimiento, financial exclusion and expulsion from the Seminole tribe in Oklahoma, and confusion about what to do next in Brackettville. At least relations between the tribe and the rest of Brackettville have never been better, Clarence believes. "The people at the fort always say to me, 'Clarence, just tell us what you need,' " he said. "For Seminole Days, the businesses here are ready to give what we need. Meat for the barbecue. Beer. Anything. We feel we have that support."

Whatever anger his people have felt for the government and the owners of the Fort Clark property is gone now, he swears: "I have never had any member of the association say anything bad to me about Fort Clark. We know our ancestors used to be there. Their blood is in the soil. It can never be taken from it. You can build all the fancy houses around or over it you want."

So now there is only about a half mile between the old village site and the new Fort Clark construction. In a decade, maybe less, a brick three-story with a satellite dish in the front yard will stand in the same place Miss Charles Emily Wilson once played with carved wooden dolls, or on top of rotting splinters from logs that a century earlier sheltered John Lapham Bullis and Gomacinda, his Seminole Negro lover.

Clarence Ward was born and raised in Brackettville. All his life, he's visited the fort, sometimes by invitation, probably more often, at least as a youngster, by sneaking on. Certainly he's walked almost every acre, but until an afternoon in summer 2000 when I took him there, the well-meaning president of the scout association hadn't known for certain where the old Las Moras Spring camp had been located. Quietly, reverently, he walked about, smiling tentatively, overwhelmed by his thoughts.

"I've been around here so many times," Clarence finally said. "I wish I'd known. I've got to bring my wife here. She's part of the Factor family, you know. This is really the place. My god." He paced, muttered to himself, and finally said it might be a good idea to see if some sort of historical marker could be placed on the site. That would be something to bring up at the next association meeting. It was a project that might get the members excited. If the Seminole Negro never got their land, at least they might have some permanent reminder for themselves and everyone else of where that land could have, and should have, been. It would also be evidence that the scout association was capable of new accomplishments. For Willie Warrior and the older members of the tribe, it would be overdue recognition of their proud history. For Clarence Ward and his generation, that same marker would symbolize a fresh start.

"We're going to survive, we're going to be strong again," promised Clarence Ward, latest and perhaps not last among a line of Seminole Negro leaders going back from Willie Warrior to Miss Charles Emily Wilson to Robert Kibbetts to John Kibbetts to John Horse to Abraham to anonymous escaped slaves. Later, on the association web site, Clarence listed modest goals for the group, including "a better and even tighter unity with the public," and closed with this hopeful message: "Stand proud, my people," he urged. "You may be tired and weary, but we still have a long way to go."

EPILOGUE

the power of one

THE OUTDOOR BATHROOMS in the association park are finished just in time for Seminole Days 2001. This pleases Clarence Ward immensely, since getting them built was one of his goals for the group—"Something that shows we're moving ahead, growing a little." The outer walls of this new, boxy little building are made from gray concrete blocks. The doors to the two separate toilets are labeled CHIEFS and SQUAWS. And, by late afternoon on their introductory Seminole Days, these toilets have backed up and a Brackettville city crew is at work outside the park trying frantically to clear the sewer line. The sickly sweet smell of human waste is as thick in the air as the smoky aroma of goat meat being sold at the barbecue pit adjacent to the malfunctioning bathrooms.

Somehow, the clogged toilets seem appropriate. Everything about Seminole Days is a little off this year. Even after the terrorist attacks in New York City and Washington, D.C., just four days earlier, Clarence and his board are determined to have the programs run on schedule. In Brackettville, those two big eastern U.S. cities are as foreign, as far removed from daily life, as Istanbul or Moscow. People in Brackettville hang out some American flags, watch the news reports of the disaster, and then get on with their own lives. There are diseases spreading among area cattle. This is what people talk about over their greasy enchilada lunches in the Krazy Chicken.

Still, the events of September 11 have a direct effect on 2001 Seminole Days. People from out of town have their flights canceled or their buses postponed, and, for the first time in many years, Seminole Days weekend finds vacancies in the Fort Clark motel. The Saturday morning parade is even more desultory than usual. Only fourteen participants—some cars, one beer truck, one uniformed pseudo-scout on horseback, a couple of kids walking and waving a banner—make up the procession. So few people come out to watch that drivers in the lead cars pause their vehicles to say hello to them. Miss Charles, due in early that morning, doesn't arrive in time to ride in the parade. It's the first time she hasn't. Two teenage girls ride on her float instead, the one fixed up to look like a hut from the scout camp along Las Moras Creek. Later, nobody laments the truncated procession or the few people who stood along the street to wave as it went by. But they all mourn Miss Charles not being part of it.

After the parade, maybe sixty or seventy Seminole Negro gather in the scout park for the traditional late-morning program. In the old days, when Miss Charles was running things, the speeches and the cakewalks and sing-alongs might last until mid-afternoon, but the 2001 version takes just more than forty-five minutes. There's a brief prayer for the terrorist attack victims, somewhat longer requests of the Lord to bless all in the park, and then remarks from three guest speakers. Two are "reenactment" specialists, men who occasionally put on old uniforms to talk to school groups about the Old West. Neither is from anywhere near Brackettville. Their regular talks concern the Buffalo Soldiers, not the Seminole Negro scouts. Each offers a token nod to local history, says it's an honor to be present, and sits down. The third speaker is a Black Seminole woman from Oklahoma who tells how her people were voted out of the blood Seminole tribe and deprived of any share in that government money. Bennie McRae, a historian from Ohio who has lots about the Seminole Negro on his web site, is master of ceremonies, not Clarence Ward or Willie Warrior, who keep their distance from each other. Afterward, there's nothing else to do for the rest of the day but drink beer and perspire. There's *cabrito* for sale, barbecued goat meat, but the flies are thick on the slices and most people who get hungry run over to the Burger 'n' Shake for fish sandwiches and fries.

Yet everyone in the park seems to have a reasonably good time. There are hugs, exclamations over pictures of new grandchildren ("His mamma and daddy couldn't come here today and bring him, well, these young folks are just so busy"), and lots of throw-your-head-back laughter. The new toilets are praised, even after they clog and begin to stink. Several people make a point of thanking Clarence for his leadership in getting them installed. He smiles, obviously relieved the parade and morning program are over.

"We haven't given up," he says more than once. "No, we haven't. We got some good spirit here still." So the parade was a little straggly, so not many people came. There still *was* a parade. Old friends are having a good time together. One more Seminole Days program is being carried out, history and ancestors are being honored. Maybe next year's will be better. Meanwhile, there's free beer.

"Come back tonight for the disco dance," Clarence calls out in mid-afternoon as people start to leave the park. "Starts when it gets dark, maybe nine o'clock." But many of the older people—and most of those who came to the park are older—think they might just head home instead, watch some TV and get to bed at a decent hour.

Clarence spends a little time reflecting. Besides the toilets in the park, there's other good news. Brackettville High teacher Kathy Bader and her history club have pursued getting a historical marker for the old village site. They've gotten most of the papers filled out, coming to Clarence for information sometimes, though he doesn't really know much more about the tribal history than they do. Willie Warrior, of course, could have helped, but he wasn't consulted. In fact, Willie says upon hearing the news that he and several other older cemetery association members living in Del Rio have already been working on getting a marker. It appears even this project will cause problems between the Seminole Negro generations.

It's a hard time for Willie and Ethel Warrior right now. Their grown son, Tony, has died unexpectedly. These days, Willie says, he and Ethel mostly "sit around moping." Still, their daughter and some other family have driven to Brackettville for 2001 Seminole Days, so there's a big group in the Warrior barracks on the Fort Clark grounds, and Ethel is spending most of her weekend cooking for them, not that she's complaining; she loves it when her relations sit around eating and visiting. When the Warrior contingent comes to the park, they all stick together in the corner farthest from where Clarence has parked his red pickup. At least Willie's showing some spark for the first time in months, running around with a clunky, older-model video camera filming different friends gnawing *cabrito* and wrinkling their noses at the sewage smell.

And, finally, Miss Charles arrives, brought by her family sometime between early afternoon and dusk, when everybody reassembles at the park for the disco dance. This year Miss Charles is resplendent in a bright turquoise dress, but it's immediately clear she's deteriorated a lot since the previous Seminole Days. She's helped out of the car and onto a folding chair in the shade under one of the oak trees—the sun is still over the horizon, it's still over ninety degrees—and there Miss Charles slumps as people line up to greet her. Her head droops, and she listlessly lifts her hand to be squeezed or shaken by each in turn. Her hand is so scrawny now that its nails poke out like talons. "So good to see you, Miss Charles," everyone says like always. "You look real nice." But this year Miss Charles doesn't have much to say back. Mostly, she mutters unintelligibly. Later, some report the only coherent thing she says the whole time is, once or twice, "For many years I was a schoolteacher."

When everyone has said hello to Miss Charles, they have no idea what to do with her next. She's just arrived, after all, so the people who brought her can't turn right around and load her back in the car. She either can't or won't talk much, and it's depressing to sit next to her and think about how sharp she used to be and how listless she is now. Finally, somebody brings a battered scrapbook with raggedy pictures pasted to its inside pages, pictures of Indians cut out of magazines and some yellowing newspaper articles about Seminole Days. This is placed in Miss Charles's lap, and she comprehends enough to flip over the pages slowly with her skinny hand, staring blankly at each page for long minutes before shakily turning to the next one. When she's seen all the pages, she turns the scrapbook over and starts at the beginning again. This occupies her for a long time, even after the sun goes down and the dim park lights barely provide more glow than a swarm of fireflies.

Around eight P.M., somebody's tape machine begins to blast out old eighties' tunes about shaking booties, and also some earlier sixties' songs like Sam and Dave's "Soul Man." A few younger people, teenagers mostly, emerge from the shadows, the girls in halter tops with lots of makeup caked on their faces, the boys in stiff jeans and clean T-shirts. None of them seem to be part of the extended Seminole Negro family. They've come because there's music and dancing. In Brackettville, any party is better than the usual nothing. The dancers shake unself-consciously while the remaining Seminole Negro sit in metal folding chairs and brush away flies and mosquitoes. In the middle of it all, underneath that same oak tree, Miss Charles sits with the scrapbook open on her lap, turning pages over and over, looking at the pictures but not really seeing. Willie and Ethel Warrior exchange last hugs with friends. They're about to go back to their barracks home and enjoy time with visiting family. Clarence Ward isn't even in the park. His wife, Audrey, had to miss most of the morning events to stay with their daughter. Afterward she told Clarence she was coming to the disco dance, but he couldn't come unless he found a baby-sitter. Apparently, he didn't.

So the tinny music pounds, the flies buzz, the sewage smell is everywhere, and it's impossible not to wonder how much longer the Seminole Negro can go on, not as individuals—most of them have made lives for themselves in this hard modern world—but as a tribe, a cohesive people held together by history and the determination to keep that history vital and alive. Honesty would compel any outsider, at least, to acknowledge that the tale-telling, the recitation of great Seminole Negro deeds and suffering and leaders that was the original focus of Seminole Days, has been replaced by socializing as the main function of the festivities. It stands to reason that very soon the handful of active association members left will decide it just isn't worth the trouble to organize a Seminole Days parade when so few people participate in it, and even fewer come out to watch it. And, if there's no parade, why bother gathering afterward on a hot September day in the scout park to listen to boring speakers? Why, in fact, even bother with Seminole Days at all?

In another few years, five or ten at the most, Miss Charles will be gone and Willie Warrior will be getting very old and Clarence Ward will probably have been replaced as association president at his own behest or by being voted out, if the association even exists anymore. More fancy houses with terraced lawns will be built adjacent to, if not over, the old village site. The cemetery will be choked with weeds, and when the searing heat and flash floods eventually combine to wear chiseled names off the headstones, no one will be left to say for certain who is buried where. Saddest of all, after the lies and betrayals—by Jesup promising freedom in Florida to any *maroons* laying down their weapons; by Marcellus Duval scheming to make the Seminole Negro his personal slaves; by the Comanche promising Wild Cat's people safe passage, then slaughtering so many of them; by the U.S. Army offering land in exchange for service, then denying the land after that service; after the blood Seminole tossed out their Black Seminole kinsmen for a few extra reparation dollars—after all this harm inflicted on the tribe by outsiders, this dismal end will be the Seminole Negro's own fault, because no one left among them could cooperate sufficiently to give the Seminole Negro a future based on the courage and determination they'd shown in the past. As Miss Charles feared, all the centuries of suffering and pluck in the face of enormous adversity will finally come to nothing. The slavers didn't finish them, nor the Seminole, nor the Comanche, nor the army. But inability to get along with one another is going to.

Or maybe not. As the flies buzz and the sewage reeks and the disco music throbs in the scout park, some of the Seminole Negro still have goals for themselves and their people. That these differ radically in scope may be less important than the fact that a few of them still have ambition, still want to rally everyone together for a common cause. They wanted their own land before they died, the one precious possession that would free them forever from serving the best interests of others at the expense of their own. That land was denied them. But ambition still flickers and could yet become flame.

Clarence Ward wants to begin collecting whatever old photographs and scout-related documents might still be hoarded by older tribal members. "I know they got them," he says, rubbing his forehead. "They take 'em out to look at when nobody else is around. What they need to understand is, it's important for our group as a whole to have everything like that, so we can put these different pieces together and make up one big collection."

That collection, Clarence believes, would form the basis for "a big ol' museum all about us, our people, and the scouts, and it would be just about us, not like that place on Fort Clark that's got one little corner about the scouts. If we had our own place, then people visiting here could learn all about us, and my association members would take a lot of pride from that. There would be a place for our kids to come and learn more. All of us would learn from it. So this museum is my next goal."

At the same time, Clarence hopes the Brackettville High history club's efforts to get a histocial marker on the old village site will be successful.

"That would be the second big thing," he says, smiling broadly at the thought. "I see that marker being dedicated, maybe, at next year's Seminole Days. After the parade we could all go out to where the old village was, and there would be speeches and unveiling the marker. It would give a whole new start to Seminole Days, just what we need right now. It would be even better than the toilets we got this year."

And with a reenergized Scout Association, Clarence believes, "We could then get more active raising money to help the people in Nacimiento. Doing for others always makes people feel good about themselves. If I can get my members involved in that, hey, I think we'll just have a lot of excitement around here again."

Sitting on his screened-in porch on the Fort Clark grounds, nursing a beer in the heat of a late fall afternoon, Willie Warrior dreams, too. He also plans a Seminole Negro museum, but not the one Clarence Ward envisions.

"Ethel and I want to gather lots of material together and have a museum in the front part of our place here," he says. "We'd do it right, get all the history right, 'cause we're the only ones left now who know it. Clarence and his people couldn't do it. They wouldn't know half of what they were looking at or talking about. Nobody with any pride in our past really takes them seriously. But Ethel and me, they'd know we'd treat their things right, the pictures and so forth. And we'd have this nice museum that all the visitors to the fort could come see, and also all the scout relatives like Cynthia Ventura, the ones who want to learn about their family's past, their history. So we're going to do this. We really are."

Willie's vision for his people goes beyond a museum. He hopes a still wider audience can be reached.

"I know our story would make a great TV miniseries, and someday somebody's going to do it, one like *Lonesome Dove* that everybody watches and talks about," he insists. "Old John Horse in Florida? That running from Indian Territory to Mexico? The Medal of Honor winners, all the scouts did, you think that wouldn't make for great TV? People believe what they see on TV, you know. Everybody around the country, around the *world,* will know about us, want to come here to meet the ones who are left. And our kids, they'd feel real proud because their people were so well known, and they'd want to know all the history again, just like I did when I was their age. A TV miniseries. That's going to be the thing."

Willie admits he has no idea of how some TV mogul will hear about the Seminole Negro, "but somebody will. You wait."

Ethel Warrior smiles as her husband spins his vision of TV fame. Her own ambition for her people still involves dollars.

"We hear about all these other tribes getting money because of old lies, old broken promises from the government," Ethel says, her usual smile replaced by a frown of concentration. "Up north, some little group got millions of dollars and land. I think they built a casino. Look at that money the Seminole in Oklahoma got. Millions, and all these years afterward. We need to put together our story, take it to the government, ask them to make right what was done wrong to us after we did what we promised as scouts. We were guaranteed land for that. We were. So we should get something now. I want to get our story written up to take to the government, but none of us know how. We need somebody to help us with it. That's what I'm praying for."

Any of these things could happen. Certainly, two of the greatest Seminole Negro assets are still intact, though who knows for how long. Anyone visiting Brackettville would be moved by the scout cemetery, with its primitive dignity. The handmade stick crosses side by side with elaborate marble headstones make the place look unique. There are the four Medal of Honor winners' markers, set off by white PVC pipe fencing and additional decorations by a Boy Scout troop that heard about the Seminole Negro and fixed up their plots as a special project. Even the newest graves, their lumpy silhouettes poking up above the rocks and caliche dust, are somehow impressive. And, as Willie Warrior likes to say, the wind always blows through the cemetery even when it's not blowing anywhere else. Maybe spirits do abide there.

And there's the old village site, desecrated with trash, favored for morning runs by joggers who have no idea of the history surrounding them, encroached upon by big, fancy houses that are the aesthetic and moral antithesis of the cozy thatched huts that once were there. But in the morning and evening deer still come there to graze, and wild turkey waddle back and forth across the narrow, pebbly road. The creek is lovely, and the breeze carries chirps and caws from the wild bird sanctuary a few hundred yards away. So what if modern-day Brackettville teens sneak over here at night for consummation, rather than contemplation of the near-ethereal beauty of the place? The old village site isn't spoiled yet, and maybe the Brackettville High kids' efforts to get a historical marker placed here will help hold off all the people and things that could ruin it.

"If the cemetery lasts, if where the old village was stays nice, then my people still have reason to stay together," Miss Charles Emily Wilson says in the summer of 1994. It is late morning, but the heat has already driven her back inside her shabby little house, back into the parlor with the groaning air conditioner that almost drowns out her reedy voice. "We are meant to survive, even though it may seem now like our kids don't care anymore, that we're just counting down the days until everyone forgets who and what we were. We haven't gotten through all these things, from Florida to Indian Territory to Mexico, and then here in Texas, just to have it all fall apart in the end."

In these last days before her mind is emptied by Alzheimer's disease, Miss Charles has her goal, too. It isn't grand, like believing the government will finally admit its mistake and give the Seminole Negro the land they were promised, or expecting millions of dollars in reparations, or a TV mini-series, or even a fancy museum devoted solely to the history of the tribe.

"We aren't getting our land before we die like John Horse told Wild Cat," Miss Charles says. "Nobody's giving us money, either, or saying they're sorry. I know this. I expect we all do. Life does not include a promise that you get what you earn and deserve. But at least we have ourselves, the things our people said and did and believed in. All I want, right now, is each day for one more person to learn our history. There is great power in one. This is what I always want, that one more person should know our story."

And now, you do.

Acknowledgments

I'm grateful to Geoff Campbell, Alyson Ward, and Bryan Curtis for outstanding research assistance. Between 1994 and 2002 I was granted extensive interviews by Miss Charles Emily Wilson, Willie Warrior, and Clarence Ward. Other in-depth interviews were conducted with Ethel Warrior, Odilia Menchaca, Cynthia Ventura, Bob Bluthardt, Ross McSwain, Max Lale, Cissy Stewart Lale, and the late Ben Pingenot, an outstanding scholar who devoted much of his life to studying the history of the Seminole Negro. My thanks are also directed to the staffs of the Texas State Historical Association in Austin, the Oklahoma Historic Association in Oklahoma City, and the Institute of Texan Cultures in San Antonio.

Assistance for this project was provided in various forms by Mike Blackman, Del Hillen, Mary Arendes, Dot and Frank Lauden, Robert Fernandez, Felix Higgins, Charles Caple, Judy Alter, James Ward Lee, Stephen G. Michaud, Kinky Friedman, Ralph Lauer, John Rush Vann, Zonk Lanzillo, Claude Crowley, Carol Vance, Broc Sears, Scott Nishimura, Doug Perry, Julie Heaberlin, Jim Witt, Ron Ennis, Jessie Milligan, Dave Ferman, and Mary Rogers. I very much appreciate the efforts of my agents, Michael and Barbara Rosenberg, to get this book published, and the willingness of Sara Carder at Tarcher/Putnam to guide me through the writing process.

The works of historian-writers Kevin Mulroy and the late Kenneth Porter were particularly invaluable. I recommend their books, *Freedom on the Border* and *The Black Seminoles,* respectively, to anyone who would like to read more about the Seminole Negro.

The Seminole Indian Scout Cemetery Association can be reached at P. O. Box 1797, Brackettville, Texas 78832, or at their web site, www.coax.net/people/lwf/sisca.html. They would be grateful for any contributions in their efforts to help their struggling kinsmen in Nacimiento, Mexico.

Everything I write is always for Nora, Adam, and Grant.

Sources

INTERVIEWS

Miss Charles Emily Wilson, founder, Seminole Indian Scouts Cemetery Association

Willie Warrior, past president and historian, Black Seminole Indian Scouts Cemetery Association

Ethel Warrior, past president, Black Seminole Indian Scouts Cemetery Association

Clarence Ward, president, Seminole Indian Scouts Cemetery Association

Gary White Deer, director, Seminole Historic Office

Izola Warrior Raspberry, scout descendant

Carol Goodloe Dimery, scout descendant

Odilia C. Menchaca, scout descendant

Cynthia Ventura, scout descendant

Janie R. Luevano, scout descendant

Wendy Goodloe, scout descendant

Faranza Halder, scout descendant

Augusta Ann Pines, scout descendant

Monika Cruz, scout descendant

Martha Ward McDonald, scout descendant

Ben Pingenot, past president, Texas State Historical Association (deceased)

Robert Bluthardt, executive director, Fort Concho Historic Site and Museum

Dr. Ian Hancock, professor of linguistics, University of Texas at Austin

Cecil Johnson, author/historian

Ross McSwain, author/historian

Bennie J. MacRae Jr., author/historian

Jerry Flemmons, author/historian (deceased)
Judy Alter, author/historian
Max Lale, past president, Texas State Historical Association
Cissy Stewart Lale, past president, Texas State Historical Association
Ben Hoover, historian, Brackettville
Kathy Bader, teacher, Brackettville High School
John Stockley, historian, Eagle Pass
Glen White, president, Fort Clark Historical Society
Staff: The Texas State Historical Association (Austin)
The Oklahoma Historic Association (Oklahoma City)
The Institute of Texan Cultures (San Antonio)

BOOKS

Africans and Seminoles: From Removal to Emancipation. Daniel F. Littlefield Jr. (Greenwood Press, 1977).

Africans in America: America's Journey Through Slavery. Charles Johnson, Patricia Smith et al. (Harcourt Brace, 1998).

The Americans: A Social History of the United States, 1587–1914. J. C. Furnas (G. P. Putnam's Sons, 1969).

American Negro Slavery: A Documentary History, Michael Mullin, ed. (University of South Carolina Press, 1976).

Andrew Jackson and His Indian Wars. Robert V. Remini (Viking, 2001).

Becoming America: The Revolution Before 1776. Jon Butler (Harvard University Press, 2000).

Black Indians: A Hidden Heritage. William Loren Katz (Atheneum, 1986).

The Black Seminoles. Kenneth W. Porter with Alcione M. Amos and Thomas P. Senter (University of Florida Press, 1996).

The Black Seminole of Texas. Doug Sivad (American Press, 1984).

Blacks in White America Before 1865: Issues and Interpretations. Robert V. Haynes (David McKay Co., 1972).

Black Society in Spanish Florida. Jane Landers (University of Illinois Press, 1999).

Black Warrior Chiefs: A History of the Seminole Negro Indian Scouts. Cloyde I. Brown (self-published, 1999).

A Brief History of Mexico. Lynn V. Foster (Facts on File Inc., 1997).

The Buffalo Soldiers. William H. Leckie (University of Oklahoma Press, 1967).

"Caribbean Region: An Overview." David Gergus. *MacMillan Encyclopedia of World Slavery.* Paul Finkelman and Joseph C. Miller, eds. (1998).

Cinco de Mayo:A Review of the Battle of Puebla. Maria Viramontes de Marin and Reymundo Marin (Marin Publications, 1990).

Chronology of World Slavery. Junius P. Rodriguez (ABC-CLIO Inc., 1999).

The Course of Mexican History. Michael C. Meyer and William L. Sherman (Oxford University Press, 1987).

Dictionary of Afro-American Slavery. Randall M. Miller and John David Smith (Greenwood Press, 1988).

Encyclopedia of Mexico: History, Society and Culture. Michael S. Werner, ed. (Fitzroy Dearborn Publishers, 1997).

Freedom on the Border: The Seminole Maroons. Kevin Mulroy (Texas Tech University Press, 1993).

Free and Slave. Jane Landers (University of Florida Press, 1996).

From Freedom to Freedom: African Roots in American Soil. Mildred Bain and Erwin Lewis, eds. (Purnell Reference Books, 1977).

From Slavery to Freedom: A History of Negro Americans. John Hope Franklin (Knopf, 1980).

The Historical Dictionary of Mexico. Donald C. Briggs and Marvin Alisky (Scarecrow Press, 1981).

A History of the Indians of the United States. Angie Debo (University of Oklahoma Press, 1983).

The History of Maximilian and Carlota of Mexico. Montgomery H. Hyde (MacMillan & Co., 1946).

Indian Removal: The Emigration of the Five Civilized Tribes of Indians. Grant Foreman (University of Oklahoma Press, 1932).

A Line in the Sand: The Alamo in Blood and Memory. Randy Roberts and James N. Olson (Free Press, 2001).

Maximilian and Juarez. Jasper Ridley (Ticknor and Fields, 1992).

The Mexican Reform 1855–1876: A Study in Liberal Nation-Building. Richard N. Sinkin (University of Texas Press, 1979).

Minorities in the New World: Six Case Studies. Charles Wagley and Marvin Harris (Columbia University Press, 1958).

Negro-Indian Relationships in the Southeast. Laurence Foster (Philadelphia Press, 1935).

The New Handbook of Texas. Ron Tyler, ed. (Texas State Historical Association, 1996).

Off the Beaten Trail. William Edward Syers (Texian Press, 1971).

"The Origins of Negro Slavery." Oscar Handlin and Mary F. Handlin. *The Origins of American Slavery and Racism.* Donald L. Noel, ed. (Charles E. Merrill Publishing Co., 1972).

The Portable Handbook of Texas. Ron Tyler, ed. (Texas State Historical Association, 2000).

Red Patriots: The Story of the Seminoles. Charles H. Coe (Editor Publishing Co., 1898; out of print).

Reminiscences of the Second Seminole War. John Bemrose (1839; reprinted University of Florida Press, 1966).

The Rise of African Slavery in the Americas. David Eltis (Cambridge University Press, 2000).

The Seminoles. Edwin C. McReynolds (University of Oklahoma Press, 1985).

Texas Siftings. Jerry Flemmons (Texas Christian University Press, 1995).

The War in Florida. Woodburne Potter (1836; out of print).

WEB SITES AND INTERNET SOURCES

The Defeat of the Spanish Armada, by Steve Goldman (http://www.historybuff.com/library/refspain.html)

The Black Seminoles' Long Road to Freedom (http://www.ccny.cuny.edu/library/News/seminoles2.html)

NEWSPAPER, REFERENCE, AND MAGAZINE ARTICLES

"'American Original' Sounds About Right." John Gonzalez (*Fort Worth Star-Telegram,* 1994).

"Black Seminoles Versus Marauders." Cecil Johnson (*Fort Worth Star-Telegram,* 1997).

"The Bonds That Tie Blacks and Native Americans." William Loren Katz (*American Legacy Magazine,* 1998).

"A Brief History of the Seminole Freedmen." Joseph A. Opala (Department of Anthropology, University of Oklahoma, 1980).

"Gathering Marks Turbulent Odyssey of Indians." A. Phillips Brooks (*Fort Worth Star-Telegram,* 1993).

"General John Lapham Bullis." Edward S. Wallace (*The Southwestern Historical Quarterly,* July 1951).

"Notes on the Origin of the Seminole Indians of Florida." James Owen Knauss (*Florida Historical Quarterly,* 1929).

"The Seminole in Mexico, 1850–1861." Kenneth W. Porter (*Hispanic American Historical Review,* 1951).

"The Seminole-Negro Indian Scouts 1870–1881." Kenneth W. Porter (*The Southwestern Historical Quarterly,* January 1952).

"Tribal Loss." Jeff Guinn (*Fort Worth Star-Telegram,* 1994).

Index